OXFORD MONOGRAPHS IN
INTERNATIONAL LAW

General Editors

PROFESSOR CATHERINE REDGWELL

Chichele Professor of Public International Law at the University of Oxford and Fellow of All Souls College, Oxford

PROFESSOR ROGER O'KEEFE

Professor of International Law at Bocconi University, Milan

Party Status to Armed Conflict in International Law

OXFORD MONOGRAPHS IN INTERNATIONAL LAW

The aim of this series is to publish important and original pieces of research on all aspects of international law. Topics that are given particular prominence are those which, while of interest to the academic lawyer, also have important bearing on issues which touch the actual conduct of international relations. Nonetheless the series is wide in scope and includes monographs on the history and philosophical foundations of international law.

RECENT TITLES IN THE SERIES

The Identity of Governments in International Law
Niko Pavlopoulos

Access to Courts for Asylum Seekers and Refugees
State Obligations under the 1951 Refugee Convention
Emma Dunlop

Gravity at the International Criminal Court
Admissibility and Prosecutorial Discretion
Priya Urs

International Law Obligations on Climate Change Mitigation
Benoit Mayer

Coastal State Jurisdiction over Living Resources in the Exclusive Economic Zone
Camille Goodman

International Law and Corporate Actors in Deep Seabed Mining
Joanna Dingwall

The Concept of an International Organization in International Law
Lorenzo Gasbarri

Necessity and Proportionality and the Right of Self-Defence in International Law
Chris O'Meara

Neutrality in Contemporary International Law
James Upcher

Geographical Change and the Law of the Sea
Kate Purcell

Statehood and the State-Like in International Law
Rowan Nicholson

Party Status to Armed Conflict in International Law
Alexander Wentker

Party Status to Armed Conflict in International Law

ALEXANDER WENTKER

OXFORD
UNIVERSITY PRESS

OXFORD
UNIVERSITY PRESS

Great Clarendon Street, Oxford, OX2 6DP,
United Kingdom

Oxford University Press is a department of the University of Oxford.
It furthers the University's objective of excellence in research, scholarship,
and education by publishing worldwide. Oxford is a registered trade mark of
Oxford University Press in the UK and in certain other countries

Published in the United States of America by Oxford University Press
198 Madison Avenue, New York, NY 10016, United States of America

British Library Cataloguing in Publication Data

Data available

Library of Congress Control Number: 2024934053

ISBN 978–0–19–890090–0

DOI: 10.1093/oso/9780198900900.001.0001

Für Viva

General Editors' Preface

Whole reservoirs of ink have been spilt over the past thirty years on the existence and classification of armed conflicts under international law. Comparatively little, however, has been written during this time on the distinction between those collective entities, whether states or non-state armed groups, that are parties to an armed conflict and those collective entities, state or non-state, that are not. Yet, as Alexander Wentker reminds us, the distinction between the parties to an armed conflict and third parties remains significant for an array of international legal purposes, ranging from the rights and obligations of neutral states in the event of international armed conflict to the amenability of individuals to target in the event of any armed conflict, international or non-international. It is on this distinction, the maintenance of which Dr Wentker supports as a matter of policy, that *Party Status to Armed Conflict in International Law* focuses. The book's chief concern is those single armed conflicts involving more than one party, state or non-state, on either or both sides—what the author terms 'multi-party' armed conflicts, in which the multiple parties on the same side are referred to as 'co-parties'. This sort of armed conflict is to be distinguished from those situations in which, even if factually more than one entity, state or non-state, may be involved alongside the other, legally they are to be considered parties to separate armed conflicts.

The principal aim of the book is to facilitate the identification of co-parties to a multi-party armed conflict, an identification 'closely connected' with the concept and classification of an armed conflict but ultimately, Dr Wentker reasons, necessarily distinct from these questions. Identifying co-parties is all the more important, he argues, insofar as—whatever the position of third parties in this regard—'co-parties have duties to take positive steps vis-à-vis the conduct of their fellow co-parties in an armed conflict'. In this light, the book advances a 'general analytical framework' for such identification, a framework for which it draws support from practice. This framework is underpinned by the claim that, despite the many and varied forms in which multi-party conflicts come, co-parties can be identified according to common criteria. At the same time, the book acknowledges that, in derogation from this general framework for co-party identification, 'special rules are conceivable, for example, for a specific type of conflict, entity, or activity—or combinations thereof', although it finds that the only special rule at present pertains to declarations of war.

Party Status to Armed Conflict in International Law is international legal scholarship of the highest order. It is deeply researched, analytically rigorous, creative, and possessed of vision. It is also fascinatingly wide-ranging and eminently readable. It makes a rich and original contribution to the literature that is guaranteed to aid and interest both intellectually and practically.

RO'K, CR
Milan and Oxford
May 2024

Acknowledgements

Along the way that led me to completing this book, I have been fortunate to have received help in countless ways, and I acknowledge those who have helped me with great pleasure and gratitude.

First, I am deeply grateful to my doctoral supervisors at the University of Oxford, Professors Dapo Akande and Miles Jackson, for their thorough advice, constant support, and warm encouragement. They have guided the doctoral thesis on which this book is based in the most wonderful way, while also leaving me with the necessary freedom to develop my ideas, and they continue to inspire my work.

I am also immensely indebted to Professor Christian Marxsen, whose research group on international peace and security law at the Max Planck Institute for Comparative Public Law and International Law in Heidelberg I have been part of for the past several years. I am enormously thankful to Christian for the patience and thoughtfulness with which he supervised my first steps as a researcher in the early stages of this project as well as for the generosity with which he has constantly provided advice and support on this project and well beyond. I would also like to thank Professor Anne Peters wholeheartedly, who has academically and professionally supported me in a great many ways throughout my time at MPIL. Being part of this institute has provided me with myriad opportunities to discuss my ideas and those of others. I am deeply grateful to the many people from whom I had the chance to learn while in Heidelberg.

My heartfelt thanks are also due to Professors Antonios Tzanakopoulos and Emily Crawford, who examined my doctoral thesis with great academic rigour and intellectual generosity. The book has benefitted from their thorough discussion of the thesis and encouragement as to its publication. To Antonios, as well as to Professor Helmut Aust of Freie Universität Berlin, I owe a particular debt, intellectually and personally, for their invaluable advice at different stages of my academic path up to this point. At the University of Oxford, I am also particularly grateful to Judge Theodor Meron and Dr Efthymios Papastravridis for the important input they provided when examining my work for the transfer and confirmation of status as on many other occasions. I should also very much like to thank Professor Catherine Redgwell, who warmly welcomed me as part of her public international law research seminars at All Souls College and Oxford's wonderful Public International Law community more widely.

Particular thanks are due to Nathalie Weizmann. The work and discussions with her at UN OCHA in New York instilled in me the first seeds of the idea for this project. As I turned the thesis into this monograph, many fruitful discussions and a collaborative project with Professor Claus Kreß have helped advanced my thinking on the themes of this book and related questions in peace and security law. I am very thankful for his thorough engagement with my work, and I have learned a great deal from working with him. In the same period of time, I have had the privilege to participate in a project on party status with Chatham House led by Elizabeth Wilmshurst. I am deeply grateful to Elizabeth and to Chatham House's International Law Programme Director Rashmin Sagoo for the opportunity to test and refine my ideas with many government legal advisers and scholarly experts. The constant exchange with the other wonderful fellow project teams members Professors Miles Jackson, Lawrence Hill-Cawthorne, Charles Garraway, and Françoise Hampson, as well as the in-depth roundtable discussions in London and many bilateral conversations with experts from government practice and academia have provided me with invaluable feedback to revise the manuscript.

Overall, I have greatly benefitted from discussing my ideas on the subject of this book with a number of bright minds over the past years. In addition to those already named, these include (in alphabetical order): Dr Ziv Bohrer, Professor Michael Bothe, Professor Emanuele Cimiotta, Professor Geoffrey Corn, Professor Ashley Deeks, Dr Anne Dienelt, Dr Jeannine Drohla, Dr Tristan Ferraro, Professor Catherine Fortin, Professor Jochen Frowein, Professor Paola Gaeta, Emanuela-Chiara Gillard, Dr Andrea Harrison, Professor Rebecca Ingber, Professor Vaios Koutroulis, Professor David Kretzmer, Professor Heike Krieger, Professor Eliav Lieblich, Professor Noam Lubell, Professor Kubo Mačák, Michael Meyer, Professor Marko Milanovic, Dr Alice Ollino, Dr Tilman Rodenhäuser, Professor Yaël Ronen, Professor Marco Sassòli, Professor Yuval Shany, Professor Paulina Starski, Professor Stefan Talmon, Professor Nicholas Tsagourias, Dr Jeroen van den Boogard, and Professor Jochen von Bernstorff.

During my work on the doctoral thesis on which the book is based, my friends and colleagues in Oxford and Heidelberg have made these places feel like home to me and have helped me in various ways. I take the liberty to single out Robert Stendel, Richard Dören, Fabian Eichberger, Florian Kriener, Felix Herbert, Josef Weinzierl, Talita de Souza Dias, Antonio Coco, Emilie McDonnell, Katie Johnston, Tsvetelina van Benthem, Irini Fasia, Anna Ventouratou, Raffaela Kunz, Silvia Steininger, Max Lesch, and Pedro Villareal. Hannes Jöbstl and Vandita Khanna have read the entire draft, and their thoughtful comments have made the book much better.

I gratefully acknowledge the generous financial and non-material support that I have received from the German National Academic Foundation, the Clarendon Fund, The Queen's College, Oxford, and the Bonavero Institute of Human Rights at the University of Oxford. I am also very much indebted to the staff at the Bodleian Law Library, the library of Freie Universität Berlin, and the library of MPIL—particularly Sandra Zikeli, Stefanie Meier, and Sara von Skerst—for their invaluable assistance in finding even the most well-hidden documents.

Finally, I owe much in life to the unconditional love and the unwavering support for every one of my steps from my parents, Annette and Hermann Wentker, and my siblings, Elisabeth and Christian. And, most of all, I could not be more profoundly grateful to my wife, Viva Welsch, whose wondrous love keeps me going every day and makes my life happy.

AW
Berlin
October 2023

Contents

Table of Cases xix
Table of Other Primary Authorities xxv
List of Abbreviations xxxix
Bibliographical Note xlvii

Introduction 1
1. Introduction 1
2. The structure of the book 4
3. The scope of the book 6

I. THE LEGAL POSITION OF PARTIES TO ARMED CONFLICTS IN INTERNATIONAL LAW

1. Parties and the Regulation of Armed Conflict through Collective Entities 11
   1. Introduction 11
   2. Parties and the collective character of armed conflict 12
      a. War as violence between collectives 12
      b. Characterising the collectives: who can be a party? 14
         i. Parties to international armed conflicts 15
         ii. Parties to non-international armed conflicts 17
   3. Parties as addressees of international law 20
      a. Party status as restrictive 20
         i. Parties as the central bearers of obligations under IHL 20
         ii. Beyond IHL: obligations imposed on parties by the UN Security Council 22
         iii. Implications of parties' obligations 24
      b. Party status as permissive 26
   4. Parties and individuals in armed conflict 34
      a. Parties and the protection of individuals in armed conflict 36
         i. Parties and individuals in the conduct of hostilities 37
            (1) International armed conflicts 37
            (2) Non-international armed conflicts 38
         ii. Parties and the protection of individuals beyond the conduct of hostilities 42

b. Individuals as addressees of international law in armed conflict 43
i. Individual rights 44
ii. Individual obligations and international criminal responsibility 46
(1) Individual criminal responsibility 46
(2) Scope of individual obligations and the relevance of party status 48
c. Interim conclusion 49
5. Parties and the geographical scope of IHL application 50
6. Conclusion 53

2. Parties and Third Parties in Armed Conflict 54
1. Introduction 54
2. Parties and neutrals 55
a. Legal positions of parties and third parties under neutrality law 56
b. Persisting existence of neutrality law in the contemporary international legal order 57
i. Room for neutrality under the UN Charter 58
ii. Neutrality in contemporary international practice 62
c. Scope of application of neutrality law 65
i. International armed conflicts 66
(1) War, armed conflict, and questions of threshold 66
(2) Automatic neutrality and the absence of intermediate statuses 67
ii. Non-international armed conflicts 69
d. Implications of party status under neutrality law 73
i. Neutral States' obligations 74
ii. Neutral States' rights and protection 75
iii. Belligerent rights 77
iv. Implications for individuals 79
3. Parties and third parties as addressees of international law in armed conflict 79
a. Obligations addressed both to parties and to third parties 80
b. Complicity and prohibitions of assistance to parties' international law violations 83
c. The duty to respect and ensure respect for IHL 84
i. Scope of application 84
ii. Content 85
(1) Internal dimension 86
(2) External dimension 86
(a) Negative duties 86
(b) Positive duties 88
4. Conclusion 92

II. THE IDENTIFICATION OF PARTIES TO ARMED CONFLICTS

3. Disentangling the Identification of Parties and the Concepts of Armed Conflict in Multiparty Conflicts 95
   1. Introduction 95
   2. Elements of the concepts of armed conflict 96
      a. War 96
      b. Armed conflict 99
         i. International armed conflict 100
            (1) Resort to armed force between States 100
            (2) Relationship to the *jus ad bellum* notion of inter-State force 103
         ii. Non-international armed conflict 106
            (1) Rationale for the intensity criterion 106
            (2) Requirements of the intensity criterion 107
            (3) Non-international armed conflicts under APII 108
   3. Multiparty conflicts and co-party status: introducing the concepts and their relevance 109
   4. Establishing multiparty conflicts and identifying co-parties 112
      a. Aggregated assessment of co-parties' activities 113
         i. Idea and implications of an aggregated assessment 113
         ii. Aggregated assessments in international practice 116
            (1) International armed conflicts 116
            (2) Non-international armed conflicts 117
               (a) Inter-State cooperation 117
               (b) Cooperation between States and armed groups as well as among multiple armed groups 120
            (3) Interim conclusion: making sense of the practice 123
         iii. Rationale and risks of aggregated assessments 125
            (1) Purpose of the conflict-related requirements for the existence of an armed conflict 126
            (2) Practical and conceptual obstacles of separate assessments 127
            (3) Normative concerns related to the implications of aggregated assessments 129
      b. Limits of aggregation 132
         i. Separate assessment of the nature and structure of each co-party 132
         ii. Forming part of a party 134
      c. Establishing multiparty non-international armed conflicts under APII 137
         i. Inter-State settings 139
         ii. Cooperation among armed groups 143
         iii. Cooperation between armed groups and the territorial State 144
      d. State cooperation with a non-State entity against a State: structural barriers to co-party status 144
   5. Conclusion 147

4. Criteria for Establishing Co-Party Status 149
1. Introduction 149
2. Charting the field of approaches to criteria for identifying co-parties 151
a. Approaches in inter-State conflicts 152
i. Classic treatises on assisting States as co-belligerents 152
ii. Delimiting neutrality and (co-)party status: distinguishing violations of neutrality obligations from the termination of neutral status 157
iii. Use of force and aggression by assistance 160
b. Approaches in non-international armed conflicts 162
i. Analogies from the inter-State context: the 'associated forces' doctrine 162
ii. Participating in pre-existing non-international armed conflicts and cooperating in 'coalitions': the ICRC's 'support-based' and 'cumulative' approaches 165
(1) The SBA 165
(2) The 'cumulative' approach 168
(3) Assessment 169
3. An analytical framework for identifying co-party status 170
a. Introduction: a general framework for identifying co-parties and the possibility of special rules 171
i. The idea of a common framework 171
ii. The possibility of special rules 173
b. Elements of a general analytical framework for identifying co-parties 174
i. Attribution 174
ii. Direct connection to military operations or hostilities 175
(1) Contouring the notions of military operations and hostilities 176
(2) Direct connection to harm 178
(a) References to 'directness' in scholarship 178
(b) References to 'directness' in international practice 179
(c) Assessing 'directness' in practice 180
iii. Coordination: requirements regarding the relationship between co-parties 182
(1) Coordination as a necessary element 182
(2) Specifying the requisite degree of coordination 185
iv. Subjective elements 189
(1) Intent to be a party? 190
(2) Subjective dimensions inherent in performing relevant coordinated conduct 191
(a) Inherent requirement of subjective dimensions 191
(b) Requisite subjective standard 193
(c) Establishment in practice 193
v. Illustrations from State practice 195

c. Special rules for identifying co-parties? 198
i. Declarations of war 198
ii. Specific types of conflicts and activities: the example of the provision of territory in inter-State settings 199
iii. Specific types of entities 202
(1) Non-State armed groups 203
(2) International organisations involved in peacekeeping operations 204
d. Temporal scope of party status 205
i. Beginning of party status 206
ii. Termination of party status 206
iii. Temporal extension of legal consequences attached to party status 208
4. Conclusion 209

5. Operationalising Party Status: Cooperation and the Implications of Identifying Co-parties 210
1. Introduction 210
2. Legal bases for different sets of positive duties of co-parties vis-à-vis their partners' conduct 213
a. Duties with respect to fellow co-parties flowing from specific party obligations 214
i. Conduct of hostilities: precautions vis-à-vis fellow co-parties 214
ii. Protection of individuals 218
b. General duty to ensure respect for IHL by fellow co-parties 220
c. The complementary relationship between the different sets of duties 222
3. A network of mutual positive duties vis-à-vis fellow co-parties: rationale and ramifications for allocating obligations in cooperation settings 224
4. Conclusion 229

Conclusion 230

Bibliography 235
Index 259

Table of Cases

INTERNATIONAL COURTS AND TRIBUNALS

Permanent Court of International Justice

German Settlers in Poland (Advisory Opion) [1923] PCIJ Series B, No 6......... 174n.132
Jurisdiction of the Courts of Danzig (Advisory Opinion) [1928] PCIJ Series B, No 15 .... 44n.227

International Military Tribunal, Nuremberg

Judgment of the Nuremberg International Military Tribunal (1 October 1946) (1947) 41 AJIL 172........ 46n.242

International Court of Justice

Accordance with International Law of the Unilateral Declaration of Independence in Respect of Kosovo (Advisory Opinion) [2010] ICJ Rep 403..................24n.84
Aerial Incident of 3 July 1988 (Iran v United States) Memorial Iran (24 July 1990) 63n.63
Application of the Convention on the Prevention and Punishment of the Crime of Genocide (Bosnia and Herzegovina v Serbia and Montenegro) (Merits) [2007] ICJ Rep 43........84n.199, 105n.68, 175n.139
Armed Activities (DRC v Uganda) (Merits) [2005] ICJ Rep 168 .... 30n.131, 89n.239
Jurisdictional Immunities of the State (Germany v Italy) Reply Germany (5 October 2010)........ 45n.234
Jurisdictional Immunities of the State (Germany v Italy) Written Statement of Greece (3 August 2011)........ 45n.234
LaGrand case (Germany v United States of America) (Merits) [2001] ICJ Rep 466........ 44n.229
Legal Consequences of the Construction of a Wall in the Occupied Palestinian Territory (Advisory Opinion) [2004] ICJ Rep 136 .... 30n.131, 59n.32, 89n.234
Legal Consequences of the Construction of a Wall in the Occupied Palestinian Territory (Advisory Opinion) Written Statement League of Arab States (January 2004) 90n.242
Legality of the Threat or Use of Nuclear Weapons (Advisory Opinion) [1996] ICJ Rep 226........ 30n.131, 31n.143, 58n.25, 62n.52, 66n.82, 67n.86, 89n.236
Military and Paramilitary Activities in and against Nicaragua (Nicaragua v United States) (Merits) [1986] ICJ Rep 14...... 60n.34, 84n.207, 86n.217, 86–87n.218, 87n.219, 104n.58, 105n.66, 145n.282
Namibia (Advisory Opinion) [1971] ICJ Rep 16................ 23n.80, 62n.52, 71n.115
Oil Platforms (Iran v United States) (Merits) [2003] ICJ Rep 161..................63n.64
Oil Platforms (Iran v United States) Counter-Memorial U.S. (23 June 1997)...... 63n.63, 159n.58
Oil Platforms (Iran v United States) Further Response Iran (24 September 2001) 117n.116, 159n.55, 159n.56
Oil Platforms (Iran v United States) Reply and Defence to Counterclaim Iran (10 March 1999)........63n.63, 117n.116, 159n.55, 159n.56

International Criminal Tribunal for the former Yugoslavia

Aleksovski (Appeal Judgment) IT-95-14/1-A (24 March 2000)................... 105n.68
Boškoski and Tarčulovski (Trial Judgment) IT-04-82-T (10 July 2008) 18n.41, 108n.83, 143n.275
Delalić (Appeal Judgment) IT-96-21-A (20 February 2001) 105n.68
Đorđević et al. (Trial Judgment) IT-05-87/1-T (23 February 2011)... 18n.41, 48n.257, 108n.83
Galić (Trial Judgment) IT-98-29-T (5 December 2003).......................... 215n.29
Gotovina (Trial Judgment) IT-06-90-T (15 April 2011)............... 206n.314, 207n.320
Haradinaj, Balaj, Brahimaj (Retrial Judgment) IT-04-84bis-T (29 November 2012) 18n.41
Haradinaj, Balaj, Brahimaj (Trial Judgment) IT-04-84-T (3 April 2008).......... 106n.76, 107n.82, 108n.83
Kordić, Čerkez (Trial Judgment) IT-95-14/2-T (26 February 2001) 105n.68
Kunarac (Appeal Judgment) IT-96-23&IT-96-23/1-A (12 June 2002) 47, 48, 48n.256, 51n.275
Miloševic (Decision on Motion for Judgment of Acquittal) IT-02-54-T (16 June 2004)..15n.19
Mladić (Trial Judgment) IT-09-92-T (22 November 2017)............. 105n.68, 186n.191
Mrkšić (Appeal Judgment) IT-95-13/1-A (5 May 2009).......................... 49n.262
Popović et al. (Trial Judgment) IT-05-88-T (10 June 2010) 48n.257
Prlić (Appeal Judgment) IT-04-74-A (29 November 2017) 105n.68
Stakić (Appeal Judgment) IT-97-24-A (22 March 2006)......................... 48n.257
Tadić (Appeal Judgment) IT-94-1-A (15 July 1999)........ 43n.221, 103, 103n.55, 105n.67, 134n.216, 134n.218, 134n.220, 175n.139
Tadić (Decision on the Defence Motion for Interlocutory Appeal on Jurisdiction) IT-94-1-A (2 October 1995).............. 15n.18, 17n.36, 48n.259, 50n.267, 50n.270, 51n.275, 99, 99n.26, 106n.73, 110n.90, 206n.316
Tadić (Trial Judgment) IT-94-1-T (7 May 1997) 106n.74, 121n.140, 121n.142

International Criminal Tribunal for Rwanda

Akayesu (Appeal Judgment) ICTR-96-4-A (1 June 2001)................ 47n.249, 47n.255
Akayesu (Trial Judgment) ICTR-96-4-T (2 September 1998)..................... 51n.275
Rutaganda (Appeal Judgment) ICTR-96-3-A (26 May 2003) 48n.257

Special Court for Sierra Leone

Brima, Kamara, Kanu (Trial Judgment) SCSL-04-16-T (20 June 2007).... 48n.257, 98n.13
Sesay, Kallon, Gbao (Trial Judgment) SCSL-04-15-T (2 March 2009)............. 48n.257
Taylor (Trial Judgment) SCSL-03-01-T (18 May 2012) 48n.257

International Criminal Court

Afghanistan (Appeal Judgment on Investigation Decision) ICC-02/17 OA4 (5 March 2020)... 48n.257, 52n.279
Afghanistan (Investigation Decision) ICC-02/17 (12 April 2019) 52n.279, 120n.138, 123n.160, 133n.213
Afghanistan (Investigation Request) ICC-02/17-7-Conf-Exp (20 November 2017) 120n.138, 122n.158, 133n.213, 189n.212, 198n.264
Al Hassan (Confirmation des Charges, Rectificatif) ICC-01/12-01/18 (8 November 2019) 18n.43
Bemba (Appeal Judgment) ICC-01/05-01/08 A (8 June 2018) 47n.253

Bemba (Confirmation of Charges) ICC-01/05-01/08 (15 June 2009) 122n.154, 125n.166, 134n.220, 189n.210, 206n.312
Bemba (Trial Judgment) ICC-01/05-01/08 (21 March 2016) 18n.41, 18n.45, 48n.257, 105n.68, 107n.82, 108n.83, 109–10, 110n.93, 122n.152, 122n.155, 124, 125n.165, 134n.214
Katanga (Trial Judgment) ICC-01/04-01/07 (7 March 2014) 18n.41, 105n.68, 107n.82, 108n.83, 121–22, 121n.143, 121n.147, 124, 133n.210, 136n.229, 136n.232, 136n.234, 186n.191, 189n.212, 197–98
Lubanga (Trial Judgment) ICC-01/04-01/06 (14 March 2012) 18n.41, 105n.68, 108n.83, 121n.148, 121n.149, 122n.151, 186n.191
Ngaïssona (Arrest Warrant) ICC-01/14-02/18 (7 December 2018) 136n.229, 136n.233
Ntaganda (Trial Judgment) ICC-01/04-02/06 (8 July 2019) 18n.41, 18n.42, 48n.257, 105n.68, 121–22, 121n.149, 122n.150, 133n.212, 134n.214, 136n.229
Yekatom (Arrest Warrant) ICC-01/14-01/18 (11 November 2018) 136n.229, 136n.233
Yekatom and Ngaïssona (Confirmation of Charges) ICC-01/14-01/18 (11 December 2019) 136n.229

European Court of Human Rights

Georgia v Russia (II) App no 38263/08 (ECtHR, 21 January 2021) 33n.160, 33n.162, 33n.163, 33n.166, 34, 112n.105
Hanan v Germany App no 4871/16 (ECtHR, 16 February 2021) 33n.166
Hassan v United Kingdom App no 29750/09 (ECtHR, 16 September 2014) 32n.150
Ukraine and The Netherlands v Russia App nos 8019/16, 43800/14 and 28525/20 (ECtHR, 25 January 2023) 34n.169
'Decision of the Court on requests for interim measures in individual applications concerning Russian military operations on Ukrainian territory' Press Release ECHR 073 (2022) 4 March 2022 . . . . 34n.168
'The European Court grants urgent interim measures in application concerning Russian military operations on Ukrainian territory' Press Release ECHR 068 (2022) 1 March 2022 . . . . 34n.168

International Tribunal for the Law of the Sea

Detention of Three Ukrainian Naval Vessels (Ukraine v Russia) (Provisional Measures, Order of 25 May 2019) ITLOS Reports 2018-2019, 283 . . . . 76n.149

World Trade Organization Dispute Settlement Body

Russia—Measures concerning Traffic in Transit (Panel Report) WT/DS512/R (5 April 2019) 31n.138, 31n.139
Saudi Arabia—Measures Concerning the Protection of Intellectual Property Rights (Panel Report) WT/DS567/R (16 June 2020) 31n.139

Court of Justice of the European Union

Case C-285/12 *Aboubacar Diakité v Commissaire général aux réfugiés et aux apatrides* (CJEU, 30 January 2014) 107n.82

Eritrea-Ethiopia Claims Commission

Eritrea–Ethiopia Claims Commission, Final Award—Ethiopia's Damages Claims (2009) 26 RIAA 631 . . . . 29n.125
Eritrea-Ethiopia Claims Commission, Partial Award: *Jus Ad Bellum*—Ethiopia's Claims (19 December 2005) 98n.13

Eritrea-Ethiopia Claims Commission, Partial Award: Prisoners of War—Ethiopia's Claim 4 (1 July 2003) 44n.232

DOMESTIC CASES

Canada

Sinnappu v Canada (Minister of Citizenship and Immigration) [1997] 2 FCR 791 .... 85n.208, 91n.252
Daniel Turp v Canada (Minister of Foreign Affairs) [2017] FC 84........ 85n.208, 91n.251

Germany

Administrative Court of Cologne, Judgment of 27 April 2016 (4 K 5467/15).. 164n.91, 211n.11
Federal Administrative Court, Judgement of 21 June 2005 (2 WD 12.04).... 64n.69, 68n.96, 84, 159n.60, 201n.283
Federal Administrative Court, Judgment of 25 November 2020 (6 C 7/19).. 119n.129, 119n.132
Federal Constitutional Court, Order of 18 November 2020 (2 BvR 477/17) 45n.234
Federal Court of Justice, Judgment of 21 February 2001 (3 StR 372/00) BGHSt 46, 292 (*Soloković*) 106n.70
Federal Court of Justice, Judgment of 6 October 2016 (III ZR 140/15)..... 120n.137, 142n.266
Federal Prosecutor General, 'Decision of 21 March 2003' (2003) 58 JZ 908 ...... 201n.284
Federal Prosecutor General, Note of 16 April 2010 (3 BJs 6/10-4) 51n.276, 120n.136, 177n.152
Federal Prosecutor General, Order of 20 June 2013 (3 BJs 7/12-4) 40n.203, 123n.161, 124n.164
Higher Administrative Court for North Rhine-Westphalia, Judgment of 19 March 2019 (4 A 1361/15)......................... 40n.203, 119n.129, 119n.131
Higher Regional Court of Cologne, Judgment of 30 April 2015 (I-7 U 4/14) 120n.137, 141n.264
Regional Court of Bonn, Judgment of 12 November 2013 (1 O 460/11) 120n.137, 141n.262

Ireland

Horgan v An Taoiseach et al [2003] 2 IR 468 .... 64n.68

Israel

The Public Committee against Torture in Israel et al v the Government of Israel et al (Targeted Killings case) HCJ 769/02 (13 December 2006) 177n.152

United Kingdom

Mohammed (Serdar) v Ministry of Defence [2014] EWHC 1369 (QB), [2014] CN 1019.. 32n.154
Mohammed (Serdar) v Ministry of Defence [2015] EWCA Civ 843, [2016] 2 WLR 247.. 32n.153, 32n.155
Mohammed (Serdar) v Ministry of Defence [2017] UKSC 2, [2017] AC 821........ 32n.156
The Queen (on the application of Campaign against Arms Trade) and The Secretary of State for International Trade and Amnesty Int'l, Human Rights Watch UK and Oxfam Int'l intervening [2017] EWHC 1726 (QB).................................... 188n.206, 227n.79

The Queen (on the application of Campaign against Arms Trade) and the Secretary of State for International Trade and Amnesty International, Human Rights Watch UK and Oxfam International intervening [2019] EWCA Civ 1020 . . . . . 188n.205, 226n.78

United States

Al-Bihani v Obama (2010) 590 F 3d 866 (DC Cir) Brief for Appellees 163n.83
Doe v Mattis (2018) 889 F 3d (DC Cir) Respondent's Factual Returns (14 February 2018) 163n.83, 164n.92
Khan v Obama (2011) 655 F 3d 20 (DC Cir) Brief for Respondents-Appellees 163n.83
Hamlily v Obama (2009) 616 F Supp 2d 63 (DC Cir) 157n.41, 163n.84
Parhat v Gates (2008) 532 F 3d 834 (DC Cir) Brief for Respondent 162n.78

Table of Other Primary Authorities

MULTILATERAL TREATIES

Agreement on Trade-Related Aspects of Intellectual Property Rights (15 April 1994) LT/UR/A-1C/IP/1
Art 73(b)(iii) 31n.139
American Convention on Human Rights (signed 22 November 1969, entered into force 18 July 1978) 1144 UNTS 123
Art 4(1) 32n.149, 130n.196
Art 27(1) 30–31
Arms Trade Treaty (signed 2 April 2013, entered into force 24 December 2014) 3013 UNTS 269
Art 6(3) 84n.200, 84n.203
Art 7(1)(b)(I) 84n.203
Art 7(3) 84n.200
Charter of the United Nations (signed 26 June 1945, entered into force 24 October 1945) 1 UNTS XVI 29–30n.129, 57–58, 61, 64, 158
Art 2(4) 29, 103
Art 2(5) 59, 83–84
Art 25. . . . . .23–24, 58, 81n.183
Art 41. 58
Art 43. 59
Art 48(1) 58n.27
Art 51. 59–60
Art 103. . . . . .58, 59
Convention on Cluster Munitions (signed 30 May 2008, entered into force 1 August 2010) 2688 UNTS 39. . . . . .26n.102
Art 1(1)(c) .84n.201
Convention on the Prevention and Punishment of the Crime of Genocide (adopted 9 December 1948, entered into force 12 January 1951) 78 UNTS 277
Art III(e). 84n.199
Convention on the Prohibition of the Development, Production, Stockpiling and Use of Chemical Weapons and on their Destruction (signed 2 September 1992, entered into force 29 April 1997)1975 UNTS 45
Art 1(1)(d) .84n.201
Convention on the Prohibition of the Use, Stockpiling, Production and Transfer of Anti-Personnel Mines and on their Destruction (signed 18 September 1997, entered into force 1 March 1999) 2056 UNTS 211 . . . . .26n.102
Art 1(1)(c) .84n.201
Convention on Prohibitions or Restrictions on the Use of Certain Conventional Weapons which may be deemed to be Excessively Injurious or to have Indiscriminate Effects (signed 10 October 1980, entered into force 2 December 1983) 1342 UNTS 137 (with Protocols I, II, and III)
Preamble. 26n.102
Art 1(1) 109n.89
Art 7(4) 15n.21
Protocol II, art 3(4). 215n.29
Protocol II, art 3(10) 215n.29
Protocol III, art 1(5). 215n.29
Convention on the Rights of the Child (opened for signature 20 November 1989, entered into force 2 September 1990) 1577 UNTS 3
Art 38(1) 84n.205
Energy Charter Treaty (opened for signature 17 December 1994, entered into force 16 April 1998) 2080 UNTS 95
Art 24(3)(a)(ii) 31n.140
Convention on the Safety of United Nations and Associated Personnel (opened for signature 15 December 1994, entered into force 15 January 1999) 2051 UNTS 363
Art 2(2) 16n.30

(European) Convention for the Protection of Human Rights and Fundamental Freedoms (adopted 4 November 1950, entered into force 3 September 1953; as amended) 213 UNTS 221
Art 1 .... 33, 34
Art 2 .... 30–31, 33n.166
Art 2(2) 32
Art 5(1) 32
Art 5(4) 32
Art 15(1) 30–31
Art 15(2) 30–31
Art 15(3) 30–31
General Agreement on Tariffs and Trade (1994) (15 April 1994) LT/UR/A-1A/1/GATT/1
Art XXI(b)(iii) 31n.138
General Treaty for Renunciation of War as an Instrument of National Policy (signed 12 August 1928, entered into force 24 July 1929) 94 LNTS 59 .... 29, 57–58
Geneva Convention (I) for the Amelioration of the Condition of the Wounded and Sick in Armed Forces in the Field (signed 12 August 1949, entered into force 21 October 1950) 75 UNTS 31
Art 1 .... 84, 85n.208, 86n.215, 87–89, 88n.228, 89n.239, 90–91, 91n.251, 212, 220–22, 222n.60, 225, 227, 228
Art 2 .... 21n.65, 97, 105n.62, 109–10, 190–91, 190n.216, 191n.224, 198–99
Art 2(1) 16–17
Art 2(3) 16–17
Art 3 .... 51, 107, 108n.85, 109–10, 137–38, 139, 142, 143, 143n.275, 228
Art 3(1) 176n.142
Art 3(2) 208n.326
Art 3(3) 17
Art 3(4) 39n.198
Arts 4–5 .... 74n.137
Art 4 .... 62n.50
Art 8(1) 62n.50
Art 10(2) 62n.50
Art 10(4) 62n.50
Art 11(2) 62n.50
Art 12 .... 208n.326
Art 13(1) 42n.217
Art 13(2)(d) 176n.141
Art 13(4) 42n.217
Art 13(5) 42n.217
Art 15 .... 21n.58, 208n.326, 208n.327, 219n.44, 220n.50
Art 17(3)–(4) 176n.142
Art 23 .... 176n.142
Art 27(1) 62n.50
Art 27(2) 62n.50
Art 27(4) 62n.50
Art 28 .... 75n.139, 176n.142
Art 31 .... 176n.142
Art 34 .... 26n.105
Art 36 .... 176n.142
Art 37(1) 62n.50
Art 37(3) 62n.50, 176n.141
Arts 40–41 .... 48n.260
Art 40 .... 176n.142
Art 43 .... 62n.50
Arts 47–48 .... 21n.67
Art 48 .... 176n.142
Arts 49–50 .... 21n.66
Arts 50–51 .... 48n.259
Art 59 .... 27n.106
Art 127 .... 21n.67
Art 129 .... 21n.66
Art 130 .... 48n.259
Art 144 .... 21n.67
Art 146 .... 21n.66
Art 147 .... 48n.259
Annex I, Art 2 .... 176n.141
Geneva Convention (II) for the Amelioration of the Condition of Wounded, Sick and Shipwrecked Members of Armed Forces at Sea (signed 12 August 1949, entered into force 21 October 1950) 75 UNTS 85
Art 1 .... 84, 85n.208, 86n.215, 87–89, 88n.228, 89n.239, 90–91, 91n.251, 212, 220–22, 222n.60, 225, 227, 228
Art 2 .... 21n.65, 97, 105n.62, 109–10, 190–91, 190n.216, 191n.224, 198–99
Art 2(1) 16–17
Art 2(3) 16–17
Art 3 .... 51, 107, 108n.85, 109–10, 137–38, 139, 142, 143, 143n.275, 228
Art 3(1) 176n.142
Art 3(2) 208n.326
Art 3(3) 17
Art 3(4) 39n.198
Art 4 .... 176n.142
Art 5 .... 62n.50
Art 8(1) 62n.50

Art 10(2) 62n.50
Art 10(4) 62n.50
Art 11(2) 62n.50
Art 12 .... 208n.326
Art 13(1) 42n.217
Art 13(2)(d) 176n.141
Art 13(4) 42n.217
Art 13(5) 42n.217
Art 15 .... 176n.141
Art 17 .... 62n.50, 176n.141
Art 18 .... 21n.58, 208n.326, 208n.327, 219n.44, 220n.50
Art 25 .... 62n.50
Art 31 .... 26n.103
Art 33 .... 176n.142
Art 38 .... 26n.104
Art 39 .... 176n.142
Art 40 .... 62n.50
Art 40(3) 176n.141
Art 42 .... 48n.260
Art 43(2) 62n.50
Arts 47–48 .... 21n.67
Arts 49–50 .... 21n.66
Arts 50–51 .... 48n.259
Art 127 .... 21n.67
Art 129 .... 21n.66
Art 130 .... 48n.259
Art 144 .... 21n.67
Art 146 .... 21n.66
Art 147 .... 48n.259

Geneva Convention (III) relative to the Treatment of Prisoners of War (signed 12 August 1949, entered into force 21 October 1950) 75 UNTS 135 49
Art 1 .... 84, 85n.208, 86n.215, 87–89, 88n.228, 89n.239, 90–91, 91n.251, 212, 220–22, 222n.60, 225, 227, 228
Art 2 .... 21n.65, 97, 105n.62, 109–10, 190–91, 190n.216, 191n.224, 198–99
Art 2(1) 16–17
Art 2(3) 16–17
Art 2(c) 68n.97
Art 3 .... 51, 107, 108n.85, 109–10, 137–38, 139, 142, 143, 143n.275, 228
Art 3(1) 176n.142
Art 3(2) 208n.326
Art 3(3) 17
Art 3(4) 39n.198
Art 4(2) 42
Art 4(A)(2) 135
Art 4(A)(2)(d) 176n.141
Art 4(B)(1) 176n.142
Art 4(B)(2) 62n.50
Art 5 .... 208n.328
Art 5(1) 209n.332
Art 8(1) 62n.50
Art 9(2)(a) 68n.97
Art 10(2) 62n.50
Art 10(4) 62n.50
Art 11(2) 62n.50
Art 17 .... 48n.260
Art 19 .... 68n.97
Art 21 .... 27n.107, 42n.215
Art 21(3) 176n.142
Art 22(2)(a) 68n.97
Art 23 .... 176n.141
Art 30(3) 68n.97
Art 31 .... 68n.97
Art 33 .... 176n.142
Art 37(1)(d) 68n.97
Art 39(1) 68n.97
Art 39(2) 48n.260
Art 43 .... 176n.142
Arts 47–48 .... 21n.67
Arts 49–50 .... 21n.66
Arts 50–51 .... 48n.259
Art 58 .... 176n.142
Art 64 .... 68n.97
Art 67 .... 176n.142
Art 75 .... 27n.106
Art 75(1) 176n.141
Art 78 44–45
Art 109 .... 176n.142
Art 109(2) 62n.50
Art 109(3) 62n.50
Art 110 .... 62n.50
Art 111 .... 62n.50, 176n.142
Art 112 .... 176n.142
Art 114 .... 62n.50
Art 115 .... 62n.50
Art 116 .... 62n.50
Art 118 .... 42n.215, 44–45, 176n.142
Art 119 .... 176n.142
Art 122 .... 62n.50
Art 127 .... 21n.67
Art 129 .... 21n.66
Art 130 .... 48n.259
Art 144 .... 21n.67
Art 146 .... 21n.66
Art 147 .... 48n.259

Geneva Convention (IV) relative to the Protection of Civilian Persons in Time of War (signed

12 August 1949, entered into force 21 October 1950) 75 UNTS 287
Art 1. . . . . . . 84, 85n.208, 86n.215, 87–89, 88n.228, 89n.239, 90–91, 91n.251, 212, 220–22, 222n.60, 225, 227, 228
Art 2. . . . . . . 21n.65, 97, 105n.62, 109–10, 190–91, 190n.216, 191n.224, 198–99
Art 2(1) 16–17
Art 2(3) 16–17
Art 3. . . . . 51, 107, 108n.85, 109–10, 137–38, 139, 142, 143, 143n.275, 228
Art 3(1) 176n.142
Art 3(2) 208n.326
Art 3(3) 17
Art 3(4) 39n.198
Art 4. 42–43
Art 4(1) 42n.219
Art 4(2) 43n.220, 62n.50, 109, 179
Art 6(2) 176n.141, 206n.314
Art 6(3) 176n.141
Art 9(1) 62n.50
Art 11(2) 62n.50
Art 11(4) 62n.50
Art 11(6) 62n.50
Art 12(2) 62n.50
Art 14. . . . . 176n.142
Art 15. . . . . 176n.142
Art 16. . . . . 21n.58, 208n.327, 219n.44, 220n.52
Art 20(2) 176n.141
Art 23. . . . . 23n.78, 27n.106
Art 24(2) 62n.50
Art 27. . . . . .27n.108
Art 28. . . . . 176n.141
Arts 35–46 . . . . .99n.20
Art 36(1) 62n.50
Art 38. . . . . .27n.108
Art 40(2) 176n.141
Art 41. . . . . .27n.108
Art 42. . . . . .27n.107
Art 43. 32
Art 45. . . . . 176n.142
Art 46. . . . . 27n.109, 176n.142
Arts 47–48 . . . . .21n.67
Arts 49–50 . . . . .21n.66
Art 49(2) 176n.142
Arts 50–51 .48n.259
Art 51(2) 176n.141
Art 53. . . . . 176n.141
Art 55. . . . . .82n.187
Art 59(3) 81n.180
Art 61(1) 62n.50
Art 70. . . . . 176n.142
Art 78. 32
Arts 79–141 .99n.20
Art 111. . . . . 27n.106, 176n.141
Art 127. . . . . .21n.67
Art 129. . . . . .21n.66
Art 130. . . . . 48n.259, 176n.142
Art 132. . . . . 176n.142
Art 132(2) 62n.50
Art 133. . . . . 176n.142
Art 134. . . . . 176n.142
Art 144. . . . . .21n.67
Art 145. . . . . 176n.142
Art 146. . . . . .21n.66
Art 147. . . . . .48n.259
Art 157. . . . . 176n.142
Hague Convention (III) relative to the Opening of Hostilities (signed 18 October 1907, entered into force 26 January 1910) 205 CTS 263
Art 1. . . . . 98, 176n.142
Hague Convention (V) respecting the Rights and Duties of Neutral Powers and Persons in Case of War on Land (signed 18 October 1907, entered into force 26 January 1910) 205 CTS 299 61
Art 1. . . . . 57n.18, 75n.141
Arts 2–4. . . . . .57n.19
Arts 2–5. . . . . 57n.14, 91n.255
Arts 6–7. . . . . .79n.169
Art 10. . . . . .75n.145
Art 11. 59
Hague Convention (XIII) concerning the Rights and Duties of Neutral Powers in Naval War (signed 18 October 1907, entered into force 26 January 1910) 205 CTS 395. 61
Art 1. . . . . 57n.17, 57n.19, 75n.141
Arts 5–6. . . . . .91n.255
Art 5. . . . . .57n.15
Art 6. . . . . .57n.13
Art 7. . . . . .79n.169
Art 9. 59
Art 13. . . . . .75n.141
Art 26. . . . . .75n.145
Hague Convention for the Protection of Cultural Property in the Event of Armed Conflict (signed 14 May 1954, entered into force 7 August 1956) 249 UNTS 215
Art 18(1) 109n.88

Hague Draft Rules of Aerial Warfare (1923)
Art 42 ... 57n.16
Art 48 ... 75n.145
International Covenant on Civil and Political Rights (opened for signature 16 December 1966, entered into force 23 March 1976) 999 UNTS 171
Art 4(1) ... 30n.134
Art 6 ... 32n.147
Art 6(1) ... 31–32, 130n.196
Protocol Additional to the Geneva Conventions of 12 August 1949, and relating to the Protection of Victims of International Armed Conflicts (Protocol I) (signed 12 December 1977, entered into force 7 December 1978) 1125 UNTS 3
Preamble ... 29–30n.129, 103–4
Art 1 ... 88
Art 1(3) ... 109n.89
Art 1(4) ... 15, 132, 144–45, 203n.293
Art 2(c) ... 62n.51
Art 3 ... 176n.141
Art 4(B)(2) ... 68n.97
Art 5 ... 80n.173
Art 8(a)–(b) ... 42n.218
Art 9(1) ... 219n.47
Art 9(2)(a) ... 62n.51
Art 10 ... 208n.326
Art 19 ... 62n.51, 74n.137
Art 22(2)(a) ... 62n.51
Art 30(3) ... 62n.51
Art 31 ... 62n.51
Art 31(4) ... 176n.142
Art 33 ... 21n.58, 176n.142, 219n.44
Art 33(1) ... 208n.327
Art 34 ... 176n.142
Art 35 ... 26n.102
Art 37(1)(d) ... 62n.51
Art 37(2) ... 176n.141
Art 39(1) ... 62n.51
Art 39(2) ... 176n.141
Art 40 ... 176n.142
Art 43 ... 42
Art 43(1)–(2) ... 37n.183
Art 43(2) ... 42, 176n.142
Art 44 ... 42
Art 44(1) ... 42
Art 44(2)–(3) ... 48n.260
Art 44(3) ... 176n.141, 176n.142, 177n.148
Art 44(5) ... 176n.141
Art 45 ... 176n.142
Art 47 ... 176n.142
Art 48 ... 20n.57, 37n.183, 37n.186, 176n.141
Art 49(1) ... 177
Art 49(4) ... 176n.142
Art 50(1) ... 37n.183, 37n.185
Art 51(1) ... 176n.141
Art 51(2) ... 37n.186
Art 51(3) ... 176n.142, 178n.154
Art 51(4)–(5) ... 211n.12
Art 51(7) ... 176n.141
Art 56(2) ... 176n.141
Art 56(5) ... 176n.142
Art 57(1) ... 21, 176n.141, 177n.149, 214n.19
Art 57(4) ... 21, 176n.141
Art 58 ... 176n.141, 218, 218n.41
Art 58(a) ... 218n.42
Art 58(b) ... 218n.43
Art 59(2) ... 176n.141
Art 60 ... 176n.142
Art 60(1) ... 176n.141
Art 60(6) ... 176n.141
Art 61 ... 176n.142
Art 64(1) ... 62n.51
Art 64(3) ... 62n.51
Art 67 ... 176n.142
Art 69 ... 82n.187
Art 70(1) ... 81n.180, 82n.187
Art 70(2) ... 23n.78, 81
Art 70(3) ... 27n.106
Art 70(4) ... 81, 82n.188
Art 70(5) ... 81
Art 73 ... 176n.142
Art 77 ... 176n.142
Art 83 ... 21n.67
Art 85 ... 21n.66
Art 85(3)–(4) ... 48n.259
Art 90 ... 25
Art 96(3) ... 15
Art 122 ... 68n.97
Protocol Additional to the Geneva Conventions of 12 August 1949, and relating to the Protection of Victims of Non-International Armed Conflicts (Protocol II) (signed 12 December 1977, entered into force 7 December 1978) 1125 UNTS 609 ... 21, 108, 113, 137
Art 1 ... 141

Art 1(1) 17–18, 108–10, 137–38, 139, 140–41, 140n.257, 142–43, 143n.275, 144, 176n.141, 176n.143
Art 1(2) 107
Art 2(2) 208n.328
Art 3(2) 140
Art 4 . . . . 176n.142
Art 6(5) 176n.142
Arts 7–8 . . . . 208n.326
Art 8 . . . . 208n.327
Art 13(1) 176n.141
Art 13(3) 39n.196, 176n.142
Art 19 . . . . .21n.67
Art 23(1) 141n.263
Protocol Additional to the Geneva Conventions of 12 August 1949, and relating to the Adoption of an Additional Distinctive Emblem (Protocol III) (signed 8 December 2005, entered into force 14 January 2007) 2404 UNTS 261
Art 7 . . . . .21n.67
Protocol to the Convention on Duties and Rights of States in the Event of Civil Strife (opened for signature 1 May 1957)
Art 2 . . . . .70n.109
Protocol (V) on Explosive Remnants of War to the Convention on Prohibitions or Restrictions on the Use of Certain Conventional Weapons which may be deemed to be Excessively Injurious or to have Indiscriminate Effects (opened for signature 28 November 2003, entered into force 12 November 2006) 2399 UNTS 100
Arts 3–6 . . . . 208n.329
Art 3 . . . . 209n.331
Rome Statute of the International Criminal Court (opened for signature 17 July 1998, entered into force 1 July 2002) 2187 UNTS 3
Art 8(2) 46n.243, 47
Art 8(2)(a)–(c) 48n.259
Art 8(2)(b)(xi) 47n.250
Art 8(2)(b)(xii) 47n.251
Art 8(2)(b)(xiii)–(xv) 47n.250
Art 8(2)(e) .48n.259
Art 8(2)(e)(x) 47n.251
Art 8(2)(e)(xii) 47n.250
Art 8(2)(f) 109–10
Art 25(4) 46n.247
Art 28 . . . . .47n.252
Art 28(a) 47n.253
Regulations concerning the Laws and Customs of War on Land, Annex to Hague Convention (IV) respecting the Laws and Customs of War on Land (signed 18 October 1907, entered into force 26 January 1910) 205 CTS 277
Art 1(4) 176n.141
Art 6(1) 176n.141
Art 22 . . . . .26n.102
Art 23(h) 176n.141
Art 29(1)–(2) 176n.141
Art 36 . . . . 176n.141
Art 37 . . . . 176n.141
Art 43 . . . . .89n.239
Art 52 . . . . 176n.141
Art 53 . . . . 176n.141
Statute of the International Court of Justice, annexed to the UN Charter (adopted 26 June 1945, entered into force 24 October 1945) 1 UNTS XVI
Art 38(1)(b) 125n.168, 227n.84
United Nations Convention on the Law of the Sea (adopted 10 December 1982, entered into force 16 November 1994) 1833 UNTS 3
Art 25 76
Art 87(1) 78n.166
Vienna Convention on the Law of Treaties (concluded 23 May 1969, entered into force 27 January 1980) 1155 UNTS 331
Art 29 . . . . .50n.267
Art 31(1) 61, 150, 219n.46, 221n.55
Art 31(3) 61, 150
Art 31(3)(b) 125–26, 227n.81
Art 32 . . . . 126n.169
Arts 34–38 . . . . 142n.267

BILATERAL TREATIES

Agreement between the State of Israel and Japan for the Liberalization, Promotion and Protection of Investment (signed 1 February 2017, entered into force 5 October 2017)
Art 15(2)(a)(i) 31n.141

UNITED NATIONS SECURITY COUNCIL

UNSC Res 27 (1 August 1947)
UN Doc S/459. . . . . .23n.75
UNSC Res 582 (24 February 1986)
UN Doc S/RES/582. . . . . .63n.61
UNSC Res 681 (20 December 1990)
UN Doc S/RES/681. . . . . .89n.241
UNSC Res 752 (15 May 1992)
UN Doc S/RES/752. . . . . .23n.76
UNSC Res 925 (6 June 1994)
UN Doc S/RES/925. . . . . .23n.76
UNSC Res 1386 (20 December 2001)
UN Doc S/RES/1386. . . . . .32n.159
UNSC Res 1509 (19 September 2003)
UN Doc S/RES/1509. . . . . .23n.76
UNSC Res 1546 (8 June 2004) UN
Doc S/RES/1546. . . . . .32n.159
UNSC Res 1612 (26 June 2005) UN
Doc S/RES/1612. . . . . .25n.94
UNSC Res 1723 (28 November 2006)
UN Doc S/RES/1723. . . . . .32n.159
UNSC Res 1890 (8 October 2009)
UN Doc S/RES/1890. . . . . .32n.159
UNSC Res 2379 (21 September 2017)
UN Doc S/RES/2379
Preamble. 25n.90
UNSC Res 2388 (21 November 2017)
UN Doc S/RES/2388
Preamble. 25n.90
UNSC Res 2439 (30 October 2018)
UN Doc S/RES/2439. . . . . .22n.72
UNSC Res 2459 (15 March 2019)
UN Doc S/RES/2459. . . .2n.14, 23n.76
UNSC Res 2475 (20 June 2019)
UN Doc S/RES/2475
Preamble. 26n.101, 82n.184
UNSC Res 2532 (1 July 2020) UN
Doc S/RES/2532. . . . . . . .2n.14, 23n.77
UNSC Res 2540 (28 August 2020)
UN Doc S/RES/2540. . . .2n.14, 22n.72
2543rd Meeting (29 May 1984)
UN Doc S/PV.2543 . . . . .159n.59
4726th Meeting (26 March 2003)
UN Doc S/PV.4726 . . . . 201n.279
9135th Meeting (22 September 2022)
UN Doc S/PV.9135 . . . .1n.3, 180n.166
Statute of the International Criminal Tribunal for Rwanda, adopted by UNSC Res 955 (8 November 1994) UN Doc S/RES/955
Art 1. . . . . .46n.243
Art 4. . . . . 46n.243, 48n.259
Statute of the International Criminal Tribunal for the former Yugoslavia, adopted by UNSC Res 827 (25 May 1993) UN Doc S/RES/827
Arts 1–3. . . . . .46n.243
Arts 2–3. . . . . .48n.259
Statute of the Special Court for Sierra Leone (adopted 16 January 2002, established pursuant to UNSC Res 1315 (14 August 2000) UN Doc S/RES/1315)
Art 1(1) 46n.243
Arts 3–4. . . . . .48n.259
Art 3. . . . . .46n.243
Art 4. . . . . .46n.243

UNITED NATIONS GENERAL ASSEMBLY

UNGA Res 3314 (XXIX) (14 December 1974) UN Doc A/RES/3314 (XXIX) (Definition of Aggression) 160n.67
Art 3(f) 83–84, 83n.198, 161, 199, 200, 200n.274
UNGA Res 43/21 (3 November 1988) UN Doc A/RES/43/21. .89n.240
UNGA Res 45/69 (December 1990) UN Doc A/RES/45/69. .89n.240
UNGA Res 59/122 (10 December 2004)
UN Doc A/RES/59/122 . . . . . .89n.240
UNGA Res 60/105 (8 December 2005) UN
Doc A/RES/60/105 . . . . .89n.240
UNGA Res 62/107 (17 December 2007)
UN Doc A/RES/62/107 . . . . . .89n.240
UNGA Res 63/96 (5 December 2008) UN
Doc A/RES/63/96 . . . . .89n.240
UNGA Res 68/81 (16 December 2013) UN
Doc A/RES/68/81 . . . . .89n.240
UNGA Res 74/88 (13 December 2019) UN
Doc A/RES/74/88 . . . . .89n.240
'Official Compendium of Voluntary National Contributions on the Subject of How International Law Applies to the Use of Information and Communications Technologies by States' UN Doc A/76/136 (13 July 2021) 65n.76
'Sixth Committee, Summary Record of the 22nd Meeting, New York, 25 October 2022, 3 p.m.'

(12 December 2022) UN Doc a/C.6/77/SR.22 90–91

UNITED NATIONS INTERNATIONAL LAW COMMISSION

Ago, Roberto, 'Seventh Report on State Responsibility—The Internationally Wrongful Act of the State, Source of International Responsibility' (1978) UN Doc A/CN.4/307 (1978) II(1) YILC 7n.24, 86–87n.218
'Articles on the Responsibility of International Organizations' UN Doc A/66/10 (2011); (2011) II(2) YILC 40 (and Commentary ibid 46) 87
Art 14.................. 83n.191, 87–88
Art 42(2)...................... 83n.192
Art 64...................... 175n.139
'Articles on the Responsibility of States for Internationally Wrongful Acts' UN Doc A/56/10 (2001); (2001) II(2) YILC 26 (and Commentary ibid 31) 87
Art 6........................ 174n.136
Art 7........................ 167n.108
Art 10.......................... 24n.86
Art 16.... 83n.191, 87, 88n.225, 200n.274
Art 16(a)...................... 87–88
Art 41(2)...................... 83n.192
Art 52(1)(b)...................... 60n.39
Art 55.................... 75, 175n.139
'Articles on the Effects of Armed Conflicts on Treaties' (2011) II(2) YILC 106 (and Commentary ibid)
Art 3.......................... 28n.122
Art 17.......................... 62n.53
Crawford, James, 'Second Report on State Responsibility' (1999) UN Doc A/CN.4/498/Add.1 ...... 59n.32, 86–87n.218
'Draft Conclusions on Subsequent Agreements and Subsequent Practice in relation to the Interpretation of Treaties, with Commentaries' (2018) UN Doc A/73/10 ..... 125n.167, 126n.169
'Guiding Principles Applicable to Unilateral Declarations of States Capable of Creating Legal Obligations' (2006) II/2 YILC 160 .... 190n.218
Lehto, Marja, 'Second report on protection of the environment in relation to armed conflict' (2019) UN Doc A/CN.4/728.......... 16n.28
Nolte, Georg, 'First Report on Subsequent Agreements and Subsequent Practice in Relation to the Interpretation of Treaties' (2013) UN Doc A/CN.4/660.......... 126n.169
'Protection of the Environment in Relation to Armed Conflicts: Comments and Observations Received from Governments, International Organizations and Others' (17 January 2022) UN Doc A/CN.4/749.......... 90–91
Report of the International Law Commission (1966) II YILC............. 125n.167
2577th Meeting of the ILC (1999) I YILC 67........... 192n.227
2672nd meeting of the ILC (2001) I YILC 34.............. 60n.37

UNITED NATIONS SECRETARIAT

OHCHR, 'Expert Group Report on the Situation of Human Rights in Yemen' (A/HRC/42/CRP.1) 3 September 2019.......... 119n.134, 138n.245, 139n.249, 142n.269
Report of the High-level Independent Panel on Peace Operations (17 June 2015) UN Doc A/70/95 ... 16n.28
Report of the Secretary-General on Children and Armed Conflict (9 June 2020) UN Doc A/74/845–S/2020/525.................. 25n.94
Report of the Secretary-General on Implementing the Responsibility to Protect (12 January 2009) UN Doc A/63/677 .... 222n.60
Secretary-General's Bulletin, 'Observance by United Nations Forces of International Humanitarian Law' (6 August 1999) UN Doc ST/SGB/1999/13 .... 16n.30
Statement at the ILC by the Under-Secretary-General for Legal Affairs and Legal Counsel

(23 May 2013) <http://legal.un.org/ola/media/info_from_lc/ILC% 20Legal%20Counsel%20statementrev3may20.pdf> 16n.30, 85n.211, 227n.80
Statement at the ILC by the Under-Secretary-General for Legal Affairs and Legal Counsel (14 May 2014) UN Doc A/CN.4/SR.3204 .... 2n.7
Statement at the ILC by the Under-Secretary-General for Legal Affairs and Legal Counsel (17 May 2016) <https://legal.un.org/ola/media/info_from _lc/mss/speeches/MSS-ILC-statement-17-May-2016-EN-FR.pdf>....... 2n.7
Statement by the Special Adviser to the UN Secretary-General (San Remo, 5 September 2013) <https://legal.un.org/ola/media/info_from _lc/POB-San-Remo-36th-Roundtable-5-September-2013.pdf>.................... 17n.33
UN Department of Peacekeeping Operations/Department of Field Support, 'Guidelines: Use of Force by Military Components in United Nations Peacekeeping Operations' (2017)........... 16n.30

UNITED NATIONS HUMAN RIGHTS COUNCIL

General Comment No. 36 Art. 6 ICCPR (30 October 2018) UN Doc CCPR/C/GC/36........ 31n.146
UN Special Rapporteur on Extrajudicial, Summary or Arbitrary Executions, 'Report - Addendum: Study on Targeted Killing' UN Doc A/HRC/14/24/Add.6 (28 May 2010)......... 164n.88
UN Special Rapporteur on Extrajudicial, Summary or Arbitrary Executions, 'Report' UN Doc A/68/382 (13 September 2013).... 129n.189, 135n.227
UN Special Rapporteur on Extrajudicial, Summary or Arbitrary Executions, 'Report: Use of armed drones for targeted killings' UN Doc A/HRC/44/38 (15 August 2020).... 100n.32, 208n.325

LEAGUE OF NATIONS

League of Nations Secretary-General, 'Legal Position Arising from the Enforcement in Time of Peace of the Measures of Economic Pressure Indicated in Article 16 of the Covenant, Particularly by a Maritime Blockade' (1927) 8 LNOJ 834 .... 97n.4

EUROPEAN UNION

Council of the European Union, 'User's Guide to Council Common Position 2008/944/CFSP' 16 September 2019 (12189/19).................. 90n.242
'Statement to the United Nations General Assembly: Humanitarian situation in Syria' 25 February 2014 (on file with the author) 90n.242

INTERNATIONAL COMMITTEE OF THE RED CROSS

'Allies, Partners and Proxies: Managing Support Relationships in Armed Conflict to Reduce the Human Cost of War' (April 2021)............. 3–4n.20, 213n.17, 213n.18, 220n.53
'International Humanitarian Law and the Challenges of Contemporary Armed Conflicts' (2003) 202n.286
'International Humanitarian Law and the Challenges of Contemporary Armed Conflicts' (2007) 38n.190
'International Humanitarian Law and the Challenges of Contemporary Armed Conflicts' (2011) 19n.47
'International Humanitarian Law and the Challenges of Contemporary Armed Conflicts' (2015) 51n.272, 51n.278, 100n.29, 102n.51, 130n.199, 167n.111, 170n.123, 193n.234, 193n.237, 206n.317
'International Humanitarian Law and the Challenges of Contemporary Armed Conflicts' (2019) 3–4n.20, 51n.277, 128n.182, 136n.230, 168n.114, 168n.115, 168n.117, 170n.124
Interpretive Guidance on the Notion of Direct Participation in

Hostilities under International Humanitarian Law (2009) . . . 37n.187, 128n.186, 166n.99
Jean-Marie Henckaerts and Louise Doswald-Beck (eds), *Customary International Humanitarian Law* vol I (CUP 2005)
r 1 . . . . 20n.57, 37n.183, 37n.186
r 3 . . . . 37n.183
r 5 . . . . 37n.185
r 6 . . . . 39n.196
r 11 . . . . 211n.12
r 15 . . . . 21n.60, 214n.19, 214n.23, 228n.88
rr 22–24 . . . . 218n.41
r 23 . . . . 218n.42
r 24 . . . . 218n.43
r 44 . . . . 214n.19
r 55 . . . . 23n.78, 82n.189
r 99 . . . . 42n.215
rr 109–111 . . . . 208n.326
rr 109–113 . . . . 220n.50
r 109 . . . . 21n.58, 219n.44, 228n.88
rr 112–114 . . . . 21n.58, 219n.44, 228n.88
rr 112–117 . . . . 208n.327
rr 116–117 . . . . 21n.58, 219n.44, 228n.88
r 139 . . . . 85n.209, 228n.89
rr 141–143 . . . . 21n.67
r 144 . . . . 84n.206, 85n.210
rr 152–153 . . . . 47n.252
r 402 . . . . 220n.51
r 509 . . . . 84n.207
'Opinion Paper: How is the Term "Armed Conflict" Defined in International Humanitarian Law?' (2008) 107n.79
'Position Paper—ICRC Engagement with Non-State Armed Groups: Why, How, for What Purpose, and Other Salient Issues' (2020) 102 IRRC 1089 . . . . 25n.91, 202–3n.290
'Questionnaire Concerning Measures Intended to Reinforce the Implementation of the Geneva Conventions of August 12, 1949: Replies Sent by Governments' (ICRC 1973) 90–91
'Report on the Third Expert Meeting on the Notion of Direct Participation in Hostilities' (2005) 192n.232
'Report on the Fifth Expert Meeting on the Notion of Direct Participation in Hostilities' (2008) 40n.202
'Resolution—Bringing IHL home' (International Conference of the Red Cross and Red Crescent 2019) 33IC/19/R1
Preamble 90n.246
Second Draft Additional Protocol to the Geneva Conventions of August 12, 1949 (1973)
Art 1 . . . . 137n.235, 139n.250
Art 3 . . . . 138n.241
Art 5 . . . . 138n.241
'The Roots of Restraint in War' (2018) 25n.92

NATO

Allied Joint Doctrine for Joint Targeting AJP-3.9 (April 2016) 189n.211

INTERNATIONAL LAW ASSOCIATION

Committee on Maritime Neutrality, 'Final Report' (1998) (*Helsinki Principles on the Law of Maritime Neutrality*) 75n.143
Committee on the Use of Force, 'Final Report on the Meaning of Armed Conflict in International Law' (2010) 62n.54, 98n.19, 100n.33
Report of the Forty-First Conference 1946 (ILA 1948) 58n.24
Study Group, 'The Conduct of Hostilities and International Humanitarian Law: Challenges of 21st Century Warfare' (2017) 93 ILS 322 . . . . 177n.149, 214n.22

INSTITUT DE DROIT INTERNATIONAL

'The Principle of Non-Intervention in Civil Wars—Resolution' (14 August 1975)
Preamble 72n.131
Art 1 . . . . 73n.134
Art 2(1) 72n.130
Art 3(b) 73n.133

OTHER

IAComHR, 'Third Report on the Human Rights Situation in Colombia' OEA/Ser.L/V/II.102 Doc 9 rev. 1 (26 February 1999) . . . 25n.93

IAComHR, 'Truth, Justice and Reparation: Fourth Report on Human Rights Situation in Colombia' OEA/Ser.L/V/II. Doc 49/13 (31 December 2013).....25n.93
International Humanitarian Fact-Finding Commission, 'Executive Summary of the Report of the Independent Forensic Investigation in relation to the Incident Affecting an OSCE Special Monitoring Mission to Ukraine (SMM) Patrol on 23 April 2017' (7 September 2017) <www.osce.org/files/f/documents/1/e/338361.pdf> 25n.96
Independent International Fact-Finding Mission Georgia Report (September 2009)............106n.69
Preparatory Commission for the ICC, Elements of Crimes (2 November 2000) PCNICC/2000/1/Add.2................47n.251
'Report on Violations of International Humanitarian and Human Rights Law, War Crimes and Crimes against Humanity Committed in Ukraine since 24 February 2022' annexed to OSCE, Note Verbale (13 April 2022) ODIHR.GAL/26/22/Rev.1 <www.osce.org/files/f/documents/f/a/515868.pdf> ... 180n.169
Report of the Committee on Study of Legal Problems of the United Nations, 'Should the Laws of War Apply to United Nations Enforcement Action?' (1952) 46 ASIL Proc 216 ... 16n.27, 205n.304

NATIONAL INSTRUMENTS

Australia

Operations Law for RAAF Commanders (2nd edn 2004)..............75n.143

Belgium

Criminal Code
Art 141bis.......................7n.31

Canada

Joint Doctrine Manual: Law of Armed Conflict at the Operational and Tactical Levels (2001).........75n.143

Costa Rica

'Costa Rica's Position on the Application of International Law in Cyberspace' 21 July 2023 <https://docs-library.unoda.org/Open-Ended_Working_Group_on_Information_and_Communication_Technologies_-_(2021)/Costa_Rica_-_Position_Paper_-_International_Law_in_Cyberspace.pdf>..............65n.76

Denmark

Criminal Code
s 101(a).........................7n.30
Danish Foreign Ministry, 'Answer to Question No 37 of 18 December 2007 by the Minister for Foreign Affairs to the Folketing - Committee on Foreign Affairs' 8 March 2008 (file no 6.B.28.a. Office of International Law) <www.ft.dk/samling/20072/almdel/uru/spm/37/svar/530893/535083.pdf>............... 141n.260
Danish Foreign Ministry, 'Proposal for a Parliamentary Resolution on the Deployment of an Additional Danish Military Contribution to Support the Effort against ISIL' (8 October 2015) B8 (2015–16)........ 197n.258, 207n.323
Military Manual on International Law Relevant to Danish Armed Forces in International Operations (2016, English Version 2019)........ 16n.29, 40n.203, 64n.73, 65n.76, 75n.143, 91n.250, 110n.92, 179n.164, 206n.309, 207n.323

France

'Déclaration Franco-Mexicaine sur le Salvador' 28 August 1981 <https://sv.ambafrance.org/XXXV-Anniversaire-de-la-Declaration-franco-mexicaine-sur-Le-Salvador> 71n.111
Décret n° 2013-364 du 29 avril 2013 portant publication de l'accord sous forme d'échange de lettres entre le Gouvernement de la République française et le Gouvernement du Mali déterminant le statut de la force « Serval » (Journal Officiel

de la République française 30 April 2013) 7426
Art 10 . . . . . 141n.258
'Letter dated 8 September 2006 from the Permanent Representative of France to the United Nations addressed to the President of the Security Council' UN Doc S/AC.51/2007/2 . . . . . 25n.94
'Ministère des armées: Droit international appliqué aux opérations dans le cyberespace' 10 September 2019 <www.defense.gouv.fr/content/download/565895/9750877/file/Droit+internat+appliqué+aux+opérations+Cyberespace.pdf> 51n.274, 52n.280, 65n.76

Germany

Address to the Nation by Federal Chancellor Scholz (8 May 2022) <https://www.bundesregierung.de/resource/2037608/883b3ea4c4c65852c8a8da991559c7e4/2022-05-08-bk-ansprache-8-mai-pdf-data.pdf?download=1> 1n.2
German Federal Government, 'Motion: continuation of the deployment of armed German forces - securing stabilisation, preventing the resurgence of IS, promoting reconciliation in Iraq and Syria' 09/09/2020 (BT Drs 19/22207) 197n.259
German Federal Ministry of Defence, *Handbuch: Humanitäres Völkerrecht in bewaffneten Konflikten* (A-2141/1) 2016 . . . . . 40n.203, 64n.73, 66n.83, 75n.146
German Federal Parliament, Stenographic Protocol Plenary Session 15/34 (19 March 2003) 201n.282
German Federal Parliament, Stenographic Protocol Plenary Session 18/144 (4 December 2015) . . . 1n.4
German Federal Parliament, Stenographic Protocol 89th Session 1st Parliamentary Inquiry Commission (25 February 2016) 119n.133
German Federal Parliament, Stenographic Protocol Plenary Session 20/33 (11 May 2022) 28n.114, 61n.41
German Navy, *Commander's Handbook: Legal Bases for the Operations of Naval Forces* (2002) 75n.143, 76n.148
Statement on Ratification of AP I (14 February 1991) 1607 UNTS 526 . . . . . 215n.29

Italy

'Comunicato della Presidenza della Repubblica sulla riunione del Consiglio Supremo di difesa del 19 marzo 2003' (2003) 86 RDI 904 . . . . . 64n.67
'Italian Position Paper on "International Law and Cyberspace" November 2021 https://www.esteri.it/mae/resource/doc/2021/11/italian_position_paper_on_international_law_and_cyberspace.pdf 65n.76

Iran

'Letter Dated 25 September 1985 from the Permanent Representative of the Islamic Republic of Iran to the United Nations Addressed to the Secretary-General' UN Doc S/17496 . . . . . 63n.62
'Letter Dated 14 August 1987 from the Permanent Representative of the Islamic Republic of Iran to the United Nations Addressed to the Secretary-General' UN Doc S/19041 . . . . . 117n.116, 159n.55

Ireland

Irish House of Representatives, 'Daéil Éireann debate 20 March 2003' vol 563 no 3 https://www.oireachtas.ie/en/debates/debate/dail/2003-03-20/4/ 202n.285

Kuwait

'Letter Dated 14 July 1988 from the Permanent Representative of Kuwait to the United Nations Addressed to the Secretary-General' (14 July 1988) UN Doc S/20015 . . . . . 159n.57

Netherlands

'Letter of the Minister of Foreign Affairs to Parliament' 5 July 2019 (Kamerstuk 33 694 Nr. 47) https://zoek.officielebekendmakingen.nl/kst-33694-47.html 65n.76

Parliamentary Debate Nr. 71 item 7 (2019-20) 14/05/2020 <https://zoek.officielebekendmakingen.nl/h-tk-20192020-71-7.html> 217n.34, 218n.40

Parliamentary Questions (Appendix) 1177 (2015-2016) 18/01/2016 https://zoek.officielebekendmakingen.nl/ah-tk-20152016-1177.html 90n.242, 90n.243

Review Committee on the Intelligence and Security Services, 'Review Report: On contributions of the MIVD to targeting' 03/08/2016 (CTIVD no 50) <https://english.ctivd.nl/investigations/review-report-50/documents/reports/2017/02/23/index> 194–95n.242, 216n.31

New Zealand

Manual of Armed Forces Law Vol 4: Law of Armed Conflict (2017).......64n.73

Peru

Peruvian Ministry of Defence, *Manual Para Las Fuerzas Armadas: Derechos Humanos, Derecho Internacional Humanitario* (2010) 16n.29, 64n.73, 75n.146

South Africa

South African Citizenship Act 1995 s 6(1)(b) 7n.28

Spain

'Salamanca Presidency Declaration' (2002) DIH/Rev.01.Corr1 (on file with the author) 16n.29

Switzerland

'Notification to the Governments of the States Parties to the Geneva Conventions of 12 August 1949 for the Protection of War Victims' 26 June 2015 https://www.eda.admin.ch/dam/eda/fr/documents/aussenpolitik/voelkerrecht/geneve/150626-GENEVE_en.pdf 15n.24

Official Records of the Diplomatic Conference on the Reaffirmation and Development of International Humanitarian Law Applicable in Armed Conflicts, Geneva (1974–1977) (Federal Political Department 1978) 15n.22, 137n.235, 138n.242, 138n.246

'Clarté et orientation de la politique de neutralité: Rapport du Conseil fédéral' 26 October 2022 <https://www.newsd.admin.ch/newsd/message/attachments/73618.pdf>...................64n.71

'Switzerland's position paper on the application of international law in cyberspace' (May 2021) <https://www.eda.admin.ch/dam/eda/en/documents/aussenpolitik/voelkerrecht/20210527-Schweiz-Annex-UN-GGE-Cybersecurity-2019-2021_EN.pdf> 65n.76

United Kingdom

Business, Innovation and Skills and International Development Committees, The use of UK-manufactured arms in Yemen (2016-17, HC 679)... 188n.204, 188n.207

'Foreign Policy Document No. 148' (1986) 57 BYIL 614 ....72n.130

Opinion of the Law Officers of 14 August 1867, reproduced in Arnold McNair, International Law Opinions, Selected and Annotated, Vol I: Peace (CUP 1956)....... 106n.78

Statement on Ratification of AP I (28 January 1998) 2020 UNTS 75 ....215n.29

United Kingdom Ministry of Defence, *The Manual of the Law of Armed Conflict* (OUP 2004) 16n.29, 75n.143, 75n.144, 76n.148, 78n.161, 102n.47, 177n.149

United States, 'Comments on ICRC Memorandum on the Applicability of International Humanitarian Law in the Gulf Region' (11 January 1991) in

S Cummins and D Stewart (eds), *Digest of United States Practice in International Law* 1991–1999 (International Law Institute 2005) 2057 . . . . 215–16n.30

United States

Authorization for Use of Military Force, Pub L No 107-40, 115 Stat 224 (2001)
s 2(a) 162n.76
Congress, 'Joint Resolution: To direct the removal of United States Armed Forces from hostilities in the Republic of Yemen that have not been authorized by Congress' (SJ Res 7) (3 January 2019) 187n.198
Digest of US Practice in International Law (2012) 27n.110
Henry Stimson, 'The Pact of Paris: Three Years of Development' Address before the Council on Foreign Relations, 8 August 1932 (Government Printing Office, Publication No. 357) 29n.123
'Letter Dated 5 May 1970 from the Permanent Representative of the United States of America to the United Nations addressed to the President of the Security Council' (S/9781) 200n.275
'Letter from the President - Supplemental 6-month War Powers Letter' 5 December 2016 https://obamawhitehouse.archives.gov/the-press-office/2016/12/05/letter-president-supplemental-6-month-war-powers-letter 164n.91
Military Commissions Act (Pub L No 109-366, 120 Stat 2600 (2006))
s 948a(1)(i) 164n.93
Military Commissions Act (Pub L No 111-84, 123 Stat 2190 (2009)) 10 USC 948a(3) (2009) 117n.118, 179n.163
Public Papers of President Nixon (1970) 200n.276
Public Papers of President Reagan (1983) 102 n.45
'Report on the legal and policy frameworks guiding the United States' use of military force and related national security operations' (December 2016) 123n.163, 162n.77
United States Department of Defense, 'Enhancing Security and Stability in Afghanistan, Report to Congress' (2016) 163n.79
United States Department of Defense, 'Enhancing Security and Stability in Afghanistan, Report to Congress' (2018) 163n.79
United States Department of Defense, *Law of War Manual* (June 2015, updated July 2023) 41n.207, 41n.210, 65n.76, 66n.83, 75n.143, 75n.144, 75n.146, 215–16n.30
United States Department of Defense, Report on Associated Forces (2014) https://www.aclu.org/sites/default/files/field_document/53-1_exhibit_51_-_report_on_associated_forces_12.1.15.pdf 163n.85
'United States: Department of Defence Report to Congress on the Conduct of the Persian Gulf War—Appendix on The Role of the Law of War' (1992) 31 ILM 615 . . . . 59n.30
United States Department of State, Cumulative Digest of United States Practice in International Law 1981-1988, book III (1995) 101n.43
United States Government Publishing Office, 'The Fight Against ISIS: Building the Coalition and Ensuring Military Effectiveness' Senate Hearing 114-197 (25 February 2015) https://www.govinfo.gov/content/pkg/CHRG-114shrg99368/html/CHRG-114shrg99368.htm 187n.196
United States Office of the Legal Counsel to the President, 'Memorandum Opinion: "Protected Person" Status in Occupied Iraq Under the Fourth Geneva Convention' (2004) 28 OpOLC 35 . . . . 115n.114, 117n.117, 179n.161, 201n.277

Abbreviations

ACDI	Anuario Colombiano de Derecho Internacional
ACHR	American Convention on Human Rights (signed 22 November 1969, entered into force 18 July 1978) 1144 UNTS 123
AFDI	Annuaire français de droit international
AJIL	American Journal of International Law
ALC	Armée de Libération du Congo
Annu Rev Polit Sc	Annual Review of Political Science
AO	Advisory Opinion
AP Commentary	Yves Sandoz, Christophe Swinarski, and Bruno Zimmermann (eds), *Commentary on the Additional Protocols of 8 June 1977 to the Geneva Conventions of 12 August 1949* (ICRC 1987)
API	Protocol Additional to the Geneva Conventions of 12 August 1949, and relating to the Protection of Victims of International Armed Conflicts (Protocol I) (signed 12 December 1977, entered into force 7 December 1978) 1125 UNTS 3
APII	Protocol Additional to the Geneva Conventions of 12 August 1949, and relating to the Protection of Victims of Non-International Armed Conflicts (Protocol II) (signed 12 December 1977, entered into force 7 December 1978) 1125 UNTS 609
APIII	Protocol Additional to the Geneva Conventions of 12 August 1949, and relating to the Adoption of an Additional Distinctive Emblem (Protocol III) (signed 8 December 2005, entered into force 14 January 2007) 2404 UNTS 261
APs	Additional Protocols
ARIO (and Commentary)	Articles on the Responsibility of International Organizations UN Doc A/66/10 (2011); (2011) II(2) YILC 40 (and Commentary ibid 46)
ARSIWA (and Commentary)	Articles on the Responsibility of States for Internationally Wrongful Acts UN Doc A/56/10 (2001); (2001) II(2) YILC 26 (and Commentary ibid 31)
ASIL Proc	Proceedings of the Annual Meeting of the American Society of International Law

ATT	Arms Trade Treaty (signed 2 April 2013, entered into force 24 December 2014) 3013 UNTS 269
AULR	American University Law Review
AUNSLB	American University National Security Law Brief
Australian Air Manual	Australia, *Operations Law for RAAF Commanders* (2nd edn 2004)
BIT(s)	bilateral investment treaty(-ies)
BYIL	British Yearbook of International Law
Canadian Manual	Canada, *Joint Doctrine Manual: Law of Armed Conflict at the Operational and Tactical Levels* (2001)
CCW	Convention on Prohibitions or Restrictions on the Use of Certain Conventional Weapons which may be deemed to be Excessively Injurious or to have Indiscriminate Effects (signed 10 October 1980, entered into force 2 December 1983) 1342 UNTS 137 (with Protocols I, II, and III)
CDDH	Diplomatic Conference on the Reaffirmation and Development of International Humanitarian Law Applicable in Armed Conflicts [Conférence diplomatique sur la réaffirmation et le développement du droit international humanitaire applicable dans les conflits armés]
Chic JIL	Chicago Journal of International Law
CIHL	Jean-Marie Henckaerts and Louise Doswald-Beck (eds), *Customary International Humanitarian Law vol I* (CUP 2005)
CIHL vol II	Jean-Marie Henckaerts and Louise Doswald-Beck (eds), *Customary International Humanitarian Law* vol II (CUP 2005)
CJEU	Court of Justice of the European Union
CJIL	Chinese Journal of International Law
Cluster Munitions Convention	Convention on Cluster Munitions (signed 30 May 2008, entered into force 1 August 2010) 2688 UNTS 39
Colum Hum Rts LR	Columbia Human Rights Law Review
Colum JTL	Columbia Journal of Transnational Law
Common Article 1	Article 1 Common to the Geneva Conventions
Common Article 2	Article 2 Common to the Geneva Conventions
Common Article 3	Article 3 Common to the Geneva Conventions
CWC	Convention on the Prohibition of the Development, Production, Stockpiling and Use of Chemical Weapons and on their Destruction (signed 2 September 1992, entered into force 29 April 1997) 1975 UNTS 45
Danish Manual	Denmark, *Military Manual on International Law Relevant to Danish Armed Forces in International Operations* (2016, English Version 2019)

diss op	dissenting opinion
DoD	[US] Department of Defense
DÖV	Die Öffentliche Verwaltung
DPH	direct participation in hostilities
DRC	Democratic Republic of Congo
Duke JCIL	Duke Journal of Comparative and International Law
ECHR	(European) Convention for the Protection of Human Rights and Fundamental Freedoms (adopted 4 November 1950, entered into force 3 September 1953; as amended) 213 UNTS 221
ECtHR	European Court of Human Rights
EECC	Eritrea–Ethiopia Claims Commission
EJIL	European Journal of International Law
EJIR	European Journal of International Relations
ELN	National Liberation Army [Ejército de Liberación Nacional] (Colombia)
EU	European Union
FARC	Revolutionary Armed Forces of Colombia [Fuerzas Armadas Revolucionarias de Colombia]
FYIL	Finnish Yearbook of International Law
GATT	General Agreement on Tariffs and Trade (1994) (15 April 1994) LT/UR/A-1A/1/GATT/1
GC	Grand Chamber (ECtHR)
GCI	Geneva Convention (I) for the Amelioration of the Condition of the Wounded and Sick in Armed Forces in the Field (signed 12 August 1949, entered into force 21 October 1950) 75 UNTS 31
GCI Commentary	ICRC (ed), *Commentary on the First Geneva Convention* (CUP 2016)
GCII	Geneva Convention (II) for the Amelioration of the Condition of Wounded, Sick and Shipwrecked Members of Armed Forces at Sea (signed 12 August 1949, entered into force 21 October 1950) 75 UNTS 85
GCII Commentary	ICRC (ed), *Commentary on the Second Geneva Convention* (CUP 2017)
GCIII	Geneva Convention (III) relative to the Treatment of Prisoners of War (signed 12 August 1949, entered into force 21 October 1950) 75 UNTS 135
GCIII Commentary	ICRC (ed), *Commentary on the Third Geneva Convention* (CUP 2020)
GCIV	Geneva Convention (IV) relative to the Protection of Civilian Persons in Time of War (signed 12 August 1949, entered into force 21 October 1950) 75 UNTS 287
GCs	Geneva Conventions

Genocide Convention	Convention on the Prevention and Punishment of the Crime of Genocide (adopted 9 December 1948, entered into force 12 January 1951) 78 UNTS 277
German Manual	German Federal Ministry of Defence, *Handbuch: Humanitäres Völkerrecht in bewaffneten Konflikten* (A-2141/1) 2016
German Navy Handbook	German Navy, *Commander's Handbook: Legal Bases for the Operations of Naval Forces* (2002)
GST	Grotius Society Transactions
GYIL	German Yearbook of International Law
Hague Air Rules	Hague Draft Rules of Aerial Warfare (1923) (reproduced in 'General Report of the Commission of Jurists at The Hague, Part II: Rules of Aerial Warfare' (1923) 17 AJIL (Supplement) 245)
Harv ILJ	Harvard International Law Journal
Harv L Pol Rev	Harvard Law and Policy Review
Harv NSJ	Harvard National Security Journal
HCIII	Hague Convention (III) relative to the Opening of Hostilities (signed 18 October 1907, entered into force 26 January 1910) 205 CTS 263
HCJ	High Court of Justice [Israel]
HCV	Hague Convention (V) respecting the Rights and Duties of Neutral Powers and Persons in Case of War on Land (signed 18 October 1907, entered into force 26 January 1910) 205 CTS 299
HCXIII	Hague Convention (XIII) concerning the Rights and Duties of Neutral Powers in Naval War (signed 18 October 1907, entered into force 26 January 1910) 205 CTS 395
Helsinki Principles	International Law Association Committee on Maritime Neutrality, 'Final Report' (1998) (*Helsinki Principles on the Law of Maritime Neutrality*)
HILJ	Harvard International Law Journal
HLR	Harvard Law Review
HLS PILAC	Harvard Law School Program on International Law and Armed Conflict
HPCR Manual	Harvard Program on Humanitarian Policy and Conflict Research, *Manual on International Law Applicable to Air and Missile Warfare* (CUP 2013)
HR	Regulations concerning the Laws and Customs of War on Land, Annex to Hague Convention (IV) respecting the Laws and Customs of War on Land (signed 18 October 1907, entered into force 26 January 1910) 205 CTS 277
HRILD	Human Rights and International Legal Discourse

Hungarian JLS	Hungarian Journal of Legal Studies
Hu V-I	Humanitäres Völkerrecht—Informationsschriften
IAComHR	Inter-American Commission on Human Rights
IACtHR	Inter-American Court of Human Rights
IC	International Conciliation
ICC	International Criminal Court
ICCPR	International Covenant on Civil and Political Rights (opened for signature 16 December 1966, entered into force 23 March 1976) 999 UNTS 171
ICCSt	Rome Statute of the International Criminal Court (opened for signature 17 July 1998, entered into force 1 July 2002) 2187 UNTS 3
ICJ	International Court of Justice
ICJ Rep	International Court of Justice—Reports of Judgments, Advisory Opinions and Orders
ICJSt	Statute of the International Court of Justice, annexed to the UN Charter
ICLQ	International and Comparative Law Quarterly
ICLR	International Criminal Law Review
ICRC	International Committee of the Red Cross
ICTR	International Criminal Tribunal for Rwanda
ICTRSt	Statute of the International Criminal Tribunal for Rwanda, adopted by UNSC Res 955 (8 November 1994) UN Doc S/RES/955
ICTY	International Criminal Tribunal for the former Yugoslavia
ICTYSt	Statute of the International Criminal Tribunal for the former Yugoslavia, adopted by UNSC Res 827 (25 May 1993) UN Doc S/RES/827
IDI	Institut de Droit International
IHFFC	International Humanitarian Fact-Finding Commission
IHL	international humanitarian law
IIFFMCG	Independent International Fact-Finding Mission on the Conflict in Georgia
ILA	International Law Association
ILC	International Law Commission
ILDC	International Law in Domestic Courts
ILM	International Legal Materials
ILS	International Law Studies
IRRC	International Review of the Red Cross
ISAF	International Security Assistance Force [Afghanistan]
ISIL	Islamic State of Iraq and the Levant
Isr LR	Israel Law Review
Isr YHR	Israel Yearbook on Human Rights
ISQ	International Studies Quarterly

ITLOS	International Tribunal for the Law of the Sea
IYIL	Italian Yearbook of International Law
Japanese YIL	Japanese Yearbook of International Law
JCIJ	Journal of International Criminal Justice
JCR	Journal of Conflict Resolution
JCSL	Journal of Conflict and Security Law
JIHLS	Journal of International Humanitarian Legal Studies
JILD	Journal of International Law and Diplomacy [Kokhsaiho Gaiko Zassi]
JoGSS	Journal of Global Security Studies
JUOFIL	Journal on the Use of Force in International Law
JZ	JuristenZeitung
Keesing's	Keesing's Record of World Events
LJIL	Leiden Journal of International Law
LNOJ	League of Nations Official Journal
LQR	Law Quarterly Review
Melb JIL	Melbourne Journal of International Law
MINUSCA	United Nations Multidimensional Integrated Stabilization Mission in the Central African Republic [Mission Multidimensionnelle Intégrée des Nations Unies pour la Stabilisation en République Centrafricaine]
MINUSMA	United Nations Multidimensional Integrated Stabilization Mission in Mali [Mission Multidimensionnelle Intégrée des Nations Unies pour la Stabilisation au Mali]
MLC [party]	Mouvement de Libération du Congo
MLLWR	Military Law and the Law of War Review
MLR	Military Law Review
MONUSCO	United Nations Organization Stabilization Mission in the Democratic Republic of Congo [Mission de l'Organisation des Nations Unies pour la Stabilisation en République Démocratique du Congo]
MP	Marine Policy
MP(s)	Member(s) of Parliament
NATO	North Atlantic Treaty Organization
NGO(s)	non-governmental organisation(s)
NILR	Netherlands International Law Review
Nordic JIL	Nordic Journal of International Law
NULR	Northwestern University Law Review
NYIL	Netherlands Yearbook of International Law
NYT	*New York Times*
NYUJILP	New York University Journal of International Law and Politics
NYULR	New York University Law Review

OCHA	Office for the Coordination of Humanitarian Affairs [UN]
ODIL	Ocean Development and International Law
OHCHR	Office of the High Commissioner for Human Rights [UN]
OSCE	Organization for Security and Co-operation in Europe
Ottawa Convention	Convention on the Prohibition of the Use, Stockpiling, Production and Transfer of Anti-Personnel Mines and on their Destruction (signed 18 September 1997, entered into force 1 March 1999) 2056 UNTS 211
PCIJ	Permanent Court of International Justice
Peruvian Manual	Peruvian Ministry of Defence, *Manual Para Las Fuerzas Armadas: Derechos Humanos, Derecho Internacional Humanitario* (2010)
Pictet Commentary GCI	Jean Pictet, *Geneva Convention for the Amelioration of the Condition of the Wounded and Sick in Armed Forces in the Field: Commentary* (ICRC 1952)
Pictet Commentary GCIV	Jean Pictet, *Geneva Convention Relative to the Protection of Civilian Persons in Time of War: Commentary* (ICRC 1958)
PTC	Pre-Trial Chamber [International Criminal Court]
QIL	Questions of International Law
RBDI	Revue belge de droit international
RCADI	Recueil des cours de l'académie de droit international de La Haye
RDI	Rivista di diritto internazionale
Rev Int Stud	Review of International Studies
RGDIP	Revue générale de droit international public
San Remo Manual	Louise Doswald-Beck (ed), *San Remo Manual on International Law Applicable to Armed Conflicts at Sea* (CUP 1995)
SBA	support-based approach
SCSL	Special Court for Sierra Leone
SCSLSt	Statute of the Special Court for Sierra Leone (adopted 16 January 2002, established pursuant to UNSC Res 1315 (14 August 2000) UN Doc S/RES/1315)
Secur Stud	Security Studies
sep op	separate opinion
SJILC	Syracuse Journal of International and Comparative Law
SYIL	Spanish Yearbook of International Law
Tallinn Manual 2.0	Michael Schmitt (ed), *Tallinn Manual 2.0 on the International Law Applicable to Cyber Operations* (CUP 2017)
Tex ILJ	Texas International Law Journal

TRIPS	Agreement on Trade-Related Aspects of Intellectual Property Rights (15 April 1994) LT/UR/A-1C/IP/1
UK	United Kingdom
UK Manual	UK Ministry of Defence, *The Manual of the Law of Armed Conflict* (OUP 2004)
UK Manual Amendment 3	UK Ministry of Defence, *Joint Service Public 383—The Manual of the Law of Armed Conflict Amendment 3* (September 2010)
UN	United Nations
UN Charter	Charter of the United Nations (signed 26 June 1945, entered into force 24 October 1945) 1 UNTS XVI
UNCLOS	United Nations Convention on the Law of the Sea (adopted 10 December 1982, entered into force 16 November 1994) 1833 UNTS 3
UNGA	United Nations General Assembly
UN OLA	Office of Legal Affairs [UN]
UNSC	United Nations Security Council
UP	University Press
U Penn LR	University of Pennsylvania Law Review
US	United States
US Manual	United States Department of Defense, *Law of War Manual* (June 2015, updated December 2016)
Va JIL	Virginia Journal of International Law
Van JTL	Vanderbilt Journal of Transnational Law
VCLT	Vienna Convention on the Law of Treaties (concluded 23 May 1969, entered into force 27 January 1980) 1155 UNTS 331
Yale LJ	Yale Law Journal
Yale L Pol Rev	Yale Law and Policy Review
YIHL	Yearbook of International Humanitarian Law
YILC	Yearbook of the International Law Commission
YJIL	Yale Journal of International Law
ZaöRV	Zeitschrift für ausländisches öffentliches Recht und Völkerrecht

Bibliographical Note

I have sought to keep the work up to date until September 2023. Developments and publications after 30 September 2023 have no longer been systematically considered.

The ideas developed more fully in this book have previously informed several other publications of mine. In particular, Chapters 1 and 4 in part draw on 'At War? Party Status and the War in Ukraine' (2023) 36 LJIL 643 and 'Kriegspartei? Sicherheitspolitischer Diskurs und Völkerrecht im Ukraine-Krieg' (2022) 75 DÖV 988. Chapters 2.3 and 5 in part draw on 'Partnered Operations and the Positive Duties of Co-Parties' (2022) 27 JCSL 159. Chapters 2.2 and 4 in part draw on 'L'Assistance d'états tiers dans la guerre d'Ukraine au regard du droit international' (2023) 68 AFDI 173 (co-authored with Claus Kreß). Chapters 3, 4, and 5 in part draw on 'Identifying Co-parties to Armed Conflict in International Law: How States, International Organisations, and Armed Groups become Parties to War' Chatham House Research Paper (2024, with Miles Jackson and Lawrence Hill-Cawthorne (contributing authors)).

Introduction

1. Introduction

Before Germany declared war on the US in the Second World War, the US maintained that the massive support it provided to the Allies still fell short of meaning that it would itself be at war with Germany.[1] More than eighty years later, many States insisted that their wide-ranging military assistance to Ukraine against Russia's full-scale invasion would not make them parties to the conflict.[2] By contrast, Russia alleged that these States had in effect become parties.[3] Similarly, when Germany decided to provide a wide range of logistical and intelligence assistance to the multinational coalition's fight against ISIL, opposition MPs raised concerns that Germany would be 'waging war' in Syria alongside the other States.[4] As part of the so-called war on terror, President Obama proclaimed that 'under domestic law, and international law, the United States is at war with al Qaeda, the Taliban, and their associated forces'.[5] US strikes against fighters of the al-Shabaab group as an alleged associate of al-Qaeda later raised questions as to whether the US also considered itself to be 'at war' with al-Shabaab.[6] The UN, for its part, was confronted

[1] 'Address of Robert H Jackson, Attorney General of the United States, Inter-American Bar Association, Havana, Cuba, March 27, 1941' (1941) 35 AJIL 348, 349.

[2] 'Press Briefing by Press Secretary Jen Psaki, March 3rd, 2022' <www.whitehouse.gov/briefing-room/press-briefings/2022/03/03/press-briefing-by-press-secretary-jen-psaki-march-3rd-2022/>; M Sermo, 'La Cobelligérance, acte de guerre ou légitime défense collective?' *Le Monde* (26 May 2022) www.lemonde.fr/idees/article/2022/05/26/la (quoting France's President and Minister of the Armed Forces); Address to the Nation by Federal Chancellor Scholz (8 May 2022) <www.bundesregierung.de/resource/blob/992814/2037608/883b3ea4c4c65852c8a8da991559c7e4/2022-05-08-bk-ansprache-8-mai-pdf-data.pdf?download=1>; 'Poland Ready to Place All Its MIG-29 Jets at the Disposal of U.S.' (*Reuters*, 8 March 2022) <www.reuters.com/world/europe/poland-ready-place-all-its-mig-29-jets-disposal-us-2022-03-08/> (quoting Poland's Prime Minister); 'West "Working Hard" to Avoid War' (*Sky News*, 28 June 2022) <https://news.sky.com/video/west-working-hard-to-avoid-war-12641856> (interview with the British Prime Minister); T Hoffmann, 'War or Peace?—International Legal Issues Concerning the Use of Force in the Russia–Ukraine Conflict' (2022) 63 Hungarian Journal of Legal Studies 206, 220 (citing statements by Hungary's government); see also 'Press Point with NATO Secretary General Jens Stoltenberg' 30 September 2022 <www.nato.int/cps/en/natohq/opinions_207788.htm>.

[3] UNSC, 9135th Meeting (22 September 2022) UN Doc S/PV.9135 17–18.

[4] German Federal Parliament, Stenographic Protocol Plenary Session 18/144 (4 December 2015) 14106, 14115.

[5] US, 'Remarks by the President at the National Defense University' 23 May 2013 <https://obamawhitehouse.archives.gov/the-press-office/2013/05/23/remarks-president-national-defense-university>.

[6] On the controversies on this point within the Obama administration, see C Savage, *Power Wars: The Relentless Rise of Presidential Authority and Secrecy* (Back Bay Books 2017) 274 ('Is the United States at War with al-Shabaab?').

Party Status to Armed Conflict in International Law. Alexander Wentker, Oxford University Press.
DOI: 10.1093/oso/9780198900900.003.0001

with the issue of whether it had become a party to the conflicts in the DRC, Mali, and the Central African Republic through the involvement of its peace operations MONUSCO,[7] MINUSMA,[8] and MINUSCA[9] in those conflicts.

All of these cases raise the question of who is 'at war'. International lawyers, however, have traditionally tended to ask, 'when does war exist?'.[10] As legal terminology has shifted away from the notion of war,[11] debates in the *jus in bello* have concentrated on the legal criteria for the existence of an armed conflict.[12] Yet, wrapped up in the question of *whether* there is an armed conflict is often a question of *who* is engaged in that conflict. Since States and armed groups tend not to go to war alone, that question has been ever present in historical and recent conflicts, as the above examples illustrate. At times, the language of being 'at war' is used as political rhetoric.[13] Frequently, however, there is an underlying legal issue, namely who is a party to the armed conflict. That question has received far less attention than the question of what constitutes an armed conflict. This is so although the parties to the conflict are referred to in hundreds of international treaty provisions and are frequently addressed by international bodies such as the UN Security Council in resolutions on situations of armed conflict.[14]

This book is about how we can tell and why it matters who is a party to an armed conflict. Asking these questions is particularly warranted in light of two sets

[7] Statement at the ILC by the Under-Secretary-General for Legal Affairs and Legal Counsel (14 May 2014) UN Doc A/CN.4/SR.3204 3; Statement at the ILC by the Under-Secretary-General for Legal Affairs and Legal Counsel (17 May 2016) <https://legal.un.org/ola/media/info_from_lc/mss/speeches/MSS-ILC-statement-17-May-2016-EN-FR.pdf> 11.

[8] B Oswald et al, 'Peace Forces at War: Implications Under International Humanitarian Law' (2014) 108 ASIL Proc 149, 154; S Mathias, 'UN Peacekeeping Today: Legal Challenges and Uncertainties' (2017) 18 Melb JIL 138, 143.

[9] P Labuda, 'The UN Goes to War in the Central African Republic: What Are the Limits of Peacekeeping?' (*Just Security*, 23 March 2017) <www.justsecurity.org/39151/war-central-african-republic-limits-peacekeeping/>; B Maganza, 'Escalation of Violence in Bangui: Has MINUSCA Become Party to a Conflict in CAR, and What Would That Mean?' (*OpinioJuris*, 28 April 2018) <http://opiniojuris.org/2018/04/16/escalation-of-violence-in-bangui-has-minusca-become-party-to-a-conflict-in-car-and-what-would-that-mean/>.

[10] Q Wright, 'When Does War Exist?' (1932) 26 AJIL 362; see Chapter 3.2.a.

[11] On the terminological shift in international law from the notions of 'war' and 'belligerents' to 'armed conflict' and 'parties to the conflict' and on the remaining legal relevance of 'war', see Chapter 1.2.; Chapter 3.2. On the contemporary significance of war as a legal concept, see also A Clapham, *War* (OUP 2021).

[12] See eg D Schindler, 'The Different Types of Armed Conflicts According to the Geneva Conventions and Protocols' (1979) 163 RCADI 121; D Carron, *L'Acte déclencheur d'un conflit armé international* (Schulthess 2016); A Cullen, *The Concept of Non-International Armed Conflict in International Humanitarian Law* (CUP 2010); N Derejko, *Identifying Non-International Armed Conflict: International Law and Practice* (CUP forthcoming); for a meta-reflection, see D Pearlstein, 'Armed Conflict at the Threshold' (2019) 58 Va JIL 369 (discussing criticism levelled against the centrality of the concept of 'armed conflict' for triggering the application of IHL); see further Chapter 3.2.b.

[13] A McNair and A Watts, *The Legal Effects of War* (4th edn, CUP 1966) 8; Clapham (n 11) xv; for the intricate connections of 'war rhetoric' and legal justifications for military action in the post-9/11 'war on terror', see F Mégret, '"War"? Legal Semantics and the Move to Violence' (2002) 13 EJIL 361.

[14] For some recent emblematic examples, see UNSC Res 2532 (1 July 2020) UN Doc S/RES/2532 [1]–[2] (adopted during the COVID-19 pandemic); UNSC Res 2540 (28 August 2020) UN Doc S/RES/2540 [8]–[9] (Somalia); UNSC Res 2459 (15 March 2019) UN Doc S/RES/2459 [1] (South Sudan).

of wider developments. These developments relate to the structure of the international legal order and the ways in which contemporary armed conflicts are fought.

On the one hand, several interrelated developments in the international legal regulation of armed conflicts call for reappraising the relevance of the status as a party. First, the blurring of the classical divide in international law between peacetime and wartime questions the traditional notion that being 'at war' comes with an entirely distinct status of rights and obligations.[15] Secondly, the 'humanisation' and 'individualisation' of international law in armed conflicts emphasise the relevance of the individual within this legal system and thus present conceptual challenges to the centrality of parties as *collective* entities.[16] Thirdly, armed conflict is increasingly regulated as a concern not merely between the parties but, rather, to the international community as a whole.[17] Analysing to what extent and in what ways the law applicable to armed conflicts is structured by reference to parties allows us to assess the impact of these developments. More widely, the book therefore aims to contribute to a clearer understanding of the structure of the current international legal framework regulating armed conflict as a whole.

On the other hand, making out who is 'at war' can be complex since armed conflicts are often fought in cooperation. For example, in the context of the US military assistance to the Saudi-led coalition in Yemen, it was reported that:

> U.S. government lawyers ultimately did not reach a conclusion on whether U.S. support for the campaign would make the United States a 'co-belligerent' in the war under international law.[18]

States have always worked together with others to wage wars.[19] Facilitated by technological advancements, cooperation is now one of the most salient features of contemporary armed conflicts.[20] The examples given at the beginning of this

[15] From a normative perspective, 'revisionist' accounts have also challenged the divide in 'traditionalist' just war theory between the morality of killing in peacetime and wartime (for the classic traditionalist view seminally, see M Walzer, *Just and Unjust Wars: A Moral Argument with Historical Illustrations* (5th edn, Basic Books 2015); for the revisionist approach, see J McMahan, *Killing in War* (Clarendon Press 2009); for an overview of the debate, see S Lazar, 'Just War Theory: Revisionists versus Traditionalists' (2017) 20 Annu Rev Polit Sci 37).

[16] Seminally T Meron, 'The Humanization of Humanitarian Law' (2000) 94 AJIL 239; D Akande, D Rodin, and J Welsh (eds), *The Individualization of War: Rights, Liability, and Accountability in Contemporary Armed Conflict* (OUP 2023).

[17] J Dill, '"The Rights and Obligations of Parties to International Armed Conflicts" from Bilateralism but Not toward Community Interest?' in E Benvenisti and G Nolte (eds), *Community Interests across International Law* (OUP 2018).

[18] W Strobel and J Landay, 'Exclusive: As Saudis Bombed Yemen, U.S. Worried about Legal Blowback' (*Reuters*, 10 October 2016) <www.reuters.com/article/us-usa-saudi-yemen-idUSKCN12A0BQ>.

[19] See eg H Grotius, *De jure belli ac pacis libri tres*, vol III (F Kelsey tr, Clarendon Press 1925) 787 (with references to ancient Greece and Rome); for further classical law of war treatises on this point, see Chapter 4.2.a.i.

[20] ICRC, 'Allies, Partners and Proxies: Managing Support Relationships in Armed Conflict to Reduce the Human Cost of War' (April 2021) 5; ICRC, 'International Humanitarian Law and the

introduction illustrate how various forms of coalitions, partnerships, and other cooperative relationships to varying degrees involve States, international organisations, or non-State armed groups in armed conflicts. These diverse cooperative patterns raise challenges in identifying parties among different cooperation partners. This book develops an account of the legal criteria for establishing party status which addresses these challenges within a single analytical framework.

2. The structure of the book

The book is organised into two parts, which together comprise five chapters.

Part I, which contains Chapters 1 and 2, situates parties within the international legal framework regulating armed conflict to assess the legal significance of party status under international law.

Chapter 1 analyses the various ways in which the rules of this body of international law are organised by reference to the parties as collective entities. The analysis demonstrates that party status continues to hold a central place in the contemporary international legal regulation of armed conflict. At one level, parties are key addressees of international law provisions regulating armed conflict. To specify what legal difference being 'at war' still makes, the chapter discusses the extent to which international law places restrictions on parties and grants them permissions that they would not otherwise have. Moving to another level, the chapter explains how the legal position of individuals in armed conflict depends on the nature of their connection to parties. This reveals that the legal positions of the parties and individuals are inextricably intertwined, balancing the collective character of the legal regulation of warfare with its humanisation and individualisation. Finally, the chapter outlines how international humanitarian law (IHL) establishes its geographical scope of application by reference to parties.

To complete the analysis of the parties' legal position, Chapter 2 considers how the parties' position relates to that of those that do not qualify as parties, referred to in this book as third parties.[21] The chapter argues that identifying and distinguishing parties and third parties still matters in a legal order that regulates war as a concern not only to parties but to all States. Party status is relevant both *in contradistinction from* and *in relation to* third-party status. First, the obligations imposed

Challenges of Contemporary Armed Conflicts' (2019) 59–61; B Cathcart, 'Coalition Warfare and the Future of the Law of Armed Conflict' in M Waxman and T Oakley (eds), *The Future Law of Armed Conflict* (OUP 2022).

[21] When referring to third parties, this thesis is mainly concerned with States who are not a party to the conflict. On whether non-State armed groups and international organisations may be addressees of IHL as third parties, see Chapter 2.3.c.i. For the different possible conceptions of third parties in international law, see generally C Chinkin, *Third Parties in International Law* (Clarendon Press 1993) 7ff.

on parties and third parties structurally differ both in kind and extent. Secondly, and relatedly, party status gives rise to obligations and rights specifically in the relationship between parties and third parties. The different layers of rules regarding third parties thus complement party status as a central regulatory reference point. In particular, these rules do not challenge the primary role of parties to ensure that armed conflicts are conducted in accordance with the protective purposes of IHL.

The analysis in Part I on why and how identifying parties to an armed conflict matters under international law sets the stage for Part II of the book. Part II provides an account of the legal framework for identifying parties. The focal point for doing so are conflicts with multiple parties on one or both sides of the same conflict. The book refers to these multiple parties as co-parties.

To lay the foundation for the account advanced in Part II, Chapter 3 disentangles the concepts of international and non-international armed conflict from the criteria for identifying parties. The chapter argues that in settings involving multiple potential co-parties, those elements of the notions of international and non-international armed conflict that specify the nature of the collective entities involved—particularly the organisation requirement in non-international armed conflicts—must be fulfilled separately by each co-party. By contrast, it is sufficient that all co-parties jointly fulfil those elements of the notions of international and non-international armed conflict that relate to the nature of the confrontation as a whole—that is, the existence of recourse to armed force in international armed conflicts and protracted armed violence in non-international armed conflicts. Accordingly, while identifying parties is intimately linked to the notions of armed conflict, the issue ultimately needs to be addressed through a distinct legal framework.

Chapter 4 responds to this often overlooked need to discern legal concepts so as to understand the identification of co-parties as a distinct legal question. Building on the parameters set out in Chapter 3, Chapter 4 develops an account of the legal criteria for establishing co-party status. The account proposes a common framework for analysing all conflict settings where co-parties need to be identified. This framework is rooted in the general structure of the legal system regulating armed conflict. It is informed by international practice and draws, in part, on concepts advanced by approaches to identifying co-parties in specific conflict settings. On this account, a co-party must knowingly perform acts with a direct connection to military operations or hostilities and thus to harm to the adversary. The acts must be coordinated with fellow co-parties in such a way that each co-party is involved in the decision-making processes on the coordinated military operations.

Chapter 5 completes Part II of the book. It explores key legal implications that flow from identifying collective entities as co-parties to multiparty armed conflicts under the framework developed in Chapters 3 and 4. In doing so, the chapter not only makes the practical significance of this account more tangible. Crucially, it also spells out the implications of the analysis in Part I on the legal position of parties in light of the legal framework that Part II proposes for identifying them. The chapter thus rounds off the book by tying Parts I and II together. To do this, it concentrates on one emblematic set of implications of party status specifically for the relationship between multiple co-parties. The central argument is that co-parties have multiple complementary sets of duties to take positive steps vis-à-vis the conduct of their fellow co-parties in an armed conflict. The resulting network of duties reflects the key role of parties to ensure that armed conflicts are carried out in accordance with the protective purposes of IHL. Accordingly, this account of the duties of co-parties is built into the established structure of this body of law. It aims to present a more refined conception of the allocation of obligations under IHL, which may contribute to addressing the protection challenges arising in co-operation settings.

3. The scope of the book

Within international law, the legal position and identification of parties to armed conflicts foremost concern IHL. Yet, the book also shows that these issues cannot be fully understood without considering their implications under other regimes of international law which may apply to parties, third parties, and individuals connected to parties, including notably the *jus ad bellum*, human rights law, and international criminal law. Some scope limitations are nonetheless necessary. The first limitation is that, within IHL, reasons of scope preclude considering the law of occupation. The second limitation concerns international counterterrorism law. For example, certain international treaties on counterterrorism exclude from their scope of application acts of armed forces during armed conflict under IHL.[22] Beyond noting here that the identification of parties may therefore also have implications in this context, the book does not further explore interactions with this body of law.

Moreover, it is helpful to clarify briefly the scope of the book regarding questions of international responsibility. Identifying parties as bearers of central sets of obligations under international law is crucial for establishing both their own responsibility for violations of these obligations and the responsibility of third parties in connection with such violations.[23] The main focus of the book is nonetheless on the primary rules that establish and flow from establishing party status,

[22] For references and discussion, see T van Poecke, F Verbruggen, and W Yperman, 'Terrorist Offences and International Humanitarian Law: The Armed Conflict Exclusion Clause' (2021) 103 IRRC 295 (also discussing similar clauses and case law at the domestic level); B Saul, 'From Conflict to Complementarity: Reconciling International Counterterrorism Law and International Humanitarian Law' (2021) 103 IRRC 157, 178–188; D O'Donnell, 'International Treaties against Terrorism and the Use of Terrorism during Armed Conflict and by Armed Forces' (2006) 88 IRRC 653.

[23] Chapter 1.3.a.iii.; Chapter 2.3.b.–c.

rather than on the secondary rules under the law of international responsibility for violations of party obligations.[24] This focus also precludes investigating the implications of a State's party status for its standing to enforce violations of international law in armed conflict.

Finally, given that the book is concerned with party status to armed conflicts in international law, it does not attempt to cover what domestic legal effects may flow from identifying parties and how this is established under domestic law. To get a sense of the wider context in which the concept of party status under international law operates, we should nonetheless briefly take note of possible interactions of that concept with domestic law.

Being 'at war' traditionally had a wide range of implications in many domestic legal systems. Some of these implications persist, while others have been added over time.[25] Relevant provisions range from 'war clauses' in insurance contracts[26] to constitutional law arrangements on the authorities competent to deploy armed forces abroad.[27] Under South African law, persons with dual citizenship lose their South African citizenship when they serve in the armed forces of a State with whom South Africa is at war.[28] Domestic criminal law also, at times, relies on international law concepts of being 'at war' or party status, for example for defining treason.[29] Such criminal law provisions have received renewed attention in the context of outlawing terrorist acts, particularly acts committed by so-called foreign fighters who have joined groups considered to be terrorist, such as ISIL. In that context, a newly introduced provision of the Danish criminal code, for example, criminalises entering the armed forces of an adverse party to an armed conflict to which Denmark is also a party.[30] Still within the counterterrorism realm, Belgian criminal law excludes the application of terrorist offences to acts of the armed forces during armed conflict.[31] This exclusion in part reflects the position

[24] On this distinction generally, see R Ago, 'Seventh Report on State Responsibility—The Internationally Wrongful Act of the State, Source of International Responsibility' (1978) UN Doc A/CN.4/307 (1978) II(1) YILC, 179; ARSIWA Commentary [3]; for criticism of its utility, see U Linderfalk, 'State Responsibility and the Primary-Secondary Rules Terminology—The Role of Language for an Understanding of the International Legal System' (2009) 78 Nordic JIL 53, 72. This focus does not exclude rules that prohibit contributing to violations by others, which Chapters 2 and 5 will address (on the primary nature of such rules, see generally M Jackson, *Complicity in International Law* (OUP 2015) 148–150).

[25] Clapham (n 11) 1–10, 169–233; McNair and Watts (n 13); M Mancini, 'The Effects of a State of War or Armed Conflict' in M Weller (ed), *The Oxford Handbook on the Use of Force in International Law* (OUP 2015).

[26] On current issues with such clauses in cyber-insurance policies in light of State-sponsored cyber operations, see eg A Shniderman, 'Prove It: Judging the Hostile-or-Warlike-Action Exclusion in Cyber-Insurance Policies' (2019) 129 Yale LJF 64.

[27] Clapham (n 11) 169–193.

[28] South African Citizenship Act 1995, s 6(1)(b).

[29] For a survey of mostly common law jurisdictions, see Clapham (n 11) 222–232.

[30] Danish Criminal Code, § 101(a); for translation and analysis, see H Højfeldt Jakobsen, 'Returning Foreign Fighters: The Case of Denmark' (2018) 100 IRRC 315, 331.

[31] Belgian Criminal Code, art 141*bis*.

under international counterterrorism treaties noted above. In their application of that provision to fighters of rebel groups in Syria in recent years, Belgian courts have referred to whether the respective group was a party to an armed conflict in the sense of international law.[32]

If domestic law provisions refer to international law notions of party status or are interpreted by competent authorities as doing so, this not only adds to the wider legal implications of identifying parties under international law. It also reveals how the respective State understands the identification of parties under international law. Against this background, instead of attempting a comprehensive or representative survey of the domestic legal effects of identifying parties, the book will emblematically discuss certain domestic provisions in analysing the concept of party status under international law.[33]

[32] For discussion, see R Bartels, 'When Do Terrorist Organisations Qualify as "Parties to an Armed Conflict" under International Humanitarian Law?' (2017) 56 MLLWR 451, 476–483; H Cuyckens and C Paulussen, 'The Prosecution of Foreign Fighters in Western Europe: The Difficult Relationship between Counter-Terrorism and International Humanitarian Law' (2019) 24 JCSL 537, 553–559; M Wéry, 'La Jurisprudence relative à la clause d'exclusion prévue à l'article 141*bis* du Code pénal: La difficile application du droit international humanitaire par les cours et tribunaux belges' (2018) 57 MLLWR 103.

[33] See notably Chapter 4.2.b.i. on the US 'associated forces' practice.

PART I

THE LEGAL POSITION OF PARTIES TO ARMED CONFLICTS IN INTERNATIONAL LAW

1

Parties and the Regulation of Armed Conflict through Collective Entities

1. Introduction

To show how the concept of party status to armed conflict is significant in international law, Part I (Chapters 1 and 2) situates the parties within the complex web of international legal rules regulating armed conflict. In doing so, Part I lays the groundwork for the analysis in Part II: before looking at how an entity can be identified as a party to an armed conflict, it is helpful to clarify what turns on this identification. Chapter 1 responds to this need by explaining in what ways the legal regulation of armed conflict is structured by reference to the parties to armed conflicts.

Across cultures and throughout history, war has been understood as collective violence. The collective entities that are 'at war', the parties to the conflict, thus appear as natural points of reference for the international legal framework regulating armed conflict. This is attested, for example, by the fact that numerous provisions in international treaties refer to parties to the conflict in various ways and Security Council resolutions frequently address parties.[1] Yet, to what extent the international legal regulation of armed conflict has been and remains conceived around parties has rarely been studied. Doing so is warranted and timely, not least in light of the increasing humanisation and individualisation of the law in this field. These trends question the relevance of conceiving the regulation of war as the regulation of collective entities. Chapter 1 explores this collective dimension of the regulation of armed conflict. It argues that parties to a conflict still hold a central position within this body of law. To make this argument, the chapter proceeds as follows.

In a preliminary step, section 2 outlines how the concepts of both international and non-international armed conflict are defined as confrontations between certain collective entities. The section then sets out the prerequisites as to their nature and organisational structure that collective entities must possess to qualify as potential parties.

As a core feature of the legal position of parties, section 3 shows that parties are central addressees of international law provisions in the field of armed conflict.

[1] n 14.

Party Status to Armed Conflict in International Law. Alexander Wentker, Oxford University Press. © Alexander Wentker 2024.
DOI: 10.1093/oso/9780198900900.003.0002

Against the background of the blurring lines between the traditional spheres of peacetime and wartime international law, the section discusses what legal difference being 'at war' still makes by spelling out *how* parties are addressed. The section specifies to what extent international law places restrictions on or grants permissions to parties both of which would not otherwise apply to these entities.

Even though war is collective in character, it is necessarily fought and suffered by individual human beings. To understand fully quite how central parties remain as regulatory reference points of international law in armed conflict, section 4 analyses the extent to which the legal position of individuals in armed conflict depends on the nature of their connection to parties. The analysis reveals how the legal positions of parties and individuals are inextricably intertwined, balancing the collective character and the humanisation and individualisation of the legal regulation of warfare.

Finally, section 5 sketches in what ways and to what extent the geographical scope of international humanitarian law (IHL) application is to be established by reference to parties to the conflict.

2. Parties and the collective character of armed conflict

The starting point to understand how and to what extent armed conflict is regulated by reference to parties is that, at the most basic level, war or armed conflict is inherently characterised as being fought between *collective* entities—the parties. To set the scene for the chapter, the section first briefly outlines this idea and the features that characterise collective entities as (potential) parties to a conflict.

a. War as violence between collectives

The collective character of warfare has historically been deeply engrained across different cultures. Historical societies in India and China are known to have distinguished collective from individual, interpersonal violence. The distinction was often reflected in separate deities for the two kinds of violence but also in distinct legal regimes.[2] Writers in ancient Greece[3] and Rome,[4] as well as in the Middle Ages,[5] already regarded violence between individuals as a matter for the domestic law enforcement of the State as the common 'superior' of these individuals.

[2] S Neff, *War and the Law of Nations: A General History* (CUP 2005) 15–20.

[3] Plato, *The Republic* (H Lee tr, Penguin 1987) 258–259; Plato, *The Laws* (T Saunders tr, Penguin 1970) 489.

[4] MT Cicero, *Philippics* (D Shackleton Bailey tr, Harvard UP 2009) 237.

[5] T Aquinas, *On Law, Morality, and Politics* (William Baumgarth and Richard Regan (eds), Hackett 1988) 221.

Conversely, war was seen as violence between collectives without a superior–subordinate relationship. This type of violence thus followed a different logic and required a distinct set of rules. As Rousseau noted, '[w]ar, then, is not a relation between men, but between states ... a state can have as an enemy only another state, not men'.[6]

With the emergence of concepts of sovereign statehood in Europe, war was conceived of as a contest between sovereigns.[7] Particularly in the nineteenth and early twentieth centuries, the formal restriction that sovereign States were the only collectives capable of being belligerents was a manifestation of Western imperialism. This conception excluded those States that were not accepted as full members of the family of nations, let alone peoples in the colonies who were deemed 'non-civilised'.[8] To some extent, the formal restriction gave way to factual considerations. Oppenheim conceded that:

> [w]henever ... a State lacking the legal qualification to make war nevertheless actually makes war, such State is a belligerent, the contention is real war, and all the rules of International Law respecting warfare apply to it.[9]

But this did not conduce Western States to apply the laws of war in the 'periphery' to colonial wars. It also did not prevent them from circumventing the full application of this law in the 'semi-periphery' to States that were not recognised as having attained the same 'civilisational' standard.[10]

Yet, beyond inter-sovereign confrontation, international law also came to acknowledge that even within a State there could be violence that defied the paradigm of domestic law enforcement. Accordingly, this type of violence was instead to be viewed through a war paradigm, as taking place between collectives. Vattel explained the rationale for applying a collective framework to so-called civil wars with the factual capabilities of the insurgents:[11]

> [w]hen a party is formed within the State which ceases to obey the sovereign and is strong enough to make a stand against him ... there exists a civil war. Civil war ... gives rise ... to two independent parties, who regard each other as enemies and acknowledge no common judge. Of necessity, therefore, these two parties

[6] J-J Rousseau, *The Social Contract* (M Cranston tr, Penguin 1968) 56.

[7] P Kalmanovitz, *The Laws of War in International Thought* (OUP 2020) 70–71, 93–96.

[8] E Colby, 'How to Fight Savage Tribes' (1927) 21 AJIL 279, 287. For critical analysis, see F Mégret, 'From "Savages" to "Unlawful Combatants": A Postcolonial Look at International Humanitarian Law's "Other"' in A Orford (ed), *International Law and Its Others* (CUP 2006); on the construction of 'civilisational' standards in the nineteenth century, see A Anghie, 'Finding the Peripheries: Sovereignty and Colonialism in Nineteenth-Century International Law' (1999) 40 Harv ILJ 1, 22–57.

[9] L Oppenheim, *International Law: A Treatise*, vol II (Longmans 1906) 86.

[10] J von Bernstorff, 'The Use of Force in International Law before World War I: On Imperial Ordering and the Ontology of the Nation-State' (2018) 29 EJIL 233.

[11] See also Kalmanovitz (n 7) 94.

> must be regarded as forming ... two separate bodies .... They have no common superior upon earth. They are therefore in the situation of two Nations which enter into a dispute and, being unable to agree, have recourse to arms.[12]

In the nineteenth century and the first half of the twentieth century, the party status of the non-State collective still depended on whether it received recognition of its belligerency. Recognition of belligerency signalled that the recognising State considered the insurgents as a party to a contest between equal collectives and not merely as a group of individuals. Under customary international law, either the State involved in civil strife itself or a third State could accord such recognition if certain conditions were met, namely that:

> (1) [the insurgents] are in possession of a certain part of the territory of the legitimate government; (2) they have set up a Government of their own; and (3) they conduct their armed contention with the legitimate Government according to the laws and usages of war.[13]

For Lauterpacht, the fulfilment of these conditions would create a duty to grant recognition, corresponding to the right of the insurgents to receive recognition.[14] State practice, however, has conceived of recognition of belligerency as an option at the discretion of States.[15]

As Chapter 3 will show, today, non-international armed conflicts automatically come into existence once certain factual prerequisites are met (pertaining to the structure of the collective entities and the nature of their confrontation).[16] Nonetheless, the 'collective' logic has not materialised to the same extent for non-State parties. In particular, still in a domestic law enforcement logic, unlike in inter-State conflicts, individuals forming part of such collectives do not hold an international law status as combatants that would shield them from prosecution for merely participating in the collective hostilities.[17]

b. Characterising the collectives: who can be a party?

The 'collective' violence paradigm has been extended beyond inter-State conflict, and both international and non-international armed conflict are characterised as

[12] E de Vattel, *Le Droit des gens, ou, Principes le la loi naturelle, appliqués à la conduite aux affaires des nations et des souverains*, vol III (C Fenwick tr, Carnegie Institution 1916) 338 (emphasis omitted).

[13] Oppenheim (n 9) 86.

[14] H Lauterpacht, *Recognition in International Law* (CUP 1947) 253.

[15] Neff (n 2) 261–264; R McLaughlin, *Recognition of Belligerency and the Law of Armed Conflict* (OUP 2020) 87–89.

[16] Chapter 3.2.b.

[17] Below 4.a.

taking place between collective entities. Yet, international law continues to distinguish between two distinct kinds of conflict regimes depending on which types of collectives confront each other as parties.

i. Parties to international armed conflicts

In international armed conflicts, understood as 'resort to armed force between States',[18] the parties' statehood remains their defining characteristic. Statehood is to be assessed by reference to the criteria under general international law,[19] which no longer leave room for discriminating among States according to alleged degrees of 'civilisation'.[20]

In addition, certain collective entities other than States can also be parties to international armed conflicts. One such case is addressed by Article 1(4) API, which extends the Protocol to 'armed conflicts in which peoples are fighting against colonial domination and alien occupation and against racist régimes in the exercise of their right of self-determination'. The provision recognises that this collective's exercise of its right to self-determination places those peoples' armed conflict with the ('colonial', 'alien', 'racist') State fully in the paradigm of a contest between formal equals. This puts such conflicts on par with inter-State conflicts. Accordingly, a declaration by the authority representing such a people under Article 96(3) API to 'undertake to apply the Conventions and this Protocol in relation to that conflict' will make that people 'a Party to the conflict with immediate effect', endowed with 'the same rights and obligations as those which have been assumed by a High Contracting Party'.[21] Controversy among States and experts has accompanied the provision since its inception, and the ambiguities surrounding the meaning of the terms of the provision leave its scope difficult to identify.[22] While the attention given to the provision has been deemed 'inversely proportional' to its practical relevance,[23] the Polisario Front notably issued a declaration under Article 96(3) API in the Western Sahara conflict in 2015.[24]

18 *Tadić* (Decision on the Defence Motion for Interlocutory Appeal on Jurisdiction) IT-94-1-A (2 October 1995).

19 *Milošević* (Decision on Motion for Judgment of Acquittal) IT-02-54-T (16 June 2004) [85]–[87].

20 J Crawford, *The Creation of States in International Law* (2nd edn, Clarendon Press 2006) 92.

21 CCW, art 7(4) allows such a declaration regarding the CCW (including its Protocols) and the GCs even where the adversary State is not a party to API.

22 Switzerland, *Official Records of the Diplomatic Conference on the Reaffirmation and Development of International Humanitarian Law Applicable in Armed Conflicts, Geneva (1974–1977)* vol VI (Federal Political Department 1978) CDDH/SR.36 41–64 (on diverging views among States at the provision's adoption); see, generally, H Wilson, *International Law and the Use of Force by National Liberation Movements* (Clarendon Press 1988) 163–168; M Bothe, KJ Partsch, and W Solf, *New Rules for Victims of Armed Conflicts: Commentary on the Two 1977 Protocols Additional to the Geneva Conventions of 1949* (reprint edn, Nijhoff 2013) 37ff.

23 K Mačák, *Internationalized Armed Conflicts in International Law* (OUP 2018) 73.

24 Switzerland, 'Notification to the Governments of the States Parties to the Geneva Conventions of 12 August 1949 for the Protection of War Victims' 26 June 2015 <www.eda.admin.ch/dam/eda/fr/documents/aussenpolitik/voelkerrecht/geneve/150626-GENEVE_en.pdf> 1. While this was the first declaration to have been accepted by the depositary, Morocco objected to this decision and denied that an armed conflict existed with the Polisario Front (ibid 1–2).

International organisations, too, can be parties to international armed conflicts. Emblematic cases are UN-led peace operations, through which the UN may become a party to an armed conflict. Ever more 'robust' mandates for such operations to use force and the blurred traditional lines between peacekeeping and peace enforcement[25] have made the issue of party status increasingly relevant to the UN.[26] Despite initial reluctance to consider forces 'acting on behalf of the organized community of nations' as waging war,[27] the possibility of the UN's and other international organisations' party status is now generally acknowledged,[28] including by States[29] and international organisations themselves.[30] While Common Article 2(1) only refers to conflicts between High Contracting Parties, some scholars have contemplated that this could be interpreted broadly as including certain international organisations (such that the Conventions would automatically apply to these organisations)[31] or that international organisations may be considered 'Powers' under Common Article 2(3) (such that the Conventions would apply to these organisations where they accept this).[32] In any event, however, international

[25] See, generally, J Sloan, *The Militarisation of Peacekeeping in the Twenty-First Century* (Hart 2011) 122–281; T Findlay, *The Use of Force in UN Peace Operations* (OUP 2002); L Howard and A Dayal, 'The Use of Force in UN Peacekeeping' (2018) 72 IO 71; M Longobardo, '"Super-Robust" Peacekeeping Mandates in Non-International Armed Conflicts under International Law' (2020) 24 SYIL 42.

[26] In most cases, UN peace operations will intervene with the consent of the territorial State such that the UN will arguably rather become a party to a non-international armed conflict (see below ii.).

[27] Report of the Committee on Study of Legal Problems of the United Nations, 'Should the Laws of War Apply to United Nations Enforcement Action?' (1952) 46 ASIL Proc 216, 217; but see D Bowett, *United Nations Forces: A Legal Study of United Nations Practice* (Stevens 1964) 498.

[28] See eg M Lehto, 'Second report on protection of the environment in relation to armed conflict' (2019) UN Doc A/CN.4/728 50; Report of the High-level Independent Panel on Peace Operations (17 June 2015) UN Doc A/70/95 [122]; O Engdahl, 'Multinational Peace Operations Forces Involved in Armed Conflict: Who are the Parties?' in K Mujezinović Larsen, C Guldahl Cooper, and G Nystuen (eds), *Searching for a 'Principle of Humanity' in International Humanitarian Law* (CUP 2012) 245; E Castrén, *The Present Law of War and Neutrality* (Suomalainen Tiedeakatemia 1954) 90; see also nn 31–32; sceptically K Johnston, 'Transformations of Conflict Status in Libya' (2012) 17 JCSL 81, 104.

[29] See eg *Danish Manual* 55 (referring specifically to the UN as a party); for references to peace operations as parties, see also eg *Peruvian Manual* 242; UK Ministry of Defence, *The Manual of the Law of Armed Conflict* (OUP 2004) [14.3]–[14.7]. For EU-led operations, see Spain, 'Salamanca Presidency Declaration' (2002) DIH/Rev01.Corr1 (on file with the author) 3.

[30] See eg Statement at the ILC by the Under-Secretary-General for Legal Affairs and Legal Counsel (23 May 2013) <http://legal.un.org/ola/media/info_from_lc/ILC%20Legal%20Counsel%20statemen trev3may20.pdf> 20. The UN remains reluctant, however, to admit its party status in concrete situations (T Gill et al, *Leuven Manual on the International Law Applicable to Peace Operations* (CUP 2017) 96). For a thorough review of international practice on the UN's party status regarding specific peace operations, see E Nalin, *L'Applicabilità del diritto internazionale umanitario alle operazioni di 'peace-keeping' delle Nazioni Unite* (Editoriale Scientifica 2018) 102–126. The applicability of IHL to peace operations' actions has been acknowledged (see notably Secretary-General's Bulletin, 'Observance by United Nations Forces of International Humanitarian Law' (6 August 1999) UN Doc ST/SGB/1999/13 [1.1]; UN DPKO/DFS, 'Guidelines: Use of Force by Military Components in United Nations Peacekeeping Operations' (2017) [8]); see also Convention on the Safety of United Nations and Associated Personnel, art 2(2).

[31] T Ferraro, 'The Applicability and Application of International Humanitarian Law to Multinational Forces' (2013) 95 IRRC 561, 575; K Mačák and N Zamir, 'The Applicability of International Humanitarian Law to the Conflict in Libya' (2012) 14 ICLR 403, 416–418.

[32] F Seyersted, *United Nations Forces in the Law of Peace and War* (Sijthoff 1966) 350–351; D Schindler, 'The Different Types of Armed Conflicts According to the Geneva Conventions and

organisations can be parties to international armed conflicts under customary international law.[33]

Finally, there are specific mechanisms by which the law governing international armed conflicts, in whole or in part, can be made applicable *inter partes* in non-international armed conflicts. One such mechanism is the recognition of non-State parties' belligerency. As Chapter 2 explains in greater detail, this remains an option under current international law available to a State party to the conflict or a third State.[34] Parties to non-international armed conflicts can also conclude special agreements on the application of IHL treaty provisions as foreseen by Common Article 3(3), and issue unilateral declarations to abide by rules of international armed conflict law.[35]

ii. Parties to non-international armed conflicts

Non-international armed conflicts are understood as 'protracted armed violence' taking place between specific collectives—the parties—namely 'between governmental authorities and organized armed groups or between such groups within a State'.[36]

Traditionally, State-like organisational structures were required for a group of individuals to be considered a collective that is capable of being a party to a civil war, as evidenced by the conditions that had to be met before recognition of belligerency could be granted.[37] In current international law, the degree of organisation that characterises an armed group as a party to a non-international armed conflict is best understood in a functional sense.[38] That is, the organisation must enable the armed group, as an identifiable collective entity, to conduct violence that is collective in character and sufficiently intense[39] as well as implement at least basic rules of IHL.[40] In practice, the functional assessment of the degree of organisation is facilitated by a non-exhaustive set of factual indicators developed in

Protocols' (1979) 163 RCADI 121, 130; contra M Zwanenburg, *Accountability of Peace Support Operations* (Nijhoff 2005) 137; D Shraga, 'The United Nations as an Actor Bound by International Humanitarian Law' (1998) 5 International Peacekeeping 64, 67; Mačák (n 23) 55.

33 See nn 28–30; see also eg Statement by the Special Adviser to the UN Secretary-General (San Remo, 5 September 2013) <https://legal.un.org/ola/media/info_from_lc/POB-San-Remo-36th-Roundtable-5-September-2013.pdf> 6–7.

34 Recognition granted by a State party to the non-international armed conflict itself will make the law of international armed conflict applicable between the parties to the conflict. Recognition by a third State will make neutrality law applicable between the third State and the parties (see Chapter 2.2.c.ii).

35 See generally S Sivakumaran, *The Law of Non-international Armed Conflict* (OUP 2012) 107ff.

36 *Tadić* (Decision on Jurisdiction) (n 18) [70].

37 n 13.

38 T Rodenhäuser, *Organizing Rebellion: Non-State Armed Groups under International Humanitarian Law, Human Rights Law, and International Criminal Law* (OUP 2018) 110–112.

39 On the intensity threshold, see Chapter 3.2.b.ii.

40 Schindler (n 32) 147; Sivakumaran (n 35) 174; for a detailed analysis of these features, see Rodenhäuser (n 38) 19–114.

international criminal jurisprudence.[41] To qualify as a potential party to an armed conflict covered by APII, Article 1(1) specifically requires—also in functional terms—that armed groups:

> under responsible command, exercise such control over a part of [the territory of the State party to the conflict] as to enable them to carry out sustained and concerted military operations and to implement this Protocol.

In non-international armed conflicts, the degree of organisation has crystallised as a baseline requirement and thus a common denominator for any collective entity, not merely armed groups, to qualify as a potential party.

Indeed, States' armed forces, too, must possess that same degree of organisation, even though, in practice, they are presumed to be sufficiently organised.[42] One may wonder whether this presumption can be rebutted[43] where armed forces lack the factual capacity to conduct sufficiently intense violence and implement IHL.[44] International criminal jurisprudence seems to be lenient in this respect. For example, in *Bemba*, the ICC considered the Central African Republic a party to a conflict with different rebel groups although it noted an 'overall disorganization' of its armed forces.[45]

Multinational forces under the aegis of an international organisation—such as UN-led peace operations—may also meet the organisation requirement. When such forces become involved in non-international armed conflicts against non-State armed groups, the respective international organisation may become a party to the conflict. Indeed, rather than automatically considering the conflict as international if an international organisation becomes a party through the involvement of multinational forces,[46] the same criteria should be applied as for classifying

[41] *Boškoski and Tarčulovski* (Trial Judgment) IT-04-82-T (10 July 2008) [199]–[203]; *Đorđević et al* (Trial Judgment) IT-05-87/1-T (23 February 2011) [1541]–[1578]; *Haradinaj, Balaj, Brahimaj* (Retrial Judgment) IT-04-84bis-T (29 November 2012) [395], [406]–[409]; *Lubanga* (Trial Judgment) ICC-01/04-01/06 (14 March 2012) [537]; *Katanga* (Trial Judgment) ICC-01/04-01/07 (7 March 2014) [1186]; *Bemba* (Trial Judgment) ICC-01/05-01/08 (21 March 2016) [134]–[136]; *Ntaganda* (Trial Judgment) ICC-01/04-02/06 (8 July 2019) [704].

[42] *Ntaganda* (Trial) (n 41) [711]; *GCI Commentary* [429].

[43] Instances where the degree of organisation of State armed forces has been explicitly examined suggest as much (see eg *Al Hassan* (Confirmation des Charges, Rectificatif) ICC-01/12-01/18 (8 November 2019) [207]). See also J Kleffner, 'The Legal Fog of an Illusion: Three Reflections on "Organization" and "Intensity" as Criteria for the Temporal Scope of the Law of Non-International Armed Conflict' (2019) 95 ILS 161, 170.

[44] For an argument that even so-called failed States can be parties to non-international armed conflicts, see R Geiß, *'Failed States': Die normative Erfassung gescheiterter Staaten* (Duncker & Humblot 2005) 233–236.

[45] *Bemba* (Trial) (n 41) [444]–[445].

[46] R Kolb, *Droit humanitaire et opérations de paix internationales* (2nd edn, Helbing Lichtenhahn 2006) 57; V Koutroulis, 'IOs Involved in Armed Conflict: The Material and Geographical Scope of Application of IHL' (2012) 42 Collegium 29, 35; E David, 'How Does the Involvement of a Multinational Peacekeeping Force Affect the Classification of a Situation' (2013) 95 IRRC 659, 664–665.

conflicts in which foreign States intervene.[47] Against this background, commentators have, for example, considered the UN to be a party with respect to the actions of several missions in recent years, including MONUSCO, MINUSCA, and MINUSMA.[48]

More widely, a functional conception of the organisation requirement allows for understanding the parties' international legal personality as part of the content of party status rather than as a limiting condition for party status.[49] While a certain degree of international personality is inherent in an entity's party status—a status which entails restrictions and permissions under international law[50]—there is no a priori *numerus clausus* of types of collective entities that can be parties to non-international armed conflicts. Instead, there is an 'open casting call'[51] to all collective entities with the requisite military capacity to conduct hostilities and implement IHL. These factual prerequisites could also be met, for example, by certain corporations.[52] The idea of such corporate belligerency may even have considerable historical pedigree in international practice and was envisaged by Grotius, for example, regarding the Dutch East India Trading Company.[53] Today, it may notably be relevant for private military and security companies.[54]

This section has shown that the very concepts of armed conflict in international law are premised on and characterised by the existence of parties as organised collectives. This provides the groundwork for analysing more specifically what role parties play in the regulation of armed conflict.

[47] ICRC, 'International Humanitarian Law and the Challenges of Contemporary Armed Conflicts' (2011) 31–32; N Zamir, *Classification of Conflicts in International Humanitarian Law: The Legal Impact of Foreign Intervention in Civil Wars* (Edward Elgar 2017) 200–205; D Akande, 'Classification of Armed Conflicts: Relevant Legal Concepts' in E Wilmshurst (ed), *International Law and the Classification of Conflicts* (OUP 2012) 69–70; O Engdahl, 'How Does the Involvement of a Multinational Peacekeeping Force Affect the Classification of a Situation: A Rebuttal to Eric David' (2013) 95 IRRC 667, 672.

[48] A Bellal (ed), *The War Report: Armed Conflicts in 2018* (Geneva Academy 2019) 87, 97, 112; B Maganza, 'From Peacekeepers to Parties to the Conflict: An IHL's Appraisal of the Role of UN Peace Operations in NIACs' (2020) 25 JCSL 209, 225–228.

[49] For an open, a posteriori conception of international legal personality as being the addressee of international provisions, see generally H Kelsen, 'Théorie générale du droit international public: Problèmes choisis' (1932) 42 RCADI 121, 141–172; R Portmann, *Legal Personality in International Law* (CUP 2010) 13, 173ff; C Brölmann and J Nijmann, 'Personality' in J d'Aspremont and S Singh (eds), *Concepts for International Law: Contributions to Disciplinary Thought* (Edward Elgar 2019) 687–688.

[50] Below 3.

[51] Crawford, 'Foreword' in Portmann (n 49) xiv.

[52] A crucial question will be whether such corporations are a separate party to the conflict in their own right, rather than merely a part of another party. On this distinction, see Chapter 3.4.b.

[53] R Giladi, 'Corporate Belligerency and the Delegation Theory from Grotius to Westlake' (2020) 41 Grotiana 349.

[54] On the possibility of such companies' party status, see L Cameron and V Chetail, *Privatizing War: Private Military and Security Companies under Public International Law* (CUP 2013) 314–315; E-C Gillard, 'Business Goes to War: Private Military/Security Companies and International Humanitarian Law' (2006) 88 IRRC 525, 546; L Vierucci, 'Private Military and Security Companies in Non-international Armed Conflicts: *Ius ad Bellum* and *Ius in Bello* Issues' in F Francioni and N Ronzitti (eds), *War by Contract: Human Rights, Humanitarian Law, and Private Contractors* (OUP 2011) 252.

3. Parties as addressees of international law

A core dichotomous distinction between peace and war has traditionally characterised international law. The 'state of war' gave rise to distinct sets of legal relations, both between the States involved and with respect to third States. The peacetime–wartime dichotomy has increasingly eroded and blurred in contemporary international law. Yet, armed conflict remains regulated as a distinct legal institution giving rise to a distinct legal position of parties, the central addressees of international law in armed conflict.[55] In essence, being in a state of war with another State had the permissive effect of freeing the respective States from restrictive peacetime rules. By contrast, current international law primarily addresses the parties in restrictive terms as bearing obligations. Nonetheless, States continue to invoke party status as granting them permissions under international law. To understand what being a party to an armed conflict means in legal terms, this section analyses both the restrictive and the permissive dimensions of party status in turn.

a. Party status as restrictive

The restrictive dimension of contemporary IHL is often regarded as the central feature of IHL's nature.[56] This section, first, briefly explains that IHL is constructed in significant parts by imposing restrictions and prescriptions on parties. Moving beyond IHL, the section notes that the Security Council frequently addresses either specific parties or all parties to an armed conflict and sometimes imposes obligations that go beyond their IHL duties. Against this background, the section then sketches how it matters to find that States, international organisations, or non-State armed groups bear obligations as parties.

i. Parties as the central bearers of obligations under IHL

Parties are the central addressees of the law relating to the means and methods of warfare as well as to the protection of individuals. This is often explicit in the text of the relevant treaty provisions. For example, the obligation to distinguish combatants and military objectives from the civilian population and civilian objects in the conduct of military operations is—naturally—explicitly addressed to the parties to the conflict.[57] The same is true of many prescriptions concerning the treatment of protected persons, such as the obligations to search for, collect, protect, and care

[55] D Kennedy, *Of War and Law* (Princeton UP 2006) 2–3, 46ff.

[56] See eg R Baxter, 'So-Called Unprivileged Belligerency: Spies, Guerrillas, and Saboteurs' (1951) 28 BYIL 323, 324; A Haque, *Law and Morality at War* (OUP 2017) 30; A Quintin, *The Nature of International Humanitarian Law: A Permissive or Restrictive Regime?* (Edward Elgar 2020) 62.

[57] API, art 48; *CIHL* r 1.

for the wounded, sick, and shipwrecked, to search for the dead and to prevent their being despoiled, and to search for missing persons.[58]

Even where obligations are passively worded—that is, where the obligations do not explicitly state whom they address—interpretation will often lead to the conclusion that they are borne by the parties.[59] For example, the obligation to take precautions in military operations under Article 57(1) API does not indicate a specific addressee.[60] Here, however, the context clarifies that the obligation is addressed to the parties. Article 57(4) API reiterates that 'each *Party to the conflict* shall ... take all reasonable precautions'.[61] Absent any reason for distinguishing operations on land from operations on the sea and in the air, the passive wording in Article 57(1) 'care shall be taken' is to be read as 'the parties to the conflict must take care'.[62] Similarly, although APII does not contain any reference to parties to the conflict, many of the obligations contained in APII should be considered as addressing parties.[63] To give another example, the recent 'Oxford Statement on the International Law Protections Against Cyber Operations Targeting the Health Care Sector' quite naturally concludes from the passively worded rule requiring respect for and protection of medical units, transport, and personnel that this obligation is borne by parties to armed conflicts.[64]

Certain sets of obligations under IHL do not specifically address parties to an armed conflict. Apart from duties imposed on third parties (discussed in Chapter 2), there are also obligations 'which shall be implemented in peacetime'.[65] These consist of obligations to enact legislation suppressing grave breaches, take measures to suppress other violations of the Conventions,[66] disseminate the Conventions (including by educating the general population and training and instructing their armed forces) as well as take other steps allowing for the implementation of obligations that will arise in armed conflict.[67] Even for some of IHL's peacetime obligations, an important rationale is that they put future parties in a position to satisfy obligations that they will have at that point.[68] Given that failures

[58] GCI, art 15; GCII, art 18; GCIV, art 16; API, art 33. The parties also bear the respective obligations under customary international law (*CIHL* rr 109, 112–114, 116–117).

[59] For potential parallel obligations of individuals, see below 4.b.ii.

[60] See also *CIHL* r 15.

[61] Emphasis added.

[62] See *AP Commentary* 680 [2191].

[63] See further Chapter 3.4.c.ii.

[64] D Akande et al, 'Oxford Statement on the International Law Protections against Cyber Operations Targeting the Health Care Sector' (*EJIL: Talk!*, 21 May 2020) <www.ejiltalk.org/oxford-statement-on-the-international-law-protections-against-cyber-operations-targeting-the-health-care-sector/>; see also D Akande et al, 'The Second Oxford Statement on International Law Protections of the Healthcare Sector during COVID-19: Safeguarding Vaccine Research' (*EJIL: Talk!*, 11 August 2020) <www.ejiltalk.org/the-second-oxford-statement-on-international-law-protections-of-the-healthcare-sector-during-covid-19-safeguarding-vaccine-research/>.

[65] Common Article 2.

[66] GCI-IV, arts 49–50, 129, 146; API, art 85.

[67] GCI-IV, arts 47–48, 127, 144; API, art 83; APII, art 19; APIII, art 7; *CIHL* rr 141–143; *GCI Commentary* [199]–[200]; *GCII Commentary* [221]–[222]; *GCIII Commentary* [232]–[233].

[68] *GCIII Commentary* [178].

to comply with these preparatory obligations are likely to materialise in violations of party obligations eventually, the former can be said to exist, at least in part, with a view to States' potential party status. Against this background, the need for such preparatory or preventive measures is the same for entities other than States that can become parties to armed conflicts.[69]

ii. Beyond IHL: obligations imposed on parties by the UN Security Council

IHL is not the only field of international law that imposes obligations on parties. States parties to an armed conflict remain bound, in principle, by all their international obligations, including notably the prohibition of the use of force as well as obligations under human rights law or trade and investment law.[70] Unlike obligations under IHL, however, these obligations do not specifically attach to party status. They are therefore not part of the restrictive dimension of party status as such. Rather, questions arise as to whether these restrictions from other bodies of international law apply less stringently to conflict parties than they otherwise would. These questions of potential permissive effects of party status are addressed in section b.

By contrast, the Security Council frequently addresses parties—either specific parties or 'all parties' to a conflict—in the language of obligations. In doing so, the Security Council often reiterates the parties' obligations under international treaty and customary law—including in particular under IHL[71]—and 'calls upon', 'demands', or 'urges' parties to comply with these obligations and 'condemns' violations thereof.[72]

Going further, however, the Security Council regularly imposes additional obligations on parties to an armed conflict, which go beyond their obligations under international treaty or customary law.[73] These obligations would then flow from the Security Council imposing them rather than from the entities' party status *ipso facto*. Importantly, however, the Security Council often chooses to specifically

[69] M Sassòli, *International Humanitarian Law: Rules, Controversies, and Solutions to Problems Arising in Warfare* (Edward Elgar 2019) 592–593. Constructing such obligations is particularly difficult for non-State armed groups, which IHL only addresses once they are parties to an armed conflict. International organisations, such as the UN, on the other hand, may well have an obligation to ensure that forces through which they may become parties are adequately trained (Maganza (n 48) 222).

[70] See b.

[71] See generally G Nolte, 'The Different Functions of the Security Council with Respect to Humanitarian Law' in V Lowe et al (eds), *The United Nations Security Council and War: The Evolution of Thought and Practice Since 1945* (OUP 2008) 521ff, 534.

[72] eg UNSC Res 2540 (28 August 2020) UN Doc S/RES/2540 [8]; UNSC Res 2439 (30 October 2018) UN Doc S/RES/2439 [6].

[73] K Polackova van der Ploeg, 'The Functional Threshold: Direct International Legal Regulation of Collective Nonstate Entities and the Law of International Peace and Security' (2020) 53 NYUJILP 71, 94–105; L Borlini, 'The Security Council and Non-State Domestic Actors: Changes in Non-Forcible Measures between International Lawmaking and Peacebuilding' (2021) 61 Va JIL 489, 527–531.

address these entities as parties to armed conflicts. In doing so, it shapes the content of party status for these entities regarding a given conflict and potentially beyond.[74]

A typical example of such Security Council-imposed obligations is the obligation to cease hostilities.[75] Usually, this obligation is imposed regarding a specific conflict.[76] However, in Resolution 2532 of 1 July 2020, adopted in the course of the COVID-19 pandemic, the Council:

> [*d*]*emands* a general and immediate cessation of hostilities in all situations on its agenda and ... [*c*]*alls* upon all parties to armed conflicts to engage immediately in a durable humanitarian pause for at least 90 consecutive days.[77]

The call for a 'humanitarian pause' shows that the obligations imposed by the Security Council may also be relevant in realms where parties already have obligations under international law—here, the obligation to facilitate humanitarian access.[78] The Security Council can concretise and thus operationalise such obligations by imposing specific measures.

Where resolutions go beyond international treaty or customary law obligations, this raises questions as to whether and when Security Council resolutions bind parties to armed conflict.[79] For States parties to an armed conflict that are members of the UN, this will depend on a case-by-case determination of whether the resolution constitutes a 'decision' under Article 25 UN Charter.[80] But also for parties other than States, in particular armed groups, the Security Council has repeatedly

[74] G Fox, K Boon, and I Jenkins, 'The Contributions of United Nations Security Council Resolutions to the Law of Non-International Armed Conflict: New Evidence of Customary International Law' (2018) 67 AULR 649 (arguing that the Council's frequent and consistent imposition of such obligations contributes to the formation of customary international law obligations).

[75] Empirical analyses have shown that this obligation has been imposed in the great majority of non-international armed conflicts in recent decades (ibid 683–684). For an early example, see UNSC Res 27 (1 August 1947) UN Doc S/459. Generally on this practice, see S Bailey, 'Cease-Fires, Truces, and Armistices in the Practice of the UN Security Council' (1977) 71 AJIL 461; C Henderson and N Lubell, 'The Contemporary Legal Nature of UN Security Council Ceasefire Resolutions' (2013) 26 LJIL 369 (discussing when such ceasefire resolutions are binding on parties).

[76] eg UNSC Res 2459 (15 March 2019) UN Doc S/RES/2459 [1] (South Sudan); UNSC Res 925 (6 June 1994) UN Doc S/RES/925 [6] (Rwanda). Where parties have previously entered into a ceasefire or peace agreement, the Council generally refers to obligations under these agreements (see eg UNSC Res 1509 (19 September 2003) UN Doc S/RES/1509 [4] (Liberia); UNSC Res 752 (15 May 1992) UN Doc S/RES/752 [1] (Bosnia and Herzegovina)).

[77] UNSC Res 2532 (1 July 2020) UN Doc S/RES/2532 [1]–[2]. For a discussion on whether this resolution qualifies as a binding 'decision', see E Pobjie, 'Covid-19 as a Threat to International Peace and Security: The Role of the UN Security Council in Addressing the Pandemic' (*EJIL: Talk!*, 27 July 2020) <www.ejiltalk.org/covid-19-as-a-threat-to-international-peace-and-security-the-role-of-the-un-security-council-in-addressing-the-pandemic/#:~:text=Recognising%20that%20the%20unprecedented%20extent,appeal%20of%20UN%20Secretary%20General>.

[78] GCIV, art 23; API, art 70(2), (4); *CIHL* r 55.

[79] For discussion, see L Borlini and R Kolb, 'Le Conseil de Sécurité des Nations Unies et les entités non-étatiques' (2021) 125 RGDIP 25, 39–45.

[80] *Namibia* (AO) [1971] ICJ Rep 16 [114].

and consistently claimed the authority to impose obligations.[81] Even though a 'unanimously convincing theory' as to the legal basis is lacking,[82] States have not seriously contested the Security Council's pragmatic assertion of authority,[83] and the ICJ also seems to have accepted it. In the *Kosovo* Advisory Opinion, the Court indicated its readiness to derive binding obligations for actors other than Member States—which would include non-State parties to armed conflict—from the Security Council's intention to impose such obligations.[84]

Having seen that parties are central addressees of obligations under IHL as well as under Security Council resolutions, it is important to note briefly what turns on establishing that a State, an international organisation, and particularly a non-State armed group, bears these obligations as a party.

iii. Implications of parties' obligations

For States and international organisations, finding that IHL imposes obligations on them as parties to armed conflict is a central step in establishing their international responsibility for violations of these obligations. If such violations are attributable to the respective State or international organisation, they may constitute internationally wrongful acts. But, establishing the obligations of parties also matters for holding third parties responsible in connection with the parties' violations of their obligations, as explored in Chapter 2.[85]

For non-State parties, the ILC acknowledged that they 'may [them]self be held responsible for [their] own conduct under international law, for example for a breach of international humanitarian law committed by [their] forces'.[86] Yet, concepts for establishing the responsibility of non-State parties under international law as well as the legal consequences flowing from such responsibility are still lacking.[87]

Nonetheless, establishing that a non-State armed group bears obligations under international law as a party matters in several respects. Indirectly, violations by non-State entities of their obligations as parties to an armed conflict may be relevant for finding third States responsible in connection with such violations, notably for assisting the non-State party.[88]

[81] K Boon, 'The UN Security Council and Non-State Actors' (2019) 113 ASIL Proc 209; A Peters, 'Article 25' in B Simma et al (eds), *The Charter of the United Nations: A Commentary*, vol I (3rd edn, OUP 2012) 803.

[82] Henderson and Lubell (n 75) 394 (suggesting that the 'implied powers doctrine' might 'most plausibly' justify this practice).

[83] Borlini (n 73) 532.

[84] *Accordance with International Law of the Unilateral Declaration of Independence in Respect of Kosovo* (AO) [2010] ICJ Rep 403 [115]–[117].

[85] Chapter 2.3.b.–c.

[86] *ARSIWA Commentary* art 10 [16].

[87] For recent explorations of the possibility to develop such a framework, see L Iñigo Alvarez, *Towards a Regime of Responsibility of Armed Groups in International Law* (Intersentia 2020); K Fortin and J Kleffner, 'Responsibility of Organized Armed Groups Controlling Territory: Attributing Conduct to ISIS' in R Bartels et al (eds), *Military Operations and the Notion of Control under International Law* (Springer 2020).

[88] Chapter 2.3.b.–c.

Moreover, the mere existence of their primary obligations in practice already serves as a basis for engagement with non-State parties by a variety of international bodies seeking compliance with obligations or enforcement of violations.[89] As noted above, the Security Council, for example, frequently calls upon all parties to non-international armed conflicts to comply with their obligations, condemns violations of these obligations, and, in doing so, even explicitly singles out particular armed groups.[90] The ICRC, for its part, engages with non-State and State parties to armed conflicts alike to seek compliance with their obligations under IHL.[91] This engagement often includes confidentially reminding them, at the outset of a conflict, of their obligations under IHL as parties, just like parties to international armed conflicts.[92] Other international bodies, too, take non-State armed groups' party obligations as a starting point for their engagement with them. This engagement may include monitoring and reporting of armed groups' compliance with their IHL obligations by, for example, the Inter-American Commission on Human Rights,[93] the UN Secretary-General and its Special Representative for Children and Armed Conflict,[94] rarely[95] by the International Humanitarian Fact-Finding Commission (established under Article 90 API),[96] and more widely by NGOs such as Geneva Call.[97]

89 A Clapham, 'Extending International Criminal Law beyond the Individual to Corporations and Armed Opposition Groups' (2008) 6 JICJ 899, 920ff.

90 See eg regarding ISIL UNSC Res 2388 (21 November 2017) UN Doc S/RES/2388 Preamble; UNSC Res 2379 (21 September 2017) UN Doc S/RES/2379 Preamble, [1]. For analysis, see P Kooijmans, 'The Security Council and Non-State Entities as Party to a Conflict' in K Wellens (ed), *International Law: Theory and Practice Essays in Honour of Eric Suy* (Nijhoff 1998); more recently Boon (n 81); Fox, Boon, and Jenkins (n 74) 665.

91 ICRC, 'Position Paper—ICRC Engagement with Non-State Armed Groups: Why, How, for What Purpose, and Other Salient Issues' (2020) 102 IRRC 1089, 1094–1095.

92 See eg A Quintin and M-L Tougas, 'Generating Respect for the Law by Non-State Armed Groups: The ICRC's Role and Activities' in E Heffes, M Kotlik, and M Ventura (eds), *International Humanitarian Law and Non-State Actors: Debates, Law and Practice* (Springer 2020); ICRC, 'The Roots of Restraint in War' (2018).

93 See eg IAComHR, 'Truth, Justice and Reparation: Fourth Report on Human Rights Situation in Colombia' OEA/SerL/V/II Doc 49/13 (31 December 2013) 17, 36–37, 49; IAComHR, 'Third Report on the Human Rights Situation in Colombia' OEA/SerL/V/II 102 Doc 9 rev 1 (26 February 1999) 48.

94 See eg 'Report of the Secretary-General on Children and Armed Conflict' (9 June 2020) UN Doc A/74/845-S/2020/525 Annexes I and II (listing State and non-State parties having committed 'grave violations'). Delisting requires implementing an action plan, supervised by the UN Security Council Working Group on Children and Armed Conflict (UNSC Res 1612 (26 June 2005) UN Doc S/RES/1612), which can recommend sanctions ('Letter dated 8 September 2006 from the Permanent Representative of France to the United Nations addressed to the President of the Security Council' UN Doc S/AC.51/2007/2, Annex [5]).

95 F Kalshoven, 'The International Humanitarian Fact-Finding Commission: A Sleeping Beauty?' (2002) 15 Hu V-I 213.

96 eg the IHFFC undertook an independent forensic investigation into the death of an OSCE observer during the conflict in eastern Ukraine (IHFFC, 'Executive Summary of the Report of the Independent Forensic Investigation in relation to the Incident Affecting an OSCE Special Monitoring Mission to Ukraine (SMM) Patrol on 23 April 2017' (7 September 2017) <www.osce.org/files/f/documents/1/e/338361.pdf>

97 E Heffes, 'Non-State Actors Engaging Non-State Actors: The Experience of Geneva Call in NIACs' in E Heffes, M Kotlik, and M Ventura (eds), *International Humanitarian Law and Non-State Actors: Debates, Law and Practice* (Springer 2020).

Evidence from contemporary conflict practice shows that, in many cases, armed groups comply with their obligations.[98] Empirical studies suggest that armed groups' behaviour regarding their obligations under IHL is often the outcome of balancing the extent to which abiding by their obligations furthers their political objectives[99] against the strategic and military costs of doing so.[100] Accordingly, the mere existence of primary party obligations is practically relevant as it may provide incentives that considerably inform armed groups' behaviour. Moreover, compliance is not the only indicator for the relevance of non-State parties' obligations under international law. These obligations also have an expressive function, which signals that the groups are considered central actors in an armed conflict.[101]

Finally, looking ahead, establishing that non-State entities bear obligations as parties to armed conflicts is an essential prerequisite for the future development of legal concepts on their international responsibility. To pave the way for such a development, it is crucial to achieve the greatest possible clarity as to the existence and scope of their party obligations in the first place.

In sum, this section has shown that party status entails obligations, and explained why this matters. The following section explores to what extent, in addition to restrictions, party status also has permissive dimensions.

b. Party status as permissive

Although party status entails obligations, it could also be understood as permitting parties to undertake certain conduct. Some support for permissive dimensions of party status can be found in IHL treaties that refer to 'rights' of parties or otherwise use permissive language regarding parties. IHL treaties, for example, speak of the rights of parties to choose methods or means of warfare,[102] control and search hospital ships[103] and board medical transport carriers,[104] and mention a 'right of requisition recognized for belligerents by the laws and customs of war'.[105]

[98] For a database compiling instances of compliance, see 'IHL in Action' <https://ihl-in-action.icrc.org>.

[99] H Jo, *Compliant Rebels: Rebel Groups and International Law in World Politics* (CUP 2015) 52ff (emphasising armed groups' search for political legitimacy).

[100] T Fazal and M Konaev, 'Homelands versus Minelands: Why Do Armed Groups Commit to the Laws of War?' (2019) 4 JoGSS 149.

[101] See eg UNSC Res 2475 (20 June 2019) UN Doc S/RES/2475, Preamble ('Reaffirming that parties to armed conflict bear the primary responsibility to take all feasible steps to protect civilians').

[102] API, art 35; see also HR, art 22 and the preambles to the CCW, the Ottawa Convention, and the Cluster Munitions Convention.

[103] GCII, art 31.

[104] ibid art 38.

[105] GCI, art 34.

To some extent, such references may simply qualify the restrictions flowing from party status. For example, the 'right' of parties to prescribe technical arrangements for relief consignments[106] essentially specifies how they may fulfil their obligation to allow and facilitate the passage of such consignments. Going further, however, such permissive language may also signal that, by virtue of its party status, a party can do something that it could not lawfully do were it not a party. Consider, for example, the permissive references to internment,[107] special measures of control and security,[108] and restrictive measures affecting individual property.[109] Beyond treaty language, States also invoke party status as accompanied with permissions that would not have otherwise existed. For example, in 2012, the US Attorney General claimed that:

> [b]ecause the United States is in an armed conflict [with al-Qaeda, the Taliban, and associated forces], we are authorized to take action [ie using force] against enemy belligerents under international law.[110]

In a similar vein, in cases before its domestic courts and before the ECtHR, the UK relied on permissions under IHL flowing from its party status in both international and non-international armed conflicts to justify the lawfulness of its conduct under human rights law.[111]

Conversely, permissive conceptions of party status sometimes also inform States' concern not to become a party.[112] Western States' repeated affirmations that they would not become parties to the armed conflict between Ukraine and Russia following Russia's full-scale invasion in 2022 and the concern with such a prospect in the wider public in the assisting States were partly driven by political and military considerations of avoiding an escalation of the conflict.[113] Officials also, however, expressed concerns that Russia would be entitled to use force against Western

[106] API, art 70(3); GCIV, art 23; GCI, art 59; see also GCIII, art 75; GCIV, art 111 (referring to rights of the parties to arrange means of transport for relief consignments).

[107] GCIII, art 21; GCIV, art 42.

[108] GCIV, arts 27, 38, 41.

[109] ibid art 46.

[110] E Holder, Speech at Northwestern University (5 March 2012) Digest of US Practice in International Law (2012) 578, 581.

[111] See below the text accompanied by nn 150–157.

[112] Parts of the following paragraphs have previously been published in a similar form (A Wentker, 'At War? Party Status and the War in Ukraine' (2023) 36 LJIL 643, 645; see also A Wentker, 'Kriegspartei? Sicherheitspolitischer Diskurs und Völkerrecht im Ukraine-Krieg' (2022) 75 DÖV 988).

[113] See Introduction, n 2.

States if they became parties to the conflict alongside Ukraine.[114] The political discourse thus hints at a permissive conception of the legal meaning of party status.

These permissive conceptions of party status are reminiscent of the traditional divide between peace and war as two separate spheres of international law. For early modern writers, such as Grotius,[115] the 'right to make war' brought with it the right to kill enemies and acquire enemy property taken in war.[116] The state of war was seen as giving rise to a set of legal relations between parties that was separate from the legal framework governing peacetime relations between States.[117] The transformation of legal relations was structurally permissive in that the constraints of peacetime rules were displaced.[118] Thus, diplomatic relations between belligerents were severed, and treaties (other than those relating to war and neutrality) automatically terminated.[119] Being at war accordingly had a permissive effect because it freed the belligerents from their peacetime obligations. Ultimately, war was envisioned as 'a legal condition in which it was entirely lawful for the two contending states to rain death and destruction upon one another'.[120]

Within the current IHL framework, establishing that a certain State or armed group is a party to an armed conflict is still relevant for the lawfulness of killing. As section 4 explores in greater detail, this finding enables applying rules to target specific categories of individuals as combatants of that State party or as fighters of that non-State party which are less restrictive than the rules for targeting civilians.[121]

In the contemporary international legal system, however, parties to an armed conflict are not placed in an entirely separate legal sphere. For example, the ILC notes that '[t]he existence of an armed conflict does not *ipso facto* terminate or suspend the operation of treaties', neither as between States parties to the armed conflict nor regarding third States.[122] Crucially for present purposes, even when they become parties, States continue to be restricted by their obligations under the prohibition of the use of force and human rights law. Both sets of restrictions challenge and nuance potential permissive dimensions of party status.

[114] See, emblematically, the statements by the German Federal Minister of Justice to parliament (German Federal Parliament, Stenographic Protocol 20/33 (11 May 2022) 2954).

[115] H Grotius, *De jure belli ac pacis libri tres*, vol II (F Kelsey tr, Clarendon Press 1925) 33.

[116] ibid 645, 663, 697.

[117] A McNair and A Watts, *The Legal Effects of War* (4th edn, CUP 1966) 3; Kennedy (n 55) 65–67.

[118] G Balladore Pallieri, 'La Notion de guerre et de combattant dans les conflits armés' (1971) 10 MLLWR 313, 315; L Hill-Cawthorne, 'Rights under International Humanitarian Law' (2017) 28 EJIL 1187, 1212 (defining 'belligerent rights' as 'rights granted to states and belligerents that permit actions that would not be permitted in peacetime').

[119] M Mancini, 'The Effects of a State of War or Armed Conflict' in M Weller (ed), *The Oxford Handbook on the Use of Force in International Law* (OUP 2015) 992, 994–995.

[120] Neff (n 2) 178.

[121] Below 4.a.i.; see also Chapter 3.4.a.iii.(3).

[122] ILC, Draft Articles on the Effects of Armed Conflicts on Treaties, art 3. For a recent review of practice on the matter, see J Zrilič, 'Armed Conflicts and the Law of Treaties: Recent Developments and Reappraisal of the Doctrine in Light of the Wars in Syria and Ukraine' (2023) 65 Japanese YIL 107.

For one, the prohibition of the use of force significantly curtails potential permissions that flow from being a party to an armed conflict. In the aftermath of the 1928 Kellogg–Briand Pact, US Secretary of State Stimson observed that the prohibition to use force entails that '[w]ar between nations … is no longer to be the source and subject of rights'.[123] Indeed, the restrictions under the *jus ad bellum* operate independently of a State's status as a party to an armed conflict.[124] The prohibition of the use of force under Article 2(4) UN Charter and customary international law continues to restrict States even when they are engaged in an armed conflict as a party, in addition to the restrictions under the *jus in bello*.[125]

The opposite view holds that once States are parties to an international armed conflict, the legality of acts of force is no longer a matter for the *jus ad bellum*, but exclusively governed by the *jus in bello*.[126] That view is difficult to square with the basic structure of the prohibition of the use of force, which applies to individual acts of force. The prohibition does not make status-based distinctions along the traditional 'spheres' of peace and war.[127] Uses of force by a party to a conflict must therefore not only comply with the *jus in bello* but must also fall within the scope of the permissive exceptions to the prohibition of the use of force to be lawful.[128] Party status as such cannot permit forcible action that is inconsistent with the *jus ad bellum*.[129]

123 Henry Stimson, 'The Pact of Paris: Three Years of Development' Address before the Council on Foreign Relations, 8 August 1932 (Government Printing Office, Publication No 357) 5. For similar statements in post-1945 scholarship, see E Lauterpacht, 'The Legal Irrelevance of the "State of War"' (1968) 62 ASIL Proc 58, 63; Baxter (n 56) 323–324; A Roberts, 'The Equal Application of the Law of War: A Principle under Pressure' (2009) 90 IRRC 931, 935.

124 C Kreß, 'The Ukraine War and the Prohibition of the Use of Force in International Law' (TOAEP Occasional Paper Series No 13 2022) 13–14.

125 G Cohen, 'Mixing Oil and Water? The Interaction between *Jus ad Bellum* and *Jus in Bello* during Armed Conflicts' (2022) 9 JUOFIL 352, 366–371 (with reference to State practice); C Greenwood, 'The Relationship between *Ius ad Bellum* and *Ius in Bello*' (1983) 9 Rev Int Stud 221, 222; J Gardam, 'Proportionality and Force in International Law' (1993) 87 AJIL 391, 404; R Sloane, 'The Cost of Conflation: Preserving the Dualism of *Jus ad Bellum* and *Jus in Bello* in the Contemporary Law of War' (2009) 34 YJIL 47, 68; see also Eritrea–Ethiopia Claims Commission, Final Award—Ethiopia's Damages Claims (2009) 26 RIAA 631 [311], [333]–[349] (awarding compensation for acts during an international armed conflict violating the *jus ad bellum* but not the *jus in bello*).

126 V Heiskanen and N Leroux, 'Applicable Law: *Jus ad Bellum, Jus in Bello*, and the Legacy of the UN Compensation Commission' in T Feighbery, C Gibson, and T Rajah (eds), *War Reparations and the UN Compensation Commission* (OUP 2015) 53–55; P Konchak, 'U.S. and Allied Involvement in the Russo-Ukrainian War: The Belligerent Status of NATO States and Its Implications' (*OpinioJuris*, 20 July 2022) <http://opiniojuris.org/2022/07/20/u-s-and-allied-involvement-in-the-russo-ukrainian-war-the-belligerent-status-of-nato-states-and-its-implications/>.

127 KL Yip, 'Separation between *Jus ad Bellum* and *Jus in Bello* as Insulation of Results, Not Scopes, of Application' (2020) 58 MLLWR 31, 35.

128 Haque (n 56) 30 (concluding that the *jus in bello* can never authorise acts of violence and should be considered as entirely prohibitive in nature); though see E Lieblich, 'The Facilitative Function of *Jus in Bello*' (2019) 30 EJIL 321, 329 (suggesting that IHL may operate as a de facto source of justification for battlefield decisions, in the absence of guidance under the *jus ad bellum* as to *how* force may be used).

129 See API, Preamble ('nothing in this Protocol or in the Geneva Conventions of 12 August 1949 can be construed as legitimizing or authorizing any act of aggression or any other use of force inconsistent with the Charter of the United Nations'); K Okimoto, *The Distinction and Relationship between* Jus ad

The traditional notion that States at war are freed from peacetime constraints is further nuanced by human rights law.[130] Human rights law is not exclusively a peacetime regime since it is clearly established that human rights law in principle also applies to armed conflict.[131] At the same time, certain human rights obligations of States are sometimes considered as becoming less restrictive[132] once States become parties to an armed conflict. To the extent that this is accepted, party status would be 'positively' permissive in the sense that otherwise unlawful conduct is lawful if carried out as a party.[133] This permissive role of party status could take three main forms. First, it could widen the possibility for a State to rely on derogation clauses. Secondly, it could induce a more lenient interpretation and application of the State's human rights obligations. Thirdly, it could even exclude the applicability of human rights obligations to the State's conduct as a party.

As to the first dimension, some room for a permissive role of party status may be built into certain human rights treaties through derogation or suspension clauses. Article 15(1) ECHR allows for derogations and Article 27(1) ACHR provides for suspensions '[i]n time of war', alongside 'other public emergency'.[134] Even if the reference to 'war' is presently understood to mean situations of international and non-international armed conflict,[135] the possibility to derogate is not necessarily tied to the status as a party to these conflicts. On the one hand, one could imagine that a State that is not a party to the conflict may rely on the derogation clause. Take, for example, a State on whose territory multiple armed groups are engaged in an armed conflict. On the other hand, a State that is a party to an armed conflict may not be able to rely on the derogation clause if the requirement of a threat to the life of the nation is understood to apply not only to other public emergencies but

Bellum *and* Jus in Bello (Hart 2011) 24. For the implications of this finding regarding traditional belligerent rights over neutrals, see Chapter 2.2.d.iii.

[130] See generally KL Yip, *The Use of Force against Individuals in War under International Law: A Social Ontological Approach* (OUP 2022) 92–104.

[131] *Legality of the Threat or Use of Nuclear Weapons* (AO) [1996] ICJ Rep 226 [25]; *Legal Consequences of the Construction of a Wall in the Occupied Palestinian Territory* (AO) [2004] ICJ Rep 136 [106]; *Armed Activities (DRC v Uganda)* (Merits) [2005] ICJ Rep 168 [216].

[132] On the different types of permissions in international human rights law, see K Trapp, 'Exemptions, Qualifications, Derogations, and Excuses in International Human Rights Law' in L Bartels and F Paddeu (eds), *Exceptions in International Law* (OUP 2020).

[133] H Kelsen, *General Theory of Norms* (M Hartney tr, OUP 1991) 98–99 (noting that behaviour 'is permitted in the positive sense if the validity of a norm which commands it is repealed or restricted', as distinct from being merely 'permitted in the negative sense if it is neither forbidden nor commanded' and thus simply 'not the object of any norm').

[134] The derogation clause in ICCPR, art 4(1), however, does not refer to war.

[135] For discussion, see M Milanović, 'Extraterritorial Derogations from Human Rights Treaties in Armed Conflict' in N Bhuta (ed), *The Frontiers of Human Rights* (OUP 2016) 67; S Wallace, *The Application of the European Convention on Human Rights to Military Operations* (CUP 2019) 200–201; W Schabas, *The European Convention on Human Rights: A Commentary* (OUP 2015) 594–595 (suggesting that both international and non-international armed conflicts are covered).

also to the war prong of the clause.[136] In any event, the very existence of the alternative category of other public emergencies considerably reduces the independent relevance of the war prong. As an aside, similar considerations apply regarding security exceptions to obligations contained in trade agreements or investment treaties[137] providing for measures 'in time of war' such as the 1994 GATT,[138] the TRIPS,[139] the Energy Charter Treaty,[140] or BITs.[141] Party status is more relevant under Article 15(2) ECHR, which contains an exception to the exclusion of derogations from the right to life for 'deaths resulting from lawful acts of war'. If a State were to avail itself of this possibility (within the confines of the requirements of Article 15(1) and (3)), acts that the State commits as a party to an international or non-international armed conflict[142] would be subject to a more permissive regime, freed from the constraints of Article 2.

Beyond derogations, a State's party status may have a permissive dimension in how it impacts the interpretation of a State's human rights obligations. In particular, as per the ICJ, whether a loss of life is 'arbitrary' in the sense of the right to life under Article 6(1) ICCPR depends on the lawfulness of the party's conduct under the law applicable in armed conflict.[143] As a party to an armed conflict, a State may accordingly take lives in a greater range of situations than the State otherwise could without violating the right to life.[144] To what extent a State's party status has a permissive effect in this respect is not, however, entirely settled. In particular, it is open to question whether a finding of lawfulness under IHL *automatically* means that the right to life is not violated.[145] More cautiously, the UN Human Rights Committee in its General Comment 36 noted that '[u]se of lethal force consistent with international humanitarian law and other applicable international law norms is, in general, not arbitrary'.[146] The references to both 'other applicable international

136 For this view, see Wallace (n 135) 203; for discussion, see I Park, *The Right to Life in Armed Conflict* (OUP 2018) 199–200.

137 On the permissive nature of exceptions in international trade and investment law, see generally C Henckels, 'Permission to Act: The Legal Character of General and Security Exceptions in International Trade and Investment Law' (2020) 69 ICLQ 557; O Suttle, 'Reasons, Institutions, Authorities: Three Models of Exceptions in World Trade Organization Law' in Bartels and Paddeu (n 132).

138 Art XXI(b)(iii). See *Russia—Measures Concerning Traffic in Transit* (Panel Report) WT/DS512/R (5 April 2019) [7.72] (interpreting 'war' as encompassing both international and non-international armed conflicts).

139 Art 73(b)(iii). See *Saudi Arabia—Measures Concerning the Protection of Intellectual Property Rights* (Panel Report) WT/DS567/R (16 June 2020) [7.241]–[7.243] (interpreting the notion as in *Russia—Traffic in Transit*).

140 Art 24(3)(a)(ii) (referring to non-precluded measures in times of 'war' and 'armed conflict').

141 See eg Israel–Japan BIT (2017), art 15(2)(a)(i) (referring to measures taken in time of 'international or non-international armed conflict').

142 Park (n 136) 204 (suggesting that it is 'generally recognized' that 'lawful acts of war' mean acts consistent with IHL in both international and non-international armed conflicts).

143 *Nuclear Weapons* (n 131) [25].

144 See below 4.a.i. for the rules of targeting individuals under IHL.

145 Haque (n 56) 36.

146 UNHRC General Comment No 36, ICCPR, art 6 (30 October 2018) UN Doc CCPR/C/GC/36 [64].

law'[147] and 'in general' considerably temper any permissive effect on the right to life.[148]

Moreover, care should be taken with generalising this permissive dimension of party status beyond the ICCPR to other human rights instruments. By contrast to the ICCPR and the ACHR,[149] the right to life under the ECHR does not refer to 'arbitrariness'. Instead, Article 2(2) ECHR exhaustively lists certain specific permissible grounds for deprivations of life. In the context of the right to liberty and security, a similar structure of enumerated grounds of exceptions did not, however, prevent the ECtHR in *Hassan* from interpreting the Convention in light of IHL provisions according to which parties to an international armed conflict may subject individuals to detention.[150] The Court also interpreted the detaining State's procedural obligation under Article 5(4) ECHR as providing for a review of the detention by a 'court' in light of Articles 43 and 78 GCIV.[151]

By 'accommodating' within Article 5(1) an additional ground for detention by parties to an international armed conflict in accordance with IHL and by allowing for additional flexibility as regards their procedural obligations, the Court ascribed a considerable permissive dimension to a State's status as a conflict party regarding detention.[152] The ECtHR explicitly limited its reasoning to international armed conflicts. In *Mohammed v Ministry of Defence*, the UK government claimed the same permissive effect under IHL in non-international armed conflicts.[153] This claim was rejected by the High Court,[154] the Court of Appeal,[155] and by Lord Reed and Lord Kerr's dissent to the Supreme Court's decision[156]—convincingly, as I have argued elsewhere.[157] The Supreme Court's majority opinion, however, left the matter open. It found that Security Council resolutions mandating the military operations in Afghanistan and Iraq provided a sufficient 'source of the international law power to detain'.[158] This permissive effect was then not a consequence of the detaining State's status as a party to a non-international armed conflict since the resolutions did not address the parties as such.[159]

147 This could, for example, include the prohibition of aggression, see ibid [70] (considering acts of aggression *ipso facto* as violations of art 6).

148 Lieblich (n 128) 333–334 (noting the change of wording from a previous draft of General Comment No 36, which provided that '[u]ses of lethal force *authorized* and regulated by and complying with international humanitarian law are, *in principle*, not arbitrary' (emphasis added)).

149 ACHR, art 4(1).

150 *Hassan v United Kingdom* App no 29750/09 (ECtHR, 16 September 2014) [104].

151 ibid [106].

152 In cases of transfers of detainees, this permissive dimension may extend to neutral States (see *GCIII Commentary* [1503)].

153 *Mohammed (Serdar) v Ministry of Defence* [2015] EWCA Civ 843, [2016] 2 WLR 247 [6].

154 *Mohammed (Serdar) v Ministry of Defence* [2014] EWHC 1369 (QB), [2014] CN 1019 [257].

155 *Mohammed* (Court of Appeal) (n 153) [251]ff.

156 *Mohammed (Serdar) v Ministry of Defence* [2017] UKSC 2, [2017] AC 821 [258]ff, [271] (Lord Reed and Lord Kerr).

157 A Wentker, 'Mohammed v Ministry of Defence' (2017) ILDC 2803.

158 *Mohammed* (Supreme Court) (n 156) [60].

159 See UNSC Res 1386 (20 December 2001) UN Doc S/RES/1386 [3]; UNSC Res 1546 (8 June 2004) UN Doc S/RES/1546 [10]; UNSC Res 1723 (28 November 2006) UN Doc S/RES/1723 [1]; UNSC Res 1890 (8 October 2009) UN Doc S/RES/1890 [2].

Finally, a State's party status may permissively impact its human rights obligations by excluding the applicability of these obligations altogether. In *Georgia v Russia (II)*, the ECtHR found there to be an exception to the jurisdiction of a State under Article 1 ECHR 'in respect of military operations ... during the active hostilities phase' of an international armed conflict.[160] The potential permissive dimension of party status stems from the categorical nature of the exclusion of effective control. Instead of treating the exclusion of effective control as a factual question to be assessed on a case-by-case basis, the Court simply assumed that, during the active hostilities phase of an international armed conflict, effective control over an area or individuals is excluded.[161] Several judges in their separate opinions as well as commentators have criticised this aspect of the Court's reasoning.[162] Indeed, conceptually, this is a step back towards the traditional separation of peacetime and wartime international law.[163] Being a party to an international armed conflict would thus mean that the respective States would be freed from their human rights obligations during the active hostilities phase of the conflict.

At present, however, the scope of this jurisdiction exception remains unclear in four respects. First, the ECtHR has not further specified the meaning of the 'active hostilities phase'.[164] While being a party to the international armed conflict would be a necessary condition, the exclusion of jurisdiction seems to be confined to certain phases of the conflict. It may also not even be relevant in all international armed conflicts. Secondly, it is unclear whether the jurisdiction exception would apply to all or only to some of the Convention rights.[165] Thirdly, the scope of the exception is further obscured since the 'special features of a case' can establish jurisdiction during the active hostilities phase of an armed conflict as well.[166] Fourthly, since the judgment only referred to international armed conflicts, the legal position of parties to non-international armed conflicts is also left unclear.[167] As a result, the shape and significance of this permissive dimension of party status vis-à-vis human rights law remain to be settled.

160 *Georgia v Russia (II)* App no 38263/08 (ECtHR, 21 January 2021) [138].

161 ibid [126], [133], [137], [142].

162 See eg ibid partly diss op Lemmens [2]–[3], partly diss op Chanturia [15]–[16]; M Milanovic, 'Georgia v. Russia No. 2: The European Court's Resurrection of Bankovic in the Contexts of Chaos' (*EJIL: Talk!*, 25 January 2021) <www.ejiltalk.org/georgia-v-russia-no-2-the-european-courts-resurrection-of-bankovic-in-the-contexts-of-chaos/>; F Tan and M Zwanenburg, 'One Step Forward, Two Steps Back? *Georgia v Russia (II)*, European Court of Human Rights, Appl No 38263/08' (2021) 22 Melb JIL 136, 144–145.

163 See also *Georgia v Russia (II)* (n 160) joint partly diss op Yudkivska, Wojtyczek, and Chanturia [1].

164 K Dzehtsiarou, 'Georgia v. Russia (II)' (2021) 115 AJIL 288, 292; Tan and Zwanenburg (n 162).

165 Tan and Zwanenburg (n 162) 144.

166 *Georgia v Russia (II)* (n 160) 329–332 (relying on this notion to establish a jurisdictional link for the obligation to investigate under ECHR, art 2); see also *Hanan v Germany* App no 4871/16 (ECtHR, 16 February 2021) [136].

167 Milanovic (n 162); Tan and Zwanenburg (n 162) 144.

Instead of consolidating its jurisprudence on this point, however, the ECtHR seems to have retreated from it somewhat.[168] In *Ukraine and the Netherlands v Russia*, the ECtHR went out of its way to confine the 'active hostilities' exception to the specific factual setting of *Georgia v Russia (II)* and concluded that:

> there can be no doubt that a State may have extraterritorial jurisdiction in respect of complaints concerning events which occurred while active hostilities were taking place. The *Georgia v. Russia (II)* judgment cannot, therefore, be seen as authority for excluding entirely from a State's Article 1 jurisdiction a specific temporal phase of an international armed conflict.[169]

In sum, permissive dimensions of party status in current international law are much more subtle and nuanced than under traditional state of war conceptions. These dimensions are confined by the prohibition of the use of force and contingent on the fine-grained interaction with human rights law. This resonates with Clapham's conclusion that war being outlawed and abolished as a legal institution 'should not mean that we carry over the Belligerent Rights that Warring States have acquired for themselves over centuries'.[170] At the same time, more sweeping permissive invocations of party status suggest that the mindset of state of war conceptions still plays a role in current international practice and legal discourse[171]—tensions with the current structures of international law notwithstanding. As Chapter 2 will show, such tensions also surround potential permissive dimensions of party status vis-à-vis third States, namely so-called belligerent rights over neutrals.[172]

To fully capture the legal relevance of party status within the contemporary regulation of armed conflict, it is crucial to look beyond the rules addressing parties themselves. The next section therefore considers how the legal position of individuals in armed conflict is regulated by reference to parties.

4. Parties and individuals in armed conflict

In addition to being addressees of international law in armed conflict themselves, parties are also crucial reference points in the regulation of armed conflict from the perspective of individuals. The role of party status for the legal position of

[168] ECHR Press Release, 'The European Court Grants Urgent Interim Measures in Application Concerning Russian Military Operations on Ukrainian Territory' (1 March 2022) 068; ECHR Press Release, 'Decision of the Court on Requests for Interim Measures in Individual Applications Concerning Russian Military Operations on Ukrainian Territory' (4 March 2022) 073.

[169] *Ukraine and the Netherlands v Russia* App nos 8019/16, 43800/14 and 28525/20 (ECtHR, 25 January 2023) [558].

[170] A Clapham, *War* (OUP 2021) 520; see also n 123.

[171] Clapham (n 170) 521.

[172] Chapter 2.2.d.iii.

individuals has been shaped both by the collective character and the increasing humanisation and individualisation of the regulation of armed conflict.

With the 'increasing professionalisation of warfare',[173] which coincided with the rise of nation States in Europe, wars were regulated as being carried out between the standing armed forces of sovereigns.[174] The collective outlook of the regulation of warfare entailed that individuals were considered as mere parts of the relevant collectives.[175] Rousseau characteristically observed: 'in war individuals are enemies wholly by chance, not as men, not even as citizens, but only as soldiers'.[176]

This vision continues, in part, to inform the protection of individuals under IHL. As members of the armed forces, individual soldiers fight for the collective and represent the State. The legal regime applicable to them as combatants reflects their status as a component of the collective. Conversely, civilians have generally been considered not to be entrusted with fighting on behalf of the collective. They are thus to be kept out of the collective hostilities and spared from its effects as far as possible. Beyond the conduct of hostilities, the protection of individuals has traditionally been conceived of in a collectivist perspective, mediated by the connection of the individuals to the collective. Rather than purely by virtue of its universal human nature, the individual is thus protected as part of a certain group (such as prisoners of war or wounded and sick members of the armed forces). That group, in turn, is frequently defined by reference to the collective entities between which the conflict takes place (ie the parties).

Yet, the legal position of the individual within international law generally, and regarding armed conflicts specifically, has seen crucial developments[177] as part of what Meron has seminally characterised as the 'humanisation' of this body of law.[178] He found trends in 'the fostering of accountability; and innovations in the formation, formulation, and interpretation of rules', spurred by the rise of human rights as an ever more significant body of law and norms at the international plane.[179] These developments are part of the broader phenomenon described as the 'individualisation of war', that is, 'a process in which individuals ... increase in importance compared with collective entities for the purposes of explaining and

173 Neff (n 2) 88, 190.

174 See eg de Vattel (n 12) 283.

175 Grotius (n 115) vol III, 650–651.

176 Rousseau (n 6) 56 (fn omitted).

177 For the historical pedigree of conceptions envisioning the individual in armed conflict as more autonomous, see Z Bohrer, 'Divisions over Distinctions in Wartime International Law' in Z Bohrer, J Dill, and H Duffy (eds), *Law Applicable to Armed Conflict* (CUP 2020) 126; T Meron, 'The Humanization of Humanitarian Law' (2000) 94 AJIL 239, 245; though see A Alexander, 'A Short History of International Humanitarian Law' (2015) 26 EJIL 109 (arguing that decisive shifts towards 'truly humanitarian' understandings of IHL occurred only in recent decades).

178 Meron (n 177) 239; T Meron, 'International Law in the Age of Human Rights' (2003) 301 RCADI 9.

179 Meron (n 177) 239.

normatively assessing the causes and conduct of war'.[180] This process has been observed from multiple disciplinary perspectives on war, including law, international relations, and moral philosophy.[181]

The humanisation and individualisation of the regulation of armed conflict could be perceived as challenging the central position of parties within this regulatory framework. However, as this section shows, rather than sidelining party status, these developments instead modify and diversify how party status is relevant to the legal position of individuals. On the one hand, humanisation and individualisation have subtly informed developments in defining protected persons categories. On the other hand, they have brought to the fore an additional dimension of the individual's legal position in armed conflict. This dimension conceives of the individual as an addressee of international law itself, namely as a subject of individual rights but also of obligations and responsibility.[182] Yet, even these rules that are addressed to the individual are structured in part by reference to party status. The connection of an individual to a party feeds into establishing that individual's international criminal responsibility and, to some extent, the scope of its obligations and rights.

To trace the development of the relationship between the legal position of parties to the conflict and individuals, section a. analyses how the connection of individuals to parties informs which rules apply to individuals as beneficiaries of protection. Section b. then assesses how party status informs how international law addresses the individual as bearing rights, obligations, and criminal responsibility.

a. Parties and the protection of individuals in armed conflict

As a corollary of the collective nature of warfare, the legal regime applicable to individuals has been traditionally conditioned on a certain status or belonging to a category determined by reference to parties. This section shows that this is still true in international armed conflicts, regarding both the conduct of hostilities and the protection granted to individuals beyond the conduct of hostilities. In non-international armed conflicts, however, the collective character of the regulation of armed conflict has not as clearly been translated into categorisations of individuals as it has in the inter-State context.

[180] J Welsh, 'The Individualisation of War: Defining a Research Programme' (2019) 53 Annals of the Fondazione Luigi Einaudi 9, 13. Similarly J Dill, 'Do Attackers Have a Legal Duty of Care? Limits to the "Individualization of War"' (2019) 11 IT 1, 4.

[181] Generally D Akande, D Rodin, and J Welsh (eds), *The Individualization of War: Rights, Liability, and Accountability in Contemporary Armed Conflict* (OUP 2023).

[182] G Blum, 'The Individualization of War: From War to Policing in the Regulation of Armed Conflicts' in A Sarat, L Douglas, and M Umphrey (eds), *Law and War* (Stanford UP 2014) 50.

i. Parties and individuals in the conduct of hostilities

(1) International armed conflicts

Which rules apply to an individual in the conduct of hostilities under the law of international armed conflict strongly depends on the nature of the connection of the individual to a State party to the international armed conflict.

As members of the armed forces of a State party to an international armed conflict, combatants are immune from criminal prosecution for merely participating in the hostilities and may be targeted so long as they are not *hors de combat*, simply by virtue of their status and regardless of whether their conduct poses any concrete threat to the other side.[183] The rationale both for the 'combatant privilege' to participate in hostilities and their status-based targetability is that they act for the sovereigns confronting each other. The individual combatant is thus legally conceived of as a mere part of the collective entity that is a party.[184]

In contrast to combatants, those individuals that are not members of the armed forces of a State party to an international armed conflict—civilians[185]—are not part of the sovereign contest and cannot be targeted based on any *status* that would identify them as a part of a collective.[186] They can only temporarily forfeit their protection from attack if their individual *conduct* sufficiently connects them to the collective hostilities. This connection is of a different nature than the status-based integration into a party's armed forces. However, the conduct-based link, too, is to be understood as a connection to one of the parties in that party's fight against the opposite side. Under the elements that the ICRC's 'Interpretative Guidance' considers as constitutive of direct participation in hostilities (DPH), that conduct-based connection consists of directly causing harm to one of the parties and being designed to do so in support of one of the parties to the detriment of another party.[187]

The rationale underpinning the status-based categorisation of individuals has been challenged precisely for reducing the individual to a mere part of a collective. Individualist, revisionist just war theorists have questioned the morality of killing simply by reference to status-based categories of individuals as members of a collective.[188] It has also been pointed out that the operational reality of contemporary

183 API, arts 43(1)–(2), 48, 50(1); *CIHL* rr 1, 3.

184 See generally K Ipsen, 'Combatants and Non-Combatants' in D Fleck (ed), *The Handbook of International Humanitarian Law* (4th edn, OUP 2021) 94.

185 API, art 50(1); *CIHL* r 5.

186 API, arts 48, 51(2); *CIHL* r 1.

187 ICRC, 'Interpretive Guidance on the Notion of Direct Participation in Hostilities under International Humanitarian Law' (2009) 16. For a thorough analysis of different approaches to the concept of DPH in international treaties, practice, and non-binding instruments, see E Crawford, *Identifying the Enemy: Civilian Participation in Armed Conflict* (OUP 2015) 53–90.

188 See eg L May, *War Crimes and Just War* (CUP 2007) 115–116; for the traditionalist and collectivist account of just war theory defending this rationale, see M Walzer, *Just and Unjust Wars: A Moral Argument with Historical Illustrations* (5th edn, Basic Books 2015) 138–144; for a critical deconstruction of revisionist morality, see M Prieto Rudolphy, *The Morality of the Laws of War: War, Law, and Murder* (OUP 2023) 113–123.

battlefields makes status-based distinctions increasingly challenging to apply.[189] A significant complicating factor is the ongoing 'civilianisation' of armed forces. This term captures the quantitative increase in the reliance on civilian contractors and employees, as well as the qualitative development in the roles that these individuals perform, including, for example, providing crucial intelligence or operating remote weapons systems.[190] Against this background, scholars including Blum and Haque have called for moving from status-based targeting to assessing on a case-by-case basis whether individuals pose a threat to justify their targetability.[191] Such proposals to decouple the legal position of the individual from its mere integration into the State party to the conflict resonate, to some extent, with conceptions envisioning the individual as an addressee of international law applicable in armed conflict, which will be outlined below.[192]

As the law on the conduct of hostilities currently stands, however, the targetability of individuals in international armed conflicts remains based on them being part of the relevant collective, the armed forces of a State party to the conflict. The following section analyses to what extent the integration into a party is also crucial in non-international armed conflicts.

(2) Non-international armed conflicts

The categorisation of individuals for purposes of the conduct of hostilities in non-international armed conflicts is less settled than that in international armed conflicts. It remains uncertain how and to what extent the legal position of the individual turns on the individual forming part of a party to the conflict. These difficulties at the individual level can, in part, be traced to tensions at the collective level.

Unlike in international armed conflicts, treaty law in non-international armed conflicts foresees no combatant status and States have consistently rejected extending international armed conflict provisions on this point, thereby preventing a development of customary international law. As there is no contest between sovereigns in which individuals would fight for their States, the traditional rationale underpinning combatant status is lacking.[193] While States domestically immunise

[189] G Blum, 'The Dispensable Lives of Soldiers' (2010) 2 JLA 117, 144–150.

[190] G Bartolini, 'The "Civilianisation" of Contemporary Armed Conflicts' in H Ruiz-Fabri, R Wolfrum, and J Gogolin (eds), *Select Proceedings of the European Society of International Law 2008*, vol II (Hart 2010); ICRC, 'International Humanitarian Law and the Challenges of Contemporary Armed Conflicts' (2007) 15.

[191] G Blum, 'The Dispensable Lives of Soldiers' in J Ohlin, L May, and C Finkelstein (eds), *Weighing Lives in War* (OUP 2017); Haque (n 56) 84ff. Contra C Finkelstein, 'The Equality of Combatants in Asymmetric War' in Ohlin, May, and Finkelstein (n 191).

[192] See b.

[193] For a challenge to this formalistic orthodox wisdom, see J Ohlin, 'The Combatant's Privilege in Asymmetric and Covert Conflicts' (2015) 40 YJIL 337, 340, 369 (suggesting that the structure of the law would allow for a combatant privilege in, at least, certain non-international armed conflicts that functionally resemble inter-State contests, along the lines of the traditional criteria for recognition of belligerency); for an exploration of the possibility of introducing a combatancy privilege in non-international armed conflicts, see C Kreß, 'Towards Further Developing the Law of Non-International Armed Conflict: A Proposal for a Jus in Bello Interno and a New Jus Contra Bellum Internum' (2014) 96

their fighters from criminal prosecution for IHL-compliant participation in the conflict,[194] they insist on remaining free to prosecute insurgents for their participation.[195]

At the same time, the regulation of non-international armed conflict does not suggest that international law equates non-State parties simply to loose bunches of individual civilians, which would be targetable only when directly participating in hostilities.[196] Instead, section 2 of this chapter has shown that non-international armed conflicts are conceived of as involving collective entities that qualify as parties through organisational features enabling them to carry out hostilities in accordance with international legal rules.[197] Yet, States remain ambivalent about the legal position of non-State parties, as evidenced by their anxiety to avoid giving any impression of conferring a more general status to these entities.[198]

The ambivalence in the treatment of non-State parties translates into persisting uncertainty as to the legal position of individual insurgent fighters under the law on the conduct of hostilities. The legal position is informed by considerations pulling in opposite directions: the recognition that these individuals fight as part of a collective on the one hand, and the rejection of a status-based approach to targeting on the other hand. Most approaches to the issue thus consider two parameters: the individual's integration into the collective entity and the individual's own function or conduct within the collective entity.

Emblematically, the ICRC's 'Interpretative Guidance' reflects both parameters. The ICRC suggests that individuals who are part of the 'organised armed groups' of a non-State party to the conflict, that is, its military wing (as distinct from its potential political or civilian subdivisions)[199] can be targeted by virtue of this membership link, akin to members of State armed forces. According to the ICRC, organised armed groups 'consist only of individuals whose continuous function it is to take a direct part in hostilities'.[200] In that sense, the contours of the relevant collective (the organised armed groups) are defined by reference to the 'function' of the individuals forming a part of it rather than the military character of the collective defining the legal position of the individual.[201] In this manner, the

IRRC 29, 39; S Sivakumaran, 'Re-envisaging the International Law of Internal Armed Conflict' (2011) 22 EJIL 219, 245 (suggesting that immunity from prosecution would provide a crucial incentive for armed groups' fighters to comply with IHL).

194 L Hill-Cawthorne, 'Persons Covered by International Humanitarian Law: Main Categories' in B Saul and D Akande (eds), *Oxford Guide to International Humanitarian Law* (OUP 2020) 104.

195 E Crawford, *The Treatment of Combatants and Insurgents under the Law of Armed Conflict* (OUP 2010) 72ff; Sivakumaran (n 35) 71.

196 APII, art 13(3); *CIHL* r 6.

197 Above 2.b.ii.

198 Common Article 3(4); Chapter 3, n 242.

199 DPH Guidance 32.

200 ibid 27.

201 D Akande, 'Clearing the Fog of War? The ICRC's Interpretive Guidance on Direct Participation in Hostilities' (2010) 59 ICLQ 180, 186.

'continuous combat function' approach combines the categorisation of the individual as a part of the collective entity—the military wing of the non-State party—with an assessment of the individual's role and the conduct that it is supposed to carry out as part of this role (ie participating in hostilities).[202] The threat posed by the specific individual thus plays a greater role than that for combatants in international armed conflicts, even if the threat is captured more abstractly than that for civilian DPH.

Although the ICRC's 'continuous combat function' approach has found some resonance in subsequent State practice,[203] the issue remains unsettled.[204] A central criticism is the perceived lack of equal treatment of State armed forces and non-State armed groups that results from adopting a narrower approach to targeting regarding the latter, as 'non-combat' members of State armed forces, such as cooks, are targetable as well.[205] Yet, treating State and non-State fighters alike in terms of their targetability might lead to more, rather than less, imbalance between them. This is the case so long as non-State fighters continue to face criminal prosecution for participation in hostilities, from which domestic law immunises their State counterparts. If actual equality was desired, it would require transferring the status-based approach from international to non-international armed conflicts and, accordingly, granting combatant status to non-State fighters.[206]

Some States and scholars have advanced alternative approaches to align the targetability of members of organised armed groups with that of members of State armed forces. Yet, these approaches, too, blend, to varying degrees, function- or conduct-based elements into the assessment of individual membership in an organised armed group. The US, for example, translates the traditional rationale for the targetability of combatants (ie that they fight for the State, to individuals belonging to armed groups). These individuals would be 'agent[s] of the group' to

[202] For the debates at the expert meetings on whether to define the continuous combat function by reference to the collective or the individual level, see ICRC, 'Report on the Fifth Expert Meeting on the Notion of Direct Participation in Hostilities' (2008) 55ff.

[203] See eg *Danish Manual* 181–182; *German Manual* [1308]; Higher Administrative Court for North Rhine-Westphalia, Judgment of 19 March 2019 (4 A 1361/15) [385]; Federal Prosecutor General, Order of 20 June 2013 (3 BJs 7/12-4) 23, 34; for a review of further practice, see N Verlinden, '"Are We at War?" State Support to Parties to Armed Conflict: Consequences under *Jus in Bello, Jus ad Bellum* and Neutrality Law' (PhD, KU Leuven 2019) 124–135.

[204] P Grzebyk, *Human and Non-Human Targets in Armed Conflicts* (CUP 2022) 180–187.

[205] M Schmitt, 'The Interpretive Guidance on the Notion of Direct Participation in Hostilities: A Critical Analysis' (2010) 1 Harv NSJ 5, 23; M Schmitt, 'International Humanitarian Law and the Targeting of Non-State Intelligence Personnel and Objects' (2020) 30 Duke JCIL 309, 339; K Watkin, 'Opportunity Lost: Organized Armed Groups and the ICRC Direct Participation in Hostilities Interpretive Guidance' (2010) 42 NYUJILP 641, 648ff; R Krebsbach, 'Totality of the Circumstances: The DoD Law of War Manual and the Evolving Notion of Direct Participation in Hostilities' (2017) 9 JNSLP 125, 150.

[206] Kreß (n 193) 39ff (proposing a symmetrical 'privilege of combatancy' coupled with an equally symmetrical '*jus contra bellum internum*' as a possible avenue for the development of the law). For an argument that fighters of non-State parties qualify for combatant status in 'internationalized' armed conflicts, see Mačák (n 23) 164ff.

which 'the organization's hostile intent may be imputed ... through [their] association with the organization'.[207] 'Functional' membership would also suffice as an alternative to 'formal' membership in an organised armed group.[208] To establish 'functional' membership, the US attaches weight to 'the extent to which the individual performs functions for the benefit of the group that are analogous to those traditionally performed by members of State militaries'.[209] The US also considers a broad set of other possible indicators, including DPH with sufficient frequency, intensity, and duration.[210] Similarly, Sivakumaran suggests accepting both a *de jure* form of membership, determined pursuant to the internal law of the armed group, and a *de facto* form, established through ongoing direct participation.[211]

All of these approaches face structural difficulties in transferring status- or category-based considerations to targeting in non-international armed conflicts. Analogies to members of States' armed forces risk being invoked to justify overbroad targeting practices, as objective evidence indicating membership will often not be as readily available as for State armed forces.[212] These risks are compounded by the potential permissive effect that the legality of such killings under broad IHL assessments may have on the legality assessment in light of the human right to life.[213] Many scholarly approaches to targeting in non-international armed conflicts thus rightly require a case-by-case assessment of objective evidence to establish membership, whatever the exact contours of the legal test against which we assess this evidence.[214]

It is important to keep in mind these difficulties and the remaining legal uncertainty on this point. At the same time, it is also crucial to note that establishing a certain non-State armed group to be a party to a non-international armed conflict will render certain individuals targetable by virtue of their connection to that non-State party. This is even if it remains unsettled how exactly the law circumscribes the group of targetable individuals and how the connection is to be established.

[207] *US Manual* 228.
[208] H Koh, 'Keynote Address: The Obama Administration and International Law' (2010) 104 ASIL Proc 207, 218.
[209] B Egan, 'Keynote Address' (2016) 110 ASIL Proc 300, 305–306.
[210] *US Manual* 230–232, 238.
[211] Sivakumaran (n 35) 360ff.
[212] C Heyns et al, 'The Right to Life and the International Law Framework Regulating the Use of Armed Drones' in D Akande et al (eds), *Human Rights and 21st Century Challenges* (OUP 2020) 174; though see Sivakumaran (n 35) 417 (noting that some armed groups do, for example, wear uniforms).
[213] Above 3.b.
[214] E Crawford, 'Who Is a Civilian? Membership of Opposition Groups and Direct Participation in Hostilities' in M Lattimer and P Sands (eds), *The Grey Zone: Civilian Protection between Human Rights and the Laws of War* (Hart 2018) 39; Heyns et al (n 212) 174; N Melzer, 'Keeping the Balance between Military Necessity and Humanity: A Response to Four Critiques of the ICRC's Interpretive Guidance on the Notion of Direct Participation in Hostilities' (2010) 42 NYUJILP 831, 890; G Gaggioli, 'Targeting Individuals Belonging to Armed Groups' (2018) 51 Van JTL 901, 914; R Mignot-Mahdavi, 'Rethinking Direct Participation in Hostilities and Continuous Combat Function in Light of Targeting Members of Terrorist Non-State Armed Groups' (2023) 105 IRRC 1028, 1046.

In addition to the legal position of individuals in the conduct of hostilities, the next section shows that protections beyond the conduct of hostilities also depend on individuals' connection to a party to the conflict.

ii. Parties and the protection of individuals beyond the conduct of hostilities

Protections granted to certain groups of persons often depend on specific connections to a party, through which international law defines different protection categories. As will be seen, however, this is only true under the law of international armed conflict.

For example, the protection of prisoners of war is granted to combatants when captured and detained by virtue of their status as part of the enemy sovereign's armed forces.[215] Under Article 4(2) GCIII, members of irregular forces also qualify as prisoners of war provided that these forces 'belong' to a party to the conflict and fulfil certain additional conditions enumerated in the provision. These conditions ensure that the individual is protected as a recognisable part of a collective, which, in turn, is sufficiently connected to a party to justify granting the status-based prisoner-of-war protection. Articles 43 and 44 API do not distinguish between members of regular and irregular forces, both of which are granted combatant status under Article 43(2) API and prisoner-of-war status under Article 44(1) API. Since, however, the customary status of the rules reflected in Article 44 API remains doubtful, the requirements of Article 4(2) GCIII remain relevant for States that have not ratified the Protocol.[216]

The special protections for other groups of persons, too, depend, to varying extents, on their connection to the parties. For example, the protection of persons *hors de combat* other than by capture, namely the wounded, sick, and shipwrecked, has also been reserved for members of the armed forces under the GCs.[217] Under API, however, these protections are extended to all wounded, sick, and shipwrecked individuals, 'whether military or civilian',[218] thus attenuating the relevance of the specific connection to a party.

Finally, how international law protects civilians also depends on how they are connected to a party. To qualify as protected persons, civilians must be in the hands of a party to the conflict of which they are not a national.[219] Nationals of a 'co-belligerent State' are excluded from the protections under GCIV while the State of which they are nationals has normal diplomatic representation in the State in whose hands they are. The same is true of nationals of neutral States, but only in

215 GCIII, arts 21, 118; *CIHL* 99.

216 *CIHL* 187ff (r 106); Y Dinstein, *The Conduct of Hostilities under the Law of International Armed Conflict* (4th edn, CUP 2022) 73–74.

217 GCI-II, art 13(1). GCI-II, art 13(4), (5) extends this protection to certain civilians not having had combatant status.

218 API, art 8(a)–(b).

219 GCIV, art 4(1).

the territory of a party.[220] Under Article 4 GCIV, the connection of an individual to a specific party qua nationality thus decisively distinguishes the applicable protective regime. In *Tadić*, the ICTY moved from nationality to the 'allegiance to a Party to the conflict'.[221] Some commentators considered this move as a step towards a more universalist conception of individual protection that is in line with the humanisation of IHL.[222] Yet, the 'allegiance' criterion continues to define an individual's protection by reference to a collective entity[223] and explicitly stresses the central role of the affiliation to a party.

In contrast to international armed conflicts, there is no similarly fine-grained distinction of categories of protected persons in non-international armed conflicts. Groups of persons to which international law grants specific protection are instead defined by the way in which the armed conflict affects these individuals.[224] Thus, the law of non-international armed conflict does not mirror the status-based categorisation of persons under the law of international armed conflicts. Indeed, the contrast regarding the protection of individuals is even more pronounced than in the realm of the conduct of hostilities.

Having considered the rules that conceive of the individual as a beneficiary of protection, the next section inquires into the relevance of party status under rules that address the individual itself by granting rights and imposing obligations and criminal responsibility.

b. Individuals as addressees of international law in armed conflict

As part of international law's humanisation and the individualisation of war, individuals are increasingly considered to be not only beneficiaries of protective obligations that are owed between collective entities, but also themselves addressees of international law that is applicable in armed conflict. This section therefore explores to what extent individuals can be conceived of as subjects of rights, obligations, and responsibility under this body of law and inquires how their position as addressees of international law is shaped by their connection to parties to the conflict.

220 ibid art 4(2).

221 *Tadić* (Appeal Judgment) IT-94-1-A (15 July 1999) [166]. For a critical discussion, see M Galvis Martínez, 'The "Allegiance" Test: Judicial Legislation and Interpretation of GCIV' (2021) JCSL 21.

222 Meron (n 177) 260; R Provost, *International Human Rights and Humanitarian Law* (CUP 2002) 39–40.

223 Blum (n 182) 53.

224 For a detailed analysis of different groups of persons benefiting from particular protection in non-international armed conflicts, see Sivakumaran (n 35) 278ff.

i. Individual rights

Individuals are increasingly considered as bearing rights not only under human rights law—which continues to apply in armed conflicts[225]—but also under IHL. Notions of individual rights under IHL have been associated with 'human rights thinking', which envisions individuals primarily as equal human beings who are entitled to universal rights by virtue of their human dignity.[226] This vision contrasts with how protective rules are structured under IHL. IHL categorises individuals as members of groups of persons that are protected conditional on their connection to parties to the armed conflict. The individual rights paradigm could thus be seen as questioning the relevance of party status for how IHL is structured.

Ascertaining the existence and scope of an individual right under international law is a matter of interpreting specific treaty provisions[227] or establishing the content of a customary rule,[228] respectively.[229] As a general matter, notions of individual rights under IHL have some ramifications in treaty law and international practice.[230] Although IHL treaties are mainly drafted in the language of obligations that impose standards of treatment (primarily on parties to a conflict or the High Contracting Parties), several provisions also refer to individual rights. For example, Articles 6/6/6/7 and 7/7/7/8 GCI-IV seem to presume that individuals have certain rights under the Conventions.[231] Article 78 GCIII speaks of a 'right' of prisoners of war to make requests or complaints, which the Eritrea–Ethiopia Claims Commission considered as reflected in customary international law.[232] International practice also provides support for certain individual rights under IHL. For example, the long-standing subsequent practice is considered to have re-interpreted Article 118 GCIII as granting an individual right to prisoners of war to release and repatriation (which, importantly, also entails an individual choice on whether or not to be repatriated).[233] Individual rights conceptions have also notably received some support—if rarely unequivocal—in practice relating to war

[225] n 131.

[226] D Luban, 'Human Rights Thinking and the Laws of War' in J Ohlin (ed), *Theoretical Boundaries of Armed Conflict and Human Rights* (CUP 2016).

[227] See *Jurisdiction of the Courts of Danzig* (AO) [1928] PCIJ Series B, No 15, 18.

[228] H Lauterpacht, 'The Subjects of the Law of Nations: Part II' (1948) 64 LQR 97, 112.

[229] *LaGrand case (Germany v United States of America)* (Merits) [2001] ICJ Rep 466 [77].

[230] For a thorough analysis of these ramifications, see Hill-Cawthorne (n 118) 1195–1211.

[231] R-J Wilhelm, 'Le Caractère des droits accordés à l'individu dans les Conventions de Genève' (1950) 32 IRRC 561, 582. Note, however, that the wording of GCI-IV, arts 7/7/7/8 does not exclude the possibility that the rights 'secured' by the Convention to individuals are rights which the Convention requires States to grant under domestic law (K Parlett, *The Individual in the International Legal System: Continuity and Change in International Law* (CUP 2011) 184).

[232] EECC, Partial Award: Prisoners of War—Ethiopia's Claim 4 (1 July 2003) [148].

[233] On this practice, see T Meron, *The Humanization of International Law* (Nijhoff 2006) 42–45; C Greenwood, 'Rights at the Frontier' in B Rider (ed), *Law at the Centre: The Institute of Advanced Legal Studies at Fifty* (Kluwer 1999) 283; Provost (n 222) 56 (taking this example to suggest that an individual rights conception becomes more compelling if the regulated situation is further removed from the conduct of hostilities); more cautiously *GCIII Commentary* [4469].

reparations.[234] Nevertheless, as the ongoing debates on an individual right to reparation illustrate, the existence and scope of individual rights under IHL remain controversial in many respects.[235]

Underlying these controversies are competing normative visions about *how* the protective purpose of IHL is best realised. Proponents of individual rights under IHL emphasise that the increased emancipation of the individual as bearing individual rights under IHL can be seen as a normative benefit in and of itself. This is because such a conception of the individual's legal position would be better aligned with a more human-centred view of international law more generally.[236] Proponents also point to potential benefits in terms of individual protection in armed conflict brought about, in part, by the norm structure of rights. This structure requires that restrictions of rights must be specifically justified, which may shift burdens of proof. It may also, more subtly, impact behaviour in armed conflict by centring the discourse in the field on requirements to justify curtailments of rights.[237]

Sceptics highlight that the same degree of protection can be achieved through obligations between collective entities and disciplinary enforcement of IHL within a collective.[238] By contrast, individual rights-oriented approaches, in the eyes of the sceptics, could risk undermining the protective benefits of the established, largely obligations-based, structure of IHL's protection scheme.[239] That structure may, for example, be more apt to protect those who are not able to invoke their rights.[240]

Depending on whether a rights-based or an obligations-based protection structure is preferred, the role accorded to party status will vary. In any event, accepting the existence of individual rights under IHL need not remove the relevance of party status. Indeed, individual rights are conceivable as shifts of certain obligations of parties as being owed to individuals too.[241] Moreover, the above examples of rights

[234] For thorough reviews of practice in favour of and against an individual right to reparation for IHL violations, see eg S Furuya, 'The Right to Reparation for Victims of Armed Conflict: The Intertwined Development of Substantive and Procedural Aspects' in S Furuya, C Correa, and C Sandoval (eds), *Reparation for Victims of Armed Conflict* (CUP 2021) 20ff; C Correa, 'Operationalising the Right of Victims of War to Reparation' in ibid 118ff; *Jurisdictional Immunities of the State (Germany v Italy)* Written Statement of Greece (3 August 2011) [40]–[42]; *Jurisdictional Immunities of the State (Germany v Italy)* Reply Germany (5 October 2010) [40]–[43]; see also Federal Constitutional Court, Order of 18 November 2020 (2 BvR 477/17) [17]–[19] (concluding that an individual right to reparation under international law does not exist as yet).

[235] Hill-Cawthorne (n 118). For an overview of the different levels of controversies regarding a potential individual right to reparation, see C Marxsen, 'Introduction: The Emergence of an Individual Right to Reparation for Victims of Armed Conflict' in Correa, Furuya, and Sandoval (n 234) 7–10.

[236] Meron (n 233) 38; A Peters, 'Direct Rights of Individuals in the International Law of Armed Conflict' (MPIL Research Paper Series, 20 December 2019) <https://papers.ssrn.com/sol3/papers.cfm?abstract_id=3506742> 8.

[237] Peters (n 236) 8ff; A Peters, *Beyond Human Rights: The Legal Status of the Individual in International Law* (CUP 2016) 231.

[238] Parlett (n 231) 225; Bohrer (n 177) 185–186.

[239] A Gross, 'Human Proportions: Are Human Rights the Emperor's New Clothes of the International Law of Occupation?' (2007) 18 EJIL 1, 7.

[240] Bohrer (n 177) 178ff.

[241] Peters (n 236) 7.

granted to prisoners of war—based on their *status*—illustrate that there may be room to integrate notions of individual rights into a system of protected persons categorised through their connection to parties. This also suggests that individual rights under IHL would be more likely to coexist, than do away, with IHL's scheme of protected persons categories and the crucial role of the individual's connection to parties within that scheme. The following section shows that this is also true for individual obligations and individual criminal responsibility.

ii. Individual obligations and international criminal responsibility

Individuals are not only addressees of rights in armed conflict, but they also bear obligations and can be held criminally responsible for certain violations of international law. As this section shows, the connection of the respective individuals to the parties significantly shapes the scope of these 'individualised' aspects of the legal position of the individual in armed conflicts.

(1) Individual criminal responsibility

As a general matter, it is accepted that individuals can bear obligations under IHL.[242] These individual obligations are crucial for establishing international criminal responsibility for war crimes. War crimes require serious violations of IHL.[243] International criminal law thus presupposes that individuals bear obligations under IHL, and international criminal law then attaches criminal sanctions for their violations (provided certain additional requirements are met).[244]

Conceptually, by criminalising certain violations of individual obligations under IHL as war crimes, international criminal law reflects an 'individualised' conception of the legal position of perpetrators of such violations.[245] In addition to the perpetrators' legal position, international criminal law may also, in part, 'individualise' victims, to the extent that international criminal justice is seen as redress for the violations of victims' rights.[246] The added individual level of responsibility and the dynamic developments in international criminal law in recent decades do not render parallel questions of State responsibility irrelevant.[247] State responsibility for violations of parties' obligations fulfils distinct functions in the

[242] *Judgment of the Nuremberg International Military Tribunal* (1 October 1946) (1947) 41 AJIL 172, 220; H Lauterpacht, *Oppenheim's International Law*, vol I (8th edn, Longmans 1955) 341; T Meron, 'International Criminalization of Internal Atrocities' (1995) 89 AJIL 554, 562; J Kleffner, 'Scope of Application of International Humanitarian Law' in Fleck (n 184) 61.

[243] ICCSt, art 8(2); ICTYSt, arts 1–3; ICTRSt, arts 1, 4; SCSLSt, arts 1(1), 3, 4.

[244] Parlett (n 231) 229ff.

[245] Blum (n 182) 67.

[246] Luban (n 226) 62; A Huneeus, 'International Criminal Law by Other Means: The Quasi-Criminal Jurisdiction of the Human Rights Courts' (2013) 107 AJIL 1 (emphasising the role of regional human rights courts' remedial and supervisory practices with respect to domestic prosecutions in strengthening this conception of criminal justice).

[247] See also ICCSt, art 25(4).

perception of justice being done for collective wrongdoing that individual criminal responsibility can never fully reflect.[248]

What is more, how an individual is connected to a party to the conflict remains relevant to the international criminal responsibility of that individual in two main ways.

First, certain war crimes and modes of liability presuppose specific connections of the relevant individuals to the parties. Although committing a war crime does not, as a general matter, require that the perpetrator be a member of the armed forces of a party,[249] several war crimes listed in Article 8(2) ICCSt presume that the perpetrator and the victim are nationals of opposing parties to the conflict[250] or that the perpetrator holds a certain position within the armed forces of a party, which, for example, enables her to declare that no quarter will be given.[251] Certain modes of liability under international criminal law, in particular command responsibility,[252] also depend on a specific position of an individual within a collective's organisational structure as well as on the character of the collective entity itself.[253] On the victim's side, connections to the parties are presupposed by those war crimes which refer to acts committed against protected persons under IHL (ie persons with a specific connection to a party).[254]

Secondly, the connection of individual perpetrators or victims of international crimes to parties may, more subtly, feed into the establishment of the nexus to an armed conflict.[255] This requirement distinguishes war crimes from ordinary crimes (which may also be committed during an armed conflict). To specify this requirement, the ICTY provided the following set of non-exhaustive factors in *Kunarac*:

[248] P Okowa, 'State Responsibility and Individual Responsibility in Internal Conflicts: Contours of an Evolving Relationship' (2009) 20 FYIL 143, 145; P Gaeta and A Jain, 'Individualisation of IHL Rules through Criminalisation for War Crimes: Some (un)intended Consequences' in Akande, Rodin, and Welsh (n 181).

[249] *Akayesu* (Appeal Judgment) ICTR-96-4-A (1 June 2001) [443]; *GCI Commentary* [2929]–[2930] with further references.

[250] See eg ICCSt, arts 8(2)(b)(xi), (xiii)–(xv), 8(2)(e)(xii).

[251] ibid arts 8(2)(xii), 8(2)(e)(x); Preparatory Commission for the ICC, Elements of Crimes (2 November 2000) PCNICC/2000/1/Add.2 30, 47

[252] ICCSt, art 28; *CIHL* rr 152–153.

[253] For example, Karsten has suggested that being a 'military commander' under ICCSt, art 28(a) presupposes a position as a superior in an entity whose 'underlying purpose is to act or be deployed as a party to an armed conflict' (N Karsten, 'Distinguishing Military and Non-Military Superiors: Reflections on the *Bemba* Case at the ICC' (2009) 7 JICJ 983, 1002). On the tensions between these collective dimensions and individualised aspects of command responsibility, see *Bemba* (Appeal Judgment) ICC-01/05–01/08 A (8 June 2018) [120]ff, sep op van den Wyngaert and Morrison [33]ff; A Galand, '*Bemba* and the Individualisation of War: Reconciling Command Responsibility under Article 28 Rome Statute with Individual Criminal Responsibility' (2020) 20 ICLR 669.

[254] Above a.ii.

[255] *Akayesu* (Appeal) (n 249) [444].

> the fact that the perpetrator is a combatant; the fact that the victim is a non-combatant; the fact that the victim is a member of the opposing party; the fact that the act may be said to serve the ultimate goal of a military campaign; and the fact that the crime is committed as part of or in the context of the perpetrator's official duties.[256]

The factors identified in *Kunarac* have been confirmed and applied in subsequent international criminal jurisprudence.[257] Note how these factors entail a specific connection of the perpetrator, victim, or relevant conduct to the parties to the conflict.

In sum, the nature of an individual's affiliation to a party matters for establishing criminal responsibility. This collective dimension is thus an important qualification to conceptualise an individual's legal position in armed conflict conveyed by international criminal law.[258]

(2) Scope of individual obligations and the relevance of party status

An obligation is imposed on an individual if the violation of the obligation is criminalised as a war crime.[259] Yet, the separate requirement for war crimes that the violation of the obligation be criminalised under international law implies that criminalised obligations of individuals are but a subset of individual obligations under IHL. Precisely which obligations IHL imposes on individuals remains uncertain.

Individual obligations under IHL do not seem to be limited to obligations that treaty provisions explicitly address to them.[260] Importantly, obligations vis-à-vis protected persons, although addressed primarily to parties,[261] have been found to be mirrored by parallel obligations that IHL implicitly imposes on specific categories of individuals. In *Mrkšić*, for example, the ICTY found:

[256] *Kunarac* (Appeal Judgment) IT-96-23&IT-96-23/1-A (12 June 2002) [59].

[257] See eg *Stakić* (Appeal Judgment) IT-97-24-A (22 March 2006) [341]; *Popović et al* (Trial Judgment) IT-05-88-T (10 June 2010) [741]; *Đorđević* (Trial) (n [1527]); *Rutaganda* (Appeal Judgment) ICTR-96-3-A (26 May 2003) [570]; *Brima, Kamara, Kanu* (Trial Judgment) SCSL-04-16-T (20 June 2007) [247]; *Sesay, Kallon, Gbao* (Trial Judgment) SCSL-04-15-T (2 March 2009) [101]; *Taylor* (Trial Judgment) SCSL-03-01-T (18 May 2012) [567]; *Bemba* (Trial) (n 41) [143]; *Ntaganda* (Trial) (n 41) [731]–[732]; *Afghanistan* (Appeal Judgment on Investigation Decision) ICC-02/17 OA4 (5 March 2020) [69].

[258] See also Blum (n 182) 68 ('What distinguishes war crimes from ordinary crimes is the collective context in which they take place.... It is violence by a collective, for a collective, against members of another collective').

[259] See the lists in GCI-IV, arts 50–51, 130, 147; API, art 85(3)–(4); ICCSt, art 8(2)(a)–(c), (e); ICTYSt, arts 2–3; ICTRSt, art 4; SCSLSt, arts 3–4. For the conditions developed by ad hoc criminal tribunals for their jurisdiction over serious violations, see *Tadić* (Decision on Jurisdiction) (n 18) [94]; for discussion, see P Gaeta, 'The Interplay between the Geneva Conventions and International Criminal Law' in A Clapham, P Gaeta, and M Sassòli (eds), *The 1949 Geneva Conventions: A Commentary* (OUP 2015) 746; Gaeta and Jain (n 248).

[260] Such as API, art 44(2)–(3); GCI, arts 40–41; GCII, art 42; GCIII, arts 17, 39(2).

[261] Above 3.a.i.

> that Geneva Convention III invests all agents of a Detaining Power into whose custody prisoners of war have come with the obligation to protect them by reason of their position as agents of that Detaining Power.[262]

Many treaty obligations of protection do not indicate a specific addressee and thus leave room for interpreting them as addressing individuals in parallel to parties to the conflict.[263] Even where an IHL obligation explicitly addresses parties, the obligation may still entail individual duties 'if individuals clearly must carry out that obligation'.[264]

As the scope of obligations of individuals under IHL remains unsettled,[265] the nature of an individual's connection to a party to the conflict can be a reasonable delimiting factor. All individuals can bear obligations under IHL. The quantitative and qualitative scope of these obligations will, however, likely differ according to the individual's connection to a party, particularly for those obligations that IHL imposes on individuals in parallel to parties. For example, while civilians, too, may bear obligations to refrain from certain abuses, specific obligations concerning the treatment of prisoners of war may be limited to persons closely linked to the Detaining Power. Party status may thus also play a role in the regulation of the individual as an addressee of obligations.

c. Interim conclusion

This section has demonstrated that the collective and individual dimensions of the legal regulation of armed conflict not only coexist but are also increasingly intertwined. As the legal position of the individual in armed conflict evolves, key aspects of this legal position remain determined by the nature of the connection between individuals and parties. Status- and category-based approaches continue to determine the legal regimes applicable to individuals under IHL by reference to their relationship with parties. This is the case both for the conduct of hostilities and the protection granted to certain groups of persons—even as the humanisation and individualisation of IHL have increasingly informed these categories. As part of this humanisation and individualisation, rules addressing parties have also been complemented with individual rights and obligations under IHL as well as with international criminal responsibility. Yet, this section has shown that even the scope of these 'individualised' aspects of the regulation of armed conflict depends, to varying extents, on the connection of the individual to the parties. In

262 *Mrkšić* (Appeal Judgment) IT-95-13/1-A (5 May 2009) [71]–[73].
263 See also *Pictet Commentary GCIV* 79; Peters (n 236) 19.
264 Meron (n 242) 563.
265 Provost (n 222) 98; Peters (n 237) 231.

sum, therefore, the increasing regulation of the individual in armed conflict has not displaced the central relevance of party status to the regulation of armed conflict, but it has subtly modified how party status is legally relevant.

The next section completes this chapter by looking at the relevance of identifying who is a party to an armed conflict for establishing *where* IHL applies.

5. Parties and the geographical scope of IHL application

The extent to which the scope of application of IHL is determined by reference to parties to the conflict is a central characteristic of parties' legal position within the international legal regulation of armed conflicts. The analysis in this chapter so far can help in understanding to whom which kinds of IHL rules apply and thus sheds light on IHL's personal scope of application. The temporal and geographical dimensions are, however, yet to be covered. The temporal scope of application will be left to a later stage of this book, as its connections to parties will be explored when the temporal scope of party status itself will be discussed.[266] The focus of this section is the geographical scope of application. It will be seen that identifying who qualifies as a party to the conflict plays a considerable role for establishing the geographical scope of application of IHL. This role, however, varies in international and non-international armed conflicts.

In international armed conflicts, IHL is generally held to apply throughout the territories of the States parties to the conflict.[267] As a baseline, establishing a State's party status is then crucial to assessing the geographical scope of the law of international armed conflict. It is also accepted, however, that IHL applies beyond the States parties' territory; IHL thus 'follows' parties if they carry out hostilities on third States' (ie neutral)[268] territory as well as in areas beyond any State's territory.[269]

In non-international armed conflicts, the extent to which the territory of States parties to the conflict, or 'the whole territory under the control of a party',[270] determines the scope of IHL application is more attenuated and controversial in several ways.

[266] Chapter 4.3.d.

[267] *Tadić* (Decision on Jurisdiction) (n 18) [68]; see, generally, VCLT, art 29.

[268] On the legal position of third States under the law of neutrality, see Chapter 2.2.

[269] E Crawford, 'The Temporal and Geographic Reach of International Humanitarian Law' in Saul and Akande (n 194) 66–69; in detail K Schöberl, 'The Geographical Scope of Application of International Humanitarian Law' (PhD, Université de Genève 2019) 98ff. For suggestions to delimit the scope of international armed conflict law beyond parties' territory to acts with a certain nexus to the conflict, see n 281.

[270] *Tadić* (Decision on Jurisdiction) (n 18) [70]; for a critical discussion, see eg N Lubell and N Derejko, 'A Global Battlefield? Drones and the Geographical Scope of Armed Conflict' (2013) 11 JICJ 65, 69.

First, it is controversial whether IHL applies to the territory of *all* States parties to a non-international armed conflict. This question is relevant in situations where several States are parties on the same side of a non-international armed conflict, a situation that Part II of the book analyses in detail. Based on its wording, object, and purpose, and in light of its drafting history, Common Article 3 does not preclude applying the law of non-international armed conflict to the territory of all States parties.[271] This would include the territory of foreign States intervening alongside the 'host' State even if the territory is geographically remote from the conflict.[272] Consider, for example, attacks by members of non-State parties on the territories of Western States intervening against these groups in other areas of the world. Or consider how 'foreign fighters' are to be treated in their (often Western) States of nationality. Although explicit practice on the matter is scarce,[273] States intervening extraterritorially in non-international armed conflicts have tended to reject the application of IHL to their own territories.[274]

Secondly, *within* the territory of a State party to a non-international armed conflict, it is accepted that IHL application is not confined to areas of active hostilities.[275] Nonetheless, as a nuance to the position that IHL applies throughout the entire territory of the State party,[276] it has been suggested that IHL only applies to conduct with a certain nexus to the conflict.[277]

Thirdly, the same idea could conversely be relied upon to *extend* the scope of application of IHL *beyond* the territory of States parties to conduct with a nexus to conflict occurring on third States' territory or in other areas. The scholarship is divided on this issue,[278] and while the ICC has recently endorsed a nexus approach

271 *GCI Commentary* [467]–[470]; [473]. On the applicability of APII in situations of inter-State co operation, see Chapter 3.4.c.i.

272 ICRC, 'International Humanitarian Law and the Challenges of Contemporary Armed Conflicts' (2015) 14; H Højfeldt Jakobsen, 'Returning Foreign Fighters: The Case of Denmark' (2018) 100 IRRC 315, 324–325.

273 *GCI Commentary* [473] ('there is insufficient identifiable State practice on [IHL's] applicability in the territory of the home State').

274 For example, as parties to a non-international armed conflict with ISIL, France and Belgium reacted through domestic law enforcement to terrorist attacks by ISIL members on their territories in 2015 and 2016, rather than by applying IHL. This choice may have been one of policy, rather than reflecting *opinio juris* that IHL did not apply (V Koutroulis, 'The Fight against the Islamic State and Jus in Bello' (2016) 29 LJIL 827, 849; V Koutroulis, 'A Clarification of the Geographical and Personal Scope of Multinational NIACs?' (2019) 49 Collegium 35, 42). Against the application of IHL to the territory of all States party to the conflict, see also France, 'Ministère des armées: Droit international appliqué aux opérations dans le cyberespace' 10 September 2019 <www.defense.gouv.fr/content/download/565895/9750877/file/Droit+internat+appliqué+aux+opérations+Cyberespace.pdf> 12.

275 *Tadić* (Decision on Jurisdiction) (n 18) [67]; *Akayesu* (Trial Judgment) ICTR-96-4-T (2 September 1998) [635]; *Kunarac* (Appeal) (n 256) [57].

276 *GCI Commentary* [459]; Federal Prosecutor General, Note of 16 April 2010 (3 BJs 6/10–4) 44.

277 *GCI Commentary* [460]; ICRC, 'International Humanitarian Law and the Challenges of Contemporary Armed Conflicts' (2019) 43.

278 In favour Lubell and Derejko (n 270) 75–76; M Schmitt, 'Charting the Legal Geography of Non-International Armed Conflict' (2014) 90 ILS 1, 15; against ICRC Challenges Report (2015) 14; P Kilibarda and G Gaggioli, 'The Globalisation of Non-International Armed Conflicts' in Lattimer and Sands (n 214) 148–149.

to the geographical scope of application of IHL,[279] France has implicitly rejected such an approach in its position paper on cyber operations.[280]

Under this approach, the scope of application of IHL is not territorially confined, and geographical factors merely feed into a broader, more flexible nexus assessment, which ultimately determines whether IHL applies to specific conduct or situations. Indeed, some proponents of this approach have suggested that the existence of a 'nexus' to the conflict would appropriately delimit the scope not only of the law of non-international armed conflict but also that of international armed conflict, both within States' territories and beyond.[281] More widely, the nexus to the armed conflict could be seen as a general additional or implicit criterion for any assessment of IHL applicability.[282]

At first sight, detaching IHL's scope of application from the parties' territory decentres parties as reference points in the application of IHL. On closer inspection of the potential contours of such a nexus concept, however, it appears that the scope of application would still be considerably determined by reference to parties, albeit more flexibly and subtly than by reference to their territory. Indeed, guidance in clarifying the requisite nexus could be sought in the factors developed for war crimes' nexus requirement in international criminal jurisprudence.[283] As seen above, these factors notably rely on the relevant individuals' affiliations to the parties and the connection of the respective acts to the parties' aims.[284] Other approaches to a nexus requirement also closely connect IHL's scope of application to parties.[285]

Thus, even if nexus approaches to the geographical scope of IHL application ultimately crystallise into positive international law, this would not mean that identifying who is a party to the conflict would become irrelevant. What is more, the nexus approach would also ascribe significance to the identification of parties other than States—notably non-State armed groups and international

[279] *Afghanistan* (Investigation Decision) ICC-02/17 (12 April 2019) [55] (finding the 'nexus with an internal armed conflict which is *required to trigger the application of international humanitarian law* as well as the Court's jurisdiction' lacking for victims captured outside Afghanistan (emphasis added)); *Afghanistan* (Appeal) (n 257) [73]–[77] (overturning this narrow understanding of the nexus).

[280] French Cyberspace Position 2019 (n 274) 12 (considering that 'cyberoperations still fall within the geographical scope of IHL, insofar as their effects must arise on the territory of the States party to the IAC and on the territory where the NIAC hostilities occur').

[281] K Schöberl, 'The Geographical Scope of Application of the Conventions' in Clapham, Gaeta, and Sassòli (n 259) 67, 83; Schöberl (n 269) 97, 111, 152; Sassòli (n 69) 187ff.

[282] E Pothelet, 'Searching for the Nexus: A Proposal to Refine the Applicability of IHL' (PhD, Geneva 2021); Sassòli (n 69) 200ff; T Rodenhäuser, 'The Legal Protection of Persons Living under the Control of Non-State Armed Groups' (2020) 102 IRRC 991, 1001.

[283] K Schöberl, 'Multinational Military Operations and the Geographical Scope of the Laws of Armed Conflict in Non-International Armed Conflict' in R Geiß and H Krieger (eds), *The 'Legal Pluriverse' Surrounding Multinational Military Operations* (OUP 2020) 27, 35.

[284] nn 255–257.

[285] See eg Lubell and Derejko (n 270) 77–78 (emphasising the importance of the fact that the conduct takes place between two parties to the conflict).

organisations—which do not have a territory and do not necessarily control territory either.

6. Conclusion

This chapter has shown that party status is a key concept in the regulation of armed conflict. This regulation remains centred in various ways around parties as the collective entities between which conflicts take place, even as the ways in which party status is legally relevant evolve. Although being a party to an armed conflict no longer brings about the separate legal sphere that being in a state of war once was, party status still comes with key sets of obligations and, in a much attenuated way, permissions. At another regulative level, the scope of protection granted to individuals in armed conflict, as well as their rights, obligations, and criminal responsibility depend on the connection of individuals to parties. The humanisation and individualisation of international law in armed conflict have thus further entangled the collective and individual dimensions of the regulation in this field. Finally, identifying who is a party to an armed conflict also matters for establishing *where* IHL applies.

Chapter 2 completes the picture on the legal position of parties with a crucial aspect left aside so far, namely how the legal position of parties relates to that of those who do not qualify as parties (ie third parties).

2

Parties and Third Parties in Armed Conflict

1. Introduction

Through the lens of traditional state of war conceptions, war might have seemed to be mainly a bilateral matter between parties. By contrast, armed conflict has long been considered and regulated as a concern to the international community and thus to all States. Structurally, this notion could be taken to question the centrality of parties as reference points in the regulation of armed conflict and the need to distinguish parties from those that do not qualify as such, which are here referred to as third parties.[1] For this distinction to be legally relevant, the duties and rights of parties and third parties must actually differ.[2] The clearer the contrast between the duties and rights of parties and third parties, the more crucial is the identification of parties. To complement the analysis in Chapter 1, of the ways in which the international legal regulation of armed conflict is structured by reference to the parties to the conflict, it is therefore necessary to consider the position of third parties too.

Chapter 2 demonstrates that the regulation of third-parties' legal position with respect to an armed conflict underscores rather than questions the need to identify and distinguish between parties and third parties. First, how international law regulates these two categories of entities remains structurally different. Both the kind and the extent of obligations imposed reflect this difference. Secondly, and relatedly, an entity's party status has implications precisely in the legal relationship to third parties. Party status gives rise to duties and rights of a party regarding third parties and vice versa.

Overall, international law requires third parties to take a posture of detachment from the conflict. As section 2 of this chapter explains, this posture stems from the law of neutrality. Neutrality law developed specifically to regulate the rights and duties of States parties to a war and of those that were not a party (neutrals) vis-à-vis one another, and it arguably still applies to contemporary international armed conflicts. In doing so, neutrality law may be regarded as an early

[1] See Introduction, n 21.

[2] D Kennedy, 'The Stages of Decline in the Public/Private Distinction' (1982) 130 U Penn LR 1349 ('[a legal] distinction must make a difference: a distinction without a difference is a failure').

Party Status to Armed Conflict in International Law. Alexander Wentker, Oxford University Press. © Alexander Wentker 2024.
DOI: 10.1093/oso/9780198900900.003.0003

expression of the community interest[3] to prevent conflicts from extending to further States,[4] though it may be questioned to what extent it has lived up to its conflict-constraining function.[5] It may have also anticipated more far-reaching developments of the role of third parties in the international legal order such as rules on complicity.

Section 3 of this chapter shows that the position of third States under neutrality law is now complemented and refined by further sets of provisions that impose obligations on third parties vis-à-vis the parties. In addition to specific protection obligations that may be addressed to them, third parties are prohibited from contributing to violations of international law applicable in armed conflict, particularly as part of the obligation to respect and ensure respect for international humanitarian law (IHL). In this sense, under these additional layers of regulation, the posture that is required of third parties remains characterised by abstention. While neutrality law requires third States to abstain from participating on either side of the conflict, third parties also bear obligations to abstain from participating in violations by the parties of their obligations. These developments should be regarded as complementing, rather than questioning, the parties' primary role in ensuring that armed conflicts are carried out in a manner that accords with IHL's protective purposes.

2. Parties and neutrals

This section, first, briefly introduces the basic scheme of the legal relations between parties and third parties under neutrality law. It then shows that this body of law retains legal relevance in the contemporary international legal order. Neutrality law automatically applies to all international armed conflicts but only exceptionally and discretionarily to non-international armed conflicts. Having set out these parameters, the section demonstrates the legal implications of an entity's party status in relation to, and in contradistinction to, third parties under neutrality law.

[3] See generally B Simma, 'From Bilateralism to Community Interest in International Law' (1994) 250 RCADI 224; G Abi-Saab, 'Whither the International Community' (1998) 9 EJIL 248; S Villalpando, 'The Legal Dimension of the International Community: How Community Interests Are Protected in International Law' (2010) 21 EJIL 387; E Benvenisti and G Nolte, 'Introduction' in E Benvenisti and G Nolte (eds), *Community Interests across International Law* (OUP 2018) 4; specifically regarding neutrality law, see H Krieger, 'Rights and Obligations of Third Parties in Armed Conflicts' in E Benvenisti and G Nolte (eds), *Community Interests across International Law* (OUP 2018) 456–457.

[4] M Bothe, 'The Law of Neutrality' in D Fleck (ed), *The Handbook of International Humanitarian Law* (4th edn, OUP 2021) 603; C Chinkin, *Third Parties in International Law* (Clarendon Press 1993) 300.

[5] Q Wright, 'The Future of Neutrality' (1928) 12 IC 353, 367; sceptically also A Clapham, *War* (OUP 2021) 70.

a. Legal positions of parties and third parties under neutrality law

The law of neutrality paradigmatically embodies the idea of third parties as detached from the conflict. This body of international law developed incrementally through international practice from the Middle Ages onwards[6] and was partly codified in the late nineteenth and early twentieth centuries[7] in what has been termed the 'golden age of neutrality'.[8]

This practice was, in part, driven by pragmatic considerations. International law confined the state of war to the relations between belligerents, while the relations between belligerents and third States remained within the realm of the laws of peace. Wars, however, often considerably affected third States as well. Third States had interests in continuing trade with other third States and belligerent States as well as interests to protect their property and maintain the integrity of their territory, free from the destruction of war. Belligerent States, in turn, possibly had interests in controlling trade relations as part of economic warfare strategies.[9] At the same time, the very notion of war as a form of settling disputes by contest would have been undermined by bystanders interfering with and thus manipulating the outcome of the 'duel'.[10] This practical significance of the relationship between belligerents and third parties required regulation. In other words, to fit the state of war between belligerents seamlessly within the realm of peace surrounding it, the legal position of third States was itself to be governed by a distinct legal status of duties and rights shaping their relationship to the belligerents.[11] The distinctiveness of war as a state of affairs thus translated into a binary categorisation of States' status into belligerents and neutrals.

The core idea of neutral status as keeping neutrals detached from the conflict is reflected both by the restrictions imposed on neutrals and the rights or protection granted to them. Neutral status is characterised by the principle of impartiality towards parties. This overarching principle informs the application of specific obligations on neutrals,[12] which fall mainly into two broad categories. First, neutral

[6] S Neff, *The Rights and Duties of Neutrals: A General History* (Manchester UP 2000) 5ff; K Wani, *Neutrality in International Law: From the Sixteenth Century to 1945* (Routledge 2017) 17–140; J Stone, *Legal Controls of International Conflict: A Treatise on the Dynamics of Disputes- and War-Law* (2nd edn, Maitland 1959) 364; P Jessup and F Deák, *Neutrality: Its History, Economics and Law—Vol I: The Origins* (Columbia UP 1935) 10–19.

[7] See notably HCV, HCXIII.

[8] C de Visscher, *Theory and Reality in Public International Law* (P Corbett tr, Princeton UP 1968) 307.

[9] E Castrén, *The Present Law of War and Neutrality* (Suomalainen Tiedeakatemia 1954) 427 (noting that 'the law of neutrality has evolved in State practice as a *compromise between conflicting interests*' (emphasis original)).

[10] S Neff, *War and the Law of Nations: A General History* (CUP 2005) 191.

[11] Castrén (n 9) 425–426.

[12] J Upcher, *Neutrality in Contemporary International Law* (OUP 2020) 77.

States bear duties of abstention with respect to the conflict, including not to assist parties, notably by supplying military material.[13] Secondly, neutral States have obligations of prevention regarding actions by parties on neutral territory, including the movement of troops or convoys, the erection or use of communication devices, the recruitment of military personnel,[14] the establishment of naval bases in neutral ports,[15] and the overflight through neutral airspace.[16]

Conversely, parties must 'respect the sovereign rights of neutral[s]',[17] chiefly the inviolability of neutral territory,[18] and not conduct certain acts on neutral territory (namely those that neutrals are required to prevent from occurring).[19] This protection traditionally depended, however, on neutrals discharging their prevention obligations. If they failed to do so with respect to one belligerent, the aggrieved side could enter neutral territory and redress the violation of neutrality by the other party.[20] Moreover, while neutrals continued to benefit from their peacetime freedom of commerce, the belligerents had the right to take certain measures restricting neutral shipping, including to visit, search, and seize contraband, as well as to set up blockades.[21]

Despite its origins in the States' pragmatic pursuit of their economic and strategic interests, neutrality law may reflect a community interest.[22] Neutrality law aims at restraining conflict by regulating neutral status as distinct from party status and requiring parties and neutrals to keep neutrals detached from the conflict.[23] It is not self-evident, however, how this scheme fits with the contemporary international legal order and the regulation of recourse to force.

b. Persisting existence of neutrality law in the contemporary international legal order

The institution of neutrality may, at first sight, appear outdated in light of the profound structural changes in international law since the development of the law of neutrality. International law is no longer indifferent to war since it prohibits the recourse to force. With the establishment of collective security mechanisms to react

13 HCXIII, art 6.
14 HCV, arts 2–5.
15 HCXIII, art 5.
16 Hague Air Rules, art 42.
17 HCXIII, art 1.
18 HCV, art 1.
19 ibid arts 2–4; HCXIII, art 1.
20 nn 142–143.
21 Below d.iii.
22 Krieger (n 3) 457 (suggesting that 'an important aspect of rendering peace a community interest is already embodied in the law of neutrality in that it is meant to promote international stability and security').
23 Bothe (n 4) 603.

to threats to and breaches of the peace, international law also makes war a concern of the international community as a whole, rather than a matter purely between warring parties. This paradigm shift inherently challenges a conception of third States as neutral bystanders, which has led commentators after the adoption of the Kellogg–Briand Pact and the UN Charter to consider neutrality to be anachronistic and obsolete.[24]

Despite this apparent tension, neutrality coexists with the UN Charter collective security system in contemporary international law. The ICJ accepted this coexistence in the *Nuclear Weapons* Advisory Opinion by holding that 'international law leaves no doubt that the principle of neutrality ... is applicable (*subject to the relevant provisions of the United Nations Charter*), to all international armed conflict'.[25] Indeed, section i. shows that the Charter's collective security system at times permits or even requires deviations from neutrality. On closer inspection, however, it leaves ample room for the continued operation of neutrality law in many cases.[26] Moreover, as will be seen in section ii., States have been unwilling to abandon the institution of neutrality.

i. Room for neutrality under the UN Charter

The extent to which neutrality law continues to determine the legal position of third parties with respect to an armed conflict depends on whether and how the UN Security Council takes action regarding that conflict under the Charter's collective security system. Three scenarios must be distinguished.

In the first scenario, the Security Council, acting under Chapter VII, identifies a party to an armed conflict as an aggressor or as having threatened or breached the peace. In such a case, the Council can impose obligations on Member States to take measures to restore the peace. Under Article 41, the Council may decide on non-forcible measures. Such a decision, however, does not necessarily prevent an individual Member State from remaining neutral. This may be because the Council determines that only some Member States carry out its decisions.[27] Moreover, the measures imposed may not necessarily conflict with Member States remaining neutral, for example when they consist merely of severing diplomatic relations. When they conflict, however, Article 103 entails that the obligation to carry out the Council's decision under Article 25 takes precedence over neutrality obligations under treaty law and arguably also over neutrality obligations under customary international law.[28]

[24] N Politis, *Neutrality and Peace* (F Macken tr, Carnegie Endowment for International Peace 1935) 80–82; ILA (ed), *Report of the Forty-First Conference 1946* (ILA 1948) 42; C Fenwick, '"The Old Order Changeth, Yielding Place to New"' (1953) 47 AJIL 84, 85–86.

[25] *Legality of the Threat or Use of Nuclear Weapons* (AO) [1996] ICJ Rep 226 [89] (emphasis added).

[26] H Kelsen, 'Théorie du droit international' (1953) 84 RCADI 1, 59–60.

[27] UN Charter, art 48(1).

[28] In favour, see eg R Bernhardt, 'Article 103' in B Simma (ed), *The Charter of the United Nations: A Commentary* (2nd edn, OUP 2002) [21]; ILC, 'Report of the Study Group—Fragmentation of International Law: Difficulties Arising from the Diversification and Expansion of International

In the second scenario, the Council, acting under Chapter VII, authorises Member States to have recourse to force. In such a case, Member States are permitted to give up their neutral status. With no agreements under Article 43 having been concluded, they are, however, under no obligation to do so. They may therefore remain neutral even when such collective enforcement action is taken. Member States remaining neutral would nevertheless bear an obligation under Article 2(5) to assist the UN-authorised enforcement action as well as an obligation not to assist the target State of such action. Their obligations under neutrality law may have to be modified as this obligation to assist would also prevail under Article 103.[29] A neutral State may thus, for example, have to discriminate between States parties acting upon Council authorisation and their opponents regarding the permission to use its territorial seas and ports (in variation of Article 9 HCXIII) or transit its airspace. The neutral State may also have to exempt UN-authorised parties from the internment of troops on neutral territory (in variation of Article 11 HCV).[30]

In the third scenario, which is the case of many armed conflicts, the Security Council neither authorises nor obliges Member States to act in a way that is contrary to neutral status. In such a case, third States may still resort to force in collective self-defence if they are requested to do so by a State that has become the victim of an armed attack.[31] By engaging in the conflict, they may lose their neutral status and become a party to the conflict. Yet, to the extent that they remain within the confines of the right to self-defence, the prohibition of using force would not be violated. Third States do not, however, bear a duty to resort to collective self-defence and may therefore remain neutral.

Whether the right to collective self-defence also justifies deviations from neutrality obligations in favour of the victim of an armed attack short of force is controversial. The orthodox position considers self-defence as an exception solely to the prohibition of the use of force.[32] Self-defence can also, however, be understood as a broader, general right, rooted in the traditional concept of self-preservation,

Law' (13 April 2006) UN Doc A/CN.4/L.682 [345]; B Fassbender, 'The United Nations Charter as Constitution of the International Community' (1998) 36 Colum JTL 529, 586; contra D Bowett, 'The Impact of Security Council Decisions on Dispute Settlement Procedures' (1994) 5 EJIL 89, 92; A Orakhelashvili, 'Article 30 1969 Vienna Convention' in O Corten and P Klein (eds), *The Vienna Conventions on the Law of Treaties*, vol I (OUP 2011) 782 [46].

[29] Upcher (n 12) 155–156; C Antonopoulos, *Non-Participation in Armed Conflict: Continuity and Modern Challenges to the Law of Neutrality* (CUP 2022) 62.

[30] 'United States: Department of Defence Report to Congress on the Conduct of the Persian Gulf War—Appendix on the Role of the Law of War' (1992) 31 ILM 615, 639; R McLaughlin, 'United Nations Mandated Naval Interdiction Operations in the Territorial Sea?' (2002) 51 ICLQ 249, 273–274; for a thorough review of practice, see Upcher (n 12) 156–160.

[31] See generally J Green, *Collective Self-Defence in International Law* (CUP 2024).

[32] J Crawford, 'Second Report on State Responsibility' (1999) UN Doc A/CN.4/498/Add.1 74; *Legal Consequences of the Construction of a Wall in the Occupied Palestinian Territory* (AO) [2004] ICJ Rep 136 sep op Higgins [35].

which would thus a fortiori also cover non-forcible measures.[33] In practical terms, relying on collective self-defence would have the disadvantage for States that they would have to immediately report their measures to the Security Council under Article 51 UN Charter.[34] Third States that assist one side in an inter-State conflict short of joining the conflict as a party themselves will generally have an interest in avoiding the escalatory signal attached to Article 51 reports.[35]

Alternatively, deviations from neutrality obligations in favour of the victim of aggression could be justified as collective countermeasures by non-injured States to redress a violation of the *erga omnes* obligation that prohibits aggression.[36] While conventional wisdom rejected the possibility of collective countermeasures,[37] there is considerable State practice and *opinio juris* today that can be read as supporting this possibility.[38] Yet, the uncertainty surrounding the permissibility of collective countermeasures persists. In addition, relying on countermeasures would come with the practical downside for States of requiring prior notification of the wrongdoing State and an offer to negotiate.[39]

Arguably, however, third States do not need to invoke collective self-defence or rely on collective countermeasures to justify their assistance to the victim of an armed attack or aggression. The neutrality obligations of non-assistance and prevention themselves contain an exception for such assistance. There is debate as to whether State practice and *opinio juris* to date—which have been reviewed thoroughly elsewhere—suffice to bear out this exception as a specific rule of customary international law.[40] To illustrate the subtle potential ramifications of such a rule in State practice and *opinio juris*, in the context of Russia's war against Ukraine,

[33] R Buchan, 'Non-Forcible Measures and the Law of Self-Defence' (2023) 72 ICLQ 1.

[34] The reporting requirement is generally regarded as a separate obligation rather than a condition of the lawfulness of self-defence—see *Military and Paramilitary Activities in and against Nicaragua (Nicaragua v United States)* (Merits) [1986] ICJ Rep 14 [200], [235]; T Ruys, *'Armed Attack' and Article 51 of the UN Charter: Evolutions in Customary Law and Practice* (CUP 2010) 72.

[35] See generally J Green, 'The Article 51 Reporting Requirement for Self-Defense Actions' (2015) 55 Va JIL 563, 620–621.

[36] P Clancy, 'Neutral Arms Transfers and the Russian Invasion of Ukraine' (2023) 72 ICLQ 527, 540.

[37] 2672nd meeting of the ILC (2001) I YILC 34, 35 (Brownlie, Elaraby).

[38] C Tams, *Enforcing Obligations* Erga Omnes *in International Law* (CUP 2005) 198–251, M Dawidowicz, *Third-Party Countermeasures in International Law* (CUP 2017) 239–284.

[39] ARSIWA, art 52(1)(b).

[40] Against such a reading of practice, see eg Upcher (n 12) 31–37; W Heintschel von Heinegg, '"Benevolent" Third States in International Armed Conflicts: The Myth of the Irrelevance of the Law of Neutrality' in M Schmitt and J Pejic (eds), *International Law and Armed Conflict: Exploring the Faultlines Essays in Honour of Yoram Dinstein* (Nijhoff 2007) 545–553 (though see W Heintschel von Heinegg, 'Neutrality in the War Against Ukraine' (*Articles of War*, 1 March 2022) <https://lieber.westpoint.edu/neutrality-in-the-war-against-ukraine/>, hinting at a change in his view in light of Russia's aggression against Ukraine); K Heller and L Trabucco, 'The Legality of Weapons Transfers to Ukraine Under International Law' (2022) 13 JIHLS 251, 263; in favour, see eg S Talmon, 'The Provision of Arms to the Victim of Armed Aggression: the Case of Ukraine ' (Bonn Research Papers on Public International Law, 6 April 2022) <https://ssrn.com/abstract=4077084>; J El-Zein, 'Das Ende des Neutralitätsrechts' (PhD thesis, University of Cologne 2023) 66–87.

the German Federal Minister of Justice justified Germany's military assistance to Ukraine by noting that:

> since the UN Charter has been in force, the old neutrality requirement, as it is still called, has been overridden to some extent. War is in principle forbidden. The only legitimate form of war is defensive war. This is expressly stipulated in the UN Charter.[41]

Whether or not there is a specific customary rule to this effect, however, the exception flows from the wider structure and purpose of the *jus ad bellum*. The purpose of the victim State's right to individual self-defence is to restore peace by allowing for the effective termination of an unlawful use of force that amounts to an armed attack. That purpose would be undermined if third States were prohibited from assisting the attacked State.[42] This reasoning informs a systematic interpretation of neutrality duties as contained in Hague Conventions V and XIII, in light of their 'context' and 'purpose' under Article 31(1), (3) VCLT. Whether or not the customary rules on neutrality—which are especially relevant to those States that are not parties to Hague Conventions V and XIII—can be interpreted,[43] systematic considerations also matter in establishing their scope by way of deduction from the rules of self-defence.[44]

Accordingly, the content of neutrality law has partly been modified by the *jus ad bellum*. This modification is limited, however, to what is necessary and proportionate to repel the armed attack against the assisted State. Beyond this specific exception, the law of neutrality can still apply. Even in situations of aggression, there

[41] German Federal Parliament, Stenographic Protocol 20/33 (11 May 2022) 2949 (translated with deepL).

[42] C Kreß, 'The Ukraine War and the Prohibition of the Use of Force in International Law' (TOAEP Occasional Paper Series No 13 2022) 18–19.

[43] In favour of the interpretability of customary international law rules, see eg P Merkouris, 'Interpreting Customary International Law: You'll Never Walk Alone' in P Merkouris, J Kammerhofer, and N Arajärvi (eds), *The Theory and Philosophy of Customary International Law and Its Interpretation* (CUP 2022); O Chasapis Tassinis, 'Customary International Law: Interpretation from Beginning to End' (2020) 31 EJIL 235; S Sur, 'La Créativité du droit international' (2013) 363 RCADI 13, 294–295; D Alland, 'L'Interprétation du droit international public' (2013) 362 RCADI 51, 82–88; A Orakhelashvili, *The Interpretation of Acts and Rules in Public International Law* (OUP 2008) 489–510; A Bleckmann, 'Zur Feststellung und Auslegung von Völkergewohnheitsrecht' (1977) 37 ZaöRV 504; against T Treves, 'Customary International Law' in A Peters (ed), *Max Planck Encyclopedia of Public International Law* (OUP) <https://opil.ouplaw.com/display/10.1093/law:epil/9780199231690/law-9780199231690-e1393?rskey=lpdCqj&result=1&prd=MPIL> [2]; M Bos, *A Methodology of International Law* (Elsevier 1984) 109–110.

[44] On the role of deductive reasoning in the—generally inductive—process of identifying custom, see eg AE Roberts, 'Traditional and Modern Approaches to Customary International Law: A Reconciliation' 95 AJIL 757, 758; CW Jenks, *The Prospects of International Adjudication* (Stevens 1964) 660–662; for evidence of the resort to this method by the ICJ, see S Talmon, 'Determining Customary International Law: The ICJ's Methodology Between Induction, Deduction and Assertion' (2015) 26 EJIL 417, 427; W Worster, 'The Inductive and Deductive Methods in Customary International Law Analysis: Traditional and Modern Approaches' (2014) 45 Geo JIL 445, 505–506.

is room for the law of neutrality. On the one hand, the States parties to conflict must observe their duties to respect neutral territory and property.[45] On the other hand, vis-à-vis an aggressor, neutrality obligations not to provide assistance are not inconsistent but in line with complicity rules under the law of State responsibility and the *jus ad bellum*.[46] While these rules have partly taken over functions of neutrality law,[47] neutrality law remains relevant because its non-assistance duties have different, less stringent requirements. They do not, for example, require specific subjective elements as complicity rules tend to do.

In sum, therefore, today's international law of peace and security leaves space for applying neutrality law. The former 'constitutes a kind of overlay network of norms under which the old law still exists, but may, to a certain extent, take on a different shape'.[48] The interplay with the collective security scheme under the Charter and the ensuing modifications to neutral status may attenuate the extent to which the neutral State's position is detached from the conflict. Looking ahead, Nasu has suggested that persisting or renewed great power rivalries may continue to give rise both to political impasses in the Security Council and to international armed conflicts in which neutrality law is 'likely to be relied upon'.[49]

ii. Neutrality in contemporary international practice

The continued existence of neutrality law seems to be presumed by references to neutral States, Powers, or countries in the GCs[50] and API,[51] as well as by pronouncements of the ICJ,[52] the ILC,[53] and the ILA.[54] Practice indeed confirms that neutrality law has survived in the contemporary international legal order.

Neutrality rarely finds prominent mention in States' pronouncements on contemporary armed conflicts, which has led one commentator to describe its existence in the post-UN Charter era as 'shadowy'.[55] However, States' reluctance to explicitly invoke neutrality need not mean that they consider neutrality obsolete. It

[45] See below 2.d.ii.

[46] See below 3.b.

[47] For a thorough study, see El-Zein (n 40) 145ff (concluding that neutrality rules do not retain independent added value here).

[48] M Bothe, 'Comments' in H Post (ed), *International Economic Law and Armed Conflict* (Nijhoff 1994) 36.

[49] H Nasu, 'The Laws of Neutrality in the Interconnected World: Mapping the Future Scenarios' in M Waxman and T Oakley (eds), *The Future Law of Armed Conflict* (OUP 2022) 124.

[50] GCI, arts 4, 8(1), 10(2), (4), 11(2), 27(1), (2), (4), 37(1), (3), 43; GCII, arts 5, 8(1), 10(2), (4), 11(2), 17, 25, 40, 43(2); GCIII, arts 4(B)(2), 8(1), 10(2), (4), 11(2), 109(2), (3), 110, 111, 114, 115, 116, 122; GCIV, arts 4(2), 9(1), 11(2), (4), (6), 12(2), 24(2), 36(1), 61(1), 132(2).

[51] Arts 2(c), 9(2)(a), 19, 22(2)(a), 30(3), 31, 37(1)(d), 39(1), 64(1), (3).

[52] *Nuclear Weapons* (n 25) [51], [74], [88]–[90], [93]. See also *Namibia* (AO) [1971] ICJ Rep 16 sep op Ammoun [13]–[16].

[53] ILC, Draft Articles on the Effects of Armed Conflicts on Treaties, art 17.

[54] ILA Committee on the Use of Force, 'Final Report on the Meaning of Armed Conflict in International Law' (2010) 1, 4, 33.

[55] P Norton, 'Between the Ideology and the Reality: The Shadow of the Law of Neutrality' (1976) 17 HILJ 249, 310.

may be that States did not deem the legal implications flowing from neutral status advantageous in that specific case. They may have considered invoking neutrality to be politically inopportune, for example, with a view to political alliances. States may also have considered that their conduct needed no justification under neutrality law because it fell within the exception for assistance to the victim State of an armed attack discussed above.

Moreover, in many major international armed conflicts since 1945, States *have* relied on different aspects of neutrality law, albeit rarely comprehensively or consistently. States have variously asserted their own neutral status with respect to a specific conflict, condemned other States' violations of neutral duties, or claimed belligerent rights against neutrals. Conflicts in which neutrality law has been relied upon in one or several of these ways include the wars between Israel and several Arab States since 1948,[56] the Korean War,[57] the war between India and Pakistan in 1965,[58] and the Falkland/Malvinas Islands War between the UK and Argentina.[59]

The Iran–Iraq War (1980–1988) saw particularly widespread invocations of different features of neutrality law. Many States explicitly asserted their neutrality,[60] various States as well as the Security Council condemned Iranian attacks on neutral shipping,[61] while Iran condemned assistance to Iraq (including by Kuwait, Saudi Arabia, and the US) as violations of neutrality duties.[62] In the *Oil Platforms* case before the ICJ (which concerned destructions of Iranian platforms by the US in reaction to Iranian attacks, inter alia, on Kuwaiti tankers previously re-flagged to the US), both parties explicitly set out their views on the continued existence and relevance of neutrality law in contemporary international law.[63] While the Court found that it did not have jurisdiction over compliance with naval warfare law in this case, it noted the damages to 'neutral shipping in Persian Gulf'.[64]

In the Gulf War of 1990–1991, several States, including Iran, Jordan, and India, asserted their neutral status, although the Security Council had identified Iraq as the aggressor and authorised a coalition of States to take forcible action.[65] The US

56 D Schindler, 'Aspects contemporains de la neutralité' (1967) 121 RCADI 221, 283, 292.
57 ibid 291.
58 C Rousseau, 'Chronique des faits internationaux' (1966) 70 RGDIP 178, 180–182 (reporting on measures taken by both parties against neutral vessels allegedly transporting contraband of war following the publication of contraband lists).
59 H Levie, 'The Falklands Crisis and the Laws of War' (1998) 70 ILS 203, 207ff.
60 S Oeter, *Neutralität und Waffenhandel* (Springer 1992) 114–122.
61 UNSC Res 582 (24 February 1986) UN Doc S/RES/582 [2].
62 'Letter Dated 25 September 1985 from the Permanent Representative of the Islamic Republic of Iran to the United Nations Addressed to the Secretary-General' UN Doc S/17496.
63 *Oil Platforms (Iran v United States)* Reply and Defence to Counterclaim Iran (10 March 1999) [7.5] ff; *Oil Platforms (Iran v United States)* Counter-Memorial US (23 June 1997) [1.18]; see already *Aerial Incident of 3 July 1988 (Iran v United States)* Memorial Iran (24 July 1990) [3.103], [4.33]ff.
64 *Oil Platforms (Iran v United States)* (Merits) [2003] ICJ Rep 161 [44].
65 Keesing's (1991) 37942; 'Refueling of Jets in India to Stop' *NYT* (20 February 1991) A13 <www.nytimes.com/1991/02/20/world/war-in-the-gulf-refueling-of-jets-in-india-to-stop.html>; see also Upcher (n 12) 151.

seemingly recognised Jordan and Iran's ability to invoke neutral status but insisted that the Council resolutions had 'modified the obligation of neutral powers to remain impartial with regard to Coalition UN members'.[66]

During the 2003 Iraq War, Italy and Ireland justified their assistance to the US and its coalition partners as being consistent with positions of 'non-belligerency'[67] and 'qualified neutrality',[68] respectively, while domestic courts in Ireland and Germany questioned the legality of such assistance in light of neutrality duties and explicitly affirmed the continued existence of neutrality law.[69]

Russia's war against Ukraine has seen relatively little explicit engagement with neutrality law, despite the wide range of military assistance that both Ukraine and Russia have received from many States.[70] Certain permanently neutral States, such as Switzerland, have, by contrast, explicitly invoked their neutral status to justify particular limitations in their assistance to Ukraine.[71] At least for States assisting Ukraine, their silence on neutrality law can be explained by political concerns to avoid the term 'neutrality', which may have been regarded as compromising their political support to Ukraine. The silence may also, however, be explained by States' view that their assistance was covered by an exception to the scope of application of neutral States' obligations because Ukraine has been the victim of an armed attack by Russia. This is evidenced, for example, by Germany's reference to neutrality law having been partly superseded by the UN Charter—which also illustrates that the even in this conflict, there has not been total silence on neutrality law on the part of States.[72]

At a general level, States seem to continue to consider neutrality law as relevant to their operational military practice. This is demonstrated by treatments devoted to neutrality law in many military manuals, including recently updated ones.[73] Neutrality law is also likely to maintain a central place in the ongoing revision of the *San Remo Manual*.[74] Moreover, pronouncements of States as well as military

[66] DoD Report Persian Gulf War 640.

[67] 'Comunicato della Presidenza della Repubblica sulla riunione del Consiglio Supremo di difesa del 19 marzo 2003' (2003) 86 RDI 904; L Appicciafuoco et al, 'Diplomatic and Parliamentary Practice' (2003) 13 IYIL 265, 288; N Ronzitti, 'Italy's Non-Belligerency during the Iraqi War' in M Ragazzi (ed), *International Responsibility Today: Essays in Memory of Oscar Schachter* (Nijhoff 2005).

[68] *Horgan v An Taoiseach et al* [2003] 2 IR 468 [124]–[125] (where the Court rejects this position).

[69] ibid [122], [124]–[125]; Federal Administrative Court, Judgement of 21 June 2005 (2 WD 12.04) [4.1.4.1.1]–[4.1.4.1.2].

[70] G Bartolini, 'The Provision of Belligerent Materials in the Russia–Ukraine Conflict: Beyond the Law of Neutrality?' (2023) 99 QIL 3, 9.

[71] Switzerland, 'Clarté et orientation de la politique de neutralité: Rapport du Conseil fédéral' 26 October 2022 <www.newsd.admin.ch/newsd/message/attachments/73618.pdf> 21.

[72] n 41.

[73] *Peruvian Manual* 301–304 [104]–[112]; *Danish Manual* 62–63; New Zealand, *Manual of Armed Forces Law Vol 4: Law of Armed Conflict* (2017) 16-1–16-15; *German Manual* 159ff; 959ff; France, *Manuel de droit des opérations militaires* (2022) 294; US, *The Commander's Handbook on the Law of Naval Operations* (2022) 7-1–7-14.

[74] On the reception of the *Manual* in international practice, see E Crawford, *Non-Binding Norms in International Humanitarian Law: Efficacy, Legitimacy, and Legality* (OUP 2021) 93, 199–201. For an

and expert manuals consider neutrality law to be applicable to outer space[75] and cyberspace.[76] This suggests that neutrality law will continue to play a role in future armed conflicts. Despite the challenges of applying a body of law that was developed against the background of nineteenth-century technological realities to the cyber realm,[77] the *Tallinn Manual* points out that:

> [t]he global distribution of cyber assets and activities, as well as global dependency on cyber infrastructure, means that cyber operations of the parties to a conflict can easily affect private or public neutral cyber infrastructure. Accordingly, neutrality is particularly relevant in modern armed conflict.[78]

The same pragmatism of States that has animated the law of neutrality since its inception now arguably keeps it alive to be invoked when it serves the interests of States, along with the conception of third parties as detached from the conflict.

Finding that neutrality law continues to exist raises questions about its application in contemporary armed conflicts.

c. Scope of application of neutrality law

This section argues that, in principle, neutrality law applies in all international armed conflicts and that it does so automatically (ie without a need for a decision of the State). This finding is crucial for the purposes of this study since it implies

equally prominent place of neutrality in another recent expert manual, see J Kraska et al, 'The Newport Manual on the Law of Naval Warfare' (2023) 101 ILS 1, 225–238.

[75] *French Manual* 294.

[76] Italy, 'Italian Position Paper on "International Law and Cyberspace"' November 2021 <www.esteri.it/mae/resource/doc/2021/11/italian_position_paper_on_international_law_and_cyberspace.pdf> 10; Netherlands, 'Letter of the Minister of Foreign Affairs to Parliament' 5 July 2019 (Kamerstuk 33 694 no 47) <https://zoek.officielebekendmakingen.nl/kst-33694-47.html>; France, 'Ministère des Armées: Droit international appliqué aux opérations dans le cyberespace' 10 September 2019 <www.defense.gouv.fr/content/download/565895/9750877/file/Droit+internat+appliqué+aux+opérations+Cyberespace.pdf> 17; Costa Rica, 'Costa Rica's Position on the Application of International Law in Cyberspace' 21 July 2023 <https://docs-library.unoda.org/Open-Ended_Working_Group_on_Information_and_Communication_Technologies_-_(2021)/Costa_Rica_-_Position_Paper_-_International_Law_in_Cyberspace.pdf> 17–18; UNGA, 'Official Compendium of Voluntary National Contributions on the Subject of How International Law Applies to the Use of Information and Communications Technologies by States' UN Doc A/76/136 (13 July 2021) 78 (Romania); Switzerland, 'Switzerland's Position Paper on the Application of International Law in Cyberspace' (May 2021) <www.eda.admin.ch/dam/eda/en/documents/aussenpolitik/voelkerrecht/20210527-Schweiz-Annex-UN-GGE-Cybersecurity-2019-2021_EN.pdf> 4–5; *Tallinn Manual 2.0* 553ff (rr 150–154); *Danish Manual* 60; *US Manual* 1032–1033.

[77] N Neuman, 'Neutrality and Cyberspace: Bridging the Gap between Theory and Reality' (2021) 97 ILS 765, 786; R Schöndorf, 'Israel's Perspective on Key Legal and Practical Issues Concerning the Application of International Law to Cyber Operations' (2021) 97 ILS 395, 397–398.

[78] *Tallinn Manual 2.0* 554; see also Nasu (n 49) 131.

that the duties and rights attached to neutral status in international armed conflicts come into play for each third State with respect to every State identified as a party to an international armed conflict. There is no intermediate or alternative status beyond the binary party–neutral categorisation. In non-international armed conflicts, neutrality law can at most be applied on a discretionary basis, though other rules of international law may require a similar posture of detachment from third States.

i. International armed conflicts

(1) *War, armed conflict, and questions of threshold*

Traditionally, the institution of neutrality was intimately connected to the state of war.[79] For the law applicable between parties, the notion of war has been mostly replaced with the notion of international armed conflict.[80] This has also affected the law of neutrality, which applies between parties and third parties. Even though the transition from war to armed conflict has not been laid down in any treaty provision on neutrality, the marginalisation of the concept of war by the concept of armed conflict in many post-1945 treaties and international practice has likely further increased the uncertainty of establishing the existence of a state of war.[81] More importantly, as soon as States become parties to an international armed conflict, the need for regulating their relationship with third States may arise. Conditioning neutral status on the existence of a state of war while party status is connected to the notion of international armed conflict is thus unhelpful. Rightly, therefore, there is great acceptance for neutrality law to apply to international armed conflicts, whether or not the conflict qualifies as 'war'.[82]

Yet, neutrality law is not consistently applied to all international armed conflicts in international practice, as noted above. To account for this inconsistency, one reading of the practice is that neutrality law does not apply to all international armed conflicts but only to those reaching a certain threshold.[83] It proves difficult, however, to set this threshold. Suggestions range from requiring a 'state of generalized hostilities' as a 'condition initiated and preserved by persistent organized fighting',[84] to the acknowledgment that it is 'impossible to establish this threshold

[79] Castrén (n 9) 34; see above 2.a.

[80] On the persisting possibility of declared wars, see Chapter 3.2.a.; for an argument that some rules of neutrality law could also apply to declared wars, see Upcher (n 12) 43–44 with reference to international practice); though see G Petrochilos, 'The Relevance of the Concepts of War and Armed Conflict to the Law of Neutrality' (1998) 31 Van JTL 575, 611; Y Dinstein, *War, Aggression and Self-Defence* (6th edn, CUP 2017) 12.

[81] n 80; Chapter 3.2.a.

[82] *Nuclear Weapons* (n 25) [89]; I Brownlie, *International Law and the Use of Force by States* (Clarendon 1963) 395–396; Heintschel von Heinegg (n 40) 560.

[83] Brownlie (n 82) 400–401; Bothe (n 4) 609; *US Manual* [15.2.1.2]; *German Manual* [1202]; *US Commander's Handbook* 7-1.

[84] Petrochilos (n 80) 605 (emphasis omitted).

in a general way' and that, therefore, '[o]ne can only say that there must be a conflict of a certain duration and intensity'.[85]

These difficulties can arguably best be mitigated by acknowledging that neutrality law applies, in principle, to the relationship between parties and third States in all international armed conflicts. The ICJ seems to have taken this view in the *Nuclear Weapons* Advisory Opinion wherein it considered neutrality law applicable 'to *all* international armed conflict'.[86] The central rights and duties flowing from neutral status—including the protection of the integrity of neutral territory and neutral duties of abstention and prevention—thus apply in every international armed conflict. This does not preclude some aspects of this body of law from applying only in those conflicts that require their application.[87] In particular, belligerent rights to visits and searches at sea or establishing blockades[88] may apply only in conflicts of a scale that justifies that parties resort to measures of control regarding neutral shipping.[89] Such a differentiation can explain why many provisions of neutrality law seem more likely to be invoked and complied with in conflicts of relatively higher intensity.[90] This reading of practice avoids the above-noted pitfalls of inferring that neutrality does not apply when States do not invoke it. At the same time, as Upcher pointed out, it would be:

> in keeping with the purpose of the law of neutrality—namely, to prevent the escalation and spread of armed conflict—that the duties of neutrality should increase as an international armed conflict increases in intensity.[91]

(2) Automatic neutrality and the absence of intermediate statuses

The dichotomous categorisation of States with respect to international armed conflicts as parties or neutrals has been challenged on grounds that neutrality is merely an optional status to which third States may choose to subject themselves.[92] This would imply the existence of an alternative (third) status for non-neutral non-parties, variably labelled 'non-belligerency' and 'benevolent' or 'qualified' neutrality. Such a status has been invoked occasionally to justify third States' deviations from neutral duties by assisting one or several parties to the conflict.[93]

[85] Bothe (n 4) 609.
[86] *Nuclear Weapons* (n 25) [89] (emphasis added).
[87] See also *GCI Commentary* [909]; Clapham (n 5) 61 (suggesting, however, that even the duties of abstention and prevention may not apply in all international armed conflicts).
[88] On these, see further below d.iii.
[89] Heintschel von Heinegg (n 40) 561.
[90] Upcher (n 12) 52.
[91] ibid 54.
[92] G Schwarzenberger, 'Jus Pacis ac Belli? Prolegomena to a Sociology of International Law' (1943) 37 AJIL 460, 470; C Greenwood, 'The Relationship between *Ius ad Bellum* and *Ius in Bello*' (1983) 9 Rev Int Stud 221, 230; Clapham (n 5) 72.
[93] For Italy's self-declared 'non-belligerency' during the Iraq War in 2003, see n 67; for similar positions taken by some States, including Italy, Spain, Turkey, and the US, at different times during the Second World War, see Schindler (n 56) 263–264; 'Address of Robert H Jackson, Attorney General

Yet, such positions have arguably not crystallised such that international law would bear out an intermediate status half-way between neutral and party.[94] Third States deviating from their neutral duties have generally not justified their conduct by reference to an intermediate status. For the most part, they have instead remained silent about the compatibility of their conduct with neutrality law, denied the facts or their violations of neutrality law, or advanced other justifications.[95] The German Federal Administrative Court also considered neutral status as applying automatically to third States in international armed conflicts.[96] The references in API to 'neutral or other States not Parties to the conflict'[97] appear to be a drafting compromise (between those favouring the wording of 'not engaged in the conflict' throughout the Protocol and those insisting on references to 'neutrals') and thus refer to the same concept with two different terms rather than acknowledge two separate categories of third States.[98]

As noted above, States may deviate from their neutrality duties if the Security Council authorises them to do so. For assistance to the victim State of an armed attack, there is also an exception to neutral States' duties of non-assistance and prevention. Conceptually, it is not helpful, however, to frame these possibilities of deviation as flowing from a special 'status'. As has been shown above, the legal implications for the lawfulness of States' conduct in these situations are more accurately conceived as flowing from an interaction between the *jus ad bellum* concepts of self-defence, armed attack, and aggression with the obligations attached to these States' neutral status. Deriving a special status from the *jus ad bellum* concepts would also seem structurally inappropriate since the *jus ad bellum* applies to specific acts and defies status-based categorisations.[99]

That neutrality law applies automatically conveys the notion that this body of law conceives of third parties as *required*—not merely *permitted*—to keep and to be kept detached from the conflict, subject to modifications under the *jus ad bellum* and the UN collective security system discussed above. Beyond what is required by these modifications, the purpose of neutrality law to constrain armed

of the United States, Inter-American Bar Association, Havana, Cuba, March 27, 1941' (1941) 35 AJIL 348, 351.

[94] Though see A Gioia, 'Neutrality and Non-Belligerency' in H Post (ed), *International Economic Law and Armed Conflict* (Nijhoff 1994) 65ff.

[95] For thorough reviews of State practice, see Heintschel von Heinegg (n 40) 545–553; Upcher (n 12) 31–37.

[96] Federal Administrative Court, Judgement of 21 June 2005 (n 69) [226].

[97] GCIII, arts 2(c), 9(2)(a), 19, 22(2)(a), 30(3), 31, 37(1)(d), 39(1), 64 API. Arts 4(B)(2), 122 also refer to 'neutral or non-belligerent Powers', while GCIII otherwise generally only refers to neutral States.

[98] Y Sandoz, 'Neutral Powers and the Conventions' in A Clapham, P Gaeta, and M Sassòli (eds), *The 1949 Geneva Conventions: A Commentary* (OUP 2015) 93.

[99] See also KL Yip, 'Separation between *Jus ad Bellum* and *Jus in Bello* as Insulation of Results, Not Scopes, of Application' (2020) 58 MLLWR 31, 35.

conflicts would unnecessarily be undermined if it were a matter of choice for third States to submit themselves to its rules or to claim a status of non-belligerent.[100]

It has been pointed out that the dichotomous distinction between party and neutral does not reflect the nuanced range of stances that third States can take vis-à-vis parties to an international armed conflict.[101] This failure, however, is inherent in the purpose of neutrality law. The purpose of neutrality law is not to give a descriptively accurate account of diverse patterns of participation but, rather, to set a standard against which we can qualify these factual patterns as either legal or illegal.

ii. Non-international armed conflicts

In contrast with international armed conflicts, there is no comparable dichotomy of party and third-party status in non-international armed conflicts since no specific third-party status is automatically triggered by the existence of a non-international armed conflict.

As seen above, the institution of neutrality in inter-State wars aimed to adapt the peacetime legal relationships with third States to the state of war between parties. There was no apparent conceptual need for such an adaptation with either party in internal conflicts. With the non-State side to the conflict, there usually would not have been peacetime international legal relations prior to the outbreak of the conflict. As regards the State party, an 'internal' conflict was, in principle, perceived as a domestic affair such that the respective State's sovereignty commanded foreign States not to interfere.[102]

The conceptual differences notwithstanding, in practice, 'internal' conflicts of a certain scale affected third States' trade and territorial interests in a way that resembled inter-State wars. They also gave rise to the parties' interests in controlling trade and making use of third States' territories. These pragmatic considerations not only drove the development of neutrality law but also fostered its extension through State practice beyond the realm of inter-State wars, namely through the institution of the recognition of belligerency. Conceptually, such recognition meant that the recognising State no longer viewed the conflict as a matter of one sovereign's internal law enforcement but, rather, as a contestation between equal collectives,[103] for which neutrality was the appropriate third-party regime. If certain conditions were fulfilled,[104] third States were free to apply neutrality law

[100] M Bothe, KJ Partsch, and W Solf, *New Rules for Victims of Armed Conflicts—Commentary on the Two 1977 Protocols Additional to the Geneva Conventions of 1949* (reprint edn, Nijhoff 2013) 550; Heintschel von Heinegg (n 40) 560.

[101] Chinkin (n 4) 301; M McDougal and F Feliciano, *Law and Minimum World Public Order* (Yale UP 1961) 412–413.

[102] See further nn 127–134.

[103] See Chapter 1.2.

[104] See Chapter 1, n 13.

between themselves and the parties[105] by recognising the non-State party's belligerency. In sum, the application of this third-party regime was limited to a strictly confined subset of conflicts, and it was optional and relative.

Yet, subject to these caveats, the option of triggering the application of neutrality law by recognising belligerency is still available to States under contemporary international law. Instances of recognition of belligerency have always been rare. From the perspective of third States, applying neutrality law was not necessarily beneficial. It subjected them to a broad set of duties with few, if any, rights to which they would not otherwise have been entitled.[106] Additionally, where the government had not recognised the belligerency of the insurgents, such recognition by a third State risked political tensions with the government.

While States' reluctance to grant recognition of belligerency is therefore understandable, claims that recognition of belligerency has fallen in desuetude and been extinguished in contemporary international law[107] appear to be overstated. As a general matter, it remains unsettled whether the mere absence of recourse to a rule of customary international law allows inferring that the rule is no longer supported by practice and *opinio juris* and thus ceases to exist or whether such an extinction presupposes practice and *opinio juris* establishing a contrary customary rule.[108] In any event, recognition of belligerency does, moreover, play a certain role in contemporary international practice. For example, international treaties have explicitly referred to it[109] and States have invoked it with respect to different conflicts in Latin America: the foreign ministers of the Andean Pact States, in a joint statement, recognised the belligerency of the Nicaraguan Sandinista National Liberation Front in 1979,[110] France and Mexico recognised El Salvadorean rebels in 1981,[111]

[105] In practice, recognition of belligerency on the part of the government opposing the insurgents may have made it difficult for third States not to follow suit by applying neutrality law (K Mačák, *Internationalized Armed Conflicts in International Law* (OUP 2018) 79).

[106] See below d.

[107] R Oglesby, *Internal War and the Search for Normative Order* (Nijhoff 1971) 100–114; T Franck and N Rodley, 'Legitimacy and Legal Rights of Revolutionary Movements with Special Reference to the Peoples' Revolutionary Government of South Viet Nam' (1970) 45 NYULR 679, 683–684.

[108] For the former view, see R Kolb, 'La Désuétude en droit international public' (2007) 111 RGDIP 577, 604–606; G Le Floch, 'La Désuétude en Droit International Public' (2007) 111 RGDIP 610, 627; M Villiger, *Customary International Law and Treaties: A Manual on the Theory and Practice of the Interrelation of Sources* (Kluwer 1997) 55; for the latter, see R Bernhardt, 'Customary International Law' in R Bernhardt (ed), *Encyclopedia of Public International Law*, vol 1 (North-Holland 1992) 901–902; I Scobbie, 'Gaza' in E Wilmshurst (ed), *International Law and the Classification of Conflicts* (OUP 2012) 303–304; generally M Glennon, 'How International Rules Die' (2005) 93 Geo LJ 939; J Kammerhofer, *Uncertainty in International Law: A Kelsenian Perspective* (Routledge 2011) 85–86.

[109] Protocol to the Convention on Duties and Rights of States in the Event of Civil Strife, art 2.

[110] Reproduced in A Gurmendi, 'The Last Recognition of Belligerency (and Some Thoughts on Why You May Not Have Heard of It)' (*OpinioJuris*, 10 December 2019) <http://opiniojuris.org/2019/12/10/the-last-recognition-of-belligerency-and-some-thoughts-on-why-you-may-not-have-heard-of-it/>; see also R Nieto Navia, '¿Hay o no hay conflicto armado en Colombia?' (2008) 1 ACDI 139, 147.

[111] 'Déclaration Franco-Mexicaine sur le Salvador' 28 August 1981 <https://sv.ambafrance.org/XXXV-Anniversaire-de-la-Declaration-franco-mexicaine-sur-Le-Salvador>. Although the declaration does not set out legal implications flowing from it, it has been understood as permitting, among other

and the Venezuelan National Assembly recognised the belligerency of the FARC and ELN rebels in Colombia in 2008.[112] It has also been suggested—though sometimes controversially—that recognition of belligerency was granted implicitly in numerous conflicts, including the Algerian rebellion against France,[113] the Biafran secession conflict in Nigeria,[114] the Namibian independence struggle,[115] the Gaza conflict in 2010,[116] as well as the conflicts in Libya,[117] Afghanistan,[118] and Yemen.[119] Finally, even armed groups, for example in the Philippines in the early 2000s, referred to the concept when reportedly claiming that their belligerency had been recognised.[120]

Recourse to recognition of belligerency could potentially also be useful in present and future non-international armed conflicts.[121] For third States, it may not only be a political tool to express support for the insurgents[122] but also to clarify their international legal relationships to parties,[123] including as regards potential claims for responsibility against the insurgent authorities.[124] From a normative perspective, Bridgeman has suggested that applying neutrality law to situations of non-international armed conflict more broadly would complement

things, the application of neutrality law—see C Fuentes, 'Salvador's Opposition' *NYT* (16 September 1981) A27.

[112] F Szesnat and A Bird, 'Colombia' in E Wilmshurst (ed), *International Law and the Classification of Conflicts* (OUP 2012) 218, 222–223.

[113] M Bedjaoui, *Law and the Algerian Revolution* (International Association of Democratic Lawyers 1961) 171–172.

[114] C Rousseau, 'Nigéria' (1968) 72 RGDIP 228, 231, 234 (reporting that, for example, Cameroun referred to its 'neutrality' in the conflict to justify the prohibition of certain products crossing its border with Biafra and that the UK did the same to justify continuing trading weapons to the Nigerian government).

[115] *Namibia* (n 52), sep op Ammoun [13].

[116] Scobbie (n 108) 302–305 (suggesting that Israel's blockade of Gaza implicitly recognised Hamas's belligerency); sceptically D Guilfoyle, 'The *Mavi Marmara* Incident and Blockade in Armed Conflict' (2011) 81 BYIL 171, 180, 191–192.

[117] SF Halabi, 'Traditions of Belligerent Recognition: The Libyan Intervention in Historical and Theoretical Context' 27 AULR 321, 372ff.

[118] J Paust, 'NIAC Nonsense, the Afghan War, and Combatant Immunity' (2016) 44 Ga JICL 555, 562–564.

[119] R McLaughlin, *Recognition of Belligerency and the Law of Armed Conflict* (OUP 2020) 237–240 (suggesting that either Pakistan's declaration of neutrality in 2015 with respect to the conflict or the establishment of a blockade by the Saudi Coalition could constitute a recognition of the Houthi rebels' belligerency); P Drew, 'Blockade? A Legal Assessment of the Maritime Interdiction of Yemen's Ports' (2019) 24 JCSL 35, 39–40 (accepting the former but rejecting the latter possibility).

[120] M Arguillas, 'The Non-Traditional Moro Elites and the Organization of Islamic Conference' (2001) 22 Phil PSJ 97, 110; Santos, 'Evolution of the Armed Conflict on the Communist Front' (Background Paper, Human Development Network Foundation 2005) <http://hdn.org.ph/wp-content/uploads/2005_PHDR/2005%20Evolution_Communist_Conflict.pdf> 10, 14; see also McLaughlin (n 119) 220.

[121] McLaughlin (n 119) 248ff; Y Lootsteen, 'The Concept of Belligerency in International Law' (2000) 166 MLR 109, 138.

[122] Gurmendi (n 110).

[123] Mačák (n 105) 81.

[124] A Cullen, *The Concept of Non-International Armed Conflict in International Humanitarian Law* (CUP 2010) 18.

the law of armed conflict that is applicable to such conflicts and may even serve protective purposes, notably regarding detention in third States and detention of neutral nationals.[125]

Nonetheless, the impartiality principle underlying the institution of neutrality conveys a legal parity between the parties—from the perspective of third States—that States are not ready to accept in a general way. This observation aligns with the ambiguities characterising the legal position of non-State parties to armed conflicts discussed in Chapter 1.[126] Neutrality thus remains an exceptional rather than general third-party status in non-international armed conflicts, confined to cases of recognition of belligerency, which are likely to remain rare.

Beyond cases of recognition of belligerency and thus neutrality law application, the principle of non-intervention may fulfil a similar role in non-international armed conflicts to some extent[127] by requiring third States to take a disinterested position in the conflict. The extent to which international law requires this detached posture vis-à-vis *both* parties to the conflict, akin to a position of neutrality in the inter-State context, is a subject of long-standing debate. The principle of non-intervention prohibits interference against the territorial State that is engaged in a non-international armed conflict. This would leave open the possibility of intervening in support of the territorial State.[128] However, as Lauterpacht had noted, the government side's ability to invite third State support may also be limited.[129] On one view, put forward notably by the IDI, '[t]hird States shall refrain from giving assistance to parties to a civil war'.[130]

Such a rule would conceive of the conflict less as a sovereign affair—for which the sovereign would be free to invite foreign assistance—and more through a war paradigm, with the ensuing legal relationship between parties and third parties. Indeed, although the IDI does not explicitly refer to notions of neutrality, the parallel to neutrality law in the IDI's approach is striking, both in the rationale and the content of the proposed rule. The IDI justifies its approach by the same combination of third States' pragmatic self-interest[131] and conflict

[125] T Bridgeman, 'The Law of Neutrality and the Conflict with Al Qaeda' (2010) 85 NYULR 1186. Such protection benefits should not be overstated, however, as in many cases human rights law may provide such safeguards.

[126] See eg Chapter 1.3.a.iii, 4.a.i.(2).

[127] See also L Ferro and N Verlinden, 'Neutrality During Armed Conflicts: A Coherent Approach to Third-State Support for Warring Parties' (2018) 17 CJIL 15, 42.

[128] M Jamnejad and M Wood, 'The Principle of Non-intervention' (2009) 22 LJIL 345, 378. This would also mean that the principle of non-intervention has no bearing on the legal relationship between parties and third parties in non-international armed conflicts in which one or several non-State armed groups confront each other. The principle would also not apply to the relationship of third parties to State parties involved in conflicts with armed groups extraterritorially.

[129] H Lauterpacht, *Recognition in International Law* (CUP 1947) 233 (referring to 'the right of the nation to decide for itself… the nature and the form of its government').

[130] IDI, 'The Principle of Non-Intervention in Civil Wars—Resolution' (14 August 1975) art 2(1). See also UK, 'Foreign Policy Document No 148' (1986) 57 BYIL 614, 616.

[131] IDI, Non-Intervention Resolution Preamble.

prevention[132] that has informed the development of the law of neutrality. Regarding the content of the rule, third States would bear duties of non-assistance as well as prevention, which are akin to neutrality duties.[133] It is then perhaps no coincidence that the IDI limited the rule—like the institution of recognition of belligerency—to conflicts qualifying as 'civil wars'. According to the IDI, 'civil wars' are characterised by the insurgent parties' aim to establish governmental control over the State (or a part thereof).[134] It is beyond the scope of the present book to assess to what extent positive international law reflects the rule that prevents States from inviting foreign assistance in civil wars.[135] Significantly for this chapter, it may simply be noted that, if that rule were to be accepted, it would specifically and automatically attach legal consequences to party status regarding the relationship to third parties in certain non-international armed conflicts.

Summing up, both the doctrine of recognition of belligerency and the principle of non-intervention provide only for a limited regulation of third-party status in non-international armed conflicts, while the alleged prohibition on third States to assist parties to civil wars would conceive of third-party status in a neutrality-like manner. This state of affairs is supplemented, to an extent, by obligations of protection or non-assistance that are imposed on third States, as section 3 of this chapter will show. Before moving to this layer of third-party regulation, it is necessary to consider why identifying that an entity qualifies as a party matters under neutrality law.

d. Implications of party status under neutrality law

Where neutrality law continues to apply, establishing the party status of an entity will determine the obligations and rights in the relationship of this entity to third parties. To assess the relevance of establishing party status from the perspective of neutrality law, this subsection analyses to what extent these obligations and rights

132 ibid; Q Wright, 'The American Civil War' in R Falk (ed), *The International Law of Civil War* (Johns Hopkins Press 1971) 106–107 (noting that in cases of 'civil strife of sufficient magnitude to constitute insurgency, but not recognized as belligerency … practice and juristic opinion, with a few exceptions, have favored impartiality and nonintervention in the interest of localization of hostilities, nonescalation and national self-determination' (footnotes omitted)).

133 IDI, Non-Intervention Resolution art 3(b).

134 ibid art 1.

135 For discussion see eg C Redaelli, *Intervention in Civil Wars: Effectiveness, Legitimacy, and Human Rights* (Hart 2020) 92–96; E de Wet, *Military Assistance on Request and the Use of Force* (OUP 2020) 76–83; T Ruys, 'Of Arms, Funding and "Non-lethal Assistance"—Issues Surrounding Third-State Intervention in the Syrian Civil War' (2014) 13 CJIL 13, 40–45; Z Vermeer, 'Intervention by Invitation and the Alleged Prohibition of Military Assistance to Governments in Civil Wars' (DPhil, University of Oxford 2018); C Nowak, *Das Interventionsverbot im Bürgerkrieg: Darstellung eines Wandels durch die Bürgerkriege in Libyen, Syrien, Irak, Jemen und Ukraine seit 2011* (Peter Lang 2018) 165–176).

differ from those that would otherwise have existed in the relationship between the respective States.

i. Neutral States' obligations

Arguably, the most important feature of neutrality for third parties is that a set of obligations is automatically triggered with respect to any party to the conflict. These obligations are essentially obligations to abstain from supporting the parties and to prevent the parties from using neutral territory.[136] From this perspective, both the existence of an (international) armed conflict and, specifically, the identification of parties thereto are crucial.

Establishing an entity's party or neutral status also plainly matters because the obligations of parties and neutrals, as well as their legal positions more generally, differ markedly. If a previously neutral State becomes a party to the conflict, it is freed from this set of obligations. But as a party, the State is then automatically subjected to a new set of obligations. From this perspective, the transition from neutral to party status changes the content of a State's restrictions under international law from requirements to stay detached from the conflict to obligations regulating how one is to carry out the conflict and, particularly, which protections are to be accorded.

This distinction between neutrals as detached from the conflict and parties as addressees of protective obligations in relation to the conflict is tempered in several respects.

First, neutral States, too, have obligations regarding protected persons in armed conflict, albeit they are more limited than the obligations of parties to the conflict. In particular, they 'shall apply by analogy' GCs I and II as well as Part II of API to wounded, sick and shipwrecked persons, and to members of the medical and religious personnel of a party, 'received or interned in their territory, as well as to dead persons found on their territory'.[137] This is to ensure that protected persons 'receive that protection wherever they may be'.[138]

The analogous application, however, does not render the distinction between neutrals and parties meaningless. This application is limited in several respects, thereby accounting for the structurally different position of neutrals. In particular, it covers only certain groups of protected persons. It notably excludes civilians which are nationals of the parties and of other neutral States who do not require treatment under IHL by neutral States. The analogous application is also limited to the territory of the neutral itself. Finally, owing to the different position of parties

[136] nn 12–16.
[137] GCI, arts 4–5; API, art 19.
[138] *GCI Commentary* [911].

and neutrals, the analogous application by a neutral does not mean that all provisions apply identically.[139]

Secondly, the image of third parties as neutrals is complemented by obligations that are imposed on all States (whether third party or party) not to be complicit in violations of international law and to respect and ensure respect for IHL. Section 3 of this chapter examines how these obligations shape the relationship between third parties and parties and the relevance of the distinction between these categories.

ii. Neutral States' rights and protection

Unlike neutral duties, the so-called neutral rights or protection that parties would need to respect at first sight do not seem to substantially differ from a State's legal position in times of peace.[140] In particular, a State's territorial integrity is protected by virtue of its sovereignty regardless of its neutral status. If anything, the 'inviolability' of neutral territory[141] appears relatively limited. This is because the neutral State's failure to prevent its territory from being used by parties traditionally entitled the aggrieved party to self-help by entering neutral territory to terminate the violation.[142] Many military and expert manuals continue to refer to this idea.[143] Under contemporary international law, however, forcible self-help measures would need to be additionally justified under the *jus ad bellum* (as self-defence).[144] Non-forcible self-help by what are otherwise unlawful measures could be seen as a particular form of a countermeasure. As a distinctive institution of international law, such non-forcible self-help could constitute a 'special rule' governing the implementation of responsibility in the sense of Article 55 ARSIWA.

Neutrals, in turn, have been considered to be permitted to resist, even by force, attempts by belligerents to violate their neutrality.[145] The rule is still found in military manuals[146] and considered to reflect customary international law.[147] In the

[139] For example, Sandoz argues that unlike parties (under GCI, art 28), neutral States may not retain medical and religious personnel against their will (Sandoz (n 98) 97).

[140] See already A Heffter, *Das Europäische Völkerrecht der Gegenwart auf den bisherigen Grundlagen* (8th edn, F Geffcken, HW Müller 1888) 331–332; Gioia (n 94) 57, 78.

[141] HCV, art 1; HCXIII, arts 1, 13.

[142] E de Vattel, *Le Droit des gens, ou, Principes le la loi naturelle, appliqués à la conduite aux affaires des nations et des souverains*, vol III (C Fenwick tr, Carnegie Institution 1916) 277; Castrén (n 9) 442; R Tucker, *The Law of War and Neutrality at Sea* (Government Printing Office 1957) 262; M Greenspan, *The Modern Law of Land Warfare* (University of California Press 1959) 538.

[143] *Danish Manual* 62; UK Ministry of Defence, *The Manual of the Law of Armed Conflict* (OUP 2004) [13.9E]; *Canadian Manual* [811(2)]; *Australian Air Manual* [12.7]; *US Manual* [15.4.2]; *German Navy Handbook* [232]; *US Commander's Handbook* 7-1; *Helsinki Principles* [2.1]; *San Remo Manual* [22]; *Tallinn Manual 2.0* r 153.

[144] *UK Manual* [1.43(a)]; *US Manual* [15.4.2]; for discussion, see Upcher (n 12) 93–98. On the relationship of permissions under the law of neutrality and the *jus ad bellum*, see below iii.

[145] HCV, art 10; HCXIII, art 26; Hague Air Rules, art 48.

[146] See eg *Peruvian Manual* 302 [106(j)], 304 [112(1)(c)]; *German Manual* 159 [1202]; *US Manual* 975 [15.4.3)].

[147] *HPCR Manual* 390.

contemporary international legal order, the rule cannot, however, provide neutrals with wider latitude to use force than what the right to self-defence under the *jus ad bellum* otherwise would (to the extent that such self-help falls within the scope of the prohibition of the use of force).

Yet, in some instances, the protection of neutrals under the law of neutrality may prove relevant. On the one hand, by detailing which acts of parties amount to violations of neutral territory, neutrality law may provide more specific regulation than the general international law rule or principle that every State's territorial integrity is protected as a core aspect of its sovereignty. On the other hand, where there is specific regulation of the extent of protection of a State's territory outside neutrality law, such as for territorial waters under the law of the sea, neutrality law may prove more protective of neutral territory. For example, a neutral State has more discretion than coastal States under the UNCLOS in restricting as well as prohibiting passage by warships of the parties through neutral waters, so long as it does not discriminate between the parties.[148] By contrast, the ITLOS held that, under the law of the sea, even warships in principle enjoy the right of innocent passage,[149] and Article 25 UNCLOS imposes more stringent conditions for restrictions of passage through the territorial sea by the coastal State than does the law of neutrality.[150] Thus, while it is true that international law protects a State's territory regardless of its neutrality, it may not necessarily do so in the same way.

Future practice will need to show whether the application of neutrality to armed conflicts that are conducted in cyberspace—accepted in principle, for example, by recent position papers of some States and by the *Tallinn Manual*[151]—ascribes particular relevance to the protection of neutrals. Neutrality law could be particularly meaningful for cyber operations that are not covered by the prohibition of the use of force and the principle of non-intervention. Debates persist on whether the sovereignty of the target State constitutes a specific rule that cyber operations can violate.[152] Relying on the protection of neutral cyberinfrastructure[153] that flows from neutral status (rather than from sovereignty) would avoid the objections raised against this conception of sovereignty 'as a rule'. The source of protective rules could, therefore, matter, leaving aside whether their content might also differ.

148 *San Remo Manual* 4 [19]; *UK Manual* [13.9B]; *German Navy Handbook* [245].

149 *Detention of Three Ukrainian Naval Vessels (Ukraine v Russia)* (Provisional Measures, Order of 25 May 2019) ITLOS Reports 2018–2019, 283 [68]; for a general discussion of the issue, see Y Tanaka, *The International Law of the Sea* (3rd edn, CUP 2019) 108–111.

150 J Farrant, 'Modern Maritime Neutrality Law' (2014) 90 ILS 198, 210–214; V Lowe, 'The Impact of the Law of the Sea on Naval Warfare' (1987) 14 SJILC 657, 669.

151 n 76.

152 For recent discussions with extensive references to the opposing views taken by States and in scholarship, see F Delerue, *Cyber Operations and International Law* (CUP 2020) 200–232; K Heller, 'In Defense of Pure Sovereignty in Cyberspace' (2021) 97 ILS 1432, 1444–1454.

153 *Tallinn Manual 2.0* 555 (r 150).

Finally, neutral rights or protection would make a difference in cases where neutrality law is applied to non-international armed conflicts.[154] In such cases, non-State parties are required to respect neutral rights and protection under international law, including the inviolability of neutral territory (while, at least on orthodox accounts, other provisions protecting States' territory do not address non-State actors).

iii. Belligerent rights

From the perspective of the parties, their status was traditionally seen as accompanied with certain rights against neutral States under neutrality law. In particular, belligerents were considered entitled to certain measures of control vis-à-vis neutral trade, such as visits and searches for and seizures of contraband and establishing blockades or maritime exclusion zones. These belligerent rights against neutrals were regarded as entailing corresponding duties of third parties to acquiesce in their exercise,[155] unlike so-called 'belligerent rights' in the relationship between parties.[156] Current international law is ambivalent about these prerogatives.

On the one hand, Clapham points out that it is inconsistent for international law to 'outlaw the recourse to war and then reward those who violate that rule with so-called "Belligerent Rights" over neutrals'.[157] He accordingly calls for a 'radical overhaul' of the rules on economic warfare at sea to give effect to the notion that no 'rights for any belligerents should flow merely from the fact of being in a State of War or in an international armed conflict'.[158]

On the other hand, State practice affirms the continued existence of the traditional belligerent rights against neutrals, as affirmed by military manuals and practice in specific conflicts.[159] Technological advances could further extend the practical relevance of such rights beyond naval warfare. In cyberspace, for example, the increasing reliance on globally distributed and interconnected

[154] See above c.ii.

[155] H Lauterpacht, *Oppenheim's International Law*, vol II (7th edn, Longmans 1952) 673. These belligerent rights would, therefore, qualify as actual 'rights' in the Hohfeldian analytical scheme (see W Hohfeld, 'Some Fundamental Legal Conceptions as Applied in Judicial Reasoning' (1913–14) 23 Yale LJ 16, 32). On the requirement for a right of one person to correspond to a duty of another person towards the former, see also H Kelsen, *Pure Theory of Law* (M Knight tr, University of California Press 1967) 126–129.

[156] H Meyrowitz, *Le Principe de l'égalité des belligérants devant le droit de la guerre* (Pedone 1970) 112; Greenwood (n 92) 228. In the Hohfeldian scheme, these so-called rights would, therefore, rather qualify as 'privileges' (Hohfeld (n 32)). On these, see Chapter 1.3.b.

[157] Clapham (n 5) 329.

[158] ibid 329, 331; A Clapham, 'Booty, Bounty, Blockade, and Prize: Time to Reevaluate the Law' (2021) 97 ILS 1200.

[159] For thorough reviews, see Farrant (n 150) 220ff; Upcher (n 12) 178–211; Neff (n 10) 200–207; E Papastavridis, *The Interception of Vessels on the High Seas: Contemporary Challenges to the Legal Order of the Oceans* (Hart 2013) 84–106; P Drew, *The Law of Maritime Blockade: Past, Present, and Future* (OUP 2017) 46–61; S Sivakumaran, 'Exclusion Zones in the Law of Armed Conflict at Sea: Evolution in Law and Practice' (2016) 92 ILS 153, 176–202.

cyberinfrastructure offers particular room and incentives for belligerent interference with neutral infrastructure.[160]

An attempt to reconcile the practice in this area with the prohibition of the use of force might take the following form. To the extent that the exercise of belligerent rights would amount to a use or threat of force, it would need to comply with the requirements of self-defence or with the terms of a Security Council resolution providing its mandate. State practice, with a few notable exceptions,[161] does not clarify the relationship of belligerent rights with the *jus ad bellum*.[162] Yet this position is a necessary corollary to the continued operation of the *jus ad bellum* in armed conflict.[163] As a result, somewhat ironically, the requirements under the law of neutrality might even further restrict the exercise of measures taken as belligerent rights. The interplay could be such that self-defence would set the outer parameters—with the broad and, to some extent, flexible requirements of an armed attack, necessity, and proportionality—within which the traditional belligerent rights could still operate.[164] Moreover, this framework would also retain relevance regarding exercises of such rights that would not amount to a use or threat of force.

In addition to the *jus ad bellum*, belligerent rights must be considered in light of the law of the sea. The development of the law of the sea has had a considerable impact on the law of naval warfare and maritime neutrality, and various aspects of the complex interplay between the two regimes have raised controversies.[165] It seems, however, that the law of the sea does not generally stand in the way of the exercise of belligerent rights. Notably, the exercise of high seas freedoms of third States, including the freedom of navigation, is subject to 'the conditions laid down ... by other rules of international law'[166] and can thus accommodate the exercise of belligerent rights.[167] Accordingly, from the perspective of the law of the sea, 'belligerent

[160] *Tallinn Manual 2.0* 554; W Heintschel von Heinegg, 'Territorial Sovereignty and Neutrality in Cyberspace' (2013) 89 ILS 123, 155.

[161] *UK Manual* [13.3].

[162] n 159.

[163] See generally Chapter 1, n 125.

[164] S Helmersen, 'The Use of Force against Neutral Ships Outside Territorial Waters' (2022) 35 LJIL 315, 325–329; Upcher (n 12) 173–175; C Greenwood, 'The Applicability of International Humanitarian Law and the Law of Neutrality to the Kosovo Campaign' (2002) 78 ILS 35, 56–57 (considering the oil embargo imposed by NATO States on the Federal Republic of Yugoslavia as a permissible blockade under the *jus in bello*, which, however, had to be cumulatively assessed under the *jus ad bellum*); similarly Antonopoulos (n 29) 157–168 (based on a review of State practice).

[165] See generally N Klein, *Maritime Security and the Law of the Sea* (OUP 2011) 259ff; R Wolfrum, 'Military Activities on the High Seas: What Are the Impacts of the U.N. Convention on the Law of the Sea' (1998) 71 ILS 501; W Heintschel von Heinegg, 'The United Nations Convention on the Law of the Sea and Maritime Security Operations' (2005) 48 GYIL 151; V Lowe, 'The Laws of War at Sea and the 1958 and 1982 Conventions' (1988) 12 MP 286.

[166] UNCLOS, art 87(1).

[167] See eg Papastavridis (n 159) 47 ('Belligerent measures may be exercised on the high seas or in the territorial seas of belligerents, but not in areas under the sovereignty of neutral states'); W Heintschel von Heinegg, 'Blockades and Interdictions' in M Weller (ed), *The Oxford Handbook of the Use of Force in International Law* (OUP 2015) 929 (concluding that 'the international law of the sea does not restrict the exercise of belligerent rights at sea').

rights' would constitute permissions of acts that may otherwise have been contrary to this body of law.

iv. Implications for individuals

Under the law of neutrality, individual nationals of neutral States are relatively less affected by the neutrality duties of their State of nationality. Unlike some duties of parties,[168] neutral duties do not translate into individual duties to, for example, abstain from certain commercial activities regarding or affecting parties. Nor has neutrality law traditionally imposed obligations on the neutral State to prevent such activities by individuals.[169]

Restrictions on individual freedom of action do, however, flow from the exercise of belligerent rights, which typically affect neutral vessels. In particular, neutral vessels are liable to seizure or attack by an aggrieved party if they engage in 'unneutral service' that favours the opposed party.[170] Similar to direct participation of individual civilians in hostilities,[171] the relationship of neutral vessels to the parties may thus affect their legal position.

In sum, identifying parties to an armed conflict continues to bear significant legal consequences under the law of neutrality for the legal positions of the respective State and third States as well as for individuals. The interplay with other rules of international law, particularly the *jus ad bellum* and the law of the sea, adds nuances to these implications but does not make them redundant. To complete the picture of the implications of establishing party status vis-à-vis third parties, the next section moves beyond the law of neutrality to consider other rules of international law that are addressed to third parties with respect to armed conflicts.

3. Parties and third parties as addressees of international law in armed conflict

In the contemporary international legal order, the law of neutrality is complemented by further layers of provisions regulating the position of third States with respect to an armed conflict. As this section shows, these provisions importantly refine the posture of neutrals as detached from or disinterested in the conflict and commit third parties more strongly to the protective purposes of international law applicable in armed conflict. In that sense, such provisions may make these protective aims community interests.

168 Chapter 1.4.b.ii.(2).

169 HCV, arts 6–7; HCXIII, art 7. For a discussion of how this traditional distinction between the State and its citizen erodes in the international practice concerning arms trade, see Upcher (n 12) 79–89.

170 See eg *San Remo Manual* [67(b)]–[(f)]; Tucker (n 142) 318ff; Farrant (n 150) 279ff.

171 Chapter 1, nn 186–187.

Different sets of obligations imposed on third parties may be distinguished. Some additional sets of obligations are imposed on third parties exclusively. For example, neutral States are, to some extent, bound by protective IHL obligations by analogy.[172] Another example of provisions that are specifically addressed to third States is the quite detailed set of rules regulating the institution of Protecting Powers that third States can assume with respect to an international armed conflict,[173] a possibility that has, however, not been resorted to since the Falkland/Malvinas conflict in 1982.[174]

Other relevant sets of obligations are imposed on all States. Some obligations that may have implications in armed conflicts are not triggered by the armed conflict itself. For example, certain IHL provisions apply in peacetime as well. Human rights obligations of States continue to apply in armed conflict, subject to lawful derogation, for parties as well as for third parties.[175] Strictly speaking, such obligations are addressed to States neither as third parties nor as parties to the conflict, although they (continue to) apply in armed conflict.[176] These obligations are therefore not of further concern here, beyond bearing their existence in mind to complete the international law framework that is applicable in armed conflict.

The focus here—in section a.—is instead on those provisions that apply specifically in situations of armed conflict and impose obligations not only on parties but also on third parties. Despite the limited overlap of the duties created by these provisions for parties and third parties, such provisions do not make the distinction between parties and third parties redundant. Indeed, even in areas where IHL imposes protective obligations on third parties, the obligations of parties may still go further, qualitatively and quantitatively.

Particularly relevant for present purposes are those obligations that concern third-parties' legal position vis-à-vis parties to a conflict. In this respect, sections b. and c. will show that neutral duties of abstention from participating in the conflict are supplemented by duties to refrain from participating in violations of obligations by the parties.

a. Obligations addressed both to parties and to third parties

Chapter 1 showed that central sets of obligations that are applicable in armed conflicts under treaty and customary IHL are addressed to parties, either explicitly

[172] nn 137–139.

[173] GCI-IV, arts 8/8/8/9, 10/10/10/11; API, art 5.

[174] Switzerland and Brazil acted as diplomatic Protecting Powers (R Kolb, 'Protecting Powers' in A Clapham, P Gaeta, and M Sassòli (eds), *The 1949 Geneva Conventions: A Commentary* (OUP 2015) 556–557).

[175] Chapter 1, n 131.

[176] As noted above, some of these obligations may apply differently to parties—see Chapter 1.3.b.

or implicitly.[177] Nevertheless, IHL also imposes certain sets of obligations on all States. This is the case not only of obligations that apply in times of peace.[178] Certain obligations arising specifically with respect to an armed conflict are also addressed to third parties and parties alike.

By way of an illustration, in the field of humanitarian relief, many—though not all—obligations are imposed both on parties and third parties, at least in international armed conflicts. The obligation to protect relief consignments and facilitate their rapid distribution under Article 70(4) API exclusively addresses parties to the conflict. By contrast, as Article 70(2) and (5) API makes clear, '[t]he Parties to the conflict and each High Contracting Party shall allow and facilitate' the passage of relief and facilitate international cooperation in that regard. Moreover, to carry out relief operations, the consent both of parties and of certain third States is required. The consent requirement, in turn, comes with an obligation not to withhold consent arbitrarily.[179] This obligation would arguably also apply to those third parties whose consent is required.[180]

Even obligations that are imposed both on parties and on third States, however, do not necessarily apply in the same way to the two categories of addressees. To illustrate, one way to withhold consent 'arbitrarily' is where its withholding violates other obligations of the respective State under international law.[181] Since parties have a wider range of IHL obligations as compared to third States, this ground of arbitrariness has a wider reach for parties regarding IHL. At the same time, as a factual matter, Akande and Gillard have suggested that third States 'are likely to have fewer security concerns' and would probably 'be entitled to withhold consent to humanitarian relief operations in fewer situations than parties to an armed conflict'.[182]

The obligations of third parties concerning humanitarian relief are sometimes reiterated by the Security Council. In this field, as well as beyond, the Council can also impose additional obligations on third States with respect to armed conflicts,[183] either by addressing them specifically or by referring to all Member States. In doing so, however, the Council does not fail to emphasise the primary role of

177 Chapter 1.3.a.i.

178 See Chapter 1, text accompanied by nn 65–69.

179 D Akande and E-C Gillard, 'Arbitrary Withholding of Consent to Humanitarian Relief Operations in Armed Conflict' (2016) 92 ILS 483.

180 The reference in API, art 70(1) to the 'agreement' of 'the Parties concerned' could be understood as also addressing third States in whose territory relief operations are initiated or through which the operations transit; for discussion, see D Akande and E-C Gillard, 'Oxford Guidance on the Law Relating to Humanitarian Relief Operations in Situations of Armed Conflict' (UN OCHA 2016) 39–41. For occupied territory, see GCIV, art 59(3).

181 Akande and Gillard (n 179) 494.

182 Akande and Gillard (n 180) 41.

183 UN Charter, art 25; see Chapter 1, nn 79–80.

parties as regards, for example, the protection of civilians in an armed conflict,[184] to which third States' obligations would appear primarily complementary in nature. Moreover, it seems that the Council addresses the parties to the conflict more frequently and more explicitly in mandatory language than third parties.[185]

The relatively wide-ranging obligations imposed on third parties in the area of humanitarian relief may be seen as a reflection of the widely shared 'community interest' at stake here, that is, access to adequate relief for civilians in need. The dynamic evolution of practice shows that third parties frequently take up a proactive role in this field.[186] It should, however, be noted that this concerns a clearly confined type of activity, which is tightly conditioned on strict impartiality and a humanitarian purpose and conducted without adverse distinction.

More generally, the humanitarian relief obligations of third parties do not question that parties bear the foremost responsibility to provide for the needs of the civilian population in the territory under their control.[187] There are also specific obligations concerning relief operations that are exclusively addressed to the parties, including the obligation to 'protect relief consignments and facilitate their rapid distribution'.[188] Moreover, in non-international armed conflicts, obligations of third States regarding humanitarian relief are considerably less clearly established. Treaty provisions in situations of non-international armed conflicts do not impose obligations on third States to allow and facilitate humanitarian assistance, and the customary rule as formulated by the ICRC's customary IHL study only addresses parties to the conflict.[189]

In sum, therefore, even in areas where third parties are addressees of specific obligations, the distinction between parties and third parties continues to matter for ascertaining the scope of a State's obligations with respect to an armed conflict. Beyond specific areas of regulation of armed conflict, certain general obligations address parties as well as third parties. In particular, rules on complicity and the general obligation to respect and ensure respect for IHL raise questions about their implications for the relationship between parties and third parties.

[184] See eg UNSC Res 2475 (20 June 2019) UN Doc S/RES/2475, Preamble ('Reaffirming that parties to armed conflict bear the primary responsibility to take all feasible steps to protect civilians'). On the Council's practice of imposing obligations on parties to armed conflict, see Chapter 1.3.b.(2).

[185] See Chapter 1.3.a.ii.; for an illustrative sample, see also the review in N Weizmann, 'Ensuring Respect for IHL as It Relates to Humanitarian Activities' in E Massingham and A McConnachie (eds), *Ensuring Respect for International Humanitarian Law* (Routledge 2020) 204–213.

[186] Weizmann (n 185) 202ff.

[187] After all, these obligations of third States are activated only when a party fails to adequately provide the civilian population in the territory under its control with the necessary supplies, API, art 70(1) (specifically for Occupying Powers, see GCIV, art 55; API, art 69).

[188] API, art 70(4).

[189] *CIHL* r 55. With great caution, the ICRC has suggested that '[i]t could be argued, at least tentatively, that this may be considered to be compulsory on the basis of the due diligence component enshrined in common Article 1' (*GCIII Commentary* [875]); see also Akande and Gillard (n 180) 41–42, 44; Weizmann (n 185) 202.

b. Complicity and prohibitions of assistance to parties' international law violations

The development of rules regulating complicity of third States has been considered as a central reflection of structural shifts towards safeguarding community interests in international law.[190] These rules bear important implications for the relationship between parties and third parties to an armed conflict. Under the general law of international responsibility, States and international organisations incur responsibility for complicity if they aid and assist in the commission of internationally wrongful acts, including those committed by parties in an armed conflict.[191] Additionally, if parties seriously breach peremptory norms of international law, other States and international organisations must not 'recognize as lawful a situation created by [such breach], nor render aid or assistance in maintaining that situation'.[192]

The duties flowing from complicity rules, at first sight, resemble neutrality duties not to assist parties to the conflict. Unlike neutrality law, however, complicity provisions also apply to parties themselves. They also crucially differ from neutrality in that neutrality duties not to assist parties flow from the mere status as a neutral, irrespective of the lawfulness of the parties' conduct. By contrast, complicity rules prohibit assistance to internationally wrongful acts and—unlike neutrality obligations—entail (derivative) responsibility for such wrongs.[193] The rationale is not to keep third parties detached from parties to a conflict altogether but, rather, from those violating international law. This connection has been considered as a crucial step towards the 'moral sophistication of international law'[194] and an 'international rule of law'.[195]

A 'network' of specific complicity rules complements the general rules.[196] Some of these may be broadly relevant to the relationship between parties and third parties as they relate to violations of primary rules that parties may violate in an armed conflict. In the realm of the prohibition of the use of force and collective security,[197] Article 3(f) of the UN General Assembly's Definition of Aggression qualifies as aggression placing one's territory 'at the disposal of another State ... for perpetrating an act of aggression against a third State'.[198] Article 2(5) UN Charter

190 Simma (n 3) 317; V Lanovoy, *Complicity and its Limits in the Law of International Responsibility* (Hart 2016) 32.

191 ARSIWA, art 16; ARIO, art 14.

192 ARSIWA, art 41(2); ARIO, art 42(2). For a thorough assessment of the relationship between these two duties as well as their relationship to the general complicity rules, see H Aust, *Complicity and the Law of State Responsibility* (CUP 2011) 325–352.

193 M Jackson, *Complicity in International Law* (OUP 2015) 125; Lanovoy (n 190) 32.

194 V Lowe, 'Responsibility for the Conduct of Other States' (2002) 101 JILD 1, 12.

195 Aust (n 192) 424.

196 ibid 376ff.

197 See generally B Nußberger, *Interstate Assistance to the Use of Force* (Nomos 2023); M Schmitt and WC Biggerstaff, 'Aid and Assistance as a "Use of Force" under the *Jus ad Bellum*' (2023) 100 ILS 186.

198 UNGA Res 3314 (XXIX) (14 December 1974) (Definition of Aggression), art 3(f).

requires Member States to 'refrain from giving assistance to any state against which the United Nations is taking preventive or enforcement action'. Specific State complicity rules also exist for genocide.[199] Prohibitions not to assist in specific international law violations can, for example, be found in the context of arms trade[200] and arms control.[201] In human rights law, too, States are 'frequently held responsible for human rights violations they have not themselves committed'.[202] These rules, however, need not be further analysed here as they do not relate to obligations addressed to the parties to an armed conflict as such.[203]

This stands on a different footing from the duty to respect and ensure respect for IHL, which, as the next section shows, also comprises a duty not to contribute to violations of IHL by others. Some features of the general complicity rules under the law of international responsibility are thus further explored in contradistinction to this duty below.[204]

c. The duty to respect and ensure respect for IHL

The obligation to respect and ensure respect under Article 1 common to GCI-IV as well as API and III,[205] is applicable to all 'High Contracting Parties'. As a matter of customary international law, the obligation applies to all States.[206] Unlike neutrality law, the obligation applies both to States parties to an armed conflict and third parties. Although it is not an obligation specifically flowing from third-party status, it is nevertheless of particular importance to third parties. This is because third parties lack the more specific obligations that parties have and because the obligation may assume particular importance for third parties in respect of IHL violations by parties.

i. Scope of application

As another crucial difference from neutrality law, the obligation to respect and ensure respect arguably applies in both international and non-international armed conflicts,[207] although its applicability to the latter remains

[199] Genocide Convention, art III(e); see *Application of the Convention on the Prevention and Punishment of the Crime of Genocide (Bosnia and Herzegovina v Serbia and Montenegro)* (Merits) [2007] ICJ Rep 43 [167].

[200] ATT, arts 6(3), 7(3).

[201] CWC, art 1(1)(d); Ottawa Convention, art 1(1)(c); Cluster Munitions Convention, art 1(1)(c).

[202] Aust (n 192) 415.

[203] Note, however, that ATT, arts 6(3), 7(1)(b)(I) refer to, inter alia, authorising the transfer of arms used to commit 'grave breaches' or 'serious violations' of IHL. Accordingly, the receiving entity's status as a party to an armed conflict may be indirectly relevant to these ATT provisions.

[204] See below 3.c.(b)(i).

[205] See also Convention on the Rights of the Child, art 38(1).

[206] *CIHL* r 144.

[207] *Nicaragua* (n 34) [220]; *CIHL* 509.

controversial.[208] Even if it is accepted, however, not all entities that may become *parties* to non-international armed conflicts would also be addressed as *third parties* by an obligation to respect and ensure respect.

Where non-State armed groups or international organisations become *parties* to armed conflicts, they are bound by the duty to respect and ensure respect as a matter of customary international law.[209] As *third parties*, however, non-State armed groups are not addressed by the obligation to respect and ensure respect.[210] This confirms the wider observation that non-State armed groups do not have an international legal status as third parties with respect to an armed conflict. The same would be true of international organisations on an understanding that strictly limits the customary duty of ensuring respect to non-party *States*.[211] By contrast, the updated ICRC Commentaries suggest that international organisations may also bear a customary international law obligation to respect and ensure respect for IHL as *third parties*, particularly where they mandate or coordinate multinational military operations without, however, becoming a party themselves.[212]

Having set out when and to whom the obligation to respect and to ensure respect is applicable, the remainder of this section focuses on its content.

ii. Content

For the purposes of this book, clarifying the content of the obligation is essential to demonstrate, first, that it is not so far-reaching as to make the distinction between parties and third parties meaningless from the point of view of the obligations that the respective entities bear. Secondly, it is also essential to clarify to what extent the obligation to ensure respect for IHL by others entails specific implications for third parties regarding violations of obligations by parties. An 'internal' and an 'external' dimension of the obligation to ensure respect can be distinguished analytically.

208 *Daniel Turp v Canada* (Minister of Foreign Affairs) [2017] FC 84 [70] (confirming the Canadian government's position against the application of Common Article 1 to non-international armed conflicts (ibid [21]); see already *Sinnappu v Canada (Minister of Citizenship and Immigration)* [1997] 2 FCR 791, 33; see alsoM Schmitt and S Watts, 'Common Article 1 and the Duty to "Ensure Respect"' (2020) 96 ILS 674, 700–702; sceptically, see also A Zimmermann, 'Humanitarian Assistance and the Security Council' (2017) 50 Isr LR 3, 20.

209 *CIHL* r 139.

210 ibid r 144 (emphasis added).

211 R Geiß, 'The Obligation to Respect and to Ensure Respect for the Conventions' in A Clapham, P Gaeta, and M Sassòli (eds), *The 1949 Geneva Conventions: A Commentary* (OUP 2015) 116–117. Implicitly, this seems to have been the understanding of the UN Under-Secretary-General for Legal Affairs when she considered that duties to ensure respect by partner forces would arise where the UN becomes a party to an armed conflict by supporting those partner forces (Statement at the ILC by the Under-Secretary-General for Legal Affairs and Legal Counsel (23 May 2013) <http://legal.un.org/ola/media/info_from_lc/ILC%20Legal%20Counsel%20statementrev3may20.pdf> 20).

212 *GCIII Commentary* [175]; see also D Shraga, 'The United Nations as an Actor Bound by International Humanitarian Law' (1998) 5 International Peacekeeping 64, 71–72; R Kolb, G Porretto, and S Vité, *L'Application du droit international humanitaire et des droits de l'homme aux organisations internationales: Forces de paix et administrations civiles transitoires* (Bruylant 2005) 154; *Wall* (n 32) [160] (vaguely hinting at this possibility).

(1) *Internal dimension*

Under the 'internal' limb, States must prevent and terminate conduct that is inconsistent with IHL by their entire population, regardless of whether the respective individual acts would be attributable to the State and regardless of whether the acting individuals violate their own obligations under IHL.[213] In this respect, there is a crucial difference to neutrality law, which, as noted, does not impose such positive obligations on neutral States regarding private individuals but merely regarding certain activities of parties on neutral territory.[214]

(2) *External dimension*

Beyond the internal dimension, the obligation to respect and ensure respect has arguably developed an *external* dimension—regarding IHL compliance by *others*. This external dimension is crucial for the purposes of this study as it entails obligations for third parties regarding violations of obligations by parties. While the development of some external dimension is increasingly accepted,[215] it remains unsettled to what extent this dimension entails not only negative duties but also duties to take positive steps.

(a) Negative duties It is well accepted that there is a *negative* external dimension flowing from the duty to respect and ensure respect, which requires States not to contribute to violations of IHL by others, chiefly parties to an armed conflict.[216] This duty of abstention is wider in several respects than the general complicity rules in the law of international responsibility, at least on their orthodox understanding.

First, it entails a prohibition not only on aiding and assisting in violations of IHL, but also on encouraging such violations.[217] This aspect goes beyond the orthodox position in the law of international responsibility, where the ILC deliberately excluded instigation from the scope of complicity.[218]

[213] Geiß (n 211) 118. On individual obligations under IHL, see Chapter 1.4.b.ii.

[214] Above 2.a.; 2.d.iv.

[215] See generally M Zwanenburg, 'The "External Element" of the Obligation to Ensure Respect for the Geneva Conventions: A Matter of Treaty Interpretation' (2021) 97 ILS 621; though see Schmitt and Watts (n 208) (rejecting the external dimension altogether as a 'reimagining' of Common Article 1 that positive international law does not reflect), see also nn 216, 227–231.

[216] *GCIII Commentary* [191]–[192]; M Sassòli, 'State Responsibility for Violations of International Humanitarian Law' (2002) 84 IRRC 401, 412–413; Ruys (n 135) 51; Aust (n 192) 389; M Milanovic, 'Intelligence Sharing in Multinational Military Operations and Complicity under International Law' (2021) 97 ILS 1269, 1326; though see V Robson, 'The Common Approach to Article 1: The Scope of Each State's Obligation to Ensure Respect for the Geneva Conventions' (2020) 25 JCSL 101, 103 (considering the negative external duty dimension as a mere corollary of the obligation to perform obligations under the GCs in good faith).

[217] *Nicaragua* (n 34) [220], [255]; see also the references in n 216.

[218] R Ago, 'Seventh Report on State Responsibility—The Internationally Wrongful Act of the State, Source of International Responsibility' (1978) UN Doc A/CN.4/307 (1978) II(1) YILC 55 [63]; Crawford (n 32) 56 [213]; *Nicaragua* (n 34) [255] ('[t]he circumstances in which one State may be

Secondly, the duty not to assist or encourage extends to violations by non-State armed groups of their IHL obligations as parties to an armed conflict.[219] This important indirect avenue to international responsibility for violations provides a crucial reason for why finding that non-State parties bear obligations under international law matters in the first place.[220] On this point, which is not included in the ARSIWA or ARIO, complicity in the law of international responsibility may, nonetheless, align with the duty to respect and ensure respect as well as with other special rules on complicity in non-State actors' international law violations, such as complicity in genocide.[221] Indeed, as Jackson puts it, 'the seriousness of the obligations that international law imposes on non-state actors supplies the logic for a complicity rule ... as a non-state analogue to the rule reflected in Article 16' which 'might be of particular relevance to state participation in violations of international humanitarian law by non-states groups'.[222] Such a rule enjoys some support in international practice.[223] Yet, the special duty not to assist in violations of IHL by non-State actors would arguably remain relevant, not least because it avoids some of the conceptual difficulties of a general rule on responsibility for complicity in acts of non-State actors.

Thirdly, the subjective element required to find that a State has violated its Common Article 1 duty by assisting or encouraging IHL violations may be lower than that for establishing responsibility for complicity under Article 16 ARSIWA/ Article 14 ARIO. '[K]nowingly contribut[ing] to violations of the Conventions by a Party to a conflict', regardless of intent, would suffice for a violation of Common Article 1.[224] While Article 16(a) ARSIWA refers to a State's 'knowledge of the

regarded as responsible for acts carried out by another State ... probably do not include the possibility of incitement'); for a challenge to this orthodoxy, see M Jackson, 'State Instigation in International Law: A General Principle Transposed' (2019) 30 EJIL 391.

[219] *Nicaragua* (n 34) [220], [255]; Milanovic (n 216) 1332; H Aust, 'Complicity in Violations of International Humanitarian Law' in H Krieger (ed), *Inducing Compliance with International Humanitarian Law: Lessons from the African Great Lakes Region* (CUP 2015) 455, 458; Geiß (n 211) 126, 130; O Hathaway et al, 'Ensuring Responsibility: Common Article 1 and State Responsibility for Non-State Actors' (2017) 95 Tex LR 539, 569.

[220] See Chapter 1.3.b.iii.

[221] *Bosnian Genocide* (n 199) [167]; for discussion, see Jackson (n 193) 202–214.

[222] Jackson (n 193) 214–215.

[223] See eg J Borger, 'The Austrian Position on Arms Embargo in Syria—Official Document' *The Guardian* (15 May 2013) <www.theguardian.com/world/julian-borger-global-security-blog/interactive/2013/may/15/austria-eu-syria-arms-embargo-pdf>; R Mackenzie-Gray Scott, 'State Responsibility for Complicity in the Internationally Wrongful Acts of Non-State Armed Groups' (2019) 24 JCSL 373 (tracing support for an 'embryonic' rule of 'non-state complicity' in State practice); see further R Mackenzie-Gray Scott, *State Responsibility for Non-State Actors: Past, Present and Prospects for the Future* (Hart 2022) 169–177; K Roithmaier, 'Holding States Responsible for Violations of International Humanitarian Law in Proxy Warfare: The Concept of State Complicity in Acts of Non-State Armed Groups' (2023) 14 EJLS 140.

[224] *GCIII Commentary* [192]; see also Netherlands, Parliamentary Questions (Appendix) 1177 (2015–2016) 18 January 2016 <https://zoek.officielebekendmakingen.nl/ah-tk-20152016-1177.html>; Milanovic (n 216) 1333 (suggesting that knowledge or even wilful blindness with 'oblique intent' would suffice, but so would direct intent without knowledge).

circumstances of the internationally wrongful act', the ILC Commentary refers to the relevant State organ's intent.[225]

(b) Positive duties Beyond the negative duty not to assist or encourage IHL violations, it is controversial whether there also exists an obligation to take *positive* steps to prevent or terminate IHL violations by parties to a conflict.[226] In its updated Commentaries to the Geneva Conventions, the ICRC firmly takes the position that such positive duties exist.[227] Although this position enjoys considerable support within certain sections of scholarship,[228] others continue to reject such duties.[229]

The ordinary meaning of the terms 'respect and ensure respect' does not provide any indications to this effect. As the preparatory work of the GCs reveals, the drafters envisaged only *internal* positive duties flowing from Common Article 1, that is, duties regarding a State's own population rather than other States or non-State parties to armed conflicts.[230] Absent any meaningful discussions on this point during the drafting process of the 1977 APs or the 2005 APIII, the wording of Article 1 API, III does not seem to have been based on a different understanding.[231] In other IHL and human rights treaty provisions, 'ensure respect' does not seem to have been understood as requiring positive steps vis-à-vis other States.[232]

Even if Common Article 1 may, therefore, initially not have comprised positive duties to ensure respect by parties, such duties are often derived from a 'dynamic

[225] ARSIWA Commentary, art 16 [5]. On the controversies and remaining uncertainties, see Aust (n 192) 230–249; Jackson (n 193) 159–162.

[226] Parts of this section have been published in a similar form elsewhere (A Wentker, 'Partnered Operations and the Positive Duties of Co-Parties' (2022) 27 JCSL 159).

[227] *GCIII Commentary* [197]ff.

[228] See eg L Condorelli and L Boisson de Chazournes, 'Quelques remarques à propos de l'obligation des états de "respecter et faire respecter" le droit international humanitaire "en toutes circonstances"' in C Swinarski (ed), *Etudes et essais sur le droit humanitaire et sur les principes de la Croix-Rouge en l'honneur de Jean Pictet* (Nijhoff 1984) 24; B Kessler, 'The Duty to "Ensure Respect" under Common Article 1 of the Geneva Conventions: Its Implications on International and Non-International Armed Conflicts' (2001) 44 GYIL 498, 505; K Dörmann and J Serralvo, 'Common Article 1 to the Geneva Conventions and the Obligation to Prevent International Humanitarian Law Violations' (2014) 96 IRRC 707, 722; Geiß (n 211) 123; Hathaway et al (n 219) 574; A Breslin, 'A Reflection on the Legal Obligation for Third States to Ensure Respect for IHL' (2017) 22 JCSL 5, 6; E Massingham and A McConnachie, 'Common Article 1: An Introduction' in E Massingham and A McConnachie (eds), *Ensuring Respect for International Humanitarian Law* (Routledge 2020) 2; C Wiesener and A Kjeldgaard-Pedersen, 'Ensuring Respect by Partners: Revisiting the Debate on Common Article 1' (2022) 27 JCSL 135, 153.

[229] See eg F Kalshoven, 'The Undertaking to Respect and Ensure Respect in All Circumstances: From Tiny Seed to Ripening Fruit' (1999) 2 YIHL 3, 54; C Focarelli, 'Common Article 1 of the 1949 Geneva Conventions: A Soap Bubble' (2010) 21 EJIL 125, 128–129; Robson (n 216) 103; Schmitt and Watts (n 208) 679; R Kolb, 'Commentaires iconoclastes sur l'obligation de faire respecter le droit international humanitaire selon l'Article 1 Commun des Conventions de Genève de 1949' (2013) 46 RBDI 513, 518–519.

[230] For a detailed review of the *travaux*, see Kalshoven (n 229) 23–28.

[231] Focarelli (n 229) 135; Robson (n 216) 104–105; but, see *GCIII Commentary* [189].

[232] Focarelli (n 229) 138–146. In the context of human rights treaties this may, however, be because jurisdictional thresholds have prevented such arguments.

interpretation'[233] in light of subsequent practice over the past decades and from a development of the customary duty to ensure respect through practice accompanied by *opinio juris*. In the *Wall* Advisory Opinion, the ICJ may have engaged in such a reading when it found that 'all the States parties to [GCIV] are under an obligation, while respecting the United Nations Charter and international law, to ensure compliance by Israel with international humanitarian law as embodied in that Convention'.[234] While not itself an instance of practice, it may be that the Court considered international practice to support its finding.

The existence of such support was, however, strongly contested by Judge Kooijmans's Separate Opinion, who also deplored that the Court failed to provide reasons for its view in this regard.[235] The *erga omnes* character of 'a great many rules of humanitarian law', which the Court emphasised immediately before reaching its finding on Common Article 1,[236] does not have any implications for the obligations incumbent on States flowing from this provision, as Judge Higgins clarified.[237] Indeed, as James Crawford noted, even if third States may have been entitled to invoke Israel's responsibility for breaching *erga omnes* provisions of IHL, they were under no obligation to do so.[238] Moreover, while the Court's finding implies that States had an obligation regarding Israel's IHL compliance, the Court's rather generic language leaves open whether this external dimension would entail taking positive measures beyond negative obligations not to encourage, aid, or assist.[239] Similar ambiguities exist in the UN General Assembly[240] and Security Council resolutions[241] addressing the position of third States vis-à-vis the Israel–Palestine conflict.

233 R Geiß, 'Common Article 1 of the Geneva Conventions Scope and Content of the Obligation to "Ensure Respect"—"Narrow but Deep" or "Wide and Shallow"?' in H Krieger (ed), *Inducing Compliance with International Humanitarian Law: Lessons from the African Great Lakes Region* (CUP 2015) 424.

234 *Wall* (n 32) [159].

235 ibid sep op Kooijmans [47]–[50].

236 ibid [157] (recalling the *Nuclear Weapons* Advisory Opinion).

237 ibid sep op Higgins [39].

238 J Crawford, 'Opinion: Third Party Obligations with respect to Israeli Settlements in the Occupied Palestinian Territories' (Report for the Trade Unions Congress 2012) <www.tuc.org.uk/sites/default/files/tucfiles/LegalOpinionIsraeliSettlements.pdf> 16.

239 This ambiguity contrasts with the *Armed Activities* case, where the Court clearly found that positive obligations to ensure respect for IHL by others flowed from HR, art 43, albeit for Occupying Powers, rather than for all third States under Common Article 1 (*Armed Activities (DRC v Uganda)* (Merits) [2005] ICJ Rep 168 [178]–[179]).

240 See eg UNGA Res 59/122 (10 December 2004) UN Doc A/RES/59/122 [3]; UNGA Res. 60/105 (8 December 2005) UN Doc A/RES/60/105 [3]; UNGA Res 62/107 (17 December 2007) UN Doc A/RES/62/107 [3]; UNGA Res 63/96 (5 December 2008) UN Doc A/RES/63/96 [3]; UNGA Res 68/81 (16 December 2013) UN Doc A/RES/68/81 [3]. Interestingly, the more explicit wording used in early UNGA resolutions has been dropped (see eg UNGA Res 43/21 (3 November 1988) UN Doc A/RES/43/21 [5]; UNGA Res 45/69 (December 1990) UN Doc A/RES/45/69 [3] ('in conformity with their obligation under article 1' (emphasis added)). More recent resolutions on the situation denouncing IHL violations by Israel do not refer to Common Article 1 or States' duties to ensure respect at all (see eg UNGA Res 74/88 (13 December 2019) UN Doc A/RES/74/88)).

241 See eg UNSC Res 681 (20 December 1990) UN Doc S/RES/681 [5].

Further, it remains uncertain whether international practice has established the positive external duty dimension for third States. Instances of practice affirming these duties have long seemed to remain relatively scarce, though there has been a noticeable increase in such instances recently.[242] Some of the practice that specifically supports an external dimension of the duty to ensure respect is explicitly limited to negative duties,[243] or simply does not specify whether the external dimension would comprise positive obligations.[244] Moreover, such duties confront persisting resistance from a number of States. Reportedly, at the 2019 International Conference of the Red Cross and Red Crescent Movement, some States strongly opposed the ICRC's views on this point.[245] This—apparently successful—resistance is reflected in the language of the resolution addressing the issue, which only mentions States' 'obligation to respect international humanitarian law', bereft of any reference to 'ensuring respect'.[246] In recent years, some States have also publicly rejected the idea of positive external duties to ensure respect under Common Article 1. In 2016, the then Legal Adviser to the US Department of State stated that the US 'do[es] not share this expansive interpretation of Common Article 1'.[247] The US Department of Defense reiterated this view in 2019,[248] and Australia joined the US in criticising the ICRC's view on positive external duties.[249] The *Danish*

[242] See eg EU Council, 'User's Guide to Council Common Position 2008/944/CFSP' 16 September 2019 (12189/19) [2.13]; EU, 'Statement to the United Nations General Assembly: Humanitarian situation in Syria' 25 February 2014 (on file with the author) 2; *Wall* (AO) Written Statement League of Arab States (January 2004) [1.18]; see also certain responses by States cited in ICRC, 'Questionnaire Concerning Measures Intended to Reinforce the Implementation of the Geneva Conventions of August 12, 1949: Replies Sent by Governments' (ICRC 1973) 20–31; for a comprehensive survey of recent instances of practice, see L Hill-Cawthorne, 'Common Article 1 of the Geneva Conventions and the Method of Treaty Interpretation' (2023) 72 ICLQ 869, 884–886.

[243] Netherlands, Parliamentary Questions 18 January 2016 (quoting the Minister of Defence stating in parliament that, with a view to the Netherlands' IHL obligations, knowledge that a partner uses shared information to commit IHL violations might entail a decision to refrain from sharing); J Charpentier, 'Pratique française de droit international' (1977) 23 AFDI 1012, 1017 (reporting that France reminded Algeria of its obligation not to assist IHL violations by others).

[244] For detailed reviews, see Hill-Cawthorne (n 242) 884–886 A Frutig, *Die Pflicht von Drittstaaten zur Durchsetzung des humanitären Völkerrechts nach Artikel 1 der Genfer Konventionen von 1949: Auf dem schmalen Grat zwischen Recht und Moral* (Helbing Lichtenhahn 2009) 88–119; Dörmann and Serralvo (n 228) 716–722.

[245] H Aly, 'Negotiations at Red Cross conference shrouded in global politics' (*New Humanitarian*, 13 December 2019) <www.thenewhumanitarian.org/news/2019/12/13/Red-Cross-IHL-conference-global-politics>.

[246] 'Resolution—Bringing IHL home' (International Conference of the Red Cross and Red Crescent 2019) 33IC/19/R1 Preamble.

[247] B Egan, 'Keynote Address' (2016) 110 ASIL Proc 300, 307 (apparently confining this criticism to *positive* external duties while accepting *negative* ones: '[a]s a matter of international law, we would look to the law of State responsibility and our partners' compliance with the law of armed conflict in assessing the lawfulness of our assistance to, and joint operations with, those military partners').

[248] 'Remarks by Defense Dept General Counsel Paul C. Ney Jr. on the Law of War' (*Just Security*, 28 May 2019) <www.justsecurity.org/64313/remarks-by-defense-dept-general-counsel-paul-c-ney-jr-on-the-law-of-war/>.

[249] J Reid, 'Ensuring Respect: The Role of State Practice in Interpreting the Geneva Conventions' (*ILA Reporter*, 2016) <http://ilareporter.org.au/2016/11/ensuring-respect-the-role-of-state-practice-in-interpreting-the-geneva-conventions-john-reid/>.

Military Manual includes a section on Common Article 1, which rather conspicuously, only refers to *internal* positive duties.[250] In the *Turp* case, the Canadian government went even further by arguing, inter alia, that Common Article 1 was not at all applicable to States with no involvement in the conflict and that the provision would not prescribe specific measures.[251] The Federal Court endorsed these views.[252] In comments to the ILC, Israel, the UK, and the US explicitly rejected the ICRC's view that Common Article 1 contained a positive external obligation for States to 'exert their influence to prevent and stop violations of the Geneva Conventions by parties to an armed conflict'.[253]

Summing up, the existence of a positive external dimension of the duty to ensure respect remains doubtful. The persisting scholarly controversies on this point and opposition by some States can plausibly be explained in light of the broader argument made in this chapter. The posture of abstention that international law generally demands of third parties aligns seamlessly with construing the duty to ensure respect by others in terms of *negative*, complicity-type duties not to aid, assist, or encourage IHL violations by parties.[254] Conversely, demanding that third parties take *positive* steps to ensure respect for IHL by parties would mean a significant rupture with the general detachment that is required of third States.[255] These frictions can arguably explain the unease that such propositions continue to face in scholarship as well as the reluctance and even rejection by certain States. This explanation then already makes room for the existence of such positive external duties for *parties*, which is in line with the overall structure of the allocation of obligations in armed conflicts between parties and third parties as two distinct categories of duty bearers. This nuance, which the debate on positive external duties to ensure respect has tended to overlook, will be explored in further detail in Chapter 5.

250 *Danish Manual* 641–642.

251 *Turp v Canada* (n 208) [21] (also denying the applicability of Common Article 1 to non-international armed conflicts). Canada has recently reiterated these views (UNGA, 'Sixth Committee, Summary Record of the 22nd Meeting, New York, 25 October 2022, 3 p.m.' (12 December 2022) UN Doc A/C.6/77/SR.22 4 [14].

252 ibid [72]; see already *Sinnappu v Canada* (n 208) 33.

253 ILC, 'Protection of the Environment in Relation to Armed Conflicts: Comments and Observations Received from Governments, International Organizations and Others' (17 January 2022) UN Doc A/CN.4/749 36 (Israel), 38 (UK, US).

254 The detached posture of third parties in armed conflict would also militate against construing the relevant complicity rules as entailing positive duties to avoid complicity by omission, in line with the prevailing position in general international law (see J Crawford, *State Responsibility: The General Part* (CUP 2013) 403; for critical analysis, see Jackson (n 193) 155–157).

255 While neutrality law also imposes positive duties to prevent the parties from using neutral territory (see HCV, arts 2–5; HCXIII, arts 5–6), these are solely aimed at safeguarding the neutral's detachment from the conflict (see above 2.a.).

4. Conclusion

As the regulation of third parties in armed conflict has evolved, the posture of abstention characterising their relationship to parties has proved remarkably resilient. That position has been refined rather than abandoned and now has multiple layers. It includes general duties of abstention from participation in the conflict under the law of neutrality as well as more nuanced duties to abstain from contributing to violations of obligations by the parties under general complicity rules and specifically as part of the duty to respect and ensure respect for IHL. These duties of third parties vis-à-vis parties supplement the centrality of party status as a regulatory reference point for international law in armed conflict.

The structural differences between the respective duties and rights of parties and third parties as well as the increasingly complex, multilayered legal relationship between parties and third parties further substantiate the findings in Chapter 1 on how identifying parties is relevant. The ground is thus prepared to turn to the legal framework governing this identification.

PART II

THE IDENTIFICATION OF PARTIES TO ARMED CONFLICTS

3
Disentangling the Identification of Parties and the Concepts of Armed Conflict in Multiparty Conflicts

1. Introduction

Part I of the book has shown why and how it matters under international law to identify parties to an armed conflict. In Part II, the book provides an account of the legal framework governing the identification of parties. The analysis focuses on conflicts with multiple parties on one or both sides of the conflict, referred to as co-parties.

As a starting point, Chapter 3 considers how and to what extent the concepts of international and non-international armed conflict inform the identification of parties. The relationship and distinction between the concepts of armed conflict and the identification of parties can best be understood, and is of particular relevance, in the context of identifying co-parties in multiparty settings.

Section 1 outlines the contours of the notions of armed conflict and shows that both international and non-international armed conflicts comprise elements that specify the nature of the collective entities involved as parties and elements that specify the nature of the confrontation between these collective entities. The subsequent sections build on this distinction and argue that the two sets of elements differ in the way they are to be assessed. The difference becomes relevant in situations wherein multiple entities appear as potential co-parties to the same armed conflict, a setting that section 2 briefly introduces. Section 3 argues that, in multiparty settings, those criteria for the existence of an armed conflict that relate to the nature of the conflict as a whole may be established by aggregating the activities of different co-parties (ie the existence of a recourse to armed force in international armed conflicts and protracted armed violence in non-international armed conflicts). Accordingly, being identified as a co-party does not require separately fulfilling these requirements so long as they are jointly fulfilled by all co-parties. By contrast, each co-party must separately fulfil the criteria related to the nature and the structure of the parties to the conflict, particularly the organisation requirement in non-international armed conflicts. This chapter thus demonstrates that, although the identification of parties is closely connected to the notions of armed conflict, it eventually requires a distinct legal framework.

Party Status to Armed Conflict in International Law. Alexander Wentker, Oxford University Press. © Alexander Wentker 2024.
DOI: 10.1093/oso/9780198900900.003.0004

2. Elements of the concepts of armed conflict

To understand how the identification of parties to armed conflicts relates to the concepts of armed conflict—and how these questions can be disentangled—it is necessary, at the outset, to outline the contours of the concepts of armed conflict.

In a preliminary step, section a. examines the concept of war and shows that it remains possible for States to declare war under current international law. This caveat notwithstanding, the *jus in bello* is centred mainly on the concepts of international and non-international armed conflict today, which section b. sets out. It will be seen that both international and non-international armed conflicts are composed of two sets of elements: first, those pertaining to the nature of the collective entities involved as parties; and, secondly, those pertaining to the nature of the factual situation of conflict that exists between these collective entities. As will be argued in the subsequent sections of this chapter, this distinction matters since the two sets of elements differ in how they are established, a difference that will become relevant where multiple entities appear as potential parties to the same armed conflict. In that sense, the distinction proves crucial for conceptually disentangling the existence of an armed conflict from the identification of parties.

a. War

Being a belligerent party traditionally meant being in a state of war.[1] Yet, what exactly brought about a state of war was never entirely settled. Historically, the matter was approached from different perspectives: as war in the 'technical', 'formal', or 'legal' sense, on the one hand, and in the 'material' sense, on the other. In the nineteenth century, these approaches were considered complementary to some extent, emphasising different aspects;[2] in the interwar period, they gave rise to entrenched divisions among States and scholars as to the legal meaning of war. These divisions came to the fore notably in controversies surrounding the then widespread practice of States resorting to forcible 'measures short of war' or 'reprisals'.[3]

The first approach conceived of war in *subjective* terms. A state of war would arise between two or more States when at least one of them had an intention to that

[1] See Chapter 1.

[2] S Neff, *War and the Law of Nations: A General History* (CUP 2005) 173.

[3] N Politis, 'Les Représailles entre états membres de la Société des Nations' (1924) 31 RGDIP 5; H Lauterpacht, 'The Pact of Paris and the Budapest Articles of Interpretation' (1934) 20 TGS 178, 180–183; I Brownlie, *International Law and the Use of Force by States* (Clarendon Press 1963) 216–229; C Wampach, *Armed Reprisals from Medieval Times to 1945* (Nomos 2020) 237–272.

effect, whether expressed explicitly, notably in a declaration of war, or implicitly, inferred from the circumstances.[4]

The second approach conceived of war in *objective* terms as consisting of armed clashes of a certain scale between the respective States.[5] The central challenge raised by this approach—defining the requisite nature and degree of material violence—was never quite resolved as regards the notion of war.[6] From today's perspective, the objective conception ultimately prevailed, given that the notions of armed conflict are understood as factual situations,[7] and, as Common Article 2 stresses, independent of whether the parties recognise that a state of war exists.[8]

At the same time, the subjective conception of war has not entirely disappeared. Although the notions of (international and non-international) armed conflict have largely replaced the concept of war as the central reference point for establishing the application of the *jus in bello*, Common Article 2 also provides for the application of the Geneva Conventions to 'declared wars'.

Declarations of war have become rare.[9] At the same time, occasional references in international practice to declared wars or a state of war indicate that States consider that war could still be declared. For example, several Arab States have regarded themselves in a state of war with Israel after 1948, as has Pakistan with respect to its conflict with India in 1965. Several States have also referred to the state of war with respect to the Falklands conflict and the Iran–Iraq conflict.[10] In its explanations for not declaring war on North Vietnam, the US implicitly acknowledged that it still considered such declarations possible under international law.[11]

[4] League of Nations Secretary-General, 'Legal Position Arising from the Enforcement in Time of Peace of the Measures of Economic Pressure Indicated in Article 16 of the Covenant, Particularly by a Maritime Blockade' (1927) 8 LNOJ 834; A McNair, 'The Legal Meaning of War, and the Relation of War to Reprisals' (1925) 11 TGS 29, 45; K Strupp, *Grundzüge des positiven Völkerrechts* (2nd edn, Röhrscheid 1922) 170–171; JB Moore, *A Digest of International Law, vol VII* (Government Printing Office 1906) 153; G Scelle, 'Règles générales du droit de la paix' (1932) 46 RCADI 327, 677; Q Wright, 'When Does War Exist?' (1932) 26 AJIL 362, 363.

[5] J Bluntschli, *Das moderne Kriegsrecht der civilisirten Staten* (Beck 1866) 1, 4; L Oppenheim, *International Law: A Treatise*, vol II (Longmans 1906) 57; T Lawrence, *The Principles of International Law* (4th edn, Macmillan 1913) 332; Politis (n 3) 12; E Borchard, '"War" and 'Peace"' (1933) 27 AJIL 114, 116; C Eagleton, 'An Attempt to Define War' (1933) 291 IC 237, 273; H Kelsen, *Principles of International Law* (Rinehart & Company 1952) 23–24.

[6] C Greenwood, 'The Concept of War in Modern International Law' (1987) 36 ICLQ 283, 286; see already Eagleton (n 5) 273–281; Brownlie (n 3) 399–400.

[7] Below b.

[8] The wording 'not recognized by one of them' is generally understood to include cases where neither of the parties considers a state of war to exist (see eg *Pictet Commentary GCIV* 21).

[9] T Fazal, 'Why States No Longer Declare War' (2012) 21 Secur Stud 557 (providing empirical data for this decline and arguing that the decline can be explained by States avoiding to label conflicts as war due to proliferating *jus in bello* restrictions); though see K Irajpanah and K Schultz, 'Off the Menu: Post-1945 Norms and the End of War Declarations' (2021) 30 Secur Stud 485 (arguing that the decline is connected to profound changes of the post-1945 regulation of the use of force); for further discussion, see T Fazal, K Irajpanah, and K Schultz, '*Jus in Bello, Jus Ad Bellum*, and the Decline in Declarations of War: An Exchange' (2021) 30 Secur Stud 893.

[10] On these cases, see Greenwood (n 6) 290–294.

[11] 'Effects of a Formal Declaration of War: U.S. Defense Department Statement' (1966) 5 ILM 791, 791–792.

Further examples include Panama's declaration of war against the US in 1989, Chad's declaration of being in a state of war with Sudan in 2005, and Sudan's declaration of war against South Sudan in 2012.[12] While rejecting Eritrea's suggestion that Ethiopia had declared war, the EECC has implicitly also acknowledged that such a declaration would have been possible.[13] Mali and Burkina Faso similarly hinted at that possibility when they declared in 2023 that 'any military intervention against Niger would be tantamount to a declaration of war against Burkina Faso and Mali'.[14] As an aside, besides these explicit and implicit acknowledgements in international practice, declarations of war continue to play a prominent role in domestic law. Quantitative surveys suggest that almost 70 per cent of the constitutions adopted between 1990 and 2015 refer to declarations of war.[15]

More generally, Chapter 2 has noted that it cannot be inferred from the absence of recourse to a rule of customary international law that the rule is extinct and could, therefore, no longer be used in the future.[16] It should also be kept in mind that historical and empirical studies suggest that resort to armed force without prior declarations of war has always been common, even during the heyday of subjective state of war conceptions from the nineteenth century to the Second World War.[17] Article 1 HCIII, which requires a declaration of war, has probably at no point in time reflected customary international law and has thus only been binding on the small number of States that had ratified the Convention.[18] A declaration of war would often constitute a threat of force, which is today prohibited under the *jus ad bellum*. As a matter of the *jus in bello*, declaring war against another State, nonetheless, remains at least a theoretical way to become a party.[19]

[12] N Zamir, *Classification of Conflicts in International Humanitarian Law: The Legal Impact of Foreign Intervention in Civil Wars* (Edward Elgar 2017) 49.

[13] EECC, Partial Award: *Jus ad Bellum*—Ethiopia's Claims (19 December 2005) [17]; see also *Brima, Kamara, Kanu* (Trial Judgment) SCSL-04-16-T (20 June 2007) [253] (noting references by the Revolutionary United Front/Armed Forces of the Revolutionary Council to the state of war).

[14] 'Burkina Faso, Mali Say Military Intervention in Niger Would Be "Declaration of War"' (France 24, 1 August 2023) <www.france24.com/en/africa/20230801-burkina-faso-and-mali-say-intervention-in-niger-would-be-declaration-of-war>.

[15] T Fazal, *Wars of Law: Unintended Consequences in the Regulation of Armed Conflict* (Cornell UP 2018) 266 (fn 37).

[16] See Chapter 2, text accompanied by n 108.

[17] JF Maurice, *Hostilities Without Declaration of War: An Historical Abstract of the Cases in which Hostilities Have Occurred Between Civilized Powers Prior to Declaration or Warning. From 1700 to 1870* (HM Stationery Office 1883) (suggesting that hostilities had been preceded by a declaration of war only in a small minority of the wars in the period surveyed); Fazal (n 9) (suggesting that throughout the nineteenth century and the first half of the twentieth century, declarations of war were made in about half of the cases of inter-State wars).

[18] Y Dinstein, *War, Aggression and Self-Defence* (6th edn, CUP 2017) 32.

[19] D Schindler, 'The Different Types of Armed Conflicts According to the Geneva Conventions and Protocols' (1979) 163 RCADI 121, 131–132; D Akande, 'Classification of Armed Conflicts' in B Saul and D Akande (eds), *The Oxford Guide to International Humanitarian Law* (OUP 2020) 33; *GCI Commentary* [207]; M Sassòli, *International Humanitarian Law: Rules, Controversies, and Solutions to Problems Arising in Warfare* (Edward Elgar 2019) 172; but see the ILA Committee on the Use of Force, 'Final Report on the Meaning of Armed Conflict in International Law' (2010) 2, 33 (concluding that such declarations 'may have evidentiary value but ... do not alone create a *de jure* state of war or armed conflict').

Such a declaration could have some practical implications. Even absent or prior to hostilities, a declaration of war could, for example, trigger the application of certain international humanitarian law (IHL) provisions, such as those concerning the treatment of enemy nationals,[20] or neutrality law.[21] A declaration of war could also be significant when issued by a State alongside its partners that are already involved in an international armed conflict.[22] As will be seen below, however, the possibility of a state of war in current international law should be limited to instances of *explicit* declarations of war.[23]

The shadowy persistence of the concept of war should not distract from the fact that the contemporary *jus in bello* primarily centres on the notions of armed conflict, which will be examined next.

b. Armed conflict

As noted at the outset of the book, there is no unitary concept of armed conflict in international law, but two kinds of armed conflict—international and non-international—are distinguished according to the nature of the collective entities involved.[24] While the concepts of international and non-international armed conflict are not defined in treaty law—a deliberate omission by the drafters[25]—the ICTY's famous *Tadić* formula has become a widely accepted definitional starting point. The ICTY found:

> that an armed conflict exists whenever there is a resort to armed force between States or protracted armed violence between governmental authorities and organized armed groups or between such groups within a State.[26]

Both international and non-international armed conflicts are conceived of as factual situations of conflicts taking place between certain collective entities. The concepts of international and non-international armed conflict thus consist of elements relating to the nature of, first, the collective entities involved as parties, and, secondly, the factual situation between them. The nature of the collective entities that may be parties to international and non-international armed conflicts has already been canvassed in Chapter 1.[27] The present section focuses on

[20] See notably GCIV, arts 35–46, 79–141.
[21] Chapter 2, n 80.
[22] Chapter 4.3.b.i.(1).
[23] ibid.
[24] Chapter 1.2.b.
[25] J Pictet, *Humanitarian Law and the Protection of War Victims* (Sijthoff 1975) 50.
[26] *Tadić* (Decision on the Defence Motion for Interlocutory Appeal on Jurisdiction) IT-94-1-A (2 October 1995) [70].
[27] Chapter 1.2.b.

the second set of elements, namely the nature of the factual situation between the parties in international and non-international armed conflicts respectively.

i. International armed conflict

(1) Resort to armed force between States

For there to be resort to armed force *between States*, the relevant act(s) must be attributable to the respective State(s).[28] It is sufficient that one State unilaterally uses force against another—the attacked State need not react by force to be a party to an international armed conflict with the attacking State.[29]

Resort to *armed force* does not require a particular intensity threshold to be met for an international armed conflict to arise, unlike the 'protracted armed violence' required for non-international armed conflicts.[30] A low threshold is not only suggested by the ICTY's language ('*whenever* there is …').[31] Excluding non-intense force between States from the concept of international armed conflict has also been seen to risk leaving such acts unregulated.[32] In its 2010 report on the meaning of armed conflict, the ILA concluded that an intensity threshold exists in international armed conflicts, based on various instances of minor incidents between States that contemporary international practice did not consider as international armed conflicts.[33] However, evidence that a lack of intensity drove the classification in those instances is rarely forthcoming, and commentators thus mostly do not read the practice as the ILA does.[34]

[28] Schindler (n 19) 131; see in detail D Carron, *L'Acte déclencheur d'un conflit armé international* (Schulthess 2016) 255ff; see also Chapter 4.3.b.i.(1).

[29] ICRC, 'International Humanitarian Law and the Challenges of Contemporary Armed Conflicts' (2015) 8; D Akande, 'Classification of Armed Conflicts: Relevant Legal Concepts' in E Wilmshurst (ed), *International Law and the Classification of Conflicts* (OUP 2012) 74; Sassòli (n 19) 170; Zamir (n 12) 56 (pointing to instances where State practice has treated unilateral uses of force as international armed conflicts).

[30] See also eg *GCI Commentary* [238]; M Milanović and V Hadzi-Vidanović, 'A Taxonomy of Armed Conflict' in N White and C Henderson (eds), *Research Handbook on International Conflict and Security Law* (Edward Elgar 2013) 274; D Kritsiotis, 'The Tremors of *Tadić*' (2010) 43 Isr LR 262, 278; Y Dinstein, *The Conduct of Hostilities under the Law of International Armed Conflict* (4th edn, CUP 2022) 1.

[31] Akande (n 29) 34.

[32] ibid 35; *GCI Commentary* [240]; though see UN Special Rapporteur on Extrajudicial, Summary or Arbitrary Executions, 'Report: Use of Armed Drones for Targeted Killings' UN Doc A/HRC/44/38 (15 August 2020) Annex [15]–[39] (suggesting, in her assessment of the killing of the Irani General Soleimani in 2020 by a US drone strike in Iraq, that single strikes are best assessed through the lens of human rights law, unaffected by the application of IHL, and should thus not be considered as an international armed conflict).

[33] ILA Report Armed Conflict 18, 26–29, 32.

[34] A Clapham, 'The Concept of International Armed Conflict' in A Clapham, P Gaeta, and M Sassòli (eds), *The Geneva Conventions: A Commentary* (OUP 2015) 15–16 (suggesting that the practice may be due to the lack of a need to apply IHL in the cases at hand, for example absent affected protected persons); M Asada, 'The Concept of "Armed Conflict" in International Armed Conflict' in M O'Connell (ed), *What Is War? An Investigation in the Wake of 9/11* (Brill 2012) 65–66 (pointing to instances of low-intensity conflicts which at least one of the States involved considered to be an international armed conflict as evidence against an intensity threshold).

Although it is therefore inapposite to conceive of international armed conflicts through the lens of an intensity threshold, the act(s) in question must still possess a certain nature or quality to be considered 'armed force' giving rise to an international armed conflict. Many authors require the act to cause harm, broadly understood, to the adversary or protected persons.[35] It also appears that those acts that can trigger an international armed conflict on their own are more narrowly confined than the range of acts that are regulated by the law of international armed conflict once an international armed conflict exists, variably referred to as 'acts of war', acts of 'hostilities', or 'military operations'.[36] Indeed, the 'acts of war' considered to form part of an existing international armed conflict may, for example, encompass preparatory or auxiliary acts to the actual use of force, such as intelligence gathering about the enemy or troop transportation,[37] which would not give rise to an international armed conflict in themselves when no international armed conflict exists as yet. Greenwood has also suggested that threats of force—he uses the example of the announcement of a blockade—would be acts of war subject to the law of international armed conflict if an international armed conflict already exists but 'will not in themselves give rise to a condition of armed conflict'.[38]

Along similar lines, Pictet's famous suggestion that the capture of a single soldier would be sufficient to trigger an international armed conflict[39]—a position that the ICRC continues to embrace[40]—remains controversial in the literature[41] and unsettled in international practice. To illustrate, consider the example of a US pilot captured by Syrian forces, having been shot down over Lebanese territory.[42] Both Syria and—as later became public—the US considered the pilot to be a prisoner of war.[43] The case is thus sometimes taken to support the view that the capture of a

[35] S Vité, 'Typology of Armed Conflicts in International Humanitarian Law: Legal Concepts and Actual Situations' (2009) 91 IRRC 69, 72; Zamir (n 12) 58–59 (considering it sufficient that such harm is 'intended or likely').

[36] On these notions, see in greater detail Chapter 4.3.b.i.(2).

[37] See eg Dinstein (n 30) 2; Chapter 4, nn 147–149.

[38] C Greenwood, 'Scope of Application of Humanitarian Law' in D Fleck (ed), *The Handbook of International Humanitarian Law* (2nd edn, OUP 2008) 57.

[39] *Pictet Commentary GCI* 32–33.

[40] *GCI Commentary* [239].

[41] In favour, see eg Vité (n 35) 72; R Kolb, *Ius in bello—Le Droit international des conflits armés* (2nd edn, Helbing Lichtenhahn 2009) 158; É David, *Principes de droit des conflits armés* (5th edn, Bruylant 2012) 126; H-P Gasser, 'International Humanitarian Law' in H Haug (ed), *Humanity for All: The International Red Cross and Red Crescent Movement* (Henry Dunant Institute 1993) 510–511; K Okimoto, *The Distinction and Relationship between Jus ad Bellum and Jus in Bello* (Hart 2011) 50; contra Sassòli (n 19) 170; Carron (n 28) 193–199; H Levie, 'The Status of Belligerent Personnel Splashed and Rescued by a Neutral in the Persian Gulf Area' (1991) 31 Va JIL 611, 616.

[42] WH Parks, 'Special Forces' Wear of Non-Standard Uniforms' (2003) 4 Chic JIL 493, 499–500 fn 11; R Goodman, 'Is the United States Already in an "International Armed Conflict" with Syria?' (*Just Security*, 11 October 2016) <www.justsecurity.org/33477/united-states-international-armed-conflict-syria/>.

[43] US Department of State, *Cumulative Digest of United States Practice in International Law 1981–1988*, book III (1995) 3456–3457; see also T Friedman, 'Syria Says Airman Seized in U.S. Raid Will not be Freed' *NYT* (6 December 1983) A 1 <www.nytimes.com/1983/12/06/world/syria-says-airman-seized-in-us-raid-will-not-be-freed.html?searchResultPosition=12>.

single soldier may constitute an international armed conflict.[44] Whether it indeed supports this position is open to question. President Reagan initially dismissed the applicability of international armed conflict law to the instance.[45] Moreover, it is unclear whether it was actually the mere capture rather than the prior shooting down of the pilot (to which the US had reacted with airstrikes on Syrian positions) that was decisive for the two States classifying the situation as one to which international armed conflict law applied.[46]

As noted above, and in contrast to the subjective conception of the state of war, the existence of an armed conflict (international or non-international) does not depend on the parties considering themselves to be engaged in a conflict. Subjective elements may, however, subtly play a role in establishing that there is resort to armed force between States. In particular, acts stemming from errors are generally not considered as giving rise to an international armed conflict if the error is one where the respective State had no knowledge of the circumstances constituting a use of force against another State[47] (as distinct from errors about whether the act qualifies as an act of force under international law).[48] One such example is where a State accidentally launches a missile or is unaware that its armed forces have penetrated into another State's territory.[49] The concept of international armed conflict thus seems to contain inherent subjective dimensions.[50] The ICRC suggests that the act of force must express or evidence 'belligerent intent', which is, however, to be objectively deduced from the circumstances in assessing whether a factual situation constitutes a resort to armed force between States.[51]

A particular threshold seems to exist for acts by which a neutral State defends itself against violations of its neutrality by a party to an international armed conflict. As noted in Chapter 2, these acts in defence of one's neutrality may include such force as is necessary to resist the (attempted) infringement of neutrality. Nonetheless, the acts would not forfeit the neutrality of the respective State.[52]

[44] See eg V Koutroulis, 'Jus ad/contra Bellum' in R Van Steenberghe (ed), *Droit international humanitaire: Un régime spécial de droit international?* (Bruylant 2013) 176.

[45] Public Papers of President Reagan (1983) 1733 ('The Syrians claim that he's a prisoner of war. Well, I don't know how you have a prisoner of war when there is no declared war between nations').

[46] See also Carron (n 28) 194.

[47] UK Ministry of Defence, *The Manual of the Law of Armed Conflict* (OUP 2004) 29; Kritsiotis (n 30) 280; J d'Asprémont and J de Hemptinne, *Droit international humanitaire: Thèmes choisis* (Pedone 2012) 49; Vité (n 35) 73; contra Zamir (n 12) 59.

[48] Carron (n 28) 397–407.

[49] For an illustration, see 'Swiss Troops Get Lost in Liechtenstein' *NYT* (3 March 2007) A3 <www.nytimes.com/2007/03/03/world/europe/03swiss.html>.

[50] N Lubell, 'Fragmented Wars: Multi-Territorial Military Operations against Armed Groups' in W Williams and C Ford (eds), *Complex Battlespaces: The Law of Armed Conflict and the Dynamics of Modern Warfare* (OUP 2019) 20.

[51] ICRC Challenges Report (2015) 8; N Melzer, *Targeted Killing in International Law* (OUP 2008) 247, 250. The contours of this subjective dimension remain opaque, particularly the requisite subjective standard. For a discussion of parallel questions specifically in relation to the identification of parties to the conflict, see Chapter 4.3.b.iii.

[52] Chapter 2.2.d.ii.

In other words, such uses of force would not give rise to an international armed conflict between the neutral State and the State having violated its neutrality.[53] Chapter 2 found indications that this idea continues to reflect good law.[54] At the same time, it sits ill with the low threshold for the existence of an international armed conflict. More broadly, the reference to self-defence is in tension with a factual conception of armed conflict since it makes the creation of an international armed conflict dependent on the legal justification of the neutral for using force. The old concept of defence of neutrality should thus only be restrictively applied to avoid frictions with the contemporary international law framework regulating armed conflict within which the concept is now embedded.

(2) Relationship to the jus ad bellum *notion of inter-State force*

A final aspect that merits closer scrutiny is whether the notion of armed force between States for an international armed conflict can be further specified by looking to the *jus ad bellum* prohibition of the use of force under Article 2(4) UN Charter and customary international law. This raises the question whether both regimes are based on the same notion of (inter-State) force.

This point was firmly embraced by Judge Shahabuddeen in his separate opinion in *Tadić*:

> whatever the context, what constitutes a use of force (a necessary element of an 'armed conflict') is so fundamental as to require constancy of principle.... That is a concept of common currency in international law. ... If there was such a use of force by one state against another, *ex definitione* the conflict was international.[55]

Importantly, drawing such a link would not challenge the crucial principle that the equal application of the *jus in bello* to all parties to the conflict must be independent of the legality of their acts under the *jus ad bellum*. To apply the law of international armed conflict, the question would merely be whether there is a prima facie use of force, whether legal or illegal.[56]

Relying on the *jus ad bellum* notion of 'force' is intuitively appealing.[57] After all, the broad underlying real-world phenomenon of inter-State force is the same. This connection comes to the fore, for example, in the Preamble of API, which begins

[53] Oppenheim (n 5) 341; similarly C Chinkin, *Third Parties in International Law* (Clarendon Press 1993) 308 ('it does not seem that a single response in self-defence should alter non-participant status into that of belligerent').

[54] Chapter 2, nn 145–147.

[55] *Tadić* (Appeal Judgment) IT-94-1-A (15 July 1999) sep op Shahabuddeen [22], [24] (emphasis original).

[56] D Akande, 'When Does the Use of Force against a Non-State Armed Group Trigger an International Armed Conflict and Why Does this Matter?' (*EJIL: Talk!*, 18 October 2016) <www.ejiltalk.org/when-does-the-use-of-force-against-a-non-state-armed-group-trigger-an-international-armed-conflict-and-why-does-this-matter/>.

[57] See Akande (n 29) 62.

by recalling the prohibition of the threat or use of force before stating that it is 'necessary nevertheless to reaffirm and develop the provisions protecting the victims of armed conflicts'.

Yet, it is neither impossible nor uncommon for different legal regimes to look at the same factual situation through the lens of similar but distinct concepts that overlap only to a certain extent. The ICJ may have hinted that the respective concepts indeed differ. In *Nicaragua*, the Court opened its 'examination of the international humanitarian law applicable to the dispute' by noting that the 'use of force *may in some circumstances* raise questions of such law'.[58] Kritsiotis takes this passage to mean that:

> [t]he Court, therefore, did not seem to hold to the view that the use of force would in all circumstances create an international armed conflict; it intimated the need to distinguish between those uses of force which would amount to an international armed conflict and those which would not.[59]

While this is a possible reading of the passage, it is not entirely clear that the Court's conception of when a use of force would be constitutive of an international armed conflict was the reason behind it hinting at the possibility that some uses of force would not 'raise questions' of IHL. The Court could also, for example, have meant that the application of IHL would not 'raise questions' worth considering because the Court considered it obvious that IHL was not violated, although there may have been an international armed conflict.

The distinction in the concept of 'force' for both purposes would be more clearly demonstrated if there were cases that international law treated as uses of force for *jus ad bellum* purposes without there being an international armed conflict or vice versa.

Before further inquiring as to whether each *use* of force would constitute an international armed conflict, and vice versa, it should be noted that the *jus ad bellum* prohibition also includes the *threat* of force. Such threats would arguably not necessarily give rise to an international armed conflict.[60] In some—but probably not all—circumstances they may be considered a declaration of war and may thus trigger the application of (some) international armed conflict law.

As regards *uses* of force, several sets of cases are worth considering. First, there may be differences in how the two regimes handle minor incidents. At the outset, it is interesting to note that the debates on a potential 'gravity threshold' for uses of force under the *jus ad bellum*[61] and a potential 'intensity threshold' for

[58] *Military and Paramilitary Activities in and against Nicaragua (Nicaragua v United States)* (Merits) [1986] ICJ Rep 14 [216] (emphasis added).

[59] Kritsiotis (n 30) 279.

[60] n 38.

[61] In favour of such a threshold, see eg O Corten, *The Law against War: The Prohibition on the Use of Force in Contemporary International Law* (Hart 2012) 51ff; contra T Ruys, 'The Meaning of "Force"

international armed conflicts bear striking similarities.[62] Yet, the debates occur separately and may, therefore, yield different outcomes. For example, Koutroulis suggests that there is a better case for the capture of a single individual soldier triggering an international armed conflict[63] than for it constituting a use of force under the *jus ad bellum*.[64] He points to the case of the US pilot captured by Syria, discussed above, which both States qualified as an international armed conflict without invoking the prohibition of the use of force.[65]

Secondly, as will be seen below, the prevailing standards developed in international jurisprudence from a *jus ad bellum* and a *jus in bello* perspective diverge precisely for the factual situation that had prompted Judge Shahabuddeen's separate opinion in *Tadić*, namely cases of assistance by foreign States to non-State groups fighting another State. As regards the *jus ad bellum*, the ICJ in *Nicaragua* found that by arming and training the contras the US had committed a prima facie violation of the prohibition to use force.[66] For an international armed conflict between the State supporting the armed group and the State fighting that group, the 'overall control' test—advanced by the ICTY's majority opinion in *Tadić*—requires material assistance as well as support at the level of coordinating military activity.[67] The 'overall control' test—rather than Judge Shahabuddeen's alternative suggestion of drawing a link to the use of force under the *jus ad bellum*—has become the settled jurisprudence of the ICTY, the SCSL, and the ICC on conflict classification.[68]

and the Boundaries of the Jus ad Bellum: Are "Minimal" Uses of Force Excluded from UN Charter Article 2(4)?' (2014) 108 AJIL 159.

[62] Compare eg the scenarios on the use of force that Corten and Ruys discuss (n 61) and the issues regarding Common Article 2 discussed in the *GCI Commentary* ([236]ff). For a suggestion that the debates on small-scale incidents under the *jus ad bellum* could inform the concept of international armed conflict, see Carron (n 28) 98ff, 231ff.

[63] For references in favour of and against such a view, see nn 30–34.

[64] Koutroulis (n 44) 175.

[65] ibid 175–176. However, in addition to the above-noted ambiguities in this case as to conflict classification (text accompanied by nn 45–46), care should be taken with drawing inferences from the non-invocation of the prohibition of the use of force. Such silence may as much be driven by other considerations as by the view that an incident did not violate the prohibition. See eg D Lewis, N Modirzadeh, and G Blum, 'Quantum of Silence: Inaction and Jus ad Bellum' (2019) HLS PILAC <http://nrs.harvard.edu/urn-3:HUL.InstRepos:40931878>; P Starski, 'Silence within the Process of Normative Change and Evolution of the Prohibition on the Use of Force: Normative Volatility and Legislative Responsibility' (2017) 4 JUOFIL 14; Ruys (n 61) 167ff.

[66] *Nicaragua* (n 58) [228].

[67] *Tadić* (Appeal) (n 55) [131].

[68] See eg *Aleksovski* (Appeal Judgment) IT-95-14/1-A (24 March 2000) [142]ff; *Delalić* (Appeal Judgment) IT-96-21-A (20 February 2001) [15]; *Kordić, Čerkez* (Trial Judgment) IT-95-14/2-T (26 February 2001) [309]ff; *Mladić* (Trial Judgment) IT-09-92-T (22 November 2017) vol 3 [3014]; *Prlić* (Appeal Judgment) IT-04-74-A (29 November 2017) vol 1 [282]ff; *Brima* (Trial) (n [251]; *Lubanga* (Trial Judgment) ICC-01/04-01/06 (14 March 2012) [541]; *Katanga* (Trial Judgment) ICC-01/04-01/07 (7 March 2014) [1178]; *Bemba* (Trial Judgment) ICC-01/05-01/08 (21 March 2016) [130]; *Ntaganda* (Trial Judgment) ICC-01/04-02/06 (8 July 2019) [727]. The ICJ conceded that the 'overall control' test 'may well be ... applicable and suitable' for conflict classification, while rejecting it for the purposes of attribution under the law of State responsibility (*Application of the Convention on the Prevention and Punishment of the Crime of Genocide (Bosnia and Herzegovina v Serbia and Montenegro)* (Merits) [2007] ICJ Rep 43 [404]).

Other international bodies[69] as well as domestic courts[70] have employed the test in that context as well, and the ICRC also follows it.[71] Debates about what constitutes an indirect use of force in such situations under the *jus ad bellum*, in turn, have not aligned with the 'overall control' test.

Overall, international law has not established conceptual uniformity between what constitutes inter-State force under the *jus ad bellum* and for the purpose of establishing the existence of an international armed conflict. There remains room for diverging developments of the concepts under the two regimes, although the practical results yielded by the concepts mostly seem to overlap. At the same time, this does not preclude looking to the *jus ad bellum*—notably for acts qualifying as aggression—as an orientation mark for *jus in bello* purposes. This point will be taken up below.[72]

ii. Non-international armed conflict

The ICTY in *Tadić* characterised non-international armed conflicts as 'protracted armed violence between governmental authorities and organized armed groups or between such groups within a State'.[73] There are thus two elements to the notion of a non-international armed conflict:[74] the first is related to the nature of the parties and the second to the nature of their confrontation. As to the first, Chapter 1 has already set out the degree of organisation that each party to a non-international armed conflict must possess.[75] As to the second, 'protracted armed violence' is commonly understood as referring to the intensity that the violence must reach.[76] This section briefly outlines the rationale for and content of this intensity criterion.

(1) Rationale for the intensity criterion

The requirement that hostilities must reach a certain scale is to be seen against its historical background. The general idea had been that civil war had to display the characteristics of inter-State war to justify treating an internal conflict as a situation of war (if recognition of belligerency was granted)[77] rather than as individual violent acts (that could be addressed purely through domestic law enforcement).[78]

[69] IIFFMCG Report (2009) vol II 302.

[70] See eg Federal Court of Justice, Judgment of 21 February 2001 (3 StR 372/00) BGHSt 46, 292 (*Soloković*) [14].

[71] *GCI Commentary* [271].

[72] Chapter 4.2.a.iii.

[73] *Tadić* (Decision on Jurisdiction) (n 26) [70].

[74] *Tadić* (Trial Judgment) IT-94-1-T (7 May 1997) [562]; for references in State practice to these two elements, see *GCI Commentary* [424]).

[75] Chapter 1.2.b.ii.

[76] *Haradinaj, Balaj, Brahimaj* (Trial Judgment) IT-04-84-T (3 April 2008) [49].

[77] nn 43–44.

[78] See eg Opinion of the Law Officers of 14 August 1867, reproduced in A McNair, *International Law Opinions, Selected and Annotated, Vol I: Peace* (CUP 1956) 143, 144 ('It is always a question of fact... whether the insurrection has or has not assumed the dimensions of war'); see also A Cullen, *The Concept of Non-International Armed Conflict in International Humanitarian Law* (CUP 2010) 17.

In that sense, the intensity requirement would further contribute to the purpose of the requirement of organisation of the parties, that is, ensuring that the armed violence is *collective* in character.[79] Today, of course, the intensity requirement is actually a distinguishing feature, rather than a commonality, of international and non-international armed conflict. As seen above, there is no comparable intensity threshold in the contemporary notion of international armed conflict. That this additional requirement to establish the collective nature of the confrontation persists can be explained by the need to distinguish such violence from that which would be regulated as a matter of domestic law enforcement. Sovereignty concerns play a central role in this distinction since States have been inclined to shield what they perceive as their internal affairs from international legal regulation.[80] Accordingly, Article 1(2) APII, which can be understood to inform the concept of non-international armed conflict under Common Article 3 and customary international law as well,[81] distinguishes non-international armed conflicts from 'situations of internal disturbances and tensions, such as riots, isolated and sporadic acts of violence and other acts of a similar nature'.

(2) *Requirements of the intensity criterion*

Turning to the content of the intensity criterion, the temporal connotation of the word 'protracted' notwithstanding, the duration of the armed violence is but one factor in assessing intensity.[82] International criminal jurisprudence has established a non-exhaustive set of indicators that may be considered in an overall assessment on a case-by-case basis. These indicators include:

> the number, duration and intensity of individual confrontations; the type of weapons and other military equipment used; the number and calibre of munitions fired; the number of persons and type of forces partaking in the fighting; the

[79] See ICRC, 'Opinion Paper: How is the Term "Armed Conflict" Defined in International Humanitarian Law?' (2008) 3 (noting that the intensity threshold may be met 'when the hostilities are of a collective character').

[80] *GCI Commentary* [416]–[417]; *Pictet Commentary GCI* 49–50.

[81] *GCI Commentary* [431]; *AP Commentary* [4473]; see also M Bothe, KJ Partsch, and W Solf, *New Rules for Victims of Armed Conflicts—Commentary on the Two 1977 Protocols Additional to the Geneva Conventions of 1949* (reprint edn, Nijhoff 2013) 719; R Abi-Saab, *Droit humanitaire et conflits internes: Origines et évolution de la réglementation international* (Henry Dunant Institute 1986) 147.

[82] *Haradinaj* (Trial) (n 76) [49]; S Sivakumaran, *The Law of Non-international Armed Conflict* (OUP 2012) 168; L Moir, 'The Concept of Non-International Armed Conflict' in A Clapham, P Gaeta, and M Sassòli (eds), *The 1949 Geneva Conventions: A Commentary* (OUP 2015) 411. International judicial decisions are not, however, entirely consistent on this point, and sometimes lean towards duration as an independent factor, see eg *Bemba* (Trial) (n 68) [139]; *Katanga* (Trial) (n 68154) [1217]; Case C-285/12 *Aboubacar Diakité v Commissaire général aux réfugiés et aux apatrides* (CJEU, 30 January 2014) para 126; for this view, see also Y Dinstein, *Non-International Armed Conflicts in International Law* (2nd edn, CUP 2021) 43–44; for discussion, see M Hrnjaz and J Simentić Popović, 'Protracted Armed Violence as a Criterion for the Existence of Non-international Armed Conflict: International Humanitarian Law, International Criminal Law and Beyond' (2020) 25 JCSL 473 (arguing against duration as an independent criterion).

number of casualties; the extent of material destruction and the number of civilians fleeing combat zones. The involvement of the UN Security Council may also be a reflection of the intensity of a conflict.[83]

(3) Non-international armed conflicts under APII

APII only applies to a more restricted category of non-international armed conflicts, defined by Article 1(1) APII as those:

> which take place in the territory of a High Contracting Party between its armed forces and dissident armed forces or other organized armed groups which, under responsible command, exercise such control over a part of its territory as to enable them to carry out sustained and concerted military operations and to implement this Protocol.

The interplay of these requirements with the identification of the parties to conflicts under APII will be addressed below.[84] At this point, suffice to note that Article 1(1) APII sets out specific requirements relating both to the nature of the parties and to the nature of their confrontation.

As to the party-related criteria, APII only applies to conflicts involving a State on one side, thus excluding those conflicts involving only non-State parties. The non-State side, in turn, must possess a particular degree of organisation, which is characterised by a 'responsible command'. The non-State party must also exercise control over territory, which is conceived of in functional terms: the control must be such 'as to enable them to carry out sustained and concerted military operations and to implement this Protocol'.

On the nature of the confrontation between parties, Article 1(1) APII is understood to require that the conflict must possess a particular degree of intensity and must accordingly be characterised by 'sustained and concerted military operations', even though, on a literal reading, the provision only requires that armed groups have the capacity to engage in such operations. Sivakumaran, for example, considers that '[t]he defining aspect of the Protocol is the intensity of the violence and the implementation of the Protocol'.[85] Some States have also, in their practice,

[83] *Haradinaj* (Trial) (n 76) [49], see also [90]–[99]; accord, with extensive reference to further case law, *Boškoski and Tarčulovski* (Trial Judgment) IT-04-82-T (10 July 2008) [177], [243]; *Đorđević et al* (Trial Judgment) IT-05-87/1-T (23 February 2011) [1523]; *Lubanga* (Trial) (n 68) [538]; *Katanga* (Trial) (n 68) [1187]; *Bemba* (Trial) (n 68) [137]–[141].

[84] Below 4.c.

[85] Sivakumaran (n 82) 186; see also Cullen (n 78) 153–154; M Bradley, 'Additional Protocol II: Elevating the Minimum Threshold of Intensity?' (2020) 102 IRRC 1125, 1130. The difference to the intensity requirement under Common Article 3 and customary international law should not be overstated, see C DeCock, 'Legal Implications Surrounding Operation "Inherent Resolve" in Iraq and Syria' (2017) 47 Isr YHR 69, 115.

apparently determined whether or not APII applies to their operations mainly based on whether they were faced with a conflict of a particular intensity.[86]

Against the background of the concepts of international and non-international armed conflict as set out in this section, the following sections will analyse how these concepts are relevant and relate to identifying parties to armed conflicts.

3. Multiparty conflicts and co-party status: introducing the concepts and their relevance

If armed conflicts under international law were, by definition, bilateral relationships of no more than two entities confronting each other, establishing that an armed conflict exists and identifying two entities as parties to that conflict would merely be two sides of the same coin. This is because, in bilateral conflict settings, an entity will be a party if it fulfils the criteria for the existence of an armed conflict in its relationship to the adverse party. As the following sections will show, however, this is not necessarily the case in multiparty conflict settings. In such settings, the identification of an entity as a party therefore more evidently gives rise to legal questions in its own right. At the outset, it is useful to briefly introduce the idea that the same armed conflict can have multiple parties on each side of the conflict and to clarify why this matters.

For international armed conflicts, Common Article 2 explicitly foresees the possibility of multiparty conflicts by referring to armed conflicts 'between two *or more* of the High Contracting Parties'.[87] Some treaties repeat this wording,[88] while others simply refer to Common Article 2.[89] The possibility of multiple parties fighting on the same side to an international armed conflict is recognised by the reference to 'co-belligerent State[s]' in Article 4(2) GCIV. The possibility is also reflected in international practice, as will be seen throughout this chapter and in subsequent chapters.

The relevant treaty provisions on non-international armed conflicts do not provide a clear answer. Unlike Common Article 2, Common Article 3 leaves open the questions as to whether more than two entities can be parties to a non-international armed conflict. Article 8(2)(f) ICCSt hints at the possibility of multiple entities fighting a non-international armed conflict by referring to the opposing sides in a non-international armed conflict in the plural form as 'governmental authorities

[86] For France's practice, see C Landais, 'Entre l'application du droit et les hostilités, cadre légal et règles d'engagement' in C Marchand (ed), *The Distinction between International and Non-International Armed Conflicts: Challenges for IHL? 38th Round Table on Current Issues of International Humanitarian Law* (Franco Angeli 2015) 132ff.

[87] Emphasis added.

[88] See eg Hague Convention for the Protection of Cultural Property in the Event of Armed Conflict, art 18(1).

[89] See eg API, art 1(3); CCW, art 1(1).

and organized armed groups'.[90] Article 1(1) APII, by contrast, could even be read as implying that, at least on the State side of a non-international armed conflict, there is only one entity, namely the territorial State ('between *its* [ie the territorial State's] armed forces and dissident armed forces').[91] States as well as international courts and tribunals have, however, in different instances considered multiple States and armed groups as parties to the same non-international armed conflict.[92] Emblematically, the ICC in *Bemba* noted:

> that while it is possible for distinct conflicts to be taking place within one territory, the mere fact of involvement of different armed groups does not mean that they are engaged in separate armed conflicts.[93]

As a terminological matter, parties on the same side of a war have traditionally been labelled 'co-belligerents',[94] understood as 'fully fledged belligerent[s] fighting in association with one or more belligerent powers'.[95] Even though the terminology has not always been consistent, the underlying idea is present in many classical treatises of the laws of war. Vattel, for example, referred to 'leagues of war' in which 'each [of the parties] becomes a principal party to the war, and all have the same friends and the same enemies. ... All the rights which war gives me against my principal enemy it gives against all his allies as well.'[96] Since the notions of 'armed conflict' and 'parties to the conflict' have, for the most part, replaced 'war' and 'belligerents' in current international law, multiple parties on the same side of an armed conflict will generally be referred to as 'co-parties', rather than 'co-belligerents', in this book.[97] It is only to capture this idea that the term will be used hereafter, both regarding international and non-international armed conflicts. At this stage, the term does not entail any conclusion as to the criteria for identifying co-parties. It does not imply that any particular concept of 'co-belligerency' is endorsed, such as that associated with patterns of US practice labelling entities as 'co-belligerents' of

[90] See also *Tadić* (Decision on Jurisdiction) (n 26) [70].

[91] Emphasis added. On the scope of APII regarding multiparty conflicts, see below 4.c.

[92] See eg *Danish Manual* 53, fn 34 (regarding Denmark's participation as 'a party to the armed conflict against ISIL in Iraq on the Iraqi side'; T Gill, 'Classifying the Conflict in Syria' (2016) 92 ILS 353, 375. See further below 3.a.ii.

[93] *Bemba* (Trial) (n 68) [129] (footnotes omitted).

[94] R Ingber, 'Co-belligerency' (2016) 42 YJIL 67, 80.

[95] M Greenspan, *The Modern Law of Land Warfare* (University of California Press 1959) 531; E Castrén, *The Present Law of War and Neutrality* (Suomalainen Tiedeakatemia 1954) 35 ('States fighting on the same side').

[96] E de Vattel, *Le Droit des gens, ou, Principes le la loi naturelle, appliqués à la conduite aux affaires des nations et des souverains*, vol III (C Fenwick tr, Carnegie Institution 1916) 261, 264; H Halleck, *International Law or, Rules Regulating the Intercourse Between States in Peace and War* (Bancroft 1861) 413.

[97] For a synonymous use of 'belligerent' and 'party to an armed conflict', see T Gill, 'Belligerents' in D Djuić and N Pons (eds), *The Companion to International Humanitarian Law* (Brill 2018) 211.

al-Qaeda (under international law) to justify increasingly extensive targeting and detention practices (notably under domestic law).[98]

Whether multiple entities qualify as co-parties to the same armed conflict is relevant in several respects.

First, it matters for the legal position of the respective entity. With respect to every armed conflict, a particular entity can only qualify as either a party or a third party. The legal position of an entity as a party, as set out in Part I of the book, only relates to the specific conflict to which the entity is a party, while it is a third party with respect to conflicts that are fought by others.

Accordingly, it is significant whether a specific entity is identified as an (additional) co-party to an armed conflict that would also exist without that co-party, rather than as a third party with respect to the conflict. Consider, for example, the number of States having joined the conflict against ISIL as part of Operation Inherent Resolve only after the US and several other States had already initiated the conflict through their first strikes. Ascertaining co-party status matters to ascertain which sets of duties and rights apply to the respective entity (namely, those of parties or of third parties).[99] It also matters for the legal position of individuals connected to that collective entity[100] as well as, for example, for the geographical scope of application of IHL in relation to that conflict.[101]

By the same token, it is crucial to distinguish whether several entities are co-parties to the same conflict or parties to separate armed conflicts. This is because, in the latter case, they would be third parties regarding the conflict fought by the other party. They would thus, for example, bear the duties of third parties towards parties to that other conflict (such as duties under neutrality law) and not the (broader) duties flowing from party status as regards protected individuals who are affected by that particular conflict. This is also the case where several entities fight separate parallel armed conflicts against the same opponent without being co-parties to a single multiparty armed conflict.[102] A party can simultaneously be involved in separate armed conflicts. Its opponents in the respective conflicts would then be third parties vis-à-vis each other. Russia, for example, has been occupying parts of Ukrainian territory since 2014 and been present with forces in eastern Ukraine without Ukraine's consent,[103] and it invaded other parts of Ukraine in 2022,[104] in parallel to the ongoing occupation of regions in Georgia

[98] For a critical discussion of this practice, see Chapter 4.2.b.i.

[99] Chapter 1.3., Chapter 2.

[100] Chapter 1.4.

[101] Chapter 1.5.

[102] As will be argued in Chapter 4.3.b.ii.(1), the mere fact of having a common opponent does not, without more, make two entities co-parties to one conflict.

[103] On the classification of the conflicts in Ukraine, see R Heinsch, 'Conflict Classification in Ukraine: The Return of the "Proxy War"?' (2015) 91 ILS 323, 352–360. See also n 107.

[104] RULAC, 'International armed conflict in Ukraine' <www.rulac.org/browse/conflicts/international-armed-conflict-in-ukraine#collapse2accord>.

(South Ossetia and Abkhazia)[105] and Moldova (Transnistria).[106] Absent additional connections between Russia's respective opponent States, Ukraine, Georgia, and Moldova would be third parties with respect to each other's conflicts with Russia. Similarly, Syria may have been involved in parallel international armed conflicts with Turkey intervening, inter alia, against Kurdish rebels on Syrian territory, and with coalition States intervening against ISIL as part of Operation Inherent Resolve (including, for example, the US, Australia, the UK, Belgium, France, and the Netherlands), both without Syria's consent.[107]

That several entities may qualify as co-parties to the same armed conflict also matters on another level, namely for establishing the criteria for the existence of an international or non-international armed conflict (outlined in section 1 of this chapter) in multiparty settings. The next section will turn to this question.

4. Establishing multiparty conflicts and identifying co-parties

Building on the idea set out in the previous section that the same armed conflict can have multiple co-parties, this section shows how the requirements for the existence of an armed conflict are established in multiparty conflicts. Doing so will help clarify the extent to which the criteria for the existence of an armed conflict inform the criteria for identifying (co-)parties to an armed conflict.

Section a. argues that the existence of an armed conflict may be established in an aggregated assessment of the activities performed by different prospective co-parties. That is, it is sufficient that the co-parties jointly fulfil the requirements for the existence of an armed conflict. By implication, the entities do not have to fulfil these requirements separately so as to be identified as co-parties. Such an aggregation is, however, only permissible for those criteria that relate to the nature of the confrontation between the potential parties (ie the existence of a recourse to armed force in international armed conflicts and protracted armed violence in non-international armed conflicts). By contrast, as section b. makes clear, the conditions related to the nature and structure of the prospective co-party itself,

[105] See eg *Georgia v Russia (II)* App no 38263/08 (ECtHR, 21 January 2021) 54–65.

[106] RULAC, 'Military occupation of Moldova by Russia' <www.rulac.org/browse/conflicts/military-occupation-of-moldova-by-russia>.

[107] For the view that non-consensual interventions on the territory of another State automatically give rise to international armed conflicts (leaving aside the potential parallel non-international armed conflicts with armed groups), see generally Akande (n 29) 53; *GCI Commentary* [262]; D Fleck, 'The Law of Non-International Armed Conflict' in D Fleck (ed), *The Handbook of International Humanitarian Law* (4th edn, OUP 2021) 638; Milanović and Hadzi-Vidanović (n 30) 296; against the view that the absence of consent by the territorial State necessarily gives rise to an international armed conflict where interventions are exclusively directed against armed groups in the respective territory N Lubell, 'The War (?) against Al Qaeda' in E Wilmshurst (ed), *International Law and the Classification of Conflicts* (OUP 2012) 432–433; Gill (n 92) 367; Sassòli (n 19) 172; Carron (n 28) 362–363.

notably the organisation requirement in non-international armed conflicts, must be met separately by each co-party.

Section c. then applies this reasoning to the particular requirements for a non-international armed conflict to be covered by APII and shows to what extent these requirements may be fulfilled jointly by all co-parties or must be fulfilled separately by each co-party.

Through the lens of the argument developed in this chapter, section d. finally explains that there is a structural limitation to the possibility of multiple entities being co-parties to the same armed conflict. The limitation concerns such conflict settings where a State and a non-State armed group cooperate against an adverse State.

a. Aggregated assessment of co-parties' activities

This section first explains the idea of aggregating the activities of multiple potential co-parties in assessing the conflict-related requirements of international and non-international armed conflicts. The section does so by contrasting aggregated and separate assessments of the activities by each co-party. In a second step, the section illustrates how the existence of an armed conflict has been established in international practice. Against this background, the section then sets out the rationale for an aggregated assessment and responds to criticism that such an assessment has faced or could face. The section concludes that each co-party's contribution need not be separately assessed so long as all co-parties, taken together, meet the conflict-related requirements for establishing an armed conflict.

i. Idea and implications of an aggregated assessment

The very possibility of multiple entities being co-parties to the same armed conflict means that the requirements for the existence of an armed conflict and for identifying an entity as a (co-)party to that conflict may differ. This is because it is conceivable in such cases that an armed conflict exists overall between the adverse sides, even if the requirements for the existence of an armed conflict are not met separately by every single co-party in its relationship to the opponent. This would mean aggregating the conduct of prospective co-parties rather than measuring their respective contributions separately against the requirements for the existence of an armed conflict.

At the outset, several clarifications are in order. First, the argument relates to how the requirements of the concepts of international and non-international armed conflict are to be assessed. It does not suggest altering these concepts altogether.[108]

[108] T Ferraro, 'The Applicability and Application of International Humanitarian Law to Multinational Forces' (2013) 95 IRRC 561, 584; Lubell (n 50) 25.

Secondly, the argument here only relates to the assessment of those elements of the concepts of international and non-international armed conflict that pertain to the nature of the confrontation between the opponents, that is, a resort to armed force in international armed conflicts and protracted armed violence in non-international armed conflicts. The argument does not concern those requirements relating to the nature of the respective entities (ie statehood in international armed conflicts, with some exceptions, and sufficient organisation in non-international armed conflicts), the assessment of which section b. will address. Thirdly, while multiple prospective co-parties may be jointly assessed against the requirements for the existence of an armed conflict, they will still need to individually fulfil other criteria to be identified as a co-party. Chapter 4 will analyse these requirements in detail. With these clarifications in mind, it is useful to set out how this aggregated assessment would play out in international and non-international armed conflicts respectively.

As regards international armed conflicts, it has been seen in section 2 of this chapter that the notion of resort to armed force between States is not to be understood as having a particular intensity threshold. Nonetheless, it requires acts of a certain nature or quality to constitute an international armed conflict. In particular, it has been noted that not all acts that would be regulated as acts of 'hostilities' or 'military operations' as part of an international armed conflict would also suffice to separately constitute an international armed conflict in the first place.[109] Indeed, in multiparty settings, there may be entities whose conduct would not constitute an international armed conflict if assessed separately but would if assessed together with the conduct of its potential co-parties.[110] Consider, for example, that States A, B, and C form a coalition as part of which A and B carry out airstrikes against State X, while State C provides air-to-air refuelling for these strikes. If it were not for the strikes by A and B, C's conduct would not constitute or form part of a resort to armed force against X. This is possible only if the activities of the potential co-parties are viewed in conjunction. An illustration for this scenario in recent international practice may be found in States like Germany and Italy having provided air-to-air refuelling to those coalition States that carry out airstrikes against ISIL on Syrian territory under Operation Inherent Resolve[111] (to the extent that one prescribes to the view that this non-consensual intervention on Syrian

[109] Above 2.b.i.(1).

[110] See alsoN Verlinden, '"Are We at War?" State Support to Parties to Armed Conflict: Consequences under *Jus in Bello*, *Jus ad Bellum* and Neutrality Law' (PhD, KU Leuven 2019) 96–98; against the view that aggregated assessments may be relevant in IACs R van Steenberghe, 'Les Interventions militaires étrangères récentes contre le terrorisme international. Seconde partie: Droit applicable (jus in bello)' (2017) 63 AFDI 37, 52; T Ferraro, 'The ICRC's Legal Position on the Notion of Armed Conflict Involving Foreign Intervention and on Determining the IHL Applicable to this Type of Conflict' (2015) 97 IRRC 1227, 1228.

[111] For reference to and analysis of practice on this case, see Chapter 4, text accompanied by nn 259–260.

territory gives rise to an international armed conflict with Syria—in addition to a non-international armed conflict with ISIL—and provided that Germany and Italy's assistance did not necessarily involve presence on Syrian territory).[112]

More difficult to imagine are scenarios in which the contributions of multiple States must be taken together to establish that an international armed conflict exists, while none of their individual contributions would suffice to do so. An example for this scenario would be a blockade that is put into place by multiple States and is only effective as long as all of these States continue to uphold their contribution.

Moreover, aggregated assessments of the contributions by multiple potential co-parties would be relevant in international armed conflicts for the application of neutrality law on the view that this body of law as a whole or at least some of its rules apply to international armed conflicts of a certain intensity only.[113] On this view, it matters whether, for establishing that a sufficiently intense international armed conflict exists, the confrontation between all co-parties and the adverse side may be assessed by aggregation or whether this assessment would have to be bilateralised. The latter solution would mean that, in the case of a multiparty international armed conflict, such as the Iraq conflict in 2003, neutrality law would have possibly only applied to the relationship of third States with the US and Iraq. By contrast, neutrality law would not have applied to the relationship with other co-parties of the US, such as Spain or Kuwait (if these States' confrontation with Iraq would not, in isolation, have been sufficiently intense for applying neutrality law on this view).[114] This solution would lead the purpose of the impartiality principle underlying neutrality law ad absurdum. It may also be practically impossible to implement, since it would mean that a third State might have been prohibited from assisting Iraq against the US but would have been allowed to support it against those other States, and vice versa.

In non-international armed conflicts, the intensity threshold means that there are considerable implications of whether or not the conduct of multiple entities is assessed separately or in aggregation against the requirements for the existence of a non-international armed conflict. Protracted armed violence could be found to exist overall, even if not all potential co-parties' activities would separately meet this requirement in the confrontation with the adverse side. Consider, for example, as a variant of the above illustration, Germany's provision of air-to-air refuelling to coalition States carrying out airstrikes against ISIL in Iraq with Iraq's consent. It is also conceivable that *none* of the prospective co-parties would separately meet

[112] On these classification issues, see n 107.

[113] Chapter 2, nn 83–85.

[114] For the US's view considering these and other States as its 'co-belligerents' in the conflict with Iraq, see US Office of the Legal Counsel to the President, 'Memorandum Opinion: "Protected Person" Status in Occupied Iraq under the Fourth Geneva Convention' (2004) 28 Op OLC 35, 44; see also below text accompanied by n 117 and Chapter 4, n 277.

the intensity threshold, but that their conduct would constitute protracted armed violence (with the adverse side) only if assessed jointly. This may, for example, be the case where several States in cooperation simultaneously carry out single strikes against an armed group, or where multiple armed groups work together to put up sufficiently intense fighting against the territorial State. Here the intensity threshold sets non-international armed conflicts apart from international armed conflicts, where there is no need to accumulate different contributions to reach such a threshold. As illustrated by the instances of practice reviewed in the following section, aggregated assessments can also considerably ease evidentiary difficulties that would arise if it were necessary to show that each entity's activities separately met the intensity threshold.[115]

To sum up, whether an aggregated or a separate assessment of multiple co-parties against the criteria for the existence of an armed conflict is required has significant implications. How these implications play out varies for international and non-international armed conflicts in light of the differences between the two concepts of armed conflict. The practical ramifications of aggregated assessments will be illustrated further by reviewing relevant instances in international practice.

ii. Aggregated assessments in international practice

International practice has not explicitly settled how the requirements for the existence of an armed conflict must be assessed in multiparty settings. Scrutinising how this assessment has been carried out in practice may, however, reveal the conception underlying the mode of assessment. Through an illustrative survey of instances of State practice and decisions by international courts and tribunals, it will be shown that many such instances can plausibly be read as being based on an aggregated assessment of the contributions by multiple co-parties.

(1) International armed conflicts

Explicit assessments of the legal requirements for international armed conflicts are scarce in international practice. This is also true in multiparty settings. While the constitutive elements of non-international armed conflicts are routinely assessed, particularly in the practice of international tribunals, this is rarer in international armed conflicts. For international armed conflicts, it is accordingly harder to pin down who among several cooperating States was in practice measured against the requirement of recourse to armed force between States.

This caveat notwithstanding, instances in practice where States assisting others in armed conflict were identified as co-parties were seemingly not based on a separate assessment of whether the conduct of each State would have constituted a resort to armed force if assessed in isolation. In particular, there are

[115] Below ii.(3).

instances where parties were considered as co-parties to an international armed conflict based on conduct that could not have constituted an international armed conflict on its own but only when seen in conjunction with the conduct of co-parties. For example, during the Iran–Iraq conflict, Iran deemed several Arab States as Iraq's co-parties, including Kuwait. Iran did so on the basis that Kuwait had, inter alia, allowed the use of its territory for military operations by Iraq against Iran and provided a range of military, logistical, and other support to the Iraqi operations.[116] Along similar lines, the US considered Kuwait and Qatar, among others, as its co-parties during the Iraq conflict beginning in 2003.[117] As a general matter, the US seems to have considered that 'direct operational support', and not only 'directly engaging in armed force', would suffice to make a State a co-party alongside the US.[118] Chapter 4 will examine these instances of practice in greater detail.[119] At this point, suffice it to note that in none of these cases were the acts of support separately assessed as to whether they constituted 'resort to armed force' that could have given rise to an international armed conflict on its own. Implicitly, they seem instead to have been considered in conjunction with the forcible acts that they facilitated. This idea can also be observed in the assessments of the existence of non-international armed conflicts, as will now be shown.

(2) Non-international armed conflicts

A range of instances from international practice of multiparty non-international armed conflicts illustrate that the intensity threshold does not seem to be assessed separately with respect to each co-party. This pattern can be observed for cooperation among States as well as cooperation of States with non-State armed groups and among such groups.

(a) Inter-State cooperation Consider, for example, the operations in Syria and Iraq carried out as part of Operation Inherent Resolve.[120] The US simply noted

[116] 'Letter Dated 14 August 1987 from the Permanent Representative of the Islamic Republic of Iran to the United Nations Addressed to the Secretary-General' UN Doc S/19041 [4]; *Oil Platforms (Iran v United States)* Reply and Defence to Counterclaim Iran (10 March 1999) [2.21]–[2.26]); *Oil Platforms (Iran v United States)* Further Response Iran (24 September 2001) [3.23]–[3.27]; for further analysis and references to international reactions, see also Chapter 4, text accompanied by nn 55–59.

[117] OLC Memo, 44.

[118] 10 USC 948a(3) (2009). For context, see Chapter 4, text accompanied by n 163.

[119] Chapter 4.2.a.ii, 3.b.i.(2), 3.c.ii.

[120] Since the coalition operated with the consent of the Iraqi government, the State practice concerning the conflict with ISIL on Iraqi territory will be categorised here as pertaining to a non-international armed conflict. While the absence of consent from the Syrian government can, on one view, give rise to an international armed conflict between Syria and the States intervening on its territory (n 107), the foreign coalition States can arguably, nevertheless, be regarded as involved in a non-international armed conflict with ISIL. See eg *GCI Commentary* [237], [404]; A Haque, 'Whose Armed Conflict? Which Law of Armed Conflict?' (2017) 45 Ga JICL 475, 482ff; Gill (n 92) 366ff; Sassòli (n 19) 171ff.

that IHL applied to the coalition operations without singling out different States and assessing their individual contributions against the intensity threshold.[121] France also noted that it was involved in a non-international armed conflict in Iraq by referring to the high intensity of the acts of the coalition as a whole rather than separately assessing the intensity of its own activities.[122] In the context of the coalition operations in Syria and Iraq, some statements of the intervening States hint at the possibility that these States could be considered parties during the initial phase of their participation in cooperative operations. This would be significant since, on orthodox accounts, single strikes would not fulfil the intensity requirement in non-international armed conflicts.[123] The instances where such strikes were considered as regulated by IHL can thus be an implicit indicator that they were not separately assessed against the intensity threshold in these cooperative settings. Canada, for example, considered IHL to apply to its first airstrikes conducted in Syria under Operation Impact in 2015.[124] Other States participating in the international coalition against ISIL seem to suggest that all of their strikes complied with IHL, which would include the first strikes upon joining the coalition, regardless of when exactly that particular State's own actions crossed the intensity threshold. For example, the Dutch Ministry of Defence reportedly stated that: '[*o*]*nly* military targets that meet the criteria of international humanitarian law are targeted. ... For *each* deployment of combat aircraft, the risk of civilian casualties has to be minimized.'[125] Similarly, the Belgian Ministry of Defence reportedly insisted that Belgium's strikes were 'fully compatible with our obligations under international humanitarian law'.[126] More generally, Koutroulis points out that none of the coalition partners seems to have denied the application of IHL to its first strikes on the basis that these would not reach the intensity threshold in the confrontation with ISIL.[127] A UN report into the situation in Iraq also found

[121] US, 'Central Command News Release: CJTF-OIR Completes Civilian Casualty Investigation' 21 May 2015 <www.centcom.mil/MEDIA/PRESS-RELEASES/Press-Release-View/Article/1093845/cjtf-oir-completes-civilian-casualty-investigation/>.

[122] Landais (n 86) 134–135.

[123] Above 2.b.ii.

[124] Canadian Department of National Defense, 'Press Release: First Airstrike Conducted in Syria under Operation Impact' 9 April 2015 <https://skiesmag.com/press-releases/firstairstrikeconductedinsyriaunderoperationimpact/>. It is important to note, however, that Canada had carried out airstrikes against ISIL in Iraq since November 2014 and continued to do so in parallel to the strikes in Syria. The airstrikes in Syria could thus be viewed as a mere extension of the non-international armed conflict with ISIL in Iraq, which had crossed the intensity threshold at that point (V Koutroulis, 'The Fight against the Islamic State and Jus in Bello' (2016) 29 LJIL 827, 841). Moreover, the potential parallel international armed conflict between the intervening States and Syria (see n 107) could allow applying IHL to the 'opening phase of hostilities' regardless of intensity questions (*GCI Commentary* [240]).

[125] Airwars, 'Cause for Concern: Civilians Killed in Coalition Strikes' (August 2015) <https://airwars.org/wp-content/uploads/2015/08/airwars-cause-for-concern-civilians-killed-by-coalition.pdf> 31 (emphasis added).

[126] ibid 29.

[127] Koutroulis (n 124) 832, 841.

the coalition States to be parties to a non-international armed conflict without distinctly assessing the intensity regarding individual States' contributions.[128]

Turning to the conflict in Yemen, the German Higher Administrative Court for North Rhine-Westphalia found the US to be involved in a non-international armed conflict in Yemen through its drone strikes in support of the Yemeni government against AQAP ('al-Qaeda in the Arab Peninsula') and groups affiliated with ISIL.[129] In this case, the US strikes may potentially have reached the non-international armed conflict threshold separately.[130] Crucially, however, the Court did not engage in such an analysis but instead assessed the intensity of the conflict as a whole.[131] The Court noted that the US had carried out strikes as part of this non-international armed conflict, that the strikes were thus governed by IHL, and that there were 'serious doubts' as to whether they complied with IHL, notably with the principle of distinction.[132] The German federal government also seems to have conceded that the US strikes in Yemen were part of an ongoing non-international armed conflict (involving the Yemeni government and armed groups as well).[133] A subsequent UN report similarly considered that the US strikes were 'to be examined through the lens of a non-international armed conflict' and that their legality had to be assessed against the applicable US obligations under IHL.[134] Importantly, the report reached its finding on the basis that the strikes had 'reportedly been launched in support of the Government of Yemen's fight against Al Qaeda as a non-State armed group', and not on the basis of a separate assessment of the intensity of the strikes in isolation.[135]

[128] OHCHR, 'Report on the Protection of Civilians in Armed Conflict in Iraq: 11 September 2014–10 December 2014' <www.ohchr.org/sites/default/files/Documents/Countries/IQ/UNAMI_OHCHR_Sep_Dec_2014.pdf> 17, 27.

[129] Higher Administrative Court for North Rhine-Westphalia, Judgment of 19 March 2019 (4 A 1361/15) [434]ff (for an unofficial translation of the oral pronouncement, see <www.ecchr.eu/fileadmin/Juristische_Dokumente/OVG_Muenster_oral_declaration_of_judgment_19_March_2019_EN.pdf>). This aspect of the judgment was upheld on appeal, see Federal Administrative Court, Judgment of 25 November 2020 (6 C 7/19) [72].

[130] R Chesney, 'Yemen Is a Hot Battlefield' (*lawfare*, 7 March 2012) <www.lawfareblog.com/yemen-hot-battlefield>; R Chesney, 'Who May Be Killed? Anwar al-Awlaki as a Case Study in the International Legal Regulation of Lethal Force' (2011) 13(2010) YIHL 3, 31–32 (who does not, however, assess the US's contribution in isolation).

[131] Higher Administrative Court North Rhine-Westphalia, Judgment of 19 March 2019 (n 129) [438].

[132] ibid [453], [456]. Although the Court does not explicitly state that the US had become a party to that non-international armed conflict, this is implicit in the Court's suggestion that the US may have violated IHL obligations incumbent on parties, as well as in the reference to 'opposite conflict parties' of the US in Yemen (ibid [499]). The findings on potential international law violations by the US were not upheld on appeal, irrespective of whether the US was a party, for reasons of evidence and the customary law status of relevant IHL provisions (Federal Administrative Court, Judgment of 25 November 2020 (n [62]–[65], [73]–[74]).

[133] German Federal Parliament, Stenographic Protocol 89th Session 1st Parliamentary Inquiry Commission (25 February 2016) 38.

[134] OHCHR, 'Expert Group Report on the Situation of Human Rights in Yemen' (A/HRC/42/CRP.1) 3 September 2019 [53].

[135] ibid.

Regarding the conflict in Afghanistan, the German Federal Prosecutor assessed alleged war crimes in connection with airstrikes carried out by US fighter jets in Kunduz on 4 September 2009. The strikes had been requested by a German colonel and had resulted in many civilian casualties. In his note on the closing of investigations in 2010, the Prosecutor General considered the Afghan government and ISAF forces to be involved (as parties) in a non-international armed conflict with the Taliban and affiliated groups, without conducting separate intensity assessments on the State side or the non-State side.[136] Tasked with assessing potential compensation claims against the Federal Republic of Germany related to this case, German courts also found that a non-international armed conflict existed 'between the Afghan security forces and the supporting ISAF troops, on one side, and the insurgent Taliban on the other side'.[137]

On the situation in Afghanistan, the ICC's Prosecutor as well as the Court broadly assessed the intensity of clashes between 'pro-government forces' and 'anti-government armed groups' and noted that the former comprised the Afghan authorities as well as international forces and pro-government militia.[138]

Finally, having identified the legal regime applicable to its intervention in the Central African Republic in support of the government, France has considered itself to be involved in a non-international armed conflict. This consideration seems to have been based on an assessment that the hostilities between the factions of the pre-existing conflict at the time of its intervention had fulfilled the requirement of intensity, rather than having been based on a separate assessment of France's own confrontations with the armed groups.[139]

In sum, the intensity threshold was not assessed separately for each potential co-party in any of these instances of inter-State cooperation.

(b) Cooperation between States and armed groups as well as among multiple armed groups Just as between States, there are similar instances of cooperation of States with non-State armed groups and between such groups in which different entities were regarded as parties to the same non-international armed conflict without a distinct assessment of whether their conduct would have met the intensity threshold in isolation.

In *Tadić*, for example, the ICTY Trial Chamber found that a non-international armed conflict was taking place in Bosnia and Herzegovina 'between the

136 Federal Prosecutor General, Note of 16 April 2010 (3 BJs 6/10-4) 43.

137 Regional Court of Bonn, Judgment of 12 November 2013 (1 O 460/11) [51] (own translation); confirmed on appeal at second and third instance, without further analysis on this point (Higher Regional Court of Cologne, Judgment of 30 April 2015 (I-7 U 4/14) and Federal Court of Justice, Judgment of 6 October 2016 (III ZR 140/15)).

138 *Afghanistan* (Investigation Request) ICC-02/17-7-Conf-Exp (20 November 2017) [125]–[128], [130], [135]–[137]; *Afghanistan* (Investigation Decision) ICC-02/17 (12 April 2019) [65]. See also nn 158–160.

139 Landais (n 86) 134.

Government of the Republic of Bosnia and Herzegovina, on the one hand, and, on the other hand, the Bosnian Serb forces, elements of the [Armed Forces of the Federal Republic of Yugoslavia] ... and various paramilitary groups'.[140] In assessing the intensity threshold, the Trial Chamber did not distinguish the activities by the different entities.[141] While this case admittedly remains somewhat ambiguous,[142] the case law of the ICC provides several more explicit examples, which merit closer inspection.

In *Katanga* and *Ntaganda*, the ICC aggregated the acts of different cooperating armed groups to assess the intensity threshold. The allegations against Katanga pertained to the 'Bogoro massacre' in 2003. The massacre occurred as part of a confrontation between the Ngiti militia, whose leader Germain Katanga was, with another armed group, the UPC (Union des Patriotes Congolais). In the preparations of its attacks, the Ngiti militia was heavily supported in various ways by the APC (Armée Populaire Congolaise), an armed group operating as the military wing of the political party, RCD-ML (Rassemblement Congolais pour la Démocratie-Mouvement de Libération). The APC logistically supported, trained, and equipped the Ngiti specifically for the Bogoro attacks, thereby ensuring their decisive military advantage over the UPC.[143] The APC also played a role in planning and coordinating the attacks.[144] Regarding the actual clashes in Bogoro, however, the Chamber found that 'there are strong indications that they [ie APC fighters] [took part in combat alongside the Ngiti] in very limited numbers' only.[145] Despite the close ties between the Ngiti and the APC, the Chamber viewed them as separate, sufficiently organised (co-)parties to the non-international armed conflict with the UPC.[146] When assessing the intensity of the hostilities, the Chamber then simply noted that: '[t]he armed conflict between the aforementioned groups was ... a protracted armed conflict between organised armed groups'.[147]

These conflict relationships, among many other conflicts taking place in the DRC at that time,[148] were also at issue in *Ntaganda*. The charges against Ntaganda, a leading figure of the UPC, related to assaults on various villages. During these assaults, the UPC clashed with, inter alia, the APC and the Ngiti militia (to which the Chamber here referred to as 'FNI/FRPI').[149] As in *Katanga*, the Chamber

[140] *Tadić* (Trial) (n 26) [566].

[141] ibid [563]–[568]; see also M Zwanenburg, 'Double Trouble: The "Cumulative Approach" and the "Support-Based Approach" in the Relationship between Non-State Armed Groups' (2021) 22(2019) YIHL 43, 48.

[142] The Court at one point speaks of 'conflicts' in the plural form (*Tadić* (Trial) (n 26) [566]) while otherwise using the singular only (see eg ibid [567]).

[143] *Katanga* (Trial) (n 68) [636]–[651]; [681].

[144] ibid [631]–[632].

[145] ibid [743].

[146] ibid [1211]. On this aspect of the judgment, see below the text accompanied by nn 211–212.

[147] *Katanga* (Trial) (n 68) [1218].

[148] On the multitude of conflicts in the DRC at the time, see generally *Lubanga* (Trial) (n 68) [543]ff.

[149] *Ntaganda* (Trial) (n 68) [33]ff; on the support relationship, see also *Lubanga* (Trial) (n 68) [544]–[545].

considered these two groups as 'allies' in the conflict with the UPC, but as separate organised armed groups.[150] The Chamber then concluded that:

> the fighting between the UPC/FPLC and the opposing organised armed groups, specifically the APC and its allies, the FNI/FRPI and the Lendu fighters, met the relevant intensity requirement.[151]

In *Bemba*, the Trial Chamber made similar findings for armed groups cooperating with State armed forces in the Central African Republic. During the relevant period, Bemba was the leader of the MLC party (Mouvement de Libération du Congo), and the Commander-in-Chief of its military branch, the ALC (Armée de Libération du Congo).[152] The charges concerned a military operation by the MLC against rebel groups in the Central African Republic, requested by the government of the Central African Republic. On the ground, the cooperation between the government forces and the MLC was such that the MLC mainly fought the opposing rebels and received assistance from the government of the Central African Republic through a small number of government forces frequently accompanying them and by way of logistical support, such as transport.[153] Through the Central African Republic government, there also seems to have been a considerable degree of coordination among different forces supporting the president.[154] The Chamber observed that this operation had taken place in the context of a non-international armed conflict 'between government authorities of the Central African Republic, supported by the MLC, amongst others, on the one hand, and the organized armed group lead by General Bozizé, on the other hand'.[155] The Chamber thus considered the Central African Republic and the MLC as co-parties.[156] It did not distinguish their respective activities in assessing the intensity threshold but, instead, assessed them together.[157]

Such patterns can also be observed in the ICC Prosecutor's and the Court's assessment of the situation in Afghanistan. The Prosecutor examined the intensity of the hostilities between the Afghan government forces, international forces, and pro-government militia, on the one hand, and the Taliban and different 'affiliated' groups (notably the Haqqani Network) on the other hand, overall, without distinguishing between the violence specifically carried out by each of the different entities.[158] Concerning the organisation requirement, however, the Prosecutor

[150] *Ntaganda* (Trial) (n 68) [711], [713], [714].

[151] ibid [725]. The FLPC—Forces Patriotiques pour la Libération du Congo—was the military wing of the UPC, see *Lubanga* (Trial) (n 68) [543].

[152] *Bemba* (Trial) (n 68) [1].

[153] ibid [411]–[412].

[154] *Bemba* (Confirmation of Charges) ICC-01/05-01/08 (15 June 2009) [242], [259].

[155] *Bemba* (Trial) (n 68) [131].

[156] See also ibid [652], [661].

[157] ibid [137]–[141], [658], [662]–[663].

[158] *Afghanistan Investigation Request* (n 138) [126], [130], [135]–[137].

clearly distinguished between the different armed groups and carefully considered each of them separately.[159] The Pre-Trial Chamber seems to have confirmed this approach, albeit without further reasoning and rather summarily. It took note of the 'protracted armed hostilities between governmental authorities and organised groups'—hinting at a joint assessment of all co-parties for intensity purposes—while finding 'that the different anti-governmental armed groups ... qualify as organised armed groups'.[160]

Similarly, in his 2013 order closing the investigation into the killing of a rebel group member (a German national) in Mir Ali (north-western Pakistan) in 2010, the German Federal Prosecutor General considered the Taliban and affiliated groups as parties to a non-international armed conflict with the Afghan government and ISAF forces in Afghanistan. In parallel, he found al-Qaeda as well as local armed groups supported by al-Qaeda to be parties to a non-international armed conflict with Pakistan. For both conflicts, the Prosecutor General concluded that the intensity requirement was met without a distinct assessment of each party's activities.[161]

Further illustrations in international practice where the intensity threshold was (explicitly or implicitly) assessed jointly for multiple co-parties will be encountered in the course of the analysis of the requirements for identifying entities as co-parties in Chapter 4. One such example is the controversial US practice of considering 'associated forces' of al-Qaeda as al-Qaeda's co-parties to the non-international armed conflict with the US. The problematic conceptual origins of this practice as well as its opaque contours are scrutinised below.[162] It may be noted at this point already, however, that the US does not seem to require each co-party to fulfil the intensity requirement separately. Instead, the US qualified groups as 'associated forces' of al-Qaeda that did not engage in intense hostilities against the US, such as al-Shabaab.[163]

(3) Interim conclusion: making sense of the practice In the multiparty conflicts analysed above, States and international judicial bodies did not separately assess whether the contribution of each co-party would have met the requirements for the existence of an international or non-international armed conflict respectively. The mere fact that they did not do so, however, does not necessarily mean that they did not consider such a separate assessment to be a legal requirement.

159 ibid [129]–[134].
160 *Afghanistan* (Investigation Decision) (n 138) [65].
161 Federal Prosecutor General, Order of 20 June 2013 (3 BJs 7/12-4) 19–21.
162 Chapter 4.2.b.i.
163 See eg US, 'Report on the Legal and Policy Frameworks Guiding the United States' Use of Military Force and Related National Security Operations' (December 2016) 17; J Johnson, 'National Security Law, Lawyers, and Lawyering in the Obama Administration—Dean's Lecture at Yale Law School, February 22, 2012' (2012) 31 Yale L Pol Rev 141, 146; S Preston, 'Policy Address: "Legal Framework for the U.S. Use of Military Force Since 9/11"' (2015) 109 ASIL Proc 331, 333.

Absent explicit statements on whether each co-party must separately fulfil the requirements for the existence of an armed conflict, these instances of international practice allow for different readings. In some cases, it may also have been the case that each co-party would have obviously met these requirements. A separate assessment would thus not have made any difference to the outcome. It could thus be claimed that there was no practical need to engage with the factual and legal complexities of separating the cooperation partners for this assessment.

Indeed, in some of the above instances, there may have been a good case for finding that each co-party would have met the requirements for the existence of an armed conflict (had the contributions been assessed in isolation). In others, however, this is less certain. First strikes by States joining their coalition partners in non-international armed conflicts may be cases in point here. Yet, these cases should, of course, be taken with a grain of salt, given the ambiguity on the part of the participating States as to whether, when, and why IHL applied. But in *Bemba*, too, it was not obvious that the Central African Republic's own involvement alongside the MLC in the non-international armed conflict taking place on its territory against Bozizé's rebels would have met the intensity requirement, given that the bulk of the fighting was done by the MLC (and other forces supporting the Central African Republic). Likewise, in *Katanga*, the APC had a very limited battlefield presence during the clashes with the UPC in Bogoro and mainly assisted the Ngiti militia. The Federal Prosecutor qualified al-Qaeda as a party to the non-international armed conflict in north-western Pakistan based on the group's support to local and transnational rebel groups, including the training of personnel, planning of attacks, and import of weapons and explosive material.[164] Assessed in isolation, this may not have sufficed to cross the intensity threshold. Further instances of practice assessed in Chapter 4 will further illustrate this point. As will be seen, the range of activities that have been considered sufficient to render the contributing entity a co-party would often not have met the requirements for an armed conflict if assessed separately.

Finally, even if the outcome as to the co-party status of a particular entity may have been different had a separate assessment been carried out, one could still object that this outcome was perhaps irrelevant to the specific legal question at hand. If that were the case, the findings on party status perhaps simply did not matter enough to the respective bodies to carry out a separate assessment for each co-party. Arguably, however, 'between' whom the conflicts took place did hold some practical relevance in the respective cases. Considering several entities as parties to the same conflict has practical advantages, especially from the perspective of a court or prosecutor. In particular, it has evidentiary benefits, as it puts the finding that an armed conflict exists on a more secure footing, notably in

[164] Federal Prosecutor's Order (20 June 2013) 8–9, 19.

non-international armed conflicts. It can also be important, for example, when the existence of a non-international armed conflict over a prolonged period (to which the criminal charges relate) is at issue. For example, in *Bemba*, considering the Central African Republic and the MLC as co-parties to the same non-international armed conflict with the opposing rebel group allowed the Chamber to find that this conflict had begun before the MLC's intervention and that the latter had then joined this conflict.[165] This finding, in turn, avoided questions as to when exactly the MLC's intervention crossed the non-international armed conflict threshold and removed possible doubts as to whether a non-international armed conflict existed throughout the entire period under review. Crucially, both the findings of the existence of a non-international armed conflict and the MLC's party status on the very first days of its intervention mattered, as is attested by allegations relating to incidents, such as rapes, on these specific days.[166] For the intensity assessment, possible doubts about whether confrontations between two opposing parties—continuously—met the intensity threshold can be eliminated by taking into consideration clashes with other co-parties. Further, if the conduct of all co-parties counts towards the same conflict's intensity, factual challenges of neatly distinguishing which co-party exactly did what amidst the 'fog of war' on the ground are considerably alleviated.

Therefore, the most plausible reading of the instances reviewed in this section is that they support the idea that the individual contribution of each co-party need not separately fulfil the requirements for the existence of an armed conflict, so long as these are fulfilled if the conduct of all co-parties is assessed in aggregation.

iii. Rationale and risks of aggregated assessments

The instances of State practice reviewed above are not sufficient to establish an 'agreement' in the sense of Article 31(3)(b). They do not suffice for a 'common understanding' among the High Contracting Parties[167] to the international treaties referring to parties to an armed conflict, which would settle how the conflict-related requirements for the existence of an armed conflict are to be assessed, absent explicit indications in the treaty texts. There also does not seem to be a general practice accepted as law in this respect.[168] No rule of customary international law can thus be said to have crystallised that would specifically address this question. Yet, the instances of State practice can be taken into consideration as supplementary

[165] *Bemba* (Trial) (n 68) [662].
[166] *Bemba* (Confirmation of Charges) (n 154) [249]ff.
[167] ILC, 'Draft Conclusions on Subsequent Agreements and Subsequent Practice in relation to the Interpretation of Treaties, with Commentaries' (2018) UN Doc A/73/10, 30 [9]; see also ILC Report (1966) II YILC 221–222 [15].
[168] ICJSt, art 38(1)(b).

means of interpreting the relevant treaty provisions,[169] and may inform the content of customary international law in resolving this question.

In that sense, the State practice and decisions by international courts and tribunals discussed above illustrate that there are at least some ramifications in international practice for jointly assessing the contributions by multiple (potential) co-parties to establish the existence of armed conflicts in multiparty settings. This section shows why allowing for the possibility of an aggregated assessment is indeed the more convincing view. It also discusses normative concerns associated with aggregated assessments that must be accommodated in considering when to conduct such assessments.

(1) *Purpose of the conflict-related requirements for the existence of an armed conflict*

Joint, rather than separate, assessments of (potential) co-parties against the conflict-related requirements for the existence of an armed conflict (ie recourse to armed force in international armed conflicts, and protracted armed violence in non-international armed conflicts) resonate better with the rationale underlying these requirements. The purpose of these requirements is to characterise the nature of the confrontation between the collective entities involved as requiring the application of IHL.[170] It makes sense to consider that this is the nature of the conflict as a whole. Indeed, where multiple entities form part of the same conflict relationship with the adverse side as (potential) co-parties, they jointly characterise the confrontation of which they are all part.

As regards the intensity requirement in non-international armed conflicts, its purpose is to distinguish whether the situation of violence is to be addressed through the framework of (domestic) law enforcement against individuals or through the inter-collective violence framework of the law of armed conflict.[171] For this paradigm distinction, it does not matter whether single opposing collective entities or multiple collective entities carry out acts that, taken together, reach the threshold of protracted armed violence. The individual law enforcement paradigm is no more appropriate in the latter case than in the former simply because multiple collective entities reach the requisite result together. The result is still inter-collective protracted armed violence. The mere fact that multiple collective entities divide up what would have sufficed if carried out by one of them individually does not justify considering their activities through the paradigm of law enforcement

169 VCLT, art 32; ILC Draft conclusions on subsequent agreements and subsequent practice, conclusion 2(4); see also G Nolte, 'First Report on Subsequent Agreements and Subsequent Practice in Relation to the Interpretation of Treaties' (2013) UN Doc A/CN.4/660 73 [107]; O Dörr, 'Article 32' in O Dörr and K Schmalenbach (eds), *Vienna Convention on the Law of Treaties: A Commentary* (2nd edn, Springer 2018) 627.

170 Above 2.b.

171 See above 2.b.(2)(a).

for isolated and sporadic individual acts of violence.[172] The sovereignty concerns underlying the intensity threshold[173] do not suggest a difference between these scenarios; indeed, where foreign States intervene alongside the territorial State, it may even be less of a matter pertaining to the territorial State's internal affairs. From the perspective of the purpose of the intensity criterion, the scenarios are equivalent. Accordingly, to treat differently the case of multiple entities reaching the intensity threshold together could allow for unwarranted circumventions of IHL application[174] and party status.[175] The same rationale applies where further collective entities join a confrontation that already qualifies as protracted armed violence and thus align themselves with that paradigm.[176]

Similarly, as regards international armed conflicts, it similarly does not matter how many States participate in a confrontation for it to qualify as recourse to armed force, which requires addressing the confrontation as a whole through the legal framework of inter-State armed conflict. This idea is reflected in the orthodox view that a neutral State would become a party to an existing international armed conflict if it would participate by performing 'acts of war'. These were understood as acts that the laws of war would regulate as part of an existing conflict but that need not give rise to an armed conflict on their own.[177] As will be seen below, moreover, particularly where States closely coordinate their operations to the point that they may be seen as jointly using force, it would be practically artificial and conceptually inadequate to determine that each of them separately uses armed force if assessed in isolation.[178]

(2) Practical and conceptual obstacles of separate assessments

Requiring a separate assessment in all cases[179] has the appeal that the established legal concepts of international and non-international armed conflict could more directly be relied upon for identifying co-parties to an armed conflict.[180] It should, however, be recalled that this would not fully resolve the legal issues of identifying

[172] See also Sassòli (n 19) 193–194.

[173] See above 2.b.(2)(a).

[174] Circumventing IHL need not mean a legal void since human rights law may still apply. The application of human rights law would, however, be subject to jurisdictional questions in the specific case and remains controversial regarding potential non-State parties; see Chapter 1.3.b.

[175] Koutroulis (n 124) 832, V Koutroulis, 'A Clarification of the Geographical and Personal Scope of Multinational NIACs?' (2019) 49 Collegium 35, 39.

[176] van Steenberghe (n 110) 47–48; Ferraro (n 110) 1231, 1239; J Parkerson, 'United States Compliance with Humanitarian Law Respecting Civilians During Operation Just Case' (1991) 133 MLR 31, 42.

[177] Chapter 4, nn 61–63.

[178] Chapter 4.3.b.ii.

[179] For such a view, see Zamir (n 12) 90–91; N Zamir, 'The Armed Conflict(s) against the Islamic State' (2016) 18(2015) YIHL 91, 109–110; C Heyns et al, 'The International Law Framework Regulating the Use of Armed Drones' (2016) 65 ICLQ 791, 808–809; M Schmitt, 'International Humanitarian Law and the Targeting of Non-State Intelligence Personnel and Objects' (2020) 30 Duke JCIL 309, 328.

[180] See Zamir (n 12) 91.

co-parties. It would not provide criteria for distinguishing when multiple entities qualify as co-parties to the same armed conflict (rather than as parties to separate armed conflicts).[181] The added value in legal certainty by relying on existing concepts is also limited, given the persisting debates and uncertainties about the contours of the concepts of international and non-international armed conflict. Moreover, assessing these standards separately for each potential co-party faces considerable practical obstacles. As the discussion of international practice has revealed above, isolating the individual contributions by the respective entities can prove difficult, particularly when multiple entities cooperate closely.[182]

Perhaps to overcome these practical obstacles, some proponents of separately assessing the intensity requirement seem to adapt this requirement itself to multiparty settings. Zamir, for example, apparently reads the intensity requirements less strictly for cooperating partners. Assessing the international operations against ISIL in Syria and Iraq, he suggests that the fact that the Syrian and Iraqi governments do not 'operate under the framework of law enforcement [ie that they are or view themselves as engaged in a non-international armed conflict governed by IHL] … is an indicator that any armed engagement … of the foreign state … against IS, would meet the requirement of intensity'.[183] Effectively, Zamir's suggestion of taking the fulfilment of the intensity threshold by the host States as indicating that their partners become (co-)parties to a non-international armed conflict[184] goes towards the very aggregated assessment of activities of multiple entities that Zamir opposes.

Similarly, Gill points out that the intensity threshold 'is not restricted to kinetic attack' but could also be met by 'forms of direct participation in hostilities which do not necessarily constitute directly performing an attack'.[185] Such acts of 'direct participation in hostilities' (DPH), however, are unlikely to suffice to give rise to a (separate) non-international armed conflict on their own, viewed in isolation from the acts of those whose attacks are being supported. After all, if they did qualify as a separate armed conflict, they would not need to be construed as DPH of the individuals committing them.[186] Implicitly, this kind of intensity assessment, too, considers contributions as relevant that reach the intensity threshold only in conjunction with acts performed by other entities.

181 On the relevance of this distinction, see above 3.

182 For conflicts involving multiple armed groups, see also ICRC, 'International Humanitarian Law and the Challenges of Contemporary Armed Conflicts' (2019) 40–42; J Kleffner, 'The Legal Fog of an Illusion: Three Reflections on "Organization" and "Intensity" as Criteria for the Temporal Scope of the Law of Non-International Armed Conflict' (2019) 95 ILS 161, 171. Caution is, however, required when relying on 'practicalities' in identifying co-parties (see Chapter 4.3.b.ii.(1)).

183 Zamir (n 12) 111.

184 For a similar suggestion, see G Gaggioli and P Kilibarda, 'Counterterrorism and the Risk of Over-classification of Situations of Violence' (2021) 103 IRRC 203, 232–233.

185 T Gill, 'Some Thoughts on the ICRC Support Based Approach' (2019) 59 QIL Zoom-in 45, 51.

186 ICRC, Interpretive Guidance on the Notion of Direct Participation in Hostilities under International Humanitarian Law (2009) 59.

Although the underlying rationale may be in line with the argument made in this chapter, as may be the results reached, modifications of the requirements for the existence of an armed conflict themselves should be resisted. Absent clear contours of such modified standards for the existence of armed conflict or criteria for when to apply these modifications, the legal uncertainty surrounding the mode of assessment of the standards would then be integrated into the very concepts of armed conflict. Masked under the cover of a purported separate assessment of the conflict-related requirements, this may actually result in greater uncertainty than not requiring a separate intensity assessment and openly acknowledging that additional criteria are required for when an aggregated assessment may be carried out. In sum, the problem is thus better situated at the level of the assessment than the content of the conflict-related requirements.[187]

Certain normative concerns associated with aggregated assessments, nonetheless, need to be considered, as will be discussed next.

(3) Normative concerns related to the implications of aggregated assessments

A key concern is that not requiring separate assessments of the conditions for the existence of an armed conflict could reduce the level of protection applicable to affected individuals.[188] This concern has been raised notably against the background of the US practice of expansively targeting members of groups that they considered to be 'associated forces' of al-Qaeda all around the world as part of the so-called 'Global War on Terror'.[189]

The normative concerns are thus associated with the implications of identifying entities as (co-)parties to armed conflicts. In particular, these concerns relate to the implications of identifying armed groups as non-State co-parties of other armed groups to a non-international armed conflict against one or several States. Chapter 1 has set out the extent to which individuals' connection to a party determines their protection. If an armed group becomes a co-party to a non-international armed conflict, this has a permissive effect for the adverse State party regarding the IHL rules applicable to targeting individuals. The extent of this permissive effect is contingent on one's view on the unsettled issue of targeting individuals connected to non-State parties in non-international armed conflicts.[190] The party status of the armed group will be relevant for those individuals whom one considers targetable as part of the group but who would not be targetable by virtue of their individual behaviour as directly participating in the conflict.[191] Under the

[187] n 108.

[188] C Heyns et al, 'The Right to Life and the International Law Framework Regulating the Use of Armed Drones' in D Akande et al (eds), *Human Rights and 21st Century Challenges* (OUP 2020) 169; Zwanenburg (n 141) 57; Gill (n 185) 50–51; Gaggioli and Kilibarda (n 184) 231.

[189] See UN Special Rapporteur on Extrajudicial, Summary or Arbitrary Executions, 'Report' UN Doc A/68/382 (13 September 2013) [61], [63]. This practice will be critically analysed in Chapter 4.2.b.i.

[190] Chapter 1.4.a.i.(2).

[191] See also the references in n 188.

ICRC's 'continuous combat function' approach to membership in armed groups (which, as seen above, enjoys considerable support),[192] the difference would concern those individuals who have the continuous role to directly participate in hostilities in general but do not do so at the relevant time.[193] It should be noted that the relevance of this permissive dimension of co-party status for the adverse side does not seem to be equally relevant where a State is identified as the co-party of another State or armed group against an armed group. This is because domestic law will still prohibit the opponent armed group from targeting members of the State armed forces. The particular relevance of these implications in the context of non-State co-parties in non-international armed conflicts has given rise to propositions to apply different, more restrictive criteria in this setting than those for identifying other entities as co-parties. Chapter 4 will discuss these propositions further.[194]

Concerns regarding lowering international legal protection are buttressed by the potential permissive impact of the legality under IHL of targeting individuals on the legality under international human rights law.[195] As discussed in Chapter 1, the legality under IHL may mean that killing is not considered 'arbitrary' under certain human rights treaty provisions on the right to life (depending on one's view on the interaction between IHL and human rights law).[196] An armed group's (co-)party status to a non-international armed conflict would thus also have a permissive effect on the scope of the adverse State's human rights obligations to the extent that, under IHL, individuals may be targeted by virtue of their connection to a collective entity that qualifies as a party.

That individuals may be targetable by virtue of a particular connection to a party to an armed conflict does not necessarily mean that individual members of a non-State party may be targeted anywhere in the world.[197] Indeed, while party status generally has significant implications for the geographical scope of IHL application, the implications of armed groups' party status to non-international armed conflicts are rather subtle, as Chapter 1 has shown.[198] On approaches that confine the geographical scope of IHL application to the territory of a State party to a non-international armed conflict, an (additional) armed group being considered a (co-)party to the conflict would not make a difference to the geographical reach of IHL's targeting rules.[199] At most, under approaches that extend the geographical

[192] Chapter 1, nn 199–203.
[193] DPH Guidance 33–34.
[194] Chapter 4.3.c.iii.(1).
[195] DPH Guidance 169; Zwanenburg (n 141) 56.
[196] Notably ICCPR, art 6(1) and ACHR, art 4(1); see Chapter 1.3.b.
[197] T Rodenhäuser, 'Armed Groups, Rebel Coalitions, and Transnational Groups: The Degree of Organization Required from Non-State Armed Groups to Become Party to a Non-International Armed Conflict' (2018) 19(2016) YIHL 3, 23.
[198] Chapter 1.5.
[199] ICRC Challenges Report (2015) 14; P Kilibarda and G Gaggioli, 'The Globalisation of Non-International Armed Conflicts' in M Lattimer and P Sands (eds), *The Grey Zone: Civilian Protection between Human Rights and the Laws of War* (Hart 2018) 148–149.

scope of IHL beyond the territory of the respective States to situations with a nexus to the conflict,[200] the party status of an armed group could play a role as a factor in assessing that nexus. Yet, while the contours of the requisite nexus would yet have to develop as a matter of positive international law, it would likely require assessing a range of different factors on a case-by-case basis.[201] The nexus would thus not be automatically fulfilled for all members of a non-State party to a conflict everywhere in the world.

Nonetheless, the concerns associated with potential permissive implications of (co-)party status must be taken seriously. It should also be kept in mind, however, that the concerns relate only to one aspect of the panorama of implications attached to identifying an entity as a co-party. In particular, party status will carry with it IHL obligations for the respective collective entity, aiming to protect individuals in armed conflict. These obligations range substantially wider than those that the respective entity would bear had it not become a party.[202] As will be seen in Chapter 5, there are also particular obligations to the benefit of protected individuals in the relationship between co-parties attached to co-party status. Additionally, the (co-)party status of a collective entity matters for those protective rules of IHL—mainly in international armed conflicts—that are applicable only to individuals with a particular connection to a party.[203] For example, for individual members of a State's armed forces, the party status of that State to an international armed conflict would mean that they benefit from prisoner of war status if they fall into the hands of the adverse side. Moreover, both in international and non-international armed conflicts, the co-party status of a collective entity may give rise to individual obligations under international law and, crucially, may feed into establishing the international criminal responsibility of individuals connected to the respective collective entity.[204]

The entire range of legal implications of identifying co-parties and the associated normative concerns or benefits must inform the criteria for when aggregated assessments of the elements establishing armed conflicts will be possible. That is, all of them must inform the criteria that the respective collective entities must meet to be considered co-parties, beyond fulfilling the (conflict-related) criteria for the existence of an armed conflict together. The background question will be to identify the situations to which the implications of party status should attach.[205]

[200] N Lubell and N Derejko, 'A Global Battlefield? Drones and the Geographical Scope of Armed Conflict' (2013) 11 JICJ 65, 75–76; M Schmitt, 'Charting the Legal Geography of Non-International Armed Conflict' (2014) 90 ILS 1, 15; E Crawford, 'The Temporal and Geographic Reach of International Humanitarian Law' in B Saul and D Akande (eds), *Oxford Guide to International Humanitarian Law* (OUP 2020) 74.

[201] Chapter 1, nn 283–285.

[202] Chapter 1.3.a.; Chapter 2.

[203] Chapter 1.4.a.ii.

[204] Chapter 1.4.b.ii.

[205] See also Chapter 4.1.

The normative concerns about the level of protection applicable to individuals as a consequence of identifying a (co-)party call for adequate restrictions to avoid enabling expansive targeting practices through permissive invocations of party status.

At the same time, where actions of individuals reflect that a collective as a whole is part of an inter-collective confrontation, it is in line with the structure of the regulation of IHL to consider the situation through the lens of party status rather than (only) of individual DPH. Chapter 4 will show that criteria pertaining to the nature of the contribution by a collective entity and nature of the relationship between the potential co-parties restrict the identification of co-parties. These criteria sufficiently accommodate the normative concerns such that a principled rejection of aggregated assessments is not necessary.

To sum up, allowing for the possibility of aggregating the contributions by potential co-parties is the more convincing account of the mode of establishing the requirements of an armed conflict that relate to the confrontation as a whole. This is not, however, the case of the requirements for establishing an armed conflict that specify the requisite nature and structure of the parties, as will now be explained.

b. Limits of aggregation

By contrast to the conflict-related requirements for the existence of an armed conflict, the requirements concerning the nature and structure of parties, that is statehood in international armed conflicts (with limited exceptions) and sufficient organisation in non-international armed conflicts,[206] must be assessed separately for each potential co-party. It is inherent in the very idea and rationale of these prerequisites that delimit the circle of potential parties that they relate to each potential party individually.

i. Separate assessment of the nature and structure of each co-party

In international armed conflicts, the rule that, in principle, only States can become parties to the conflict by definition means that a potential party must itself fulfil the requirements for statehood. Alternatively, it must be one of the limited types of other collective entities that may become parties to an international armed conflict (ie as a national liberation movement under Article 1(4) API or as an international organisation).[207]

Although there is no such *numerus clausus* of types of collective entities in non-international armed conflicts, the rationale for the organisation requirement as defining the nature and structure that an entity must possess to be capable of being a party necessarily entails a separate assessment. The purpose of the organisation

[206] Chapter 1.2.b.
[207] Chapter 1.2.b.i.

requirement is to distinguish at what point a group of individuals must be considered and addressed as a collective entity from the perspective of IHL.[208] As seen above, this point is understood in functional terms as the capability to conduct intense violence of a collective nature in accordance with the rules of IHL. Up until that point, individuals can participate in a conflict between collectives as individuals only. Their legal position is accordingly regulated by rules addressing them as individuals, notably those on DPH. Below the organisation threshold, there is no collective entity that is separate from these individuals to which international legal regulation could attach. That a group of individuals engage in violence along with other collectives does not necessarily affect its own organisational structures. If it is indeed the case that a certain group of individuals possess the requisite organisational structures only if assessed together with another group of individuals, this would necessarily mean that there is only one organised collective comprising both groups, a question that will be further explored below.

For these reasons, it is convincing that most voices in the literature that allow for the possibility to aggregate contributions by multiple potential co-parties regarding the assessment of the intensity criterion insist on separately assessing the organisation criterion.[209] This distinction between the two elements is also reflected in the above-reviewed international practice in which aggregated intensity assessments have been undertaken. For example, in *Katanga*, before the ICC assessed the intensity of the non-international armed conflict as a whole, it separately assessed the respective organisational structures of the different armed groups.[210] The Court found that 'in January 2003, if not before, each of those groups, namely, the UPC, the APC and the Ngiti militia ... had a sufficient degree of organisation'.[211] The reference to the different armed groups as separate entities in assessing the organisation requirement seems to have been conscious. Indeed, at other points in the judgment, the Court assessed the organisational ties of the different subgroups within the Ngiti militia in great detail, concluding that they formed one larger party rather than several separate groups.[212] Similarly, regarding the ICC's Afghanistan investigations, the Prosecutor separately assessed the relevant armed groups for their degree of organisation before grouping their conduct together for intensity purposes.[213] Further instances of separate organisation

[208] Chapter 1.2.a., b.ii.

[209] For example Lubell (n 50) 25; Kilibarda and Gaggioli (n 199) 133; T Ferraro, 'Military Support to Belligerents: Can the Provider Become a Party to the Armed Conflict?' (2019) 49 Collegium 47, 53; but see R Bartels, 'When Do Terrorist Organisations Qualify as "Parties to an Armed Conflict" under International Humanitarian Law?' (2017) 56 MLLWR 451, 472.

[210] *Katanga* (Trial) (n 68) [1207]–[1211].

[211] ibid [1211].

[212] ibid [679]–[681]; [1209]; [1365]; see also *Ntaganda* (Trial) (n 68) [719].

[213] *Afghanistan Investigation Request* (n 138) [74]–[75], [129]–[134]; see also *Afghanistan* (Investigation Decision) (n 138) [65].

assessments coupled with aggregated intensity assessments have been noted above.[214]

ii. Forming part of a party

As a consequence of the need for each potential (co-)party to separately fulfil the requirements on the nature and structure of the entity—particularly, the degree of organisation in non-international armed conflicts—the only way for multiple entities to be assessed together in this respect is if they actually are parts of one single (potential) party to the conflict. It would then suffice that the overarching entity meets the requirements for being a party rather than its constituent sub-entities. Violent acts by different subgroups could then also be considered in the intensity assessment, and the legal implications of party status in terms of, for example, targetability and individual criminal responsibility would arise for individuals linked to the subgroups.[215] For present purposes, clarifying the point at which several entities form part of the same party is also useful for another reason. This point, by implication, sets the upper limit on how close the ties between multiple entities may still be for them to be identifiable as separate co-parties.

On one approach, two collective entities have to be considered as one party to an armed conflict if one exercises what the ICTY has labelled 'overall control'[216] over the other. According to the ICTY, a foreign State has overall control over an armed group engaged in a non-international armed conflict with another State if it 'has a role in organising, coordinating or planning the military actions of the military group, in addition to financing, training and equipping or providing operational support to that group'.[217] The result would be the existence of an international armed conflict between the two States,[218] and—although this is not always explicitly spelled out—the armed group would be considered to be absorbed by the State exercising overall control.[219] The consequence that the armed group is no longer a separate party in its own right stems from the idea that a State exercising overall control over an armed group acts *through* the armed group acting on its behalf (or rather the individuals making up the group).[220] Beyond the specific scenario of a State supporting an armed group against another State, the ICRC

[214] See eg *Ntaganda* (Trial) (n 68) [704]–[715]; *Bemba* (Trial) (n 68) [657]–[661]; see generally above a.ii.(2).

[215] Heyns et al (n 188) 169–170.

[216] *Tadić* (Appeal) (n 55) [131].

[217] ibid [137] (emphasis omitted). For jurisprudence of different international criminal tribunals endorsing this test, see n 68.

[218] *Tadić* (Appeal) (n 55) [162].

[219] *GCI Commentary* [406]; Ferraro (n 110) 1250, 1252; Zamir (n 12) 122; K Fortin, 'Symposium: Further Thoughts on an IAC with Three Parties and the Capacity of Armed Groups to Adhere to International Norms' (*OpinioJuris*, 18 January 2019) <http://opiniojuris.org/2019/01/18/symposium-further-thoughts-on-an-iac-with-three-parties-and-the-capacity-of-armed-groups-to-adhere-to-international-norms/>.

[220] See eg *Tadić* (Appeal) (n 55) [84]; [122]; *Bemba* (Confirmation of Charges) (n 154) [223].

considers the ICTY's legal construction to be generalisable to other conflict settings. Accordingly, where a State, an armed group, or an international organisation were to overall control over a non-State party to a non-international armed conflict with another non-State party, the respective entities would have to be considered as one party.[221]

It is doubtful, however, that 'overall control', as understood by the ICTY, indeed bears out a relationship of absorption or merging. As Mačák has rightly pointed out, the elements constituting overall control do not actually convey a notion of control in a 'dictionary sense' and, thus, make the label 'overall control' a 'misnomer'.[222] Indeed, even if another entity provides material assistance and participates in the organisation, coordination, and planning of military operations, this would still leave the entity receiving such assistance with considerable autonomy.[223] Accordingly, it seems reasonable that the entity receiving such support may still qualify as a separate (co-)party rather than being deemed absorbed as part of another party.

These objections against understanding 'overall control' as having an effect of merging or absorption, a fortiori, also militate against relying on the requirement of 'belonging' under Article 4(A)(2) GCIII to determine when multiple collective entities constitute one party to an armed conflict.[224] This would set the bar yet lower since a mere de facto agreement between the respective entities that one fights on behalf of the other could then suffice[225] such that it would appear even less compelling that this should effectively merge the two entities.[226]

Instead, for several entities to form part of one party, they must be integrated into a common set of military organisational structures.[227] What exactly this integration requires depends on the type of entity into which the other is integrated and how the military apparatus is organised.

221 Ferraro (n 110) 1238–1240.

222 K Mačák, *Internationalized Armed Conflicts in International Law* (OUP 2018) 46 (fn 128).

223 K Mačák, 'Symposium: Internationalized Armed Conflicts—Four Concluding Thoughts' (*OpinioJuris*, 23 January 2019) <http://opiniojuris.org/2019/01/23/symposium-internationalized-armed-conflicts-four-concluding-thoughts/>.

224 In favour of relying on this concept (by analogy), see eg R Goodman, 'Al-Qaeda, the Law on Associated Forces and "Belonging to" a Party (Did the New UN Drones Reports Get It Right?)' (*Just Security*, 18 October 2013) <www.justsecurity.org/2191/al-qaeda-law-forces-belonging-to-party-drones-reports/>; E Nohle, 'Drawing the Line between Armed Groups under IHL' (*Humanitarian Law and Policy*, 22 July 2016) <https://blogs.icrc.org/law-and-policy/2016/07/22/drawing-line-armed-groups/> (albeit understanding this requirement restrictively as 'a structural relationship' among groups sharing a 'hierarchical structure, chain of command and disciplinary system'); for criticism of the analogy, see K Heller, 'The Use and Abuse of Analogy in IHL' in J Ohlin (ed), *Theoretical Boundaries of Armed Conflict and Human Rights* (CUP 2016) 274–275.

225 K Del Mar, 'The Requirement of "Belonging" under International Humanitarian Law' (2010) 21 EJIL 105, 109; *GCIII Commentary* [1004]–[1007]; Mačák (n 222) 173–174.

226 Rodenhäuser (n 197) 19.

227 Schindler (n 19) 131; Lubell (n 50) 22; Targeted Killings Report 2013 (A/68/382) [62]; Heyns et al (n 179) 808–809.

For a State and an armed group to be considered as part of one single party, the armed group must be subordinated within the hierarchical chains of command and control that characterise State militaries, and it must be subjected to the State's system of sanctions so that its operational autonomy is sacrificed.[228]

For multiple armed groups to be considered integrated into one single party, international criminal jurisprudence requires the overarching 'umbrella' group itself to fulfil the organisation requirement.[229] In this respect, it must be borne in mind that different command and control arrangements may suffice to fulfil the requisite degree of organisation. Armed groups may, but need not (and frequently do not), have state-like, centralised, vertically structured chains of command and control. They can also organise themselves in a decentralised, horizontal manner.[230] Rodenhäuser has thus suggested that different subgroups 'can be considered as one collective entity with a certain command structure and the abilities to engage in military violence and to ensure respect for basic IHL' if that overarching collective entity has 'the ability to coordinate military activities and to distribute logistics' as well as the 'authority to determine the overall military objectives and the internal rules that all sub-groups have to follow'.[231]

International criminal jurisprudence seems relatively lenient in this respect. For example, in *Katanga*, the ICC found the Ngiti militia, a network of local subgroups, to form one sufficiently organised armed group. This was even though the Court was unable to conclude that the group had a centralised command structure.[232] The ICC attached weight to the existence of a central leadership figure[233] and to the coherence among the different subgroups.[234]

To sum up, so far, it has been shown that the requirements for the existence of an armed conflict as to the nature of the confrontation and the requirements related to the nature of the parties differ in the way in which they may be established. The following section explores how this distinction plays out in the assessment of the particular requirements for a non-international armed conflict to be covered by APII in multiparty settings.

[228] Mačák (n 222) 179.

[229] *Ngaïssona* (Arrest Warrant) ICC-01/14-02/18 (7 December 2018) [6]–[8], [13]; *Yekatom* (Arrest Warrant) ICC-01/14-01/18 (11 November 2018) [6]–[8], [15]; *Yekatom and Ngaïssona* (Confirmation of Charges) ICC-01/14-01/18 (11 December 2019) [61]–[62], [72]–[73]; see also *Katanga* (Trial) (n 68) [679], [1209]; *Ntaganda* (Trial) (n 68) [714]. See also K Dörmann and T Rodenhäuser, 'Contemporary Challenges for International Humanitarian Law' in J Crawford et al (eds), *The International Legal Order: Current Needs and Possible Responses Essays in Honour of Djamchid Momtaz* (Brill 2017) 680.

[230] ICRC Challenges Report (2019) 40.

[231] T Rodenhäuser, *Organizing Rebellion: Non-State Armed Groups under International Humanitarian Law, Human Rights Law, and International Criminal Law* (OUP 2018) 84.

[232] *Katanga* (Trial) (n 68) [1365].

[233] ibid [1360]; see also *Ngaïssona* (Arrest) (n 229) [6]; *Yekatom* (Arrest) (n 229) [6].

[234] *Katanga* (Trial) (n 68) [679]–[681], [1209].

c. Establishing multiparty non-international armed conflicts under APII

The particular requirements for a non-international armed conflict to be regulated by APII raise issues in multiparty conflicts as to whether each co-party must separately meet them for APII to apply to its actions. As explained above, Article 1(1) limits the Protocol's scope of application to conflicts between States on one side and dissident armed forces or non-State armed groups on the other. Article 1(1) therefore excludes conflicts between non-State armed groups.[235] Settings involving multiple potential parties may, however, still arise on both sides of the conflicts within the realm of APII.

Establishing to whom APII applies matters. Although APII falls significantly short of the API's dense regulatory framework, it still provides considerably more detailed rules than does Common Article 3. Of course, according to the ICRC's customary IHL study, most provisions of APII also reflect customary international law and customary IHL may already go beyond APII in some respects.[236] But to what extent that is actually so remains debated.[237] The ICRC study also left open whether the customary equivalents of APII's provisions would apply to all non-international armed conflicts or only to those meeting the threshold of APII,[238] and international judicial practice has been inconsistent in that respect.[239] Against that background, establishing whether and to what extent APII applies to the acts of co-parties is relevant, at least for the added clarity and legal certainty.[240]

Before further exploring these questions, it is worth clarifying that parties to the conflict are the central addressees of APII, notwithstanding that APII does at no point explicitly refer to them. The obligations under APII are generally set out in the passive voice, thus obscuring the duty bearers. The ICRC's 1973 Draft of APII still contained numerous references to parties to the conflict, including two provisions addressing the implications of party status under the Protocol in

235 The ICRC's Draft did not foresee this exclusion, see ICRC Second Draft Additional Protocol to the Geneva Conventions of August 12, 1949 (1973), art 1, 33. Some States deplored the restriction during the adoption of the Protocol, see eg Switzerland, *Official Records of the Diplomatic Conference on the Reaffirmation and Development of International Humanitarian Law Applicable in Armed Conflicts, Geneva (1974–1977)*, vol VII (Federal Political Department 1978), CCDH/SR.50, 100 (Italy).

236 *CIHL* xxxv.

237 Sivakumaran (n 82) 282; J Bellinger and W Haynes, 'A US Government Response to the International Committee of the Red Cross Study Customary International Humanitarian Law' (2007) 89 IRRC 443, 448 (rejecting the ICRC's finding on the extent to which the APs reflect customary international law).

238 M Bothe, 'Customary International Humanitarian Law: Some Reflections on the ICRC Study' (2006) 8(2005) YIHL 143, 175 (regretting the silence of the study on this point); for discussion M Sassòli, 'Taking Armed Groups Seriously: Ways to Improve Their Compliance with International Humanitarian Law' (2010) 1 JIHLS 5, 20; R van Steenberghe, 'La Légalité de la participation de la Belgique à la lutte armée contre l'Etat islamique en Irak' (2015) 134 Journal des Tribunaux 641, 647.

239 For a critical assessment, see Sivakumaran (n 82) 66.

240 See also van Steenberghe (n 110) 64, fn 171.

general.[241] The deletion of these provisions and careful avoidance of references to parties were probably a concession to those States eager to avoid giving any impression of putting the non-State side in the conflict on an equal legal footing with the State.[242] Yet, naturally, the rules set out in APII are 'based on the existence of two or more parties confronting each other'[243] in the conflict situation triggering the application of APII. Even if APII does not use the term 'parties', this idea is implicit in Article 1(1), which refers to conflicts 'between its armed forces and dissident armed forces or other organized armed groups'. Moreover, as Article 1(1) makes clear, APII 'develops and supplements' Common Article 3, which explicitly imposes obligations on parties. There can, therefore, be no doubt that APII, too, imposes obligations of protection on parties.[244]

By the same token, it should be noted that APII addresses, if implicitly, State and non-State parties alike, just as Common Article 3 does.[245] The reference to the ability of armed groups to 'implement this Protocol' in Article 1(1) presupposes as much. Draft Article 5, which would have explicitly clarified this point, was deleted during the adoption of the Protocol.[246] Statements of numerous States during the Diplomatic Conferences, however, testify to the fact that they considered APII to follow Common Article 3's logic of equally binding State and non-State parties.[247] Accordingly, scholarly debates generally turn on *how* the binding force of APII (and IHL more generally) on non-State armed groups is best conceptualised in legal terms rather than on *whether* IHL can bind non-State parties in the first place.[248]

With these clarifications in mind, it can now be assessed whether and how APII applies to co-parties in multiparty non-international armed conflicts. Different possible multiparty constellations will be distinguished: first, instances of multiple States as co-parties; secondly, instances of multiple cooperating armed groups; and, thirdly, instances of cooperation between the territorial State and armed groups.

[241] Second Draft AP, arts 3, 5.

[242] Bothe, Partsch, and Solf (n 81) 696. This concern is voiced, for example, in Zaire's voting explanation (Official Records vol VII, CCDH/SR.50, 104). In the context of the adoption of APII, other States considered, however, that these changes did not make any legal difference, see eg ibid 85–86 [3] (Norway), [4] (Italy), [5] (Belgium); see also below n 247.

[243] *AP Commentary* 1345 [4442]; see also S Junod, 'Additional Protocol II: History and Scope' (1983) 33 AULR 29, 35–36.

[244] Statements of States during the Diplomatic Conferences preceding the adoption of APII also support this conclusion, see n 247.

[245] Yemen Report 2019 (n 134) [49].

[246] Official Records vol VII, CDDH/SR.50, 86 [9].

[247] ibid CDDH/SR.49, 76 (Belgium); CCDH/SR.50, 101 (Italy); CCDH/SR.50, 101 (Netherlands).

[248] A Cassese, 'The Status of Rebels under the 1977 Geneva Protocol on Non-International Armed Conflicts' (1981) 30 ICLQ 416; S Sivakumaran, 'Binding Armed Opposition Groups' (2006) 55 ICLQ 369; Sassòli (n 238) 12ff; A Bellal and E Heffes, 'Yes, I Do: Binding Armed Non-State Actors to IHL and Human Rights Norms Through Their Consent' (2018) 12 HRILD 120.

i. Inter-State settings

If additional States qualify as co-parties of the State on whose territory a non-international armed conflict takes place, this raises questions about whether APII may also apply to these co-parties. In its 2019 investigation report on the situation in Yemen, a UN expert group found as much:

> The member States of the coalition supporting the Government of Yemen became parties as 'co-belligerents' to the pre-existing non-international armed conflict between Yemen and the Houthis, from the time of the coalition intervention in March 2015. The members of the coalition are bound to respect all applicable international humanitarian law, *including ... the second Additional Protocol of 1977*.[249]

The finding that APII applies not only to Yemen but also to its co-parties is not self-evident. The reference in Art 1(1) to '*its* armed forces'[250] (ie the armed forces of the High Contracting Party in whose territory the conflict takes place) is often taken to indicate that the Protocol only applies to the territorial State, provided it has ratified the Protocol.[251] According to this reading, co-party States operating extraterritorially would be regulated by Common Article 3 and customary IHL. APII would cover the forces of other States only if they are integrated into the armed forces of the territorial State.[252]

While intuitive at first sight, this conclusion does not necessarily follow from Article 1(1)'s wording. Indeed, on its face, when Article 1(1) refers to conflicts taking place 'between' the territorial State's armed forces and dissident forces or armed groups, it does not require that the conflict is *exclusively* 'between' such forces. Arguably, a conflict in which the territorial State fights insurgents together with other States as its co-parties is still 'between' that State and the insurgents. Of course, the matter would be different if *only* foreign States fought the insurgents, without the territorial State being a party. Article 1(1)'s wording excludes this scenario. However, so long as the territorial State fights non-State parties, as Article 1(1) requires, that provision's wording should not be taken to exclude the territorial State's co-parties from the scope of the Protocol, simply because it does not explicitly include them.[253] The wording leaves the issue open.

249 Yemen Report 2019 (n 134) [50] (emphasis added).

250 Emphasis added. This restriction was not foreseen by the ICRC's Draft—see Second Draft AP, art 1.

251 Akande (n 29) 55; Melzer (n 51) 57; DeCock (n 85) 114.

252 Akande (n 29) 55. This integration would mean that these forces would form part of one party to the same armed conflict and the respective States would not qualify as separate co-parties. See above b.

253 C McDougall, 'The *Inspector-General of the Australian Defence Force Afghanistan Inquiry Report* and the Applicability of Additional Protocol II to Intervening Foreign Forces' (2023) 105 IRRC 992, 1009.

In an attempt to counter narrow readings of Article 1(1)'s wording, van Steenberghe notes that, during the diplomatic conferences preceding the adoption of APII, 'extra-territorial non-international armed conflicts' (ie conflicts involving foreign States alongside the territorial State, were not explicitly discussed). He suggests that the phenomenon did not actually exist in State practice at the time. Therefore, he concludes, the fact that the application of APII to States acting extraterritorially has not been foreseen does not imply that the drafters intended to exclude this scenario from APII's scope of application.[254]

The empirical claim that extraterritorial interventions in support of States fighting insurgents on their territory were an unknown practice at the time of the diplomatic conferences preceding the adoption of the 1977 APs is not quite accurate.[255] Indeed, fears of foreign interventionism into non-international armed conflicts were a central concern raised by many States during the diplomatic conferences and has even found its way into the text of APII as a safeguard clause in Article 3(2).

Yet, these concerns related to foreign interventions supporting insurgents, rather than consensual interventions supporting the territorial State. It is plausible that States were aware of the possibility of foreign interventions on both sides of non-international armed conflicts but only perceived this practice as a concern worth regulating to the extent that it risked affecting their sovereignty. The preparatory work does not support the conclusion that States understood Article 1(1) as excluding co-parties of the territorial State from the scope of application of APII. It would, therefore, be consistent with the drafting history of Article 1(1) to understand its wording as allowing for the application of APII to co-parties of the territorial State.[256]

The rationale for such a broader understanding would be that multiple (potential) co-parties may be assessed together for establishing the existence of requirements relating to the nature of the armed conflict, building on the broader argument of this chapter. Provided that Article 1(1)'s requirements are fulfilled overall, APII would thus cover co-parties on the State side of the conflict. A joint assessment here would mean that, so long as the armed forces of the territorial State (which has ratified APII) are involved in an armed conflict with dissident forces or other non-State armed groups in the sense of APII,[257] the fulfilment of

[254] van Steenberghe (n 110) 57, 60.

[255] For an extensive review of interventions alongside the territorial State in State practice, including prior to the adoption of APII, see G Nolte, *Eingreifen auf Einladung* (Springer 1999) 65ff, 261ff.

[256] Dinstein (n 82) 117; Vité (n 35) 80; A Bellal, G Giacca, and S Casey-Maslen, 'International Law and Armed Non-state Actors in Afghanistan' (2011) 93 IRRC 47, 60; tentatively also N Lubell, *Extraterritorial Use of Force against Non-State Actors* (OUP 2010) 100 (fn 79); K Schöberl, 'Multinational Military Operations and the Geographical Scope of the Laws of Armed Conflict in Non-International Armed Conflict' in R Geiß and H Krieger (eds), *The 'Legal Pluriverse' Surrounding Multinational Military Operations* (OUP 2020) 43.

[257] The wording of art 1(1) requires the involvement of the armed forces of the territorial State; though see van Steenberghe (n 110) 60 (suggesting that the territorial State need not be involved so long as the conflict takes place on the territory of a High Contracting Party).

Article 1(1) by the territorial State would also 'count' for its potential co-parties and would bring them within APII's scope.

Although subsequent practice in applying APII has to further elucidate this matter, there are instances that support applying the Protocol to co-parties. For example, in the status of forces agreement concerning France's intervention in Mali in 2013, the two States considered APII applicable to both France and Mali's military operations.[258] A representative of the French Ministry of Defence indicated that France deemed APII applicable even prior to the conclusion of the status of forces agreement.[259] Concerning the conflict in Afghanistan, the Danish government noted that:

> [i]t is the government's view that a non-international armed conflict as defined in Article 1 of Additional Protocol II ... is taking place in Afghanistan, between, on the one hand, the legitimate Afghan government and its international allies, including Denmark, and, on the other hand, one or more hostile organised armed groups.... This understanding is shared ... by our closest allies in Afghanistan.[260]

This statement suggests that Denmark considered APII applicable also to foreign States as Afghanistan's co-parties in the non-international armed conflict. Similarly, in its assessment of potential compensation claims against the German federal government related to the 2009 Kunduz strikes discussed above,[261] the German court of first instance deemed APII applicable to operations by States conducted as part of ISAF, thus not limiting the application of the Protocol to hostilities between the Afghan forces themselves and the Taliban.[262] The court of second instance noted difficulties with this view given that APII entered into force with respect to Afghanistan only *after* the strikes,[263] but did not take issue with the application of APII to intervening States as such.[264] Having found that APII had been complied with, the Court left open the question as to whether the Protocol could

[258] France, Décret n° 2013-364 du 29 avril 2013 portant publication de l'accord sous forme d'échange de lettres entre le Gouvernement de la République française et le Gouvernement du Mali déterminant le statut de la force « Serval » (Journal Officiel de la République française 30 April 2013) 7426 Article 10 ('conformément aux règles applicables du droit international humanitaire ... notamment ... Protocole II').

[259] Landais (n 86) 132.

[260] Danish Foreign Ministry, 'Answer to Question No 37 of 18 December 2007 by the Minister for Foreign Affairs to the Folketing—Committee on Foreign Affairs' 8 March 2008 (file no 6.B.28.a. Office of International Law) <www.ft.dk/samling/20072/almdel/uru/spm/37/svar/530893/535083.pdf> (translated with DeepL); see also O Engdahl, 'Multinational Peace Operations Forces Involved in Armed Conflict: Who Are the Parties?' in K Mujezinović Larsen, C Guldahl Cooper, and G Nystuen (eds), *Searching for a 'Principle of Humanity' in International Humanitarian Law* (CUP 2012) 263 fn 4.

[261] nn 136–137.

[262] Regional Court of Bonn, Judgment of 12 November 2013 (n 137) [51]–[53].

[263] Afghanistan acceded to APII on 24 June 2009. APII entered into force regarding Afghanistan six months thereafter, see APII, art 23(1).

[264] Higher Regional Court of Cologne, Judgment of 30 April 2015 (n 137) [36], [58].

be applied although the strikes had occurred before APII had entered into force for Afghanistan.[265] The Federal Court of Justice, at third instance, confirmed these findings and also referred to APII to assess the legality of the acts by the German commanders under international law.[266]

Even if it is accepted in principle that APII can also cover the territorial State's co-parties, this possibility is limited to those co-parties that are High Contracting Parties of APII. It would contravene the rule that treaties cannot bind third States without their consent (*pacta tertiis* rule)[267] to suggest that APII could bind States that have not ratified the Protocol[268] because they become a co-party alongside a territorial State bound by APII. Accordingly, such States remain regulated by Common Article 3 and customary IHL.

The different conflicts in Yemen illustrate this point. Regarding the non-international armed conflict between the Yemeni government and the Saudi-led coalition States, on the one hand, and the Houthis, on the other hand, the 2019 UN report found both Yemen and its co-parties to be bound by APII, since all of these States had ratified the Protocol.[269] The matter would be different for the parallel non-international armed conflict between Yemen and AQAP (and affiliated groups). If one considers the US to be a party to that conflict through its drone strikes supporting the Yemeni government,[270] APII could still apply only to Yemen but not to the US, since the latter has not ratified the Protocol.[271] Similarly, in the conflict with the Taliban (and other armed groups), APII can apply to Afghanistan, which has ratified APII, but not to the US.[272] To the extent that other foreign States, which cooperated with Afghanistan alongside the US to varying extents in different phases of this conflict,[273] were considered parties to that conflict, APII may also have bound those other States that had ratified the Protocol.[274]

To conclude, although international law has not settled this matter entirely, there is a good case for considering the territorial State's co-parties in non-international armed conflicts under Article 1(1) APII as bound by the Protocol. The conditions are that the territorial State is a party to that conflict and that both the territorial State and its co-parties have ratified the Protocol. This possibility reveals

[265] ibid [35].
[266] Federal Court of Justice, Judgment of 6 October 2016 (n 137) [47]ff.
[267] VCLT, arts 34–38. See also eg R Geiß and M Siegrist, 'Has the Armed Conflict in Afghanistan Affected the Rules on the Conduct of Hostilities?' (2011) 93 IRRC 11, 16.
[268] Bellal, Giacca, and Casey-Maslen (n 256) 61 (fn 69); van Steenberghe (n 110) 60, though see, for the opposite view, R van Steenberghe and P Lesaffre, 'The ICRC's "Support-Based Approach": A Suitable but Incomplete Theory' (2019) 59 QIL, Zoom-in 5, 17.
[269] Yemen Report 2019 (n 134) [51].
[270] nn 129–135.
[271] <https://ihl-databases.icrc.org/applic/ihl/ihl.nsf/States.xsp?xp_viewStates=XPages_NORMStatesParties&xp_treatySelected=475>.
[272] Geiß and Siegrist (n 267) 16.
[273] See generally F Hampson, 'Afghanistan 2001–2010' in E Wilmshurst (ed), *International Law and the Classification of Conflicts* (OUP 2012).
[274] See also Bellal, Giacca, and Casey-Maslen (n 256) 60.

an interesting additional dimension to the implications of co-party status. In such cases, the co-parties of the territorial State are regulated by provisions going beyond what would have applied to their actions if they were parties to a separate non-international armed conflict with the respective armed groups (for example where the territorial State consents to the intervention but is not itself a party to the conflict).

Beyond inter-State settings, issues of establishing to whom APII applies may also arise in conflicts involving multiple non-State co-parties or non-State co-parties of the territorial State. These scenarios will be examined next.

ii. Cooperation among armed groups

The 'non-State side' of a non-international armed conflict under APII consists of 'dissident armed forces or other organized armed groups which, under responsible command, exercise such control over a part of its territory as to enable them to carry out sustained and concerted military operations and to implement this Protocol'. The requirements for armed groups to qualify as parties under APII are thus higher than those under Common Article 3 and customary IHL.[275] In situations of multiple non-State co-parties, this raises the question of whether each non-State armed group must separately fulfil these requirements.

The use of the plural form ('forces', 'groups') allows for the possibility of APII covering multiple co-parties on the non-State side.[276] But the wording of Article 1(1) also clearly requires each armed group to possess the requirements of being under responsible command and exercising sufficient control over territory. There is little room for jointly assessing different armed groups to also include groups under APII that do not on their own possess these features.[277]

This is consistent with the above finding that only the intensity requirement in non-international armed conflicts, and not the organisation requirement, can be assessed jointly for multiple co-parties. Being under 'responsible command' as well as possessing the capacity to carry out sustained and concerted military operations and to implement APII are features that relate to a party's degree of organisation. Each party must separately possess these inherent qualities of any non-State party to a conflict under APII.

By contrast, the requirement of sustained and concerted military operations in Article 1(1) APII relates to the conflict as a whole.[278] Regarding this requirement, making a case for jointly assessing the contributions of different cooperating non-State parties is therefore in line with the general distinction of conflict- and party-related criteria proposed in this chapter.

[275] *Boškoski* (Trial) (n 83) [197]; though see Rodenhäuser (n 231) 54 (stating that the difference between the requirements of art 1(1) APII and Common Article 3 should not be exaggerated).

[276] See also Bellal, Giacca, and Casey-Maslen (n 256) 60 fn 64.

[277] See also Hampson (n 273) 252.

[278] Above 2.b.ii.(3).

iii. Cooperation between armed groups and the territorial State

The territorial State may not only have States as co-parties but also non-State armed groups. Examples include as the scenario underlying the ICC's *Bemba* case discussed above. In that case, the Central African Republic government had requested and received an intervention from the Congolese MLC armed group to support the government's fight against the rebels.[279] The same rationale that has justified considering APII to bind States that are co-parties of the territorial State applies to its *non-State* co-parties. An ensuing question would be whether such non-State co-parties would also have to meet the heightened organisation requirements under Article 1(1) APII for the non-State opponents of the territorial State. Even though Article 1(1) explicitly sets these organisational requirements only for potential non-State parties opposing the territorial State, the provision arguably presumes that parties on both sides must possess these features. In line with the idea that each co-party must separately meet the requirements relating to the nature of the party, the better view is also to demand this from non-State co-parties of the territorial State.[280]

In sum, also regarding the requirements for APII to regulate multiparty non-international armed conflicts, the criteria related to the nature of the conflict as a whole must be distinguished from the criteria related to the nature of each party. The preceding sections have analysed how the concepts of armed conflict relate to identifying the parties in situations in which multiple (co-)parties qualify as parties to the same armed conflict. Before concluding this chapter, a final clarification regarding the type of conflict settings to which these findings extend is in order.

d. State cooperation with a non-State entity against a State: structural barriers to co-party status

There is a structural limitation to the possibility that multiple entities may qualify as parties to the same armed conflict. This limitation flows from who can be a party to an international and non-international armed conflict respectively. In constellations where a State and a non-State armed group cooperate against another State, the two States cannot be parties to the same non-international armed conflict on opposite sides. If they are to be viewed as adverse parties to an armed conflict, this inter-State conflict is, by definition, international in character. Conversely, if

[279] nn 153–154.

[280] See also van Steenberghe and Lesaffre (n 268) 18 (arguing that APII would not apply to foreign armed groups controlling territory *outside* rather than *within* the host State's territory).

the non-State armed group is to be viewed as a party to an armed conflict with the opposed State, this will generally be a non-international armed conflict given that armed groups can, in principle, only be a party to non-international armed conflicts (except if they qualify as a national liberation movement under Article 1(4) API).[281] This limitation to co-party status can be explained through the lens of the argument made in this chapter: each potential co-party must separately fulfil the requirements for the existence of an armed conflict related to the nature of the entity. In this setting, the nature of the respective entities bars them, in principle, from becoming parties to the same armed conflict.

The logical consequence would be that a non-State armed group and a State co-operating against another State can only be parties to separate, parallel conflicts—a non-international and an international armed conflict respectively—with their common adversary.[282] On a popular view, however, there will only be an international armed conflict, and not a separate non-international armed conflict, if the relationship between the cooperating entities is such that the State wields 'overall control' over the armed group.[283] The armed group would then be considered 'absorbed' by the State and thus part of a party to an international armed conflict.[284] As seen above, however, it is doubtful that the elements of the 'overall control' test indeed bear out such a merging of two collective entities. It is doubtful because these elements still allow for considerable autonomy of the two entities.[285] On another view, the armed group is deemed to remain a party in its own right (up to the point at which it is integrated into the State party). This would mean that a separate non-international armed conflict persists, on orthodox accounts at least.[286] Accordingly, neither of these views would lead to a finding of co-party status in the sense of this chapter.

Nonetheless, there have been propositions that move in the direction of a functional equivalent to co-party status in this setting. First, according to the view that considers the armed group to be part of a State party to an international armed conflict in situations of overall control, it has been suggested that the IHL obligations under the law of international armed conflict binding the State party could, as regards conduct by the armed group, be adapted 'functionally to what the group is actually able to comply with.'[287] This adaptation could be seen as a step towards treating the armed group and the State as separate duty bearers and thus

281 Chapter 1.2.b.ii.
282 Akande (n 29) 44, 48–49; see also *Nicaragua* (n 58) [219].
283 nn 219, 221. For references on the 'overall control' test, see nn 68–71.
284 nn 216–220.
285 nn 222–223.
286 See below n 290 for an alternative view.
287 Sassòli (n 19) 176; see also T Gal, 'Unexplored Outcomes of *Tadić*: Applicability of the Law of Occupation to War by Proxy' (2014) 12 JICJ 59, 73–75.

separate parties (to the same armed conflict). Secondly, where the armed group is considered a party to a non-international armed conflict with the adverse State in parallel to the international armed conflict between the two States, it has been suggested that the parallel international armed conflict might be taken into account in the intensity assessment for establishing a non-international armed conflict. As a result, this threshold would require less than the protracted armed violence that the armed group would have to engage in if assessed in isolation.[288] This view would be similar to the aggregated intensity assessment that this chapter has proposed for (potential) co-parties.

Moreover, the overall control requirement for a State to become a party to an international armed conflict by supporting an armed group in a non-international armed conflict conceptually implies some sort of joint assessment of the acts of the armed group conducting hostilities and the State supporting the group, akin to the argument made in this chapter for co-parties. After all, were it not for the violent conduct of the armed group against the adverse State, the exercise of overall control by the supporting State would not, without more, have constituted an international armed conflict between the two States.[289]

Going further, Mačák has argued that the armed group should at some point be considered a co-party in its own right to the international armed conflict alongside the State. According to Mačák, the armed group becomes a party to the international armed conflict once the State and the armed group can be said to be jointly, rather than autonomously, using force.[290] This standard would not require that the two entities be in a subordination relationship but that their military operations be intertwined to the point that they could no longer be properly distinguished.[291] This construction avoids the criticism that it would be artificial to consider the State and the armed group as parties to separate conflicts even in situations of close cooperation and the practical difficulties of distinguishing the separate conflicts in such situations.[292] At the same time, Mačák's construction better reflects the factual situation on the ground than considering the two as merged despite retaining some operational autonomy.[293] It would mean, however, to effectively waive the requirement that a party to an international armed conflict must qualify as a State and, instead, to consider closely cooperating with a State to be sufficient. In other words,

[288] L Blank, 'Symposium: The Interplay between IAC and NIAC—Questions and Consequences' (*OpinioJuris*, 16 January 2019) <http://opiniojuris.org/2019/01/16/symposium-the-interplay-between-iac-and-niac-questions-and-consequences/>.

[289] Sassòli (n 19) 175.

[290] Mačák (n 222) 103–104.

[291] ibid.

[292] T Meron, 'Classification of Armed Conflict in the Former Yugoslavia: Nicaragua's Fallout' (1998) 92 AJIL 236, 237–238; K Johnston, 'Transformations of Conflict Status in Libya' (2012) 17 JCSL 81, 101.

[293] Mačák (n 222) 103; Mačák (n 223).

the proposition would amount to a sort of joint assessment of the two entities regarding the statehood requirement. As previously argued in this chapter, there are important reasons of principle—stemming from the purpose of the party-related requirements for the existence of an armed conflict—which militate for separately assessing these requirements for each potential co-party.[294] It remains to be seen whether this proposal gains traction.[295] It can, however, be doubted that States will have much appetite to enlarge the circle of entities that may become parties to international armed conflicts.

In summary, the parameters of the analytical framework for identifying co-parties, as discerned so far, may provide conceptually helpful tools to understand the controversies as to who qualifies as a party to an armed conflict (and to which conflict) in situations of State-armed group cooperation against another State. However, since this conflict setting structurally cannot give rise to situations of co-party status, the setting will not be a focal point for its own sake in the further analysis of the framework for identifying co-parties to armed conflict. At the same time, factual similarities remain between the cooperation relationships underlying this setting and cooperation constellations that may result in co-party status. Against this background, the concepts developed in the rich jurisprudence and wealth of scholarship on this particular setting may provide some conceptual inspiration for present purposes. These concepts will, therefore, be occasionally picked up in the next chapter, keeping in mind the different purposes for which these concepts have been developed.

5. Conclusion

The analysis of multiparty conflicts has revealed that establishing the existence of an armed conflict and identifying (co-)parties to an armed conflict are closely related and yet distinct legal questions with related but distinct requirements. The questions and requirements are related since the co-parties must overall meet the requirements for an armed conflict. They are, nonetheless, distinct because it is arguably sufficient that the conflict-related conditions for the existence of an armed conflict be met by aggregating the co-parties' contributions, while each co-party separately fulfils the requirements relating to the nature of a potential party.

[294] Above b.

[295] For criticism, see eg Fortin (n 219); E Pothelet, 'Symposium: Three Questions to the Author' (*OpinioJuris*, 21 January 2019) <http://opiniojuris.org/2019/01/21/symposium-three-questions-to-the-author/>; for tentative support, see B Maganza, 'Which Role for Hybrid Entities Involved in Multi-Parties NIACs? Applying The ICRC's Support-Based Approach to the Armed Conflict in Mali' (2019) 59 QIL Zoom-in 25, 39–40.

The criteria for when the activities by multiple entities can be jointly assessed as co-parties to the same armed conflict cannot be inferred from the concepts of armed conflict itself. Nor do the concepts of armed conflict provide criteria for when multiple entities that do separately fulfil the requirements for the existence of an armed conflict in their relationship to the adversary qualify as co-parties to the same armed conflict.

Chapter 4 turns to these questions and, building on the parameters set out in this chapter, develops an account of the legal criteria for identifying co-parties to armed conflicts.

4

Criteria for Establishing Co-Party Status

1. Introduction

Based on the findings of Chapter 3, the starting point for developing an account of the legal criteria for identifying co-parties is as follows. On the one hand, international law requires classifying *certain* factual situations as instances of multiple co-parties to the same armed conflict. On the other hand, few, if any, clear rules exist specifically for identifying *which* situations must be classified as such. Chapter 3 set out some parameters. It argued that each co-party must separately fulfil 'party-related' requirements (concerning the requisite nature and structure of the collective entity). By contrast, it is sufficient that the contributions by all co-parties taken together fulfil the 'conflict-related' requirements (concerning the nature of the confrontation between the collective entities) for the existence of an international or non-international armed conflict respectively. There remains an open question, however, on when to conduct this aggregated assessment and when to consider multiple entities as co-parties in situations where no aggregation of their acts would be necessary to fulfil the requirements for the existence of an armed conflict.

In other words, international law assumes that co-party status can exist and that there is a path to get to this result—without, however, setting out this path in treaty or customary rules designed or developed specifically for this purpose. At the same time, the contours of this path would be crucial both to develop a more refined conceptual understanding of the regulation of armed conflict and to approach the identification of co-parties in practice.

Against this background, Chapter 4 aims to present a conceptually helpful and practically plausible account to draw the path to identifying co-parties. To meet both its conceptual and its practical aims, the chapter does not develop the account from scratch. Section 2 critically reviews key approaches that have been suggested to identify co-parties in specific conflict settings, in inter-State and non-international armed conflicts, respectively. Section 3 then develops a common analytical framework for identifying co-parties in multiparty armed conflicts.

In doing so, the analysis builds in part on structural considerations pertaining to the system of the international legal framework regulating armed conflict. Based on the findings in Part I of the book, the framework aims to suggest a conceptualisation of the delimitation between party status and third-party status that is

Party Status to Armed Conflict in International Law. Alexander Wentker, Oxford University Press. © Alexander Wentker 2024.
DOI: 10.1093/oso/9780198900900.003.0005

appropriate in light of the legal consequences of identifying an entity as either a party or a third party.

This means, to some extent, working backwards from the regulation of the implications of party status to discern the assumptions underlying this legal framework about the factual situation that co-parties are presupposed to be in. The guiding question will therefore be to which factual situation it is appropriate to attach the respective legal consequences. Chapters 1 and 2 of this book have shown how the legal positions of parties and third parties within the regulatory framework of armed conflict structurally differ and that this dichotomous differentiation is worth maintaining. The delimitation between the two statuses should reflect that the legal implications of party status situate parties as the principal collective subjects in armed conflict, bearing central sets of obligations with respect to that conflict, possessing certain—nuanced—permissions, and triggering corresponding (potentially far-reaching) changes of the law applicable to individuals. Extending this status to actors that are only remotely connected to the conflict would distort this conception of centrality and the interplay between parties and third parties. The position of abstention required of third parties seems more fitting for such entities. Conversely, an overly narrow conception of party status could yield equally distorted results if collective actors who play a central role within a coordinated framework are qualified as third parties.

Methodologically, it may be recalled here that these structural considerations inform a systematic interpretation of the treaty provisions that refer to parties to the conflict, that is, an interpretation in light of the 'context' of the provisions, as well as their 'purpose' under Article 31(1), (3) VCLT. Regarding customary rules referring to parties to the conflict, those same systematic considerations equally matter. This is so, regardless of whether one subscribes to the interpretability of customary international law as methodological matter, because systematic, deductive considerations pertaining to the structure of the legal system feed into the process of identifying the existence and content of rules of customary international law.[1]

Beyond the above considerations regarding the structure and system of the international legal framework that regulates armed conflicts, the legal implications attached to identifying an entity as a (co-)party to an armed conflict also give rise to normative or policy concerns—in particular, pertaining to the permissibility of targeting individuals—as discussed in the previous chapters.[2] These concerns will be accommodated in considering where the line delimiting party and third-party status is to be drawn.

In addition to a refined conceptual understanding of the legal framework, guidance is required on how to practically approach the identification of co-parties. The concrete legal consequences that flow from identifying an entity as a

[1] See Chapter 2, nn 43–44.
[2] Chapter 1.4.a.i.; Chapter 3.4.a.iii.

co-party (set out in Chapters 1 and 2) mean that this finding is practically relevant. Consequently, the need for this identification will arise in actual international practice. A central practical consideration is the context in which the assessment is made, that is: when, by whom, in relation to what, and for what purpose.

Given the varied implications of party status, the need for identifying co-parties arises not only *ex post*, such as in judicial proceedings, but also with a view to actual conflict settings. Here, the assessment has to be made *ex ante*. In conflict settings, time, evidence, and other resources to establish whether nuanced doctrinal criteria have been met will typically be much more constrained than they are in *ex post* settings. Concepts that can only be applied with the benefit of hindsight are, therefore, practically insufficient to cater to military needs. It is beyond the scope, and thus not the aim, of the present study to offer comprehensive military guidance to issues of co-party identification in practice. Nonetheless, to illustrate how the conceptual elements put forward here could be operationalised, suggestions will be made at different stages of the analysis on how the general criteria may be assessed in practice. These suggestions affirm and buttress the practical workability of the proposed concepts.

In this regard, the analytical framework also aims to align with the existing international practice. At the same time, practice that explicitly addresses these questions proves to be scarce and often ambiguous. The prospect of international practice settling on clearly discernible criteria for co-party identification thus appears slim. The rare instances where States specify whom they identify as parties are unlikely to produce much conceptual clarity on a specific criterion. Structurally, such clarity could rather be expected, for example, of international and domestic courts and tribunals or treaty bodies. These institutions are more attuned to articulating and refining doctrinal concepts through their jurisprudence. As we have seen, however, questions of identifying parties typically arise incidentally in judicial proceedings and are particularly prone to be dealt with implicitly. Nuanced considerations that could illuminate relevant criteria are, therefore, improbable. Against this background, instances from international practice will, for present purposes, mainly illustrate the practical relevance and workability of the proposed conceptual elements.

2. Charting the field of approaches to criteria for identifying co-parties

While no common framework for establishing co-party status has been suggested as yet, relevant elements of solution have been advanced from different angles for certain kinds of multiparty conflict settings, both for international and non-international armed conflicts (as well as historically already for inter-State wars). To prepare the ground for developing an account of the legal criteria for identifying co-parties, section 2 analyses what insights these approaches can yield for understanding the identification of co-parties under international law and to what extent they reveal issues that require further thought and clarification.

a. Approaches in inter-State conflicts

Inter-State conflict was the focus of the laws of war for centuries. Issues of ascertaining party status in cooperation settings thus first arose in the inter-State context. Section i. retraces the approaches developed in classic treatises in this regard and critically assesses their analytical value for understanding the criteria for identifying co-parties under current international law. Sections ii. and iii. then scrutinise the extent to which the content of two sets of rules prohibiting specific cooperative acts with warring States, namely neutrality law and the prohibition of the use of force, could be relied on to specify the criteria for co-party identification in international armed conflicts.

i. Classic treatises on assisting States as co-belligerents

Cooperation in warfare is probably as old as warfare itself. The legal implications regarding party status have been explicitly addressed by writers throughout the past centuries. Without rehearsing what Parry has succinctly labelled 'nineteenth century … catalogues of the praises of famous men'[3], there are good reasons to consider some key historical writings on this particular subject. First, although formally even the most eminent legal scholars 'are not legislators, nor lawmakers in international relations',[4] many of these scholars' writings had a notable influence on State practice during and beyond their lifetime.[5] Secondly, given the relatively scarce scholarly attention paid to this issue since the Second World War, the classical treatments of belligerent status in multiparty settings continue to be among the more developed approaches to date. Thirdly, in light of present-day practice claiming to rely on allegedly well-established traditional understandings of co-belligerency,[6] clarifications about the historical evolution of the relevant concepts may prove insightful. Therefore, by briefly reviewing key classical writings, this section will sketch how the understanding of the contours and operation of co-party status has developed. This will prepare the ground for critically analysing

[3] C Parry, *The Sources and Evidences of International Law* (Manchester UP 1965) 103.

[4] M Lachs, 'Teachings and Teaching of International Law' (1976) 151 RCADI 161, 169. On the relevance of international legal academic discourse as a social phenomenon, see G Hernandez, 'The Responsibility of the International Legal Academic: Situating the Grammarian within the "Invisible College"' in J d'Aspremont, T Gazzini, and A Nollkaemper (eds), *International Law as a Profession* (CUP 2017) 174ff; O Schachter, 'Invisible College of International Lawyers' (1977–78) 72 NULR 217.

[5] See eg for Vattel nn 22–23.

[6] Below b.i.

to what extent earlier understandings can still shed light on the issue in contemporary international law.

Grotius suggested 'that he is counted in the ranks of the enemy who supplies a hostile army with what is directly useful for war'. Conversely, 'we must call ally and friend not only him who takes post beside us in battle, but also him who openly supplies all the things necessary for waging war'.[7] The point that States assisting others in war can become parties alongside their cooperation partners was elaborated by Wolff, about a century after Grotius, who argued that:

> he who allies himself to my enemy, as by sending him troops or subsidies, or by assisting him in any manner, engages in war against me, and therefore becomes a participant in the war. Therefore, since one is an enemy when a war exists between him and me, he who allies himself with my enemy, as by sending troops or subsidies, or by assisting him in war in any manner, is my enemy.[8]

To better understand the legal construct underlying the identification of co-parties in such cases, it is essential to recall that Grotius and Wolff, like many writers of their time, considered that (under the law of nations) waging war had to be preceded or accompanied by a declaration of war.[9] To consider assisting States as co-belligerents, this view required a twofold legal twist. On the one hand, Grotius noted that '[a] war declared against any one ... is held to be declared at the same time ... upon all who will join him as allies'.[10] Declarations of war were thus implicitly extended to the opponent's present and future co-belligerents.[11] By the same token, the assisting State itself did not need to declare war explicitly to be considered a co-belligerent. As Wolff explained, that State 'declare[d] by that very fact that he wishes to be a participant in the war carried on against me'.[12]

Other writers were more reluctant to consider assisting States as co-belligerents. Writing before Grotius, Gentili had cautioned that 'because some hostile act is committed by such giving of aid, that does not necessarily constitute war'.[13] Vattel later raised similar objections to Wolff's position. While Vattel agreed that 'every ally of my enemy is himself my enemy',[14] he disagreed that a State would automatically be

[7] H Grotius, *De jure belli ac pacis libri tres*, vol II (F Kelsey tr, Clarendon Press 1925) 787 (approvingly referring to the position of the Byzantine writer Procopius).

[8] C Wolff, *Jus gentium methodo scientifica pertractatum*, vol II (J Drake tr, Clarendon Press 1934) 376.

[9] Grotius (n 7) 633; Wolff (n 8) 366ff. For a prominent proponent of the opposite view, see C van Bynkershoek, *Quaestionum Juris Publici libri duo*, vol II (T Frank tr, Clarendon Press 1930) 18ff. On declarations of war see Chapter 3.1.a. and below 3.b.iii.(1)(a), 3.c.

[10] Grotius (n 7) 646.

[11] Wolff (n 8) 378.

[12] ibid 377.

[13] A Gentili, *De jure belli libri tres*, vol II (J Rolfe tr, Clarendon Press 1933) 140.

[14] E de Vattel, *Le Droit des gens, ou, Principes le la loi naturelle, appliqués à la conduite aux affaires des nations et des souverains*, vol III (C Fenwick tr, Carnegie Institution 1916) 264.

a (co-)belligerent if it 'do[es] no more than give [the adversary] a definite amount of help, either by allowing certain troops to be raised or by advancing money'.[15] Instead, it would give the aggrieved State a just cause to wage war against the other State.[16] Crucially, this left the aggrieved State with discretion on triggering the legal effects of belligerent status or maintaining peaceful relations.[17]

Both Gentili and Vattel pointed to a body of practice in line with their position. Gentili, then Regius Professor at Oxford, noted the Queen of England's frequent subsidies and arms supplies to Belgium against Spain.[18] Vattel, in turn, stressed that other States had tolerated the Swiss practice of regularly assisting parties in war, which had 'given rise to the *custom* of not regarding such assistance ... as an act of hostility'.[19] The reference to practice supporting one's position[20] is undoubtedly a crucial methodological development for the discipline of international law more broadly.[21] Conclusions drawn from this practice on the state of (customary) international law at the time should, however, be taken with a grain of salt. Indeed, both Gentili and Vattel essentially justify the specific practice and interests of the rulers of their respective States.

Nonetheless, Vattel's conceptions, in particular, concretely shaped State practice during his lifetime (through his activities as a diplomat)[22] and beyond (through the influence of his writings on subsequent political decision-makers).[23] This was especially so in the US,[24] where his ideas were taken up by influential authors like Wheaton and Halleck.[25] Other subsequent writers, however, were more critical towards Vattel's concepts and rejected Vattel's conceptualisation of assistance as a 'just cause' to make war against the State providing the assistance.[26]

[15] ibid 265.

[16] ibid 265–266.

[17] ibid 265.

[18] Gentili (n 13) 140.

[19] de Vattel (n 14) 265 (emphasis added).

[20] Subsequent writers have questioned to what extent Swiss practice supported Vattel's legal position. See eg C Calvo, *Le Droit international: Théorique et pratique*, vol IV (5th edn, Rivière 1896) 105–106.

[21] See generally F Iurlaro, *The Invention of Custom: Natural Law and the Law of Nations, c.1550–1750* (OUP 2021) 103–104, 189.

[22] See eg G Martens, *Précis de droit des gens, fondé sur les traités et l'usage* (W Cobbett tr, Cobbett and Morgan 1802) 319–320 (approvingly referring to an 'opinion of the minister of the Elector of Saxony relative to the ... alliance of 1746 between Austria and Russia'—Vattel was then in the service of the Elector of Saxony).

[23] P Allott, *The Health of Nations: Society and Law beyond the State* (CUP 2002) 416.

[24] V Chetail, 'Vattel and the American Dream: An Inquiry into the Reception of the *Law of Nations* in the United States' in P-M Dupuy and V Chetail (eds), *The Roots of International Law/Les Fondements du droit international: Liber amicorum Peter Haggenmacher* (Brill 2014).

[25] H Wheaton, *Elements of International Law* (8th edn, reprint Clarendon Press [1866] 1936) 434; H Halleck, *International Law or, Rules Regulating the Intercourse between States in Peace and War* (Bancroft 1861) 419.

[26] Calvo (n 20) 106; F Martens, *Traité de droit international* (A Léo tr, Maresq 1883) 196; A Heffter, *Das Europäische Völkerrecht der Gegenwart auf den bisherigen Grundlagen* (8th edn, F Geffcken, HW Müller 1888) 252.

Through his highly influential treatise, Oppenheim emblematically set out how conceptions of identifying co-parties in cooperation settings evolved into the twentieth century. When several States cooperated on either side of a war, Oppenheim considered that there could be 'accessory' belligerent parties, which 'provide help and succour only in a limited way to a principal belligerent party at war with another State'.[27] Along the lines of previous writers, updated to reflect technological evolutions in warfare, Oppenheim listed a wide range of acts that could have this effect, including:

> paying subsidies, sending a certain number of troops or men-of-war to take part in the contention, granting a coaling station to the men-of-war of a principal party, allowing the latter's troops a passage through their territory, and the like.[28]

Oppenheim clearly stated that '[s]uch accessory party becomes a belligerent through rendering help'[29]—without the discretion (advocated by Vattel) for the adverse party not to regard the accessory as a belligerent.[30] Crucially, moreover, Oppenheim advocated an objective conception of the state of war.[31] He thus ascribed the legal consequences regarding belligerent status directly to the acts of the cooperating States, rather than construing them as an implicit declaration of war. The distinction between 'principal' and 'accessory' belligerents seems to have been explanatory. It did not entail any difference in the legal implications of the respective belligerent statuses. The notion of 'accessory' conveyed that the (co-)belligerent status of an assisting State depended on the belligerent status of the State receiving support.

Subsequent editors of *Oppenheim's International Law* left these passages essentially unchanged, until and including the (so far) latest edition of the second volume by Hersch Lauterpacht in 1952.[32] This suggests that these ideas still made sense to them, even amidst an international legal framework for war that had profoundly changed after the two World Wars. This framework was now shaped by the prohibition to use force and the UN Charter system of collective security, on the one hand, and substantial developments in the *jus in bello* with the 1949 GCs, on the other hand. Of course, the changes were still fairly recent in 1952 and the GCs were not yet widely ratified. Still, Lauterpacht devoted extensive commentary to

[27] L Oppenheim, *International Law: A Treatise*, vol II (Longmans 1906) 87.
[28] ibid.
[29] ibid.
[30] Other nineteenth-century writers followed Vattel's account regarding discretion, see eg Heffter (n 20) 252–253 (also citing international practice).
[31] Oppenheim (n 27) 57. See also S Neff, *War and the Law of Nations: A General History* (CUP 2005) 175.
[32] H Lauterpacht, *Oppenheim's International Law*, vol II (7th edn, Longmans 1952) 253–254.

these developments in that very same last edition of *Oppenheim*.[33] He can, therefore, be hardly suspected of having failed to appreciate their impact.

To assess the analytical value of the historical scholarly accounts for present purposes, it is nonetheless important to consider that these accounts were written in light of legal implications of co-belligerent status that differed from the implications of identifying co-parties under current international law. In particular, the prohibition of the use of force means that an assisting State's party status no longer implies that the opponent can 'rightfully wage war' against it, a background assumption of the accounts from previous centuries. At the same time, Part I of the book has shown that the central aim of the accounts—drawing a distinction between parties and third parties—has not lost its significance, although the legal content of the respective statuses has evolved.

The accounts reviewed here accommodated the identification of co-parties without requiring that the potential co-party separately meet the requirements that would be necessary to give rise to a separate war (namely a declaration of war or material acts of war of a sufficient scale).[34] This is in line with the findings of Chapter 3. Regarding the underlying construct of identifying co-parties, the rather shadowy persistence of the possibility of declared wars in contemporary international law[35] sounds a note of caution about whether factual behaviour may still be construed as an implicit declaration of war, as section 3 of this chapter will explain.[36] Regarding the actual legal criteria, however, many accounts left open the exact requirements that would have to be met to establish co-party status in a given case. Some writers have suggested a certain connection to the hostilities,[37] an aspect that will still prove significant today.[38] Most authors have merely listed types of activities that could give rise to co-belligerency. While helpful to illustrate that no specific type of activity was required, the open-ended enumerations do not remove the need for legal criteria for those accounts that did not defer establishing an assisting State's co-party status to the discretion of the adverse State. This need for criteria persists. As will be argued in section 3, discretion on this point would be inconsistent with the system of the international legal framework regulating armed conflict.[39]

The following sections consider to what extent rules prohibiting certain acts of assistance in armed conflict, stemming from neutrality law and the prohibition of the use of force, could be relied on to specify the criteria for identifying co-parties.

33 See notably ibid 177ff, 634ff, 645–646. Lauterpacht's treatment of the laws of war considers the GCs throughout (see eg ibid 353ff).

34 See generally Chapter 3.2.a.

35 Chapter 3.2.a.

36 Below 3.b.iii.(1).

37 Heffter (n 20) 248 (considering as participation in hostilities acts that 'strengthened the attack or defence system of one belligerent Power against the other' (own translation)). See also Calvo (n 20) 106.

38 Below 3.b.i.(2).

39 Below 3.b.iii.(1).

ii. Delimiting neutrality and (co-)party status: distinguishing violations of neutrality obligations from the termination of neutral status

The legal relationship between parties to an international armed conflict and third States (ie neutrals, has traditionally been—and arguably remains in part—regulated by the law of neutrality).[40] Given the lack of rules specifically developed to draw a line as to when a State moves from neutral status to (co-)party status, there remains a temptation to rely on the content of the rules of neutrality law themselves.[41] The cardinal distinction between compliance with the rules attached to neutral status and the termination of neutral status is generally accepted.[42] Nonetheless, there have been persistent suggestions that a neutral State would become a party through 'significant' or 'substantial', and 'systematic' violations of its neutrality obligations not to provide assistance to parties and prevent them from using neutral territory.[43] This section argues that the temptation driving such propositions should be resisted.[44]

Proposals to draw on qualified violations of neutrality law have not been specifically justified. While they are sometimes claimed to have been traditionally widely accepted,[45] the classical treatises discussed in the preceding section suggest otherwise. Oppenheim (and later Lauterpacht), for example, saw no difficulty in maintaining both a distinction between violations of neutrality obligations (even the most serious ones)[46] and the termination of neutrality, as well as the idea that States could become co-belligerents by assisting another belligerent.[47]

[40] See Chapter 2.2.

[41] For such reliance on neutrality violations, see eg O Hathaway and S Shapiro, *The Internationalists: How a Radical Plan to Outlaw War Remade the World* (Simon & Schuster 2017) 91; V Lanovoy, *Complicity and Its Limits in the Law of International Responsibility* (Hart 2016) 202; *Hamlily v Obama* (2009) 616 F Supp 2d 63 (DC Cir) 75.

[42] J Kunz, *Kriegsrecht und Neutralitätsrecht* (Springer 1935) 221; Lauterpacht (n 32) 672, 752; M Bothe, 'The Law of Neutrality' in D Fleck (ed), *The Handbook of International Humanitarian Law* (4th edn, OUP 2021) 611; R Tucker, *The Law of War and Neutrality at Sea* (Government Printing Office 1957) 258–259; F Russo, 'Neutrality at Sea in Transition: State Practice in the Gulf War as Emerging International Customary Law' (1988) 19 ODIL 381, 387; C Chinkin, *Third Parties in International Law* (Clarendon Press 1993) 306; H Haug, *Neutralität und Völkergemeinschaft* (Polygraphischer Verlag 1962) 17; U Pieper, *Neutralität von Staaten* (Peter Lang 1996) 83.

[43] C Bradley and J Goldsmith, 'Congressional Authorization and the War on Terrorism' (2005) 118 HLR 2047, 2112; T Bridgeman, 'The Law of Neutrality and the Conflict with Al Qaeda' (2010) 85 NYULR 1186, 1200; N Weizmann, 'The End of Armed Conflict, the End of Participation in Armed Conflict, and the End of Hostilities: Implications for Detention Operations under the 2001 AUMF' (2016) 47 Colum Hum Rts LR 204, 226ff; N Weizmann, 'Are the U.S. and U.K. Parties to the Saudi-led Armed Conflict against the Houthis in Yemen?' (*Just Security*, 22 September 2016) <www.justsecurity.org/33095/u-s-u-k-parties-saudi-led-armed-conflict-houthis-yemen/>.

[44] See also J Upcher, *Neutrality in Contemporary International Law* (OUP 2020) 63; C Schaller, 'Der völkerrechtliche Rahmen für Waffenlieferungen an die Ukraine' (2023) 60 AVR 439, 451.

[45] See eg N Verlinden, '"Are We at War?" State Support to Parties to Armed Conflict: Consequences under *Jus in Bello, Jus ad Bellum* and Neutrality Law' (PhD, KU Leuven 2019) 306; Bradley and Goldsmith (n 43) 2111–2112.

[46] Oppenheim (n 20) 388; Lauterpacht (n 32) 671–672, 752.

[47] nn 27–29.

It may, of course, be the case that the same conduct that would be manifestly contrary to the duties of a neutral State would *also* make that State a party to the conflict. In that sense, it may be possible to consider neutrality law as a rough yardstick in identifying co-parties. The value of this yardstick would remain limited owing to the lack of clarity on what 'significant', 'substantial', and 'systematic' neutrality violations would require.

At any rate, however, it would be problematic to draw a legal connection between the two distinct questions. Legally speaking, one does not follow from the other. Leaving aside the conceptual difficulty of construing an act as violating an obligation from a status that the act itself terminates, the connection would mistake the very purpose of neutrality law. The purpose of neutrality law is to contain the effects of war by regulating the relationship between parties and neutrals. This regulation includes duties on neutrals and remedies to a party aggrieved by violations. These remedies can be exercised against the neutral to enforce its abstention from the conflict *as a neutral*, despite its violations of neutrality law.[48]

Another reason not to connect the loss of neutral status to the violation of neutrality obligations stems from the interplay of neutrality law with the collective security system under the UN Charter.[49] Consider the case of a neutral State engaging in activities that would be contrary to its neutral duties but are authorised by the Security Council under Chapter VII, such as assisting a State facing aggression by another State. Here, the neutral does not commit a violation of its neutrality duties if the authorisation is taken to exclude the applicability of neutrality law or modify its content[50] (rather than merely to preclude the wrongfulness of an act that prima facie violates neutrality law).[51] There would no longer be a violation to which the loss of neutral status could be connected. Connecting the termination of neutral status to the violation of neutral duties may, therefore, entail that Security Council authorisations could prevent a State from becoming a (co-)party that would otherwise have qualified as such.[52] This consequence seems problematic given that establishing party status has significant implications for the application of international humanitarian law (IHL). It would be inconsistent with the overall system of the regulation of armed conflict and the notion that the application of IHL is triggered by factual situations regardless of the will of States.[53]

Further, distinguishing between violations of neutrality duties and co-party status better aligns with international practice, which has not established a legal connection in this respect.[54] To illustrate, in the Iran–Iraq War, Iran considered

[48] Chapter 2.2.a., d.
[49] Chapter 2.2.b.i.
[50] For this view, see Bothe (n 42) 605–607.
[51] For this view, see Upcher (n 44) 153–154.
[52] C Greenwood, 'Scope of Application of Humanitarian Law' in D Fleck (ed), *The Handbook of International Humanitarian Law* (2nd edn, OUP 2008) 58 (accepting this consequence).
[53] See also Verlinden (n 45) 309–310.
[54] For a thorough review of practice, see Upcher (n 44) 57–63.

that Kuwait had become a co-party of Iraq by assisting Iraq by, inter alia, military logistical support, and intelligence provision, and allowing its territory to be used by Iraq.[55] Iran did not, however, seem to regard this conclusion as a legal consequence of Kuwaiti violations of neutrality law. Conversely, in the *Oil Platforms* case, Iran alleged that the US had systematically violated its duties as a neutral by assisting Iraq and Kuwait in the Iran–Iraq War.[56] These violations did not lead Iran to conclude that the US had itself become a co-party of those States. Kuwait itself and various other States reacted that Kuwait had maintained neutral status without justifying this by reference to the lawfulness of Kuwait's conduct under neutrality law. Kuwait denied the facts alleged by Iran,[57] and other States admitted Kuwait's assistance but noted that Kuwait was not 'militarily engaged'[58] or 'directly involved' in the conflict[59] and was, thus, not a party. The 2003 Iraq War yields similar illustrations. For example, German courts raised 'grave concerns' that Germany violated its neutrality duties by allowing the US to use German territory, without even hinting at the possibility that such violations might have rendered Germany a party to the conflict.[60]

A more promising starting point is to consider, like Lauterpacht, that 'acts of war' will make a neutral State a party,[61] or, in contemporary terminology, 'participation in hostilities'[62]—rather than violations of neutrality obligations. The contours of what this would require have not received much attention. Greenwood has clarified that to make a neutral State a co-party, the 'act of war' would not need to be such that it would have given rise to an international armed conflict on its own in the first place. Instead, 'direct support to the military operations of one of the belligerents' would suffice, provided that it is 'directly related, i.e. closely related in space and time, to measures harmful to the adversary'.[63] Similarly, Upcher has required that 'there must be some sort of direct, causal link between the neutral's action and an act of belligerency'.[64] Beyond these occasional hints, on which section

[55] 'Letter Dated 14 August 1987 from the Permanent Representative of the Islamic Republic of Iran to the United Nations Addressed to the Secretary-General' UN Doc S/19041 [4]; *Oil Platforms (Iran v United States)* Reply and Defence to Counterclaim Iran (10 March 1999) [2.21]–[2.26]; *Oil Platforms (Iran v United States)* Further Response Iran (24 September 2001) [3.23]–[3.27].

[56] *Oil Platforms*, Reply Iran (n 55) [7.9]; *Oil Platforms*, Further Response Iran (n 55) [3.32]–[3.38].

[57] 'Letter Dated 14 July 1988 from the Permanent Representative of Kuwait to the United Nations Addressed to the Secretary-General' (14 July 1988) UN Doc S/20015.

[58] 'The US Plan to Protect Kuwaiti Ships in the Gulf by Putting Them under US Flags' (1987) 26 ILM 1429, 1430; see also *Oil Platforms (Iran v United States)* Counter-Memorial US (23 June 1997) [1.17], [1.66].

[59] R Siekmann, 'Netherlands State Practice for the Parliamentary Year 1986–1987' (1988) 19 NYIL 279, 390; see similarly UNSC, 2543rd Meeting (29 May 1984) UN Doc S/PV.2543 [12] (Morocco).

[60] Federal Administrative Court, Judgement of 21 June 2005 (2 WD 12.04) [4.1.4.1.1]–[4.1.4.1.2].

[61] Lauterpacht (n 32) 753.

[62] Bothe (n 42) 611.

[63] Greenwood (n 52) 58; see also Upcher (n 44) 63 ('direct military support').

[64] Upcher (n 44) 63.

3 of this chapter will pick up, the delineation between neutral and co-party status remains opaque.

iii. Use of force and aggression by assistance

Akin to propositions of relying on neutrality law, specification of the legal criteria for co-party identification could also be sought in another central rule that prohibits specific acts of cooperation—the prohibition of the use of force.[65] The patterns of cooperation in inter-State armed conflict that give rise to challenges for identifying co-parties also raise issues under the *jus ad bellum*. In particular, such cooperation patterns raise questions about the extent to which assistance by States to uses of force by other States is itself covered by the prohibition of the use of force. The content of the prohibition of the use of force in this respect could then be relied on to delimit the factual patterns that give rise to co-party status to an international armed conflict.

At the outset, the findings of the book so far do not suggest that the same criteria necessarily govern the two sets of legal questions. To recall, Chapter 3 has found no necessary identity between the concepts of use of force under the *jus ad bellum* and resort to armed force constituting an international armed conflict under the *jus in bello*. In any event, an identity of concepts at that level would not necessarily impact the rules on identifying co-parties. This is because, as Chapter 3 has shown, co-party status to an international armed conflict does not require performing acts that would be sufficient in isolation to give rise to a separate international armed conflict.

Nonetheless, prohibitions of assistance under the *jus ad bellum* could potentially serve as practical yardsticks for establishing whether the respective State has become a party to an international armed conflict, notably where such assistance constitutes an act of aggression (ie a particularly serious use of force).[66] In this respect, Okimoto has argued that the acts enumerated in the 1974 Definition of Aggression[67] undoubtedly amount to an international armed conflict and that in all cases in which the Security Council had so far identified a situation as an 'act of aggression', there had been an international armed conflict under IHL.[68]

[65] On the continuing application of the prohibition to use force even once an armed conflict has begun, see Chapter 1, n 125.

[66] See eg C McDougall, *The Crime of Aggression under the Rome Statute of the International Criminal Court* (2nd edn, CUP 2021) 93; see ibid 106–120 for a thorough review of UNSC and UNGA practice as well as ICJ decisions on this point.

[67] Annexed to UNGA Res 3314 (XXIX) (14 December 1974) (Definition of Aggression).

[68] K Okimoto, *The Distinction and Relationship between Jus ad Bellum and Jus in Bello* (Hart 2011) 131–133.

Accordingly, if specific acts of inter-State assistance are covered by the prohibition of aggression, this indicates that the State performing such acts will likely also qualify as a party to an international armed conflict, even if one does not legally follow from the other.[69]

Going further, it remains possible that such *jus ad bellum* rules will come to be regarded as legally determinative of questions of party status if accepted in future practice. By way of an illustration, section 3 will explore this possibility for one particularly relevant *jus ad bellum* rule in this respect, namely the rule contained in Article 3(f) of the Definition of Aggression. That rule qualifies as aggression allowing territory placed at the disposal of another State to be used for an act of aggression.[70] Generally, however, the scholarly debates have framed the issues arising from inter-State cooperation for the scope of the prohibition of the use of force and co-party identification in separate terms.[71] International practice also does not seem to have established a legal connection in this respect.[72] Conceptually, even if it is accepted that acts constituting a use of force or aggression necessarily also make the respective State a party to an international armed conflict, this may not solve all legal issues for present purposes. In particular, *jus ad bellum* rules do not seem to provide general criteria for when a State would be a *co*-party, rather than a party to a separate international armed conflict.[73]

In summary, although concepts of co-party status have a considerable historical pedigree in inter-State settings, the criteria for identifying (co-)parties in international armed conflicts have not been specified so far. Relying on the content of neutrality obligations and the prohibition on the use of force can, at best, provide rough yardsticks. Co-party identification in international armed conflicts has thus remained underdeveloped, to the point that it has been suggested to rely on more specific approaches recently advanced for non-international armed conflicts[74] (in contrast with analogies from the inter-State context for identifying co-parties in non-international armed conflicts).[75] The next section turns to these approaches.

[69] See also V Koutroulis, 'Jus ad/contra Bellum' in R Van Steenberghe (ed), *Droit international humanitaire: Un régime spécial de droit international?* (Bruylant 2013) 173 (pointing out that the UNSC practice does not draw a legal connection between the respective concepts and that future practice could deviate from this line).

[70] Below 3.c.ii.

[71] See eg Verlinden (n 45) (discussing both questions separately); though see recently R van Steenberghe, 'Military Assistance to Ukraine: Enquiring the Need for Any Legal Justification under International Law' (2023) 28 JCSL 231, 235–236 (suggesting a connection in the opposite direction of the proposition discussed here, ie that the test for becoming a co-party could inform the test for when inter-State assistance amounts to a use of force).

[72] nn 274–285.

[73] Below 3.c.ii.

[74] n 127.

[75] Below b.i.

b. Approaches in non-international armed conflicts

With non-international armed conflicts being the prevalent type of conflict in international practice today, their international legal regulation has increasingly received the attention of States and scholars. Although identifying co-parties has rarely been at the forefront of these debates, such issues have notably arisen in two contexts: first, for cooperating armed groups in the so-called war on terror and, secondly, for foreign States militarily supporting the territorial State engaged in a non-international armed conflict. In these contexts, two sets of emblematic approaches to identifying co-parties in specific conflict settings have developed, advanced by the US and the ICRC, respectively. These approaches have shaped the scholarly debate on the matter and merit closer scrutiny.

i. Analogies from the inter-State context: the 'associated forces' doctrine

One approach to identifying co-parties to non-international armed conflicts has emerged in the context of the so-called war on terror through the US practice of considering armed groups as 'associated forces' of other armed groups with which they cooperate and with which the US is engaged in armed conflict. In the aftermath of 9/11, Congress enacted the Authorization for Use of Military Force (AUMF), authorising the President to:

> use all necessary and appropriate force against those nations, organizations, or persons he determines planned, authorized, committed or aided the terrorist attacks that occurred on September 11, 2011, or harbored such organizations or persons.[76]

US administrations have interpreted this provision to include the use of force against 'associated forces' of al-Qaeda and the Taliban, at which the reference to 'organizations' in the AUMF is generally seen to be aimed.[77] This practice has developed in the context of justifying and expanding the authority of the US President under domestic law—namely regarding targeting and detention. Nonetheless, US administrations have made it clear that who qualifies as an 'associated force' needs to be assessed by reference to the US's understanding of international law. In particular, the administrations have understood the notion of 'associated forces' as informed by the 'well established concept of "co-belligerents" in the law of IAC'.[78]

[76] Authorization for Use of Military Force, Pub L No 107-40, 115 Stat 224 (2001), s 2(a).

[77] See eg US, 'Report on the Legal and Policy Frameworks Guiding the United States' Use of Military Force and Related National Security Operations' (December 2016) 3.

[78] *Parhat v Gates* (2008) 532 F 3d 834 (DC Cir) Brief for Respondent 30; J Johnson, 'National Security Law, Lawyers, and Lawyering in the Obama Administration—Dean's Lecture at Yale Law School, February 22, 2012' (2012) 31 Yale L Pol Rev 141, 146.

Conversely, the US's understanding of 'associated forces' now also informs whom the US identifies as (co-)parties to armed conflicts with the US.[79]

The idea underlying these alleged connections to international law concepts from the inter-State context can be traced to an argument advanced in a 2005 article by Bradley and Goldsmith, both having just left positions within the Bush administration. In essence, Bradley and Goldsmith argued that groups providing support to al-Qaeda could be considered its 'co-belligerents' if this support would have amounted to 'systematic or significant' violations of neutrality obligations had it been provided to a party to an international armed conflict by a third State.[80] Many scholars have rightly criticised this position.[81] Since violations of neutrality obligations, even if 'systematic or significant' do not in and of themselves terminate neutral status, the rule in international armed conflicts that Bradley and Goldsmith have sought to apply by analogy to non-international armed conflicts does not exist in the first place.[82]

Despite this conceptual flaw underpinning the 'associated forces' doctrine, the US executive[83] and courts[84] have embraced Bradley and Goldsmith's position. Since the Obama administration, the executive requires cumulatively that, to qualify as an 'associated force', 'the entity must be an organized, armed group that has entered the fight alongside al-Qa'ida or the Taliban' and is 'a co-belligerent with al-Qa'ida or the Taliban in hostilities against the United States or its coalition partners'.[85] These criteria hardly allow for a clear assessment of who is to be viewed as covered by the concept of an 'associated force'. Pointing out the lack of determinacy of the US's concept of 'associated forces', Ingber suggests that there may, in fact, be different competing understandings within the executive. The precise criteria of these understandings may not be entirely settled or may even be purposefully obscured by secrecy and ambiguity.[86]

[79] US DoD, 'Enhancing Security and Stability in Afghanistan, Report to Congress' (2016) 9; US DoD, 'Enhancing Security and Stability in Afghanistan, Report to Congress' (2018) 9.

[80] Bradley and Goldsmith (n 43) 2111–2112.

[81] See eg K Heller, 'The Use and Abuse of Analogy in IHL' in J Ohlin (ed), *Theoretical Boundaries of Armed Conflict and Human Rights* (CUP 2016) 270ff; R Ingber, 'Untangling Belligerency from Neutrality in the Conflict with Al-Qaeda' (2011) 47 Tex ILJ 75, 97. But see in favour of Bradley and Goldsmith's argument eg D Mortlock, 'Definite Detention: The Scope of the President's Authority to Detain Enemy Combatants' (2010) 4 Harv L Pol Rev 375, 395; B Farley, 'Targeting Anwar al-Aulaqi: A Case Study in US Drone Strikes and Targeted Killing' (2011) 2 AUNSLB 57, 74.

[82] Above a.ii.

[83] *Al-Bihani v Obama* (2010) 590 F 3d 866 (DC Cir) Brief for Appellees 31; *Khan v Obama* (2011) 655 F 3d 20 (DC Cir) Brief for Respondents-Appellees 42; *Doe v Mattis* (2018) 889 F 3d (DC Cir) Respondent's Factual Returns (14 February 2018) 14.

[84] See eg *Hamlily v Obama* (n 41) 70, 74–75.

[85] Johnson Yale Speech, 146; S Preston, 'Policy Address: "Legal Framework for the U.S. Use of Military Force Since 9/11"' (2015) 109 ASIL Proc 331, 333; Frameworks Report (2016) 4; Remarks by Acting Department of State Principal Deputy General Counsel William Castle, 'Congressional Authorizations on Use of Force—Speech at the NYC Bar Association' 11 December 2017 <www.scribd.com/document/366923593/Dod-Acting-General-Counsel-William-Castle-NYC-Bar-Remarks-Aumf-Dec-11#download&from_embed>; US, Report on Associated Forces (2014) <www.aclu.org/sites/default/files/field_document/53-1._exhibit_51_-_report_on_associated_forces_12.1.15.pdf> 2.

[86] R Ingber, 'Co-belligerency' 42 YJIL 67, 84–85.

The least problematic is the requirement that associated forces be organised armed groups. This requirement is in line with the idea advanced in Chapter 3 that sufficient organisation is an inherent characteristic that all parties to non-international armed conflicts must fulfil.[87] It should be noted, however, that the US does not seem to have consistently applied this criterion in line with the organisation requirement under international law.[88] The requirement that the respective group be a 'co-belligerent' of al-Qaeda or the Taliban (under international law) is question-begging for the purposes of setting out the US's view on precisely this concept. Given that the executive has, at different times, explicitly endorsed Bradley and Goldsmith's argument on co-belligerency as flowing from violations of neutrality law by analogy,[89] it would be plausible to regard this as a reference to such an understanding of co-belligerency.

At the same time, the additional requirement that the group must have 'entered the fight alongside al-Qa'ida or the Taliban' could be taken to suggest that the group in question must actively conduct hostilities.[90] However, although the exact meaning of this phrase has been left open, its application in US practice to different groups does not indicate such an understanding. Indeed, the US has also considered armed groups as 'associated forces' even when they did not actively conduct hostilities against the US. This has notably been the case of al-Shabaab, an Islamist group active mainly in and around Somalia, which (allegedly) cooperates with al-Qaeda on various levels of its fight against the US without, however, itself conducting combat operations against the US.[91] The US's qualification of al-Shabaab as an 'associated force' of al-Qaeda engaged in an armed conflict with the US does not specify, however, which requirements the conduct of the respective groups and the links between different cooperating armed groups regarding the armed conflict must meet.

To sum up, some form of 'associated forces' doctrine is by now deeply entrenched in US practice throughout several consecutive administrations[92] across all branches of power.[93] This is despite the doctrine's flawed conceptual

[87] Chapter 3.4.b.

[88] UN Special Rapporteur on Extrajudicial, Summary or Arbitrary Executions, 'Report—Addendum: Study on Targeted Killing' UN Doc A/HRC/14/24/Add.6 (28 May 2010) [55].

[89] n 83.

[90] Ingber (n 86) 94–97.

[91] US, 'Letter from the President—Supplemental 6-Month War Powers Letter' 5 December 2016 <https://obamawhitehouse.archives.gov/the-press-office/2016/12/05/letter-president-supplemental-6-month-war-powers-letter>; Frameworks Report (2016) 17; C Savage, *Power Wars: The Relentless Rise of Presidential Authority and Secrecy* (Back Bay Books 2017) 274ff (on the internal controversies within the Obama administration). Interestingly, the German federal government concluded that al-Shabaab had been a party to a non-international armed conflict with the US in Somalia already in 2012 (ie long before the US publicly referred to al-Shabaab as an 'associated force' of al-Qaeda). The German government seems to have believed this also to be the US's position—see Administrative Court of Cologne, Judgment of 27 April 2016 (4 K 5467/15) [17].

[92] *Doe v Mattis* (Respondent's Factual Returns) (n 13 ('longstanding consensus').

[93] In addition to the cases discussed in this section, for references to 'associated forces' in legislation, see eg Military Commissions Act (Pub L No 109-366, 120 Stat 2600 (2006)) s 948a(1)(i).

underpinnings, ambiguous contours, and problematic wider normative repercussions in light of the implications for rules applicable to targeting and detaining individuals under international law.[94] The exact content of this practice is hard to pin down and subject to constant evolution. With this caveat in mind, a first key parameter of the concept is that co-parties to non-international armed conflicts must each possess a sufficient degree of organisation. Secondly, armed groups co-operating with other groups conducting combat operations can also become their co-parties under the 'associated forces' doctrine, even if they do not themselves carry out such operations against the adversary.

ii. Participating in pre-existing non-international armed conflicts and cooperating in 'coalitions': the ICRC's 'support-based' and 'cumulative' approaches

The ICRC has put forward more elaborate and specific criteria than the associated forces doctrine to establish when entities providing support to a party to a pre-existing non-international armed conflict can themselves be considered (co-)parties to that conflict. In addition to this 'support-based' approach (SBA), the ICRC has subsequently advanced an approach to identify armed groups that coordinate and cooperate in 'coalitions' as co-parties—the 'cumulative' approach. This section critically analyses the content and scope as well as the rationale and conceptual underpinnings of these approaches so as to assess their contributions in developing a framework of the legal criteria for identifying co-parties.

(1) The SBA

The ICRC summarises its SBA as follows:

> [i]n the ICRC's view, a third power supporting one of the belligerents can be regarded as a party to the pre-existing NIAC when the following conditions are met: (1) there is a pre-existing NIAC taking place on the territory where the third power intervenes; (2) actions related to the conduct of hostilities are undertaken by the intervening power in the context of that pre-existing conflict; (3) the military operations of the intervening power are carried out in support of one of the parties to the pre-existing NIAC; and (4) the action in question is undertaken pursuant to an official decision by the intervening power to support a party involved in the pre-existing conflict.[95]

[94] Chapter 3.4.a.iii.(3) and below 3.c.iii.(1).

[95] T Ferraro, 'The ICRC's Legal Position on the Notion of Armed Conflict Involving Foreign Intervention and on Determining the IHL Applicable to this Type of Conflict' (2015) 97 IRRC 1227, 1231.

Once these conditions are met, the support is 'graft[ed] onto [the] pre-existing NIAC'.[96] This integrates the support provider into that conflict (as a party) alongside the party receiving the support, without the support provider having to meet the intensity threshold separately.[97] In the ICRC's view, therefore, this rationale conceptually accounts for element (1) of the SBA (ie the need for a pre-existing non-international armed conflict). A more practical explanation for this element is that the approach was developed with particular conflict settings in mind—notably, the interventions by multiple States in Afghanistan[98]—which mapped onto the scheme of further co-parties joining a pre-existing conflict.

The second and third elements of the SBA must be understood as implicitly informed by the constitutive elements of civilian direct participation in hostilities (DPH), as proposed by the ICRC's Interpretive Guidance.[99] This conceptual background is essential to specify the content of these relatively broadly worded criteria. Element (2) leaves open the nature of the 'relation' between the act of support and the conduct of hostilities. In its explanation of this criterion, however, the ICRC relies on aspects of the 'direct causation' test developed in the DPH context. The ICRC specifically builds on the idea that actions forming part of coordinated military operations can be deemed to directly cause harm if they form an 'integral part' of a coordinated military operation that causes harm in one step.[100] In that sense, the ICRC explains that the support provided must be an 'integral part of the collective conduct of hostilities'[101] as part of the pre-existing conflict,[102] in the sense that it must 'have a direct impact on the opposing party's ability to conduct hostilities'.[103] This would not require that the support as such 'cause[s] direct harm to the opposing party'. Instead, it would be sufficient if the support 'has an impact on the enemy *only in conjunction with* other acts undertaken by the supported party'.[104] Element (3) is understood by the ICRC in light of the 'belligerent nexus' concept developed for civilian DPH. The ICRC suggests assessing whether 'the

[96] T Ferraro, 'The Applicability and Application of International Humanitarian Law to Multinational Forces' (2013) 95 IRRC 561, 584.

[97] T Ferraro, 'International Humanitarian Law, Principled Humanitarian Action, Counterterrorism and Sanctions: Some Perspectives on Selected Issues' (2021) 103 IRRC 109, 116; Ferraro (n 95) 1231.

[98] B Oswald et al, 'Peace Forces at War: Implications under International Humanitarian Law' (2014) 108 ASIL Proc 149, 159 (response Ferraro); on the diverging views of States participating in the operations in Afghanistan as to their party status, see O Engdahl, 'Multinational Peace Operations Forces Involved in Armed Conflict: Who Are the Parties?' in K Mujezinović Larsen, C Guldahl Cooper, and G Nystuen (eds), *Searching for a 'Principle of Humanity' in International Humanitarian Law* (CUP 2012) 235–236.

[99] 'Q&A Session' (2019) 49 Collegium 58 (paraphrasing a response by the ICRC's Senior Legal Adviser Ferraro acknowledging that these concepts had been relied on in the framing of the SBA); on the constitutive elements of DPH as understood by the ICRC, see ICRC, Interpretive Guidance on the Notion of Direct Participation in Hostilities under International Humanitarian Law (2009) 16.

[100] DPH Guidance 54ff.

[101] Ferraro (n 96) 585 (fn 72).

[102] Ferraro (n 95) 1231.

[103] Ferraro (n 96) 585.

[104] ibid 585 (emphasis original).

military action of the third party ... can be reasonably and objectively interpreted as action designed to support one of the parties to the conflict to the detriment of the other'.[105]

Finally, the 'official decision' required by element (4) aims to ensure that the collective entity, the prospective party, as such becomes involved in the conflict, rather than only individuals. Accordingly, the requirement purports to exclude acts that result from errors or are ultra vires.[106] Although the focus on the involvement of the collective entity as such is an essential clarification in light of the reliance on individual DPH criteria by elements (2) and (3), this requirement raises both conceptual and practical issues. Conceptually, the requirement seems to commingle two sets of underlying issues that would have benefited from being unpacked on their own terms.

First, when an individual can be said to act for a State, an international organisation, or another collective entity is essentially a question of attribution.[107] In this respect, the ICRC's approach purports to distinguish itself from the general rules on attribution in international law[108] but fails to explain what would support the existence of a special rule of attribution in this realm.[109]

Secondly, the requirement embodies a certain subjective dimension of 'belligerent intent'.[110] The ICRC does not, however, clarify the requisite subjective standard. This clarification would have been not only conceptually beneficial but also practically helpful to effectively fulfil the aim to exclude errors. While an official decision may be a manifestation of a subjective element, it may not be necessary to ensure that the conduct did not stem from error since, for example, the mental state of the collective could also be tacitly formed. Conversely, an official decision may also not be *sufficient* in this respect since errors can also occur at the level of collective decision-making.

The scope of conflict settings to which the ICRC and scholars have applied the SBA has gradually expanded. The approach had initially been developed in the context of multinational forces intervening in support of a host State engaged in a non-international armed conflict.[111] Beyond the context of multinational forces' operations, the ICRC subsequently extended the SBA, first to support provided by States or international organisations to any conflict party, including to non-State

[105] Ferraro (n 95) 1234; for the parallel definition of 'belligerent nexus' in the DPH context, see DPH Guidance 58ff.

[106] Ferraro (n 96) 587.

[107] See in more detail below 3.b.i.(1).

[108] See ARSIWA, art 7 on the attribution of ultra vires acts.

[109] n 139.

[110] Ferraro (n 96) 587.

[111] ICRC, 'International Humanitarian Law and the Challenges of Contemporary Armed Conflicts' (2015) 22–23; Ferraro (n 96) 562.

parties fighting other non-State parties,[112] and then to support provided by non-State armed groups to a party.[113]

(2) *The 'cumulative' approach*

Adding to the extension of the scope of the SBA, the ICRC has more recently put forward another approach to the identification of co-parties in non-international armed conflicts. According to the ICRC, if multiple armed groups operate in 'some sort of coalition' by 'objectively and effectively adopt[ing] a collective approach to fighting against a common enemy', their contributions should be aggregated in assessing the intensity requirement, provided that they separately meet the organisation requirement.[114] Implicitly, the ICRC thus considers the respective armed groups as co-parties in these circumstances.

The rationale underlying the approach is primarily pragmatic:

> it would be unrealistic to expect States to operate under different paradigms – either the law-enforcement or the conduct-of-hostilities paradigm – to respond to the different groups that *operate together*.[115]

As with the SBA, the ICRC suggests that the 'cumulative' approach may be extended beyond its original setting 'to States coalescing with others States and/or NSAG(s) [non-State armed group(s)] in order to fight NSAG(s)'.[116] This extension inevitably raises questions about how the two approaches relate to each other. Both would apply to cooperation settings involving States, international organisations, and armed groups. The only remaining scope distinction is that the SBA can be applied only if a non-international armed conflict already existed when these entities entered into cooperation. On its face, the 'cumulative' approach could, however, also cover this situation to establish the co-party status of cooperating entities, even if no aggregation would be necessary, in that case, to establish the intensity (which would have been met already). While the ICRC apparently acknowledges this, it seems to consider the SBA as the more specific approach for this constellation and hints at a carve-out to the cumulative approach in this respect.[117]

[112] Ferraro (n 95) 1228.

[113] T Ferraro, 'Military Support to Belligerents: Can the Provider Become a Party to the Armed Conflict?' (2019) 49 Collegium 47, 53; K Dörmann and T Rodenhäuser, 'Contemporary Challenges for International Humanitarian Law' in J Crawford et al (eds), *The International Legal Order: Current Needs and Possible Responses Essays in Honour of Djamchid Momtaz* (Brill 2017) 682. On the criticism of this extension, see n 120 and accompanying text.

[114] J Nikolic, T de Saint Maurice, and T Ferraro, 'Aggregated Intensity: Classifying Coalitions of Non-State Armed Groups' (*Humanitarian Law and Policy*, 7 October 2020) <https://blogs.icrc.org/law-and-policy/2020/10/07/aggregated-intensity-classifying-coalitions-non-state-armed-groups/>; ICRC, 'International Humanitarian Law and the Challenges of Contemporary Armed Conflicts' (2019) 40.

[115] ICRC Challenges Report (2019) (n 114) 40 (emphasis original).

[116] Nikolic, de Saint Maurice, and Ferraro (n 114) fn 12.

[117] ibid fn 5; see also ICRC Challenges Report (2019) (n 114) 41.

These difficulties of reconciling the two approaches also highlight the more general failure of the ICRC to explain why the pre-existence—as opposed to the joint creation—of a conflict would be a sound reason to apply a different test for identifying co-parties. If there actually is no convincing ground for distinguishing whether a pre-existing armed conflict is joined or a conflict is jointly created—as section 3 of this chapter argues[118]—that requirement of the SBA should not be adhered to.

(3) Assessment

Overall, the ICRC's SBA has the merit of putting forward relatively detailed criteria that can readily apply to practical scenarios with a prospect of delivering reasonably clear outcomes as to the identification of co-parties. The ICRC has achieved this pragmatically, notably by drawing on its previous work on the elements constituting civilian DPH.

Room for conceptual clarification and refinement persists, nonetheless, for example regarding the degree of coordination required between the acts of potential co-parties. Specifying the requisite coordination would have been crucial to the extent that the SBA relies on the 'integral part' variant of direct causation, designed for 'coordinated operations'. This is more so apparent for the 'cumulative' approach, which places 'coordination and cooperation' front and centre, but, instead of clarifying the requisite standard to assess this, it merely defers to an open-ended list of relevant circumstances.[119] Discerning the requisite degree of coordination could also help counter the criticism of over-inclusiveness raised against the ICRC approaches, particularly against their application to cooperation among armed groups, in light of normative concerns of unduly expanding States' targeting authority.[120]

The ICRC's pragmatic approach also entails several inherent limitations that must be considered in devising an account of the legal criteria for identifying co-parties.

First, to make the approaches less vulnerable to the criticism that they lacked a basis in law,[121] it would have been helpful to situate them more firmly within the general system of the legal framework regulating armed conflict and to clarify how the exact requirements have been arrived at,[122] instead of simply asserting their

118 See below 3.a.i.

119 Nikolic, de Saint Maurice, and Ferraro (n 114). For criticism, see G Gaggioli and P Kilibarda, 'Counterterrorism and the Risk of Over-classification of Situations of Violence' (2021) 103 IRRC 203, 230.

120 M Zwanenburg, 'Double Trouble: The "Cumulative Approach" and the "Support-Based Approach" in the Relationship between Non-State Armed Groups' (2021) 22(2019) YIHL 43, 56–58; T Gill, 'Some Thoughts on the ICRC Support Based Approach' (2019) 59 QIL Zoom-in 45, 50–51; see also Chapter 3.4.a.iii.(3) and below 3.c.iii.(1).

121 N Tsagourias and G Biggio, 'Cyber Peacekeeping Operations and the Regulation of the Use of Lethal Force' (2022) 99 ILS 37, 54; Zwanenburg (n 120) 54–55; Gill (n 120) 52.

122 See also R van Steenberghe, 'Les Interventions militaires étrangères récentes contre le terrorisme international. Seconde partie: Droit applicable (jus in bello)' (2017) 63 AFDI 37, 53–55; R van

consistency with the intensity requirement in non-international armed conflicts[123] and pointing out their practical reasonableness.[124]

Secondly, clarifying the conceptual underpinnings of the suggested criteria could also have helped ensure that they effectively perform the work they are supposed to do (as discussed above for the 'official decision' requirement and the underlying issues of attribution and subjective elements).

Thirdly, the focus on devising practically workable solutions to specific conflict settings when the need to do so arose also fostered a piecemeal approach. On the one hand, this section has shown that the subsequent extension of such insular solutions may have led to two competing approaches for the same settings, which can only be reconciled by drawing arguably arbitrary distinctions. On the other hand, there remain significant gaps. In particular, as seen in Chapter 3, the need to identify co-parties also arises if no aggregation of the actions of the respective entities is required.[125] Moreover, the previous chapters of the book have shown that a need to identify co-parties also exists in international armed conflicts—contrary to what the ICRC's official position suggests[126]—which may explain suggestions (including from other voices within the ICRC) to extend to international armed conflicts the reasoning of the ICRC accounts discussed in this section.[127]

To sum up, the analysis of the ICRC's approaches has revealed a need for further conceptualisation. This need will be addressed by the account of co-party identification that section 3 of this chapter develops. This account can, however, also build on the valuable contributions of the ICRC approaches that have been identified in this section.

3. An analytical framework for identifying co-party status

Section 2 of this chapter has charted the field of possible approaches to criteria establishing party status in different conflict settings. Informed by that review, section 3 presents an analytical framework for identifying co-parties in multiparty armed conflicts. To develop this account, the section proceeds as follows.

Steenberghe and P Lesaffre, 'The ICRC's "Support-Based Approach": A Suitable but Incomplete Theory' (2019) 59 QIL, Zoom-in 5, 20 (suggesting a more explicit reliance on DPH criteria).

123 ICRC Challenges Report (2015) (n 111) 23; *GCIII Commentary* [480]; Ferraro (n 113) 51.

124 ICRC Challenges Report (2019) (n 114) 40.

125 See Chapter 3.3

126 Ferraro (n 95) 1228.

127 C Droege and D Tuck, 'Fighting Together and International Humanitarian Law: Setting the Legal Framework (1/2)' (*Humanitarian Law and Policy*, 12 October 2017) <https://blogs.icrc.org/law-and-policy/2017/10/12/fighting-together-international-humanitarian-law-setting-legal-framework-1-2/>; Verlinden (n 45) 150–152.

In a preliminary step, section a. argues that all constellations where co-parties are to be identified can be analysed through a common framework and explains how this general framework relates to potential special rules for identifying co-parties in specific situations.

Against this background, section b. sets out the key conceptual elements of the proposed general framework. Subsection i. explains that the conduct of a (potential) co-party must consist of acts that can be attributed to that collective entity. Subsection ii. explains that this conduct must possess a direct connection to harm to the adversary. Subsection iii. analyses the requisite relationship between the (potential) co-parties and argues that there must be a sufficient degree of co-ordination between the respective entities. The coordination requirement can be understood as fulfilled where each co-party is involved in the decision-making processes on the coordinated military operations. Subsection iv. examines the relevance of subjective elements to the identification of co-parties. It will be clarified that the intention of an entity to be a party is irrelevant for identifying the entity as having party status, except where such intent is expressed in a declaration of war. Crucially, however, it will also be explained that inherent subjective dimensions of knowledge are contained in the requisite coordinated contributions that co-parties must make under the framework proposed here.

Section c. then turns to potential special rules for identifying co-parties that would co-exist alongside the general framework and take precedence of the general requirements for specific situations. The section finds that no such special rules are presently established other than the rule on declarations of war and discusses potential candidates and rationales for other special rules regarding specific types of conflicts, activities, and entities.

Finally, section d. complements the analysis of the identification of co-parties by specifying at which points in time co-party status begins and ends.

a. Introduction: a general framework for identifying co-parties and the possibility of special rules

i. The idea of a common framework

As seen throughout Chapters 3 and 4, questions of identifying co-parties arise in a variety of different conflict settings. A core idea underlying the argument of this book is that all of these settings can, in principle, be analysed through the same general framework of co-party identification.

Differences relating to whether the co-party status is to an international or non-international armed conflict are sufficiently accommodated in the parameters set out in Chapter 3, that is each co-party must separately meet the party-related requirements as to its nature and at least jointly meet the conflict-related requirements as to the nature of the confrontation. Both of these sets of criteria vary for international and non-international armed conflicts. Within these parameters, the remaining question of when multiple entities may be considered co-parties to that conflict is structurally the same.

Moreover, a different framework is not needed regardless of whether the potential co-parties jointly initiate a conflict or whether one of them joins a pre-existing armed conflict.[128] Chapter 3 has argued that there is no qualitative difference—from the perspective of being identified as a party—between a single party that separately fulfils the conflict-related requirements in its relationship with the adverse side and multiple co-parties jointly doing so (whether or not each co-party would fulfil them if assessed in isolation). Accordingly, it is also immaterial whether a pre-existing armed conflict is joined or whether an armed conflict is jointly created (ie whether the conflict-related requirements are met before or after the respective entity begins contributing to the conflict). A multiparty conflict is constituted and shaped by the contributions of different co-parties in the relationship to the adverse side on an ongoing basis. The fact that different contributions are connected as part of that armed conflict means that it is unnecessary, and even structurally inappropriate, to distinguish, for the purposes of identifying entities as co-parties, whether a contribution would have sufficed in isolation to give rise to an armed conflict. Not having to apply a different framework once an armed conflict exists may also alleviate practical difficulties in specific cooperative settings of determining whether an armed conflict already existed before a particular contribution was made or not.

Since the underlying question of what makes the respective entities co-parties to an armed conflict is common to all these scenarios, it is reasonable to conceive of all of them through the same analytical lens in response to that question. This does not mean that applying each element of a general framework will raise equal difficulties in different factual scenarios. For those potential co-parties whose actions in the relationship to the adverse side would not separately fulfil the conflict-related requirements, certain criteria relating to the nature of their conduct must be met.[129] These criteria will, by definition, be fulfilled for entities that would have separately met the conflict-related requirements had their contribution been assessed in isolation. Yet, the central issue of the connection between the entities and their contributions remains the same.

In sum, the same analytical framework can in principle be applied for conceptualising the identification of co-parties whether the conflict is an international or non-international armed conflict, whether no, some, or all participating entities would independently fulfil the conflict-related requirements for the existence of an

[128] For the ICRC's suggestion of distinct approaches depending on the pre-existence of a non-international armed conflict, see above 2.b.ii.

[129] See below b.i. on the requirement of a direct connection to military operations or hostilities.

armed conflict through their conduct, and whether a certain contribution is made before or after these criteria have been met.

ii. The possibility of special rules

That the issue of co-party identification can be soundly conceptualised through a general analytical framework, as proposed here, does not mean that international law cannot also develop special rules confined to specific constellations in which co-parties are to be identified. Indeed, general rules—flowing from the structure of the overarching framework—and special rules—originating in specific treaty rules or patterns of practice accepted as law—may operate in parallel. Wherever a special rule would regulate a particular constellation, the special rule would govern the identification of co-parties in this situation. The special rule would apply even where it produces results that are inconsistent with those that would have followed from an application of the general framework. The interplay between the general framework and special rules in this sense can be imagined along the lines of the relation between what James Crawford has described as 'isolated/positive' rules and 'structural/systematic' rules:

> Rules can thus be 'isolated' or 'positive', or they can be structural or systematic, deriving part at least of their validity from the assumption that international law is a system, not merely a set of primary norms. A 'positive' rule can, if sufficiently established, contradict the rule which would otherwise be induced or inferred from more basic 'structural' rules. But such a rule is relatively 'brittle' or unstable, in the sense that it requires the sustenance of a continued consensus to support it.[130]

Such special rules are conceivable, for example, for a specific type of conflict, entity, or activity—or combinations thereof. As will be seen, except for the special rule on declarations of war, no special rule can presently be said to have emerged. Yet, different potential candidates for such special rules can be made out based on tendencies in international practice or suggestions in scholarship. These propositions and the rationales underlying them will be addressed below to complement the elements of the general framework put forward here.[131]

[130] J Crawford, 'International Law and Foreign Sovereigns: Distinguishing Immune Transactions' (1983) 54 BYIL 75, 86 (footnotes omitted).

[131] Below c.

b. Elements of a general analytical framework for identifying co-parties

Having clarified the overarching aim of the general framework, we can now turn to the elements of this framework. In a first step, it will be clarified that the relevant individual conduct must be attributable to a collective entity for that entity to become a co-party. In a second step, it needs to be specified what characterises the conduct that allows the identification of a collective entity as a co-party. In a third step, the requisite characteristics of the relationship between different co-parties and their contributions will be examined.

i. Attribution

Collective entities can act in the real world only through individuals.[132] The very idea of an activity by a collective entity presupposes that conduct of individuals can be considered as that of the collective entity, that is, that the conduct can be attributed to the collective entity.[133] In this basic sense, however, attribution is equally presupposed by international law in purely bilateral conflict settings whenever acts of individuals are taken to constitute activities between collective entities,[134] whether this is for the purpose of establishing the existence of an armed conflict through hostile acts between collectives or for regulating the conduct of hostilities between parties. Attribution, in this sense, is thus not specific to the identification of co-parties and, therefore, need not be analysed here in greater depth.

Nonetheless, it should be noted that attribution is an implicit element in identifying co-parties and that this element can prove problematic in practice. For example, when it emerged in 2015 that UK pilots had been embedded with US forces carrying out strikes against ISIL in Syria (in parallel to the UK's overt participation in operations against ISIL in Iraq), the UK government claimed that 'UK personnel embedded within other nations' armed forces operate as members of that military'.[135] This claim suggested that it was not the UK that was acting through these individuals in such cases.[136]

[132] *German Settlers in Poland* (AO) [1923] PCIJ Series B, No 6, 22.

[133] ARSIWA Commentary 35 [5].

[134] See L Condorelli and C Kreß, 'The Rules of Attribution: General Considerations' in J Crawford et al (eds), *The Law of International Responsibility* (OUP 2010) 222 ('the question of attribution can be raised in relation to any conduct of the State in relation to which a norm of international law attaches any legal significance').

[135] UK Ministry of Defence, 'UK Embedded Forces' (Statement UIN HLWS139) 20 July 2015 <https://questions-statements.parliament.uk/written-statements/detail/2015-07-20/HLWS139>; UK Ministry of Defence, 'Defence in the Media: 18 July 2015' <https://modmedia.blog.gov.uk/2015/07/18/defence-in-the-media-18-july-2015/>.

[136] See also D Akande, 'Embedded Troops and the Use of Force in Syria: International and Domestic Law Questions' (*EJIL: Talk!*, 11 September 2015) <www.ejiltalk.org/embedded-troops-and-the-use-of-force-in-syria-international-and-domestic-law-questions/> (showing that, since the UK retained authority over the personnel, the conduct of these forces was still attributable to the UK under ARSIWA, art 6).

Particular difficulties in determining which entity, among several collective entities involved, has acted for the purposes of being identified as a party may also arise in multinational operations under the aegis of international organisations. In such operations, rules on attribution can help identify who is to be considered a party to the conflict: the respective international organisation(s), the force contributing Member States, both of the former, or the multinational operation as such.[137]

To establish that it was indeed a particular State or international organisation that has acted in the sense of international law, the rules on attribution under the law of international responsibility can be relied on,[138] in the absence of special attribution rules on this question.[139] For non-State armed groups, concepts of attribution are so far lacking[140]—although the notion that they can become parties to an armed conflict and the regulation of their activities as parties logically presume that certain acts can be attributed to them.

Importantly, it is sufficient that the individual conduct constituting each (potential) co-party's *own* contribution can be considered as conduct of that collective entity. If entity A's contribution consists, for example, in providing air-to-air refuelling or targeting intelligence, it suffices that these acts are attributable to A. The acts that A's cooperation partner, B, carries out in relation to A's conduct—for example, a consecutive airstrike—need not be attributable to A.

Once it is established that it is indeed a collective entity that acts, the question is what characterises the acts that will make the collective a co-party.

ii. Direct connection to military operations or hostilities

To approach the character of the conduct identifying an entity as a co-party, it is helpful to discern the nature of the relationship between adverse parties that is embodied in the idea of being a party to an armed conflict. This conflict relationship

[137] Engdahl (n 98) 252–257; Ferraro (n 96) 588–595; R Kolb, G Porretto, and S Vité, *L'Application du droit international humanitaire et des droits de l'homme aux organisations internationales: Forces de paix et administrations civiles transitoires* (Bruylant 2005) 151–155; B Maganza, 'From Peacekeepers to Parties to the Conflict: An IHL's Appraisal of the Role of UN Peace Operations in NIACs' (2020) 25 JCSL 209, 221–225; B Maganza, 'Which Role for Hybrid Entities Involved In Multi-Parties NIACs? Applying the ICRC's Support-Based Approach to the Armed Conflict in Mali' (2019) 59 QIL Zoom-in 25, 30–34.

[138] See also N Zamir, *Classification of Conflicts in International Humanitarian Law: The Legal Impact of Foreign Intervention in Civil Wars* (Edward Elgar 2017) 119 (suggesting relying on State responsibility rules for determining whether a State has acted, albeit in the context of conflict classification).

[139] See ARSIWA, art 55; ARIO, art 64; *Application of the Convention on the Prevention and Punishment of the Crime of Genocide (Bosnia and Herzegovina v Serbia and Montenegro)* (Merits) [2007] ICJ Rep 43 [401]. For a discussion and rejection of the idea of special rules of attribution in IHL, see M Milanovic, 'Special Rules of Attribution of Conduct in International Law' (2020) 96 ILS 295, 317–331. In particular, the ICTY's 'overall control' test was intended as a general attribution standard under the law of international responsibility, *Tadić* (Appeal Judgment) IT-94-1-A (15 July 1999) [131]; but see R Jorritsma, 'Where General International Law Meets International Humanitarian Law: Attribution of Conduct and the Classification of Armed Conflicts' (2018) 23 JCSL 405, 430 (considering the ICTY to have recognised a special rule of attribution).

[140] See Chapter 1.3.b.iii.

is characterised and constituted by the acts that the parties perform against each other. Contemporary international law refers to these acts, traditionally called 'acts of war', variously as 'military operations'[141] or 'hostilities'.[142] Both international and non-international armed conflicts are understood as characterised by the occurrence of military operations or hostilities.[143] The occurrence of these acts is not only required to give rise to an armed conflict in the first place but also constitutes the conflict on an ongoing basis and determines its scope (including its extension in time). If these are the acts that characterise the relationship between adverse parties, then, by implication, international law presupposes that the contribution by each (co-)party consists, at a granular level, of acts constituting or forming part of military operations or hostilities.

This idea has long been reflected in the view that a neutral State would have to perform 'acts of war' to forfeit its neutral status—and thereby become a party—as opposed to merely violating neutrality duties.[144] The idea continues to be reflected in approaches to identifying parties to non-international armed conflicts. The ICRC in its SBA, for example, requires 'actions related to the conduct of hostilities' and 'military operations' that the respective entity carries out.[145]

To characterise the contribution required for identifying co-parties, the contours of the concepts of 'military operations' and 'hostilities' will thus provide the starting point for the analysis. These contours will then be refined by specifying the requisite direct connection of the conduct to such military operations or hostilities.

(1) Contouring the notions of military operations and hostilities

The notions of military operations and hostilities have been considered by some as used almost synonymously in relevant treaties.[146] Whether or not the notions are indeed fully synonymous and thus interchangeable in all respects is not decisive here. Instead, the following considerations apply to both notions as they are used in treaties. Treaty law defines neither of the notions. Despite the absence of

[141] See eg HR, arts 36, 37, 52, 53; GCI, Annex I, art 2; GCIII, arts 23, 75(1); GCIV, arts 6(2), 6(3), 20(2), 28, 40(2), 51(2), 53, 111; API, arts 3, 39(2), 44(3), 44(5), 51(1), 51(7), 56(2), 57(1), 57(4), 58, 59(2), 60(1), (6); APII, arts 1(1), 13(1). Sometimes, the treaties only speak of 'operations'—see eg HR, arts 1(4), 29(1)–(2), 36; GCI, art 13(2)(d); GCII, art 13(2)(d); GCIII, art 4 A(2)(d); API, arts 37(2), 48 or 'operations of war', HR, arts 6(1), 23(h); GCI, art 37(3); GCII, arts 15, 17, 40(3).

[142] See eg HCIII, art 1; Title Section II HR; Common Article 3(1); GCI, arts 17(3)–(4), 23, 28, 31, 36, 40, 48; GCII, arts 4, 33, 39; GCIII, arts 4(B)(1), 21(3), 33, 43, 58, 67, 109, 111, 112, 118, 119; GCIV, arts 14, 15, 45, 46, 49(2), 70, 130, 132, 133, 134, 145, 157; API, arts 31(4), 33, 34, 40, 43(2), 44(3), 45, 47, 49(4), 51(3), 56(5), 60, 61, 67, 73, 77; APII, arts 4, 6(5), 13(3).

[143] On both concepts, see Chapter 3.2. For international armed conflicts, see also N Melzer, *Targeted Killing in International Law* (OUP 2008) 247 ('the existence of an international armed conflict is simply determined by the actual occurrence of unilateral or mutual hostilities'); for non-international armed conflicts, note also the reference in APII, art 1(1) to 'sustained and concerted military operations'.

[144] Oppenheim (n 20) 314, 388; Lauterpacht (n 32) 671, 752; Greenwood (n 52) 58. See above 2.a.ii.

[145] Ferraro (n 95) 1231.

[146] Melzer (n 143) 271–272 (fns 163–171).

precise definitions, some yardsticks can be discerned to delimit the range of conduct covered.

The first yardstick is that the notions are *broader* than 'attacks', which Article 49(1) API defines as 'acts of violence against the adversary, whether in offence or in defence'. In addition to attacks, military operations/hostilities have been understood to cover a considerably wider range of activities,[147] including non-violent activities preparing[148] or supporting attacks.[149]

At the same time, the notions are not infinite. Not all actions which are (potentially) covered by the regulation of armed conflict are relevant for identifying parties. International law also prohibits, prescribes, or otherwise regulates a range of other activities of parties in relation to a conflict, notably regarding the protection of individuals affected by the conflict.[150] These activities, however, relate to protection needs arising as a consequence of the conflict relationship between parties and do not as such constitute this relationship. Activities in relation to protected individuals can also be carried out by other actors, such as humanitarian organisations, without risking being identified as a party. By contrast, the law on the conduct of hostilities regulates military operations and hostilities as constituting the conflict relationship between the adverse parties.

Military operations or hostilities in this sense are characterised as the resort to 'means or methods of injuring the enemy',[151] that is, 'acts which by their nature or purpose are intended to cause actual harm to the personnel and equipment of the armed forces'.[152] It has been pointed out that not all activities somehow related to the conflict relationship between parties are relevant and that hostilities (or military operations) are narrower than 'the entire war effort'.[153]

[147] *Tallinn Manual 2.0* 415; M Bothe, KJ Partsch, and W Solf, *New Rules for Victims of Armed Conflicts—Commentary on the Two 1977 Protocols Additional to the Geneva Conventions of 1949* (reprint edn, Nijhoff 2013) 344.

[148] See eg API, art 44(3) ('military operation preparatory to an attack').

[149] Y Dinstein, *The Conduct of Hostilities under the Law of International Armed Conflict* (4th edn, CUP 2022) 2 (referring to the notion of hostilities as including, among others, intelligence gathering and various types of logistical support); *AP Commentary* 680 (considering the notion of 'military operations' under API, art 57(1) to include 'any movements, manoeuvres and other activities whatsoever carried out by the armed forces with a view to combat'); similarly Bothe, Partsch, and Solf (n 147) 408; ILA Study Group, 'The Conduct of Hostilities and International Humanitarian Law: Challenges of 21st Century Warfare' (2017) 93 ILS 322, 380; UK Ministry of Defence, *The Manual of the Law of Armed Conflict* (OUP 2004)[5.32].

[150] See Chapter 1.3.a.i.

[151] DPH Guidance 43; see alsoDinstein (n 149) 2.

[152] *AP Commentary* [1942]; see also eg *The Public Committee against Torture in Israel et al v the Government of Israel et al* (Targeted Killings case) HCJ 769/02 (13 December 2006) [33]; Federal Prosecutor General, Note of 16 April 2010 (3 BJs 6/10-4) 61.

[153] *AP Commentary* [1679]; see alsoD Akande, 'Clearing the Fog of War? The ICRC's Interpretive Guidance on Direct Participation in Hostilities' (2010) 59 ICLQ 180, 188.

(2) *Direct connection to harm*

Against this background, the conduct's requisite character can be refined as demanding a relationship of proximity or 'directness' to injury or harm to the adversary. Treaty law does not frame the issue in the language of 'directness' in the present context—unlike civilian 'direct' participation in hostilities.[154] Nonetheless, that framing seems to be a common denominator between different approaches to identifying co-parties. This will now be shown briefly, first, regarding references to the notion of directness in scholarship, and, secondly, regarding illustrations from international practice. In a third step, a way to assess 'directness' in practice will be suggested.

(a) References to 'directness' in scholarship Scholars have frequently referred to a 'direct' connection to harm when identifying the contributing entity as a party to the conflict, as seen in section 2 of this chapter. Grotius already hinted at this notion when he referred to assisting a belligerent with 'what is *directly* useful for war'.[155] Greenwood required '*direct* support to the military operations of one of the belligerents' to mark the threshold from neutrality to co-party status. He specifies that support to an act of war 'shall generally be rated as an act of war of the supporting State if it is *directly* related, i.e. closely related in space and time, to measures harmful to the adversary'.[156] Upcher noted that '*direct* military support or . . . some sort of *direct, causal link* between the neutral's action and an act of belligerency' would suffice to constitute 'co-belligerency'.[157]

Similarly, in the context of a State supporting a non-State party fighting another State, Mačák has suggested that the ICTY's overall control test (required for a State supporting an armed group to become a party to an international armed conflict with the opposing State) can be understood as requiring that 'the third state's involvement is *directly causally related* to the consequences of the insurgents' conduct', 'such as injury, death, damage, or destruction'.[158]

Finally, the ICRC in its SBA to identifying co-parties joining non-international armed conflicts takes the criterion to mean that the intervening State's actions are 'related to the conduct of hostilities' as requiring a '*direct* impact on the opposing party's ability to conduct hostilities'.[159]

[154] API, art 51(3).
[155] Grotius (n 7) 787 (emphasis added).
[156] Greenwood (n 52) 58 (emphasis added).
[157] Upcher (n 44) 63 (emphasis added).
[158] K Mačák, *Internationalized Armed Conflicts in International Law* (OUP 2018) 45–46 (emphasis added).
[159] Ferraro (n 96) 585 (emphasis added).

(b) References to 'directness' in international practice International practice also provides references to 'directness' to specify the character of the conduct that allows identifying an entity as a co-party. During the Iran–Iraq War, in the context of approving arms sales to Kuwait (which Iran accused of cooperating with Iraq), the Netherlands were of the view that:

> Kuwait is at present not *directly involved* in the armed conflict between Iraq and Iran in the region and there is no reason to suppose that it will become a belligerent of its own accord in the foreseeable future.[160]

In the context of the invasion of Iraq in 2003, the US considered that 'especially when a State's specific contribution has no *direct nexus* with belligerent or hostile activities', it would not suffice to make that State a 'co-belligerent' of the US against Iraq (in the sense of Article 4(2) GCIV).[161] In the same memorandum, the US also implicitly emphasised the relevance of the directness of the connection of the contribution to military operations when it noted that States would be its 'co-belligerents' if they 'allow their territory to be used *as a base for [combat] operations*'.[162] In the Military Commissions Acts, the US later seems to have understood as its co-party 'any State or armed force *directly engaged* along with the United States in such hostilities … or providing *direct operational support* to the United States in connection with such hostilities'.[163]

Using similar wording, in assessing whether it has become a party, the Danish government considers 'the character and scope of the overall *active* military contribution' made by Denmark.[164]

During its full-scale invasion of Ukraine, Russia reacted with fierce condemnations to reports about the provision of military intelligence, including specific targeting data, to Ukraine by several Western States. In doing so, Russia partly used 'directness' language to support its claim that these States had become parties to the conflict alongside Ukraine. The speaker of Russia's State Duma considered that 'the aid of American intelligence forces' meant that 'Washington essentially coordinates and develops military operations, thereby directly participating in the hostilities against our country'.[165] At a later stage, Russia's Foreign Minister Lavrov

[160] Siekmann (n 59) 390 (emphasis added); see also Upcher (n 44) 61.

[161] US Office of the Legal Counsel to the President, 'Memorandum Opinion: "Protected Person" Status in Occupied Iraq under the Fourth Geneva Convention' (2004) 28 Op OLC 35, 45 (emphasis added).

[162] ibid 44 (emphasis added).

[163] Military Commissions Act (Pub L No 111-84, 123 Stat 2190 (2009)) 10 USC 948a(3) (2009) (emphasis added). While this definition was used for the purposes of domestic law, it is plausible that it reflects the US position as a matter of international law, since the same act defines 'hostilities' as 'any conflict subject to the laws of war' (10 USC 948a(9) (2009)).

[164] *Danish Manual* 53 (emphasis added).

[165] C Vakil, 'Russian Official Claims US Participating in Direct Hostilities with His Country' *The Hill* (7 May 2022) <https://thehill.com/policy/defense/3480589-russian-official-claims-us-participating-in-direct-hostilities-with-his-country/>.

more generally connected 'directness' language and the notion of party status when he claimed that 'Western countries are directly involving themselves in the Ukrainian conflict and becoming party to it'.[166]

While the US rejected the claim that it did indeed directly participate in hostilities or was directly involved in the conflict, its own position may be read as being compatible with the underlying criterion invoked by Russia. The US, at least in the early days of the invasion, denied that the intelligence it provided was sufficiently specific 'explicitly to target and kill Russian soldiers'.[167] This factual denial seems to suggest that such activities could, indeed, make the US a co-party. The overarching concern not to become or be regarded as a co-party to the conflict also seems to have informed decision-making within the US administration. Referring to the decision-making within the Pentagon, the Chairman of the House of Representatives' Armed Services Committee noted that sharing intelligence for 'real-time targeting ... steps over the line to making us participating in the war. So the Pentagon is really struggling and walking that very fine line'.[168]

In similar terms, an OSCE expert report concluded that States supporting Ukraine or Russia would only become co-parties to the international armed conflict through 'acts that would constitute direct participation in the hostilities by persons attributable' to them.[169]

(c) Assessing 'directness' in practice At the same time, no test for assessing this 'directness' of the connection to military operations or hostilities in identifying co-parties has yet been established as a matter of international law. For practical purposes, orientation could be sought in the 'direct causation of harm' criterion put forward by the ICRC's Interpretive Guidance as an element that is constitutive of civilian DPH. In that context, the ICRC has suggested requiring that the relevant activity causes harm to the adversary in one causal step.[170]

Where multiple collective entities coordinate patterns of intertwined acts, it may not, however, be feasible to analytically single out individual contributions and arrange them into a causal chain, such that the number of causal steps to harm to the adversary could be counted. In the context of civilian DPH, the ICRC's Interpretive Guidance has thus suggested a variant of the direct causation test. This

[166] UNSC, 9135th Meeting (22 September 2022) UN Doc S/PV.9135 17–18.

[167] N Bertrand and K Lillis, 'US Officials Say Biden Administration Is Sharing Intelligence with Ukraine at a "Frenetic" Pace after Republicans Criticize Efforts' (*CNN*, 4 March 2022) <https://edition.cnn.com/2022/03/04/politics/us-ukraine-intelligence/index.html>.

[168] K Dilanian, 'Biden Administration Walks Fine Line on Intelligence-Sharing with Ukraine' (*NBC News*, 4 March 2022) <www.nbcnews.com/news/investigations/biden-administration-walks-fine-line-intelligence-sharing-ukraine-rcna18542>.

[169] 'Report on Violations of International Humanitarian and Human Rights Law, War Crimes and Crimes against Humanity Committed in Ukraine since 24 February 2022' annexed to OSCE, Note Verbale (13 April 2022) ODIHR.GAL/26/22/Rev 1 <www.osce.org/files/f/documents/f/a/515868.pdf> 5.

[170] DPH Guidance 53.

variant attempts to address the parallel problem of assessing the proximity or 'directness' of coordinated contributions operating in conjunction with one another. This may also be a practically helpful way to approach the assessment of the 'directness' of harm for identifying co-parties.[171] According to this variant, acts forming an 'integral part of a concrete and coordinated tactical operation' are considered as causing harm in one step.[172]

Applying similar reasoning to identifying co-parties would mean that conduct has a sufficiently 'direct' connection to harm to the adversary where it constitutes military operations causing harm to the adversary in one step or forms an integral part of (a set of) coordinated military operations that do so.

By way of illustration, not only executing one's own or joint airstrikes but also providing air-to-air refuelling to the fighter jets that carry out the strikes may bear out a sufficiently direct connection to harm. Other forms of logistical support, such as troop transportation to the front lines, may similarly be sufficiently connected to harm. Along similar lines, intelligence provision for a concrete military operation may suffice,[173] as distinct from the mere routine intelligence provision under a standing arrangement.[174] Assisting with military advisers in the preparation or execution of a concrete operation may also suffice: as noted above, all stages of the decision-making process can be deemed to form part of the operation. Finally, cyber operations may also directly cause harm in and of themselves or as part of kinetic operations into which they may integrated.[175] As will be seen at different points throughout this chapter, examples of co-party identification taken from international practice frequently involve combinations of several of these activities.

By contrast, the provision of weapons—of whatever type—or other supplies will usually not be part of a concrete military operation but rather sustain the 'general war effort', as would, a fortiori, financial or political support.[176] The same can be said of general combat training, as distinct from the preparatory advice and guidance with a view to a concrete military operation, which could possess the requisite direct connection to harm. This is in line with the consistent and repeated statements by States supporting Ukraine following Russia's full-scale invasion that neither their political and financial support, nor their delivery of weapons—including

[171] This variant of the direct causation requirement has informed how the ICRC assesses the requirement of a 'direct' relation of support to the conduct of hostilities in its SBA, see nn 101–102.

[172] DPH Guidance 54–55. The Guidance does not specify what degree of coordination would be required for a 'coordinated' operation. For present purposes, this degree can be understood in the same way as the coordination requirement which the next section will address (see ii.(2)).

[173] See also Tsagourias and Biggio (n 121) 52.

[174] On potential complexities see text accompanied by n 240.

[175] *Tallinn Manual 2.0* 383; *GCIII Commentary* [288].

[176] See also Ferraro (n 96) 585.

heavy artillery, tanks, and fighter jets—and other material, nor the combat training of Ukrainian troops made them co-parties to the conflict.[177]

iii. Coordination: requirements regarding the relationship between co-parties

The previous sections have analysed the requisite conduct by a collective entity to establish co-party status. This section turns to the requisite relationship between potential co-parties and their contributions. It will first be argued that there must be a degree of coordination between the prospective co-parties as regards their respective contributions to the conflict. It will then be specified what degree of coordination is required.

(1) Coordination as a necessary element

As a matter of terminology at the outset: if cooperation means broadly 'working together', then coordination can be understood as the element that connects contributions by different entities such that they work together.[178] Put differently, coordinated contributions constitute a relationship of cooperation. Coordination is, therefore, for present purposes, a necessary aspect of cooperation. The two terms cannot be separated and should not be understood to refer to different modalities of working together.[179]

In this basic sense, coordination in armed conflict takes a great variety of forms and degrees. It may amount to (prospective) parties establishing institutionalised structures to agree on details of strikes and carrying them out jointly. Arguably, however, simply providing and receiving assistance already means that contributions by different entities are brought together, which implies a degree of coordination. One may think of, for example, the provision of air-to-air refuelling by State A to fighter jets of State B in between specific airstrikes. The point here is not that any degree of coordination is *sufficient* for co-party status, but that *some* coordination is *necessary* as a baseline. Before further enquiring which kind and level of coordination are required, it is important to emphasise that, legally and conceptually, coordination plays a crucial role. As the element that ties cooperation

[177] See eg France, Press Conference of the Ministry of Foreign Affairs (26 January 2023) <https://twitter.com/francediplo/status/1618906329925718016?s=66&t=yQX2QgElwKQBP1VR-SbK7Q>; 'Bundesregierung: Ausbildung von Soldaten kein Kriegseintritt' *SZ* (2 May 2022) <www.sueddeutsche.de/politik/konflikte-bundesregierung-ausbildung-von-soldaten-kein-kriegseintritt-dpa.urn-newsml-dpa-com-20090101-220502-99-126669>; see also Introduction n 2.

[178] See 'co-ordination, n.' (*OED Online*, OUP September 2020) <www.oed.com/view/Entry/41066>; 'co-operation, n.' (*OED Online*, OUP September 2019) <www.oed.com/view/Entry/41037>; 'coordination' (*CED Online*, CUP) <https://dictionary.cambridge.org/dictionary/english/coordination>; 'co-operation' (*CED Online*, CUP) <https://dictionary.cambridge.org/dictionary/english/cooperation>.

[179] But see Zwanenburg (n 120) 52 (suggesting that '[c]ooperation implies a stronger link between two entities, because it entails common activities' while coordination merely requires 'an understanding … on when, where or how they will carry out activities individually').

partners' contributions together, coordination sets the foundation for considering them as co-parties to the same armed conflict.

Potential alternative justifications or rationales for grouping together different entities as co-parties appear insufficient. In particular, it is not the mere fact of fighting a common opponent that makes entities co-parties.[180] Indeed, Chapter 3 has already noted that one entity can be simultaneously engaged in separate armed conflicts with different entities.[181] For example, the fact that Russia is fighting (alongside Syria) Syrian opposition groups while simultaneously fighting ISIL does not, without more, make Russia's respective opponents co-parties to the same armed conflict. Nor can it, without more, be assumed that Russia and the US-led coalition of States fighting ISIL as part of Operation Inherent Resolve are co-parties to one single armed conflict with that group.[182]

The mere geographical and temporal proximity of the conduct of different entities also does not provide a sufficient justification per se for grouping together the respective entities, contrary to what Kleffner suggests.[183] The main rationale for relying on such factors is to respond to the practical complexities of distinguishing multiple conflict relationships that exist simultaneously in the same area (eg to assess the intensity criterion for the existence of a non-international armed conflict). The practical realities of complex conflict situations should inform any conceptualisation of the identification of party status that purports to be operable. However, that a practical advantage is gained by relying on geographical and temporal proxies for proximity as independent legal criteria is doubtful. The practicability of such criteria would require clearly delimiting the relevant geographical and temporal space.[184] Any such delimitation is bound to be 'context-specific'[185] rather than universal. Yet, if sufficient geographical and temporal proximity depends on what is practical in each context, then this risks undermining the practicability of such an assessment. Indeed, whether distinguishing the conduct of different entities is practically feasible will depend on when, by whom, and for what purpose the assessment is to be done. That is, different things may be 'practicable'

[180] N Lubell, 'Fragmented Wars: Multi-Territorial Military Operations against Armed Groups' in W Williams and C Ford (eds), *Complex Battlespaces: The Law of Armed Conflict and the Dynamics of Modern Warfare* (OUP 2019) 25; but see C Redaelli, 'A Common Enemy: Aggregating Intensity in Non-international Armed Conflicts' (*Humanitarian Law and Policy*, 22 April 2021) <https://blogs.icrc.org/law-and-policy/2021/04/22/common-enemy/>.

[181] Chapter 3.3.

[182] For reports on failed attempts of Russia and the US to coordinate their military operations against ISIL, see eg C Muñoz, 'U.S, Russia Suspend Talks on Joint Operations in Syria as Cease-fire Deal Fails' *Washington Times* (20 September 2016) <www.washingtontimes.com/news/2016/sep/20/us-russia-suspend-talks-joint-operations-syria-cea/>.

[183] J Kleffner, 'The Legal Fog of an Illusion: Three Reflections on "Organization" and "Intensity" as Criteria for the Temporal Scope of the Law of Non-International Armed Conflict' (2019) 95 ILS 161, 177; similarly Redaelli (n 180) (who relies on these factors in addition to the requirement of a common enemy).

[184] See also Zwanenburg (n 120) 51.

[185] Kleffner (n 183) 177.

for courts in *ex post* settings than for actors involved in the conflict. Crucially, even among these actors on the ground, capabilities to distinguish will significantly vary. Moreover, remote technologies in warfare would raise additional questions regarding how to assess, for example, whether acts of cyber warfare by multiple entities are geographically proximate and, more generally, whether geographical parameters can adequately capture such conflict relationships at all.

Similarly, as regards temporal proximity, the mere simultaneous occurrence of different acts need not make it impossible to distinguish between those who carry them out. Given that the possibility of different parallel conflicts is a standard feature of the contemporary conflict landscape, it is also doubtful that simultaneous occurrence of acts should in and of itself be a rationale to group them together.

All this shows that elevating geographical and temporal proximity to independent—and sufficient—legal criteria in the identification of co-parties may aggravate, rather than resolve, the practical concerns that these 'proxies' aim to address. Such concerns are, therefore, better accommodated by considering geographical and temporal proximity as potential practical evidence in assessing the proximity of the coordination of the actions of different potential co-parties.

A stronger connection between the conduct of different co-parties is, therefore, required. An element of coordination can best provide that connection. In situations where the acts of multiple entities need to be aggregated to establish the conflict-related requirements for the existence of an armed conflict (particularly, the intensity requirement in non-international armed conflicts), there must be a justification for treating them as equivalent to a situation in which one single party fulfils these requirements on its own with respect to the opponent. Coordination arguably justifies this equivalence as it allows partners to divide labour and combine the potential of their respective contributions in a way that makes a qualitative difference to mere accumulations of separate, parallel action against a common enemy.[186] Along the same lines, where entities separately meet the requirements for the existence of an armed conflict, there must be a reason for not treating them as parties to separate parallel conflicts with the same adversary. Absent coordination, there appears to be no sufficient connection between their contributions. These entities are best viewed as parties to separate armed conflicts and, accordingly, as third parties with respect to each other's conflicts.

Indeed, it is the coordination of the acts performed by different entities that connects them in a conceptually satisfactory way such that they build on one another as contributions to one conflict with a common adversary. As seen in section 2 of this chapter, approaches vary in their framing and delimitation on this point, but, at least implicitly, coordination is a widely shared baseline requirement. Practice also illustrates this point: in the instances reviewed so far, when States or

[186] See Chapter 3.4.a.iii.

international courts and tribunals have identified multiple entities as co-parties, there mostly seems to have been some discernible degree of coordination between them.[187]

When there are more than two co-parties on the same side of a conflict, it suffices for them to coordinate with one of their fellow co-parties if that co-party, in turn, coordinates with others.[188] For example, States A, B, and C can be co-parties if States A and C do not directly coordinate but each only coordinate with State B. Accordingly, it is sufficient for all the contributions from co-parties to be connected through a link of coordination, even if some co-parties do not directly coordinate with some of the others.

Finally, it is worth clarifying the relationship between the coordination requirement discussed here and the above reference to acts forming part of a 'coordinated' operation.[189] In the latter context, coordination is merely a tool to establish that a contribution directly causes harm because the direct relationship cannot be established by considering the contribution in isolation from the other contributions that are part of the very same operation. Where a potential co-party carries out a military operation by itself that directly causes harm, the tool of coordination in that sense is not required to establish directness. Nonetheless, coordination with military operations carried out by others will be required to establish the co-party status of the respective entities. In other words, coordination of different contributions can, but need not, take place at the 'micro-level' of the same concrete operation—and if it does take place at the 'micro-level', this is relevant to assess the direct connection to harm. Consider the example of an airstrike that is jointly planned by two partners for which one partner provides the targeting intelligence and the refuelling while the other partner's fighter jet strikes. Coordination may, however, also occur at the 'macro-level' between different operations by several potential co-parties. For example, partners may divide up the targets that they have jointly identified as relevant to defeat the adversary and then strike separately. The bottom line of the present section is that coordination *must* occur, whether at the micro- or the macro-level or both.

(2) *Specifying the requisite degree of coordination*

Having argued that an element of coordination between the contributions of the respective entities is a prerequisite to co-party status, it needs to be specified how this element of coordination can be understood and, particularly, what degree of coordination is required.

[187] Chapter 3.4.a.ii., 4.b., 4.c.; Chapter 4.2.a.ii., 2.b.i., 3.b.i.(2); see also below (2).

[188] This paragraph has previously been published in a similar form (A Wentker, 'At War? Party Status and the War in Ukraine' (2023) 36 LJIL 643, 651).

[189] See above the text accompanied by nn 172–174.

Degrees of coordination can be envisioned as a sliding scale. The upper limit of how closely the two entities may intertwine their actions is that they must continue acting as two separate collective entities, so that they can be identified as two co-parties rather than as sub-divisions of one party. Chapter 3 has shown that this point would be reached when the two entities effectively combine their activities as part of one single organisational structure.[190] At the lower end of what might still loosely be understood as 'coordination', there are only minimal connections between the actions of the respective entities. Consider, for example, entities that merely inform each other of the time and location of their strikes against a common enemy but otherwise operate entirely independently.

On this sliding scale or spectrum, a helpful parameter to understand the degree of coordination required for co-party status is whether the respective entities are involved in the decision-making processes as to whether and how the (coordinated) military operations are carried out. This would include a certain role in the process leading up to the decisions on whether and how their partner carries out their (parts of the) military operations. As Mačák has argued in a related context, having 'a role in the making of strategic and tactical decisions as to how to engage the common enemy' such that '[t]he aligned conflict parties can thus be said to participate jointly in the organization, coordination, or planning of their military operations'[191] would mean that their 'activities are sufficiently intertwined' for treating them as parties to a single armed conflict.[192] This would also specify the ICRC's suggestion that the respective entities must be 'essentially operating in some sort of a coalition, objectively and effectively demonstrating a collective approach of the fighting'.[193]

Emphasising involvement in the decision-making process is appropriate in light of the legal position that comes with being identified as a (co-)party to the conflict. Indeed, the primary role assigned to parties under international law to ensure that the conflict is carried out in a manner that accords with IHL seems to presuppose that the parties concretely determine how the conflict with the adverse side is carried out. This position relates to the conflict relationship with the adverse side as a whole,[194] and the conflict relationship with the adverse side is constituted and shaped by the military operations of all co-parties. It, therefore, seems reasonable to require co-parties to also have some involvement in the strategic, tactical, and operational decision-making that shapes their partners' contributions (ie those

[190] See Chapter 3.3.b.

[191] This wording relies on the second element of the 'overall control' test as developed in international criminal jurisprudence (see eg *Mladić* (Trial Judgment) IT-09-92-T (22 November 2017) [3014]; *Lubanga* (Trial Judgment) ICC-01/04-01/06 (14 March 2012) [541]; *Katanga* (Trial Judgment) ICC-01/04-01/07 (7 March 2014) [1178]).

[192] Mačák (n 158) 102–103.

[193] Nikolic, de Saint Maurice, and Ferraro (n 114).

[194] For the idea that the legal position of the parties always relates to the specific conflict to which they are a party, see Chapter 3.3.

which the respective co-party does not carry out itself).[195] This does not mean that co-parties need to delegate decisions regarding their own contributions to their fellow co-parties. It would suffice that they coordinate their decisions as to whether and how their respective contributions occur in a way that these effectively build on one another and that the co-parties can be said to involve each other in the decision-making that determines the (coordinated) military operations.

One way in which involvement in decision-making processes can occur is through more or less institutionalised coordination structures. Recent conflicts provide illustrations of such structures.

For example, States contributing to the US-led coalition against ISIL as part of Operation Inherent Resolve coordinated their activities, inter alia, through dedicated headquarters in Kuwait. Additionally, a 'Combined Joint Operations Center' in Baghdad was established specifically to coordinate the operations of the Coalition forces and those of Iraqi forces.[196]

In support of the Saudi-led coalition against the Houthi rebels, the US temporarily embedded with the 'Coalition Command Center' in Riyadh[197] a 'Joint Combined Planning Cell', 'in which members of the United States Armed Forces assist[ed] in aerial targeting and help[ed] to coordinate military and intelligence activities'.[198] This framework reportedly enabled the US to be considerably involved in concrete decision-making on specific military operations.[199] The coordination assistance was coupled with wide-ranging military support to the

[195] On the relevance of co-parties' involvement in the decision-making processes for obligations relating to the conduct of their fellow co-parties, see further Chapter 5.2.a.i.

[196] US Central Command, 'Combined Joint Operations Center–Baghdad Brings Coalition together for Operation Inherent Resolve' (18 January 2017) <www.centcom.mil/MEDIA/NEWS-ARTICLES/News-Article-View/Article/1052365/combined-joint-operations-center-baghdad-brings-coalition-together-for-operatio/>; US Government Publishing Office, 'The Fight against ISIS: Building the Coalition and Ensuring Military Effectiveness' Senate Hearing 114–197 (25 February 2015) <www.govinfo.gov/content/pkg/CHRG-114shrg99368/html/CHRG-114shrg99368.htm>; B Ackermann, 'Is War on ISIS Illegal?' *NYT* (5 May 2016) A25 <www.nytimes.com/2016/05/05/opinion/is-americas-war-on-isis-illegal.html?searchResultPosition=1>; Global Coalition, 'Spain's Military Contribution to the Coalition' 12 May 2021 <https://theglobalcoalition.org/en/spains-military-contribution-to-the-coalition/>; Global Coalition, 'Military: Major General Chris Ghika' 12 July 2019 <https://theglobalcoalition.org/en/on-the-line-major-general-chris-ghika/>.

[197] Saudi Arabia, 'News Release: The Coalition to Restore Legitimacy in Yemen Announces Resuming Humanitarian and Commercial Access to All Ports under the Control of the Legitimate Government of Yemen' 12 November 2017 <www.saudiembassy.net/news/coalition-restore-legitimacy-yemen-announces-resuming-humanitarian-and-commercial-access-all>.

[198] US Congress, 'Joint Resolution: To direct the removal of United States Armed Forces from hostilities in the Republic of Yemen that have not been authorized by Congress' (SJ Res 7) (3 January 2019); see also US, 'Statement by NSC Spokesperson Bernadette Meehan on the Situation in Yemen' 25 March 2015 <https://obamawhitehouse.archives.gov/the-press-office/2015/03/25/statement-nsc-spokesperson-bernadette-meehan-situation-yemen>.

[199] D Sanger and E Schmitt, 'Biden Signals Break with Trump Foreign Policy in a Wide-Ranging State Dept. Speech' *NYT* (4 February 2021) A1 <www.nytimes.com/2021/02/04/us/politics/biden-foreign-policy.html?action=click&module=Spotlight&pgtype=Homepage> ('At a flight operations room in the capital, Riyadh, Saudi commanders sat near American military officials who provided intelligence and tactical advice, mainly aimed at stopping the Saudis from killing Yemeni civilians').

Saudi-led coalition, including air-to-air refuelling for fighter jets and the provision of targeting intelligence.[200] Although the US government ultimately abandoned support over pressure from Congress,[201] it reportedly maintained that the US had not become a co-party of Saudi Arabia,[202] a view that seems inconsistent with the US's approaches to identifying co-parties in other contexts.[203]

In addition to the US, the UK also had personnel in the Joint Combined Planning Cell to advise the Saudi-led coalition.[204] The government, nonetheless, insisted that the UK had not become a co-party of Saudi Arabia,[205] a position that the High Court accepted.[206] To justify this position, the government stressed that the UK did not have a sufficient role in the decision-making processes on the military operations by the Saudi-led coalition.[207]

In the conflict between Libya's Government of National Accord with rebels led by General Haftar, Turkey announced in early 2020 that it would support the government, by, inter alia, establishing an operations centre to facilitate the coordination of the military operations against the rebels.[208] An earlier episode of armed

[200] C Daugirdas and J Mortenson, 'United States Strikes Houthi-Controlled Facilities in Yemen, Reaffirms Limited Support for Saudi-Led Coalition Notwithstanding Growing Concerns about Civilian Casualties' (2017) 111 AJIL 523; J Galbraith, 'Congress Signals Concern over U.S. Role in Aiding Saudi Arabia's Activities in Yemen' (2019) 113 AJIL 159, 160.

[201] K Eichensehr, 'Biden Administration Launches Reset in Relations with Saudi Arabia, Withdraws Support for Saudi-Led War in Yemen' (2021) 115 AJIL 545, 549.

[202] S Oakford, 'One American's Failed Quest to Protect Civilians in Yemen' *The Atlantic* (17 August 2018) <https://perma.cc/PM9Q-6H3V> ('In an email, the Pentagon spokesperson Rebecca Rebarich wrote that the United States "is not a party to the Yemeni civil war and is not investigating strikes conducted by the Saudi-led coalition"'). Earlier reports had suggested that 'U.S. government lawyers ultimately did not reach a conclusion on whether U.S. support for the campaign would make the United States a "co-belligerent" in the war under international law' (W Strobel and J Landay, 'Exclusive: As Saudis Bombed Yemen, U.S. Worried about Legal Blowback' (*Reuters*, 10 October 2016) <www.reuters.com/article/us-usa-saudi-yemen-idUSKCN12A0BQ>).

[203] See eg above 2.b.i.; 3.b.i.(2); below c.ii. See also O Hathaway et al, 'Yemen: Is the U.S. Breaking the Law?' (2019) 10 Harv NSJ 1, 59 ('[I]t is possible that such support is sufficient to involve the U.S. in the NIAC between those states and the Houthis'); contra J Hursh, 'International Humanitarian Law Violations, Legal Responsibility, and US Military Support to the Saudi Coalition in Yemen: A Cautionary Tale' (2020) 7 JUOFIL 122, 141.

[204] Business, Innovation and Skills and International Development Committees, *The Use of UK-Manufactured Arms in Yemen* (2016–17, HC 679) 30–31.

[205] *The Queen (on the application of Campaign against Arms Trade) and the Secretary of State for International Trade and Amnesty International, Human Rights Watch UK and Oxfam International intervening* [2019] EWCA Civ 1020 [83] (quoting a ministerial statement on this point).

[206] *The Queen (on the application of Campaign against Arms Trade) and The Secretary of State for International Trade and Amnesty Int'l, Human Rights Watch UK and Oxfam Int'l intervening* [2017] EWHC 1726 (QB) [181].

[207] UK Secretary of State for Foreign and Commonwealth Affairs, 'Saudia Arabia' (Statement UIN HCWS716) 23 May 2018 <https://questions-statements.parliament.uk/written-statements/detail/2018-05-23/HCWS716> ('[T]he UK is not a member of the Saudi-Led Coalition. We do not have any role in setting Coalition policy, or in executing air strikes'); House of Commons Report Yemen (2016) 30 ('[The Minister of State for Defence Procurement] told us that UK liaison officers in the air operations centre were not involved in targeting decisions, but instead conducted training on doctrine for using UK-supplied weapons systems and provided advice on targeting processes').

[208] C Gall, 'As Libya Faces a Growing Conflict, Turkey Deploys Troops to Back Its Government' *NYT* (6 January 2020) A6 <www.nytimes.com/2020/01/05/world/europe/erdogan-turk

conflict in Libya provides a similar illustration: in 2011, NATO forces and rebel groups reportedly coordinated their military operations through a 'joint operations centre'.[209]

As a final illustration, in the armed conflicts underlying the proceedings against Jean-Pierre Bemba before the ICC, the Central African Republic government had set up a centre to coordinate the military operations in support of the government, including those by the Congolese armed group MLC led by Bemba.[210]

The respective role played by different partners in decision-making processes can also be reflected and specified in formalised arrangements. For example, for operations by multiple Member States under the auspices of NATO, NATO's 'Allied Joint Doctrine for Joint Targeting' standardises the input of the respective troop-contributing States during the targeting process. In this respect, the Doctrine, for example, specifies that national targeting experts represent States at the Allied Command Operations Headquarters.[211]

Yet, while institutionalisation and formalisation of coordination between partners are helpful evidence to discern involvement in decision-making processes, such involvement can also occur in more ad hoc, informal ways.[212]

To specify the contours of the elements of the analytical framework set out so far, a crucial question is whether these elements can be understood in entirely objective terms or whether, and to what extent, they also have subjective dimensions to them.

iv. Subjective elements

The proper role of States' 'mindset' for establishing whether they are at war has long troubled international lawyers.[213] These troubles continue to resurface in contemporary debates, which reveal that not all aspects thereof are settled. It is, therefore, useful to clarify the extent to which subjective elements inform and complement the analytical framework for identifying parties armed conflicts.

Different levels to which subjective elements may relate must be distinguished. Section (1) will clarify that, with the limited exception of declarations of war, it is irrelevant whether an entity intends or knows of its status as (co-)party for that status to produce legal effects. By contrast, as section (2) will argue, subjective elements are relevant to establish that the requirements for identifying co-parties

ish-troops-libya.html?searchResultPosition=1>; 'Libya Conflict: Turkey Sends Troops to Shore Up UN-backed Government' (*BBC*, 6 January 2020) <www.bbc.com/news/world-africa-51003034>.

209 S Ghasemilee, 'Libyan Rebels, NATO in Joint Military Operations against Qaddafi Forces' (*Alarabiya*, 16 April 2011) <https://english.alarabiya.net/articles/2011/04/16/145587>.

210 *Bemba* (Confirmation of Charges) ICC-01/05-01/08 (15 June 2009) [259].

211 NATO, Allied Joint Doctrine for Joint Targeting AJP-3.9 (April 2016) 3-3.

212 For illustrations, see *Afghanistan* (Investigation Request) ICC-02/17-7-Conf-Exp (20 November 2017) [58]; similarly *Katanga* (Trial) (n 191) [631]ff (discussed in detail in Chapter 3.4.a.ii.(2)).

213 See above Chapter 3.2.a.

(as developed in the preceding sections) are fulfilled because these requirements have an inherent subjective dimension. The requisite subjective standard is arguably knowledge, which can, in practice, be objectively deduced from the factual circumstances.

(1) *Intent to be a party?*

One way in which the intent of a State to be at war may still play a role is if that intent is expressed in a declaration of war,[214] which, as already noted, remains an option available to States.[215] States can also declare war jointly or declare to join inter-State conflicts as a co-party to one side against the other.[216] In such situations, whether multiple States are considered as co-parties to one multiparty conflict or as parties to separate declared wars or international armed conflicts would need to be established by discerning the intent of the potential co-parties[217] based on an interpretation of the declarations as unilateral acts.[218]

The possibility of declarations of war should, however, be understood restrictively. In particular, contemporary international law leaves no room for considering purely factual conduct by States as an *implicit* declaration of war, as classical writers doctrinally constructed the co-belligerent status of States assisting others.[219] This restriction is not only suggested by the wording of Common Article 2, which refers to *declared* wars. Allowing for such constructions of implicit declaration of war could entirely undermine the general requirements for establishing co-party status in international armed conflicts. Indeed, it could entail considering a potentially infinite range of conduct as giving rise to party status. Construing a wide range of acts as implicit declarations of war would also sit uneasily with the broader context of IHL treaties. The primary reference points for these treaties are concepts of armed conflict rather than war.[220] Since States hardly ever declare war anymore, there is no reasonable basis for reading the intention of doing so into their factual conduct. On the contrary, 'there is probably a presumption that nations do not

[214] D Akande, 'Classification of Armed Conflicts' in B Saul and D Akande (eds), *The Oxford Guide to International Humanitarian Law* (OUP 2020) 34 ('Whether [declarations of war] are to be regarded as bringing into effect IHL is essentially a question of intention').

[215] Chapter 3.2.a.

[216] See also Lubell (n 180) 24. The possibility of such a combination of a declared war with an international armed conflict appears to be in line with Common Article 2's wording. It would arguably not be reasonable to treat State A declaring to join State B as parties to separate conflicts against State C and thus as third parties (neutrals) in their relation to one another. By virtue of its declaration to join a conflict, the respective State should be seen as giving up its third-party status with respect to both parties to that conflict.

[217] This could theoretically present challenges where a State declares to join other States that have not issued a declaration of war. The accordance of will would then have to be discerned by other means.

[218] See generally ILC, 'Guiding Principles Applicable to Unilateral Declarations of States Capable of Creating Legal Obligations' (2006) II/2 YILC 160.

[219] Above 2.a.i.

[220] Chapter 3.2.

intend to create a state of war'.[221] Factual patterns of States' conduct are thus arguably best assessed through the lens of the general framework suggested here for identifying party status.

Where the elements of this framework are met, party status is an automatic legal consequence. It is an effect independent of whether or not it is intended, known, or accepted or whether any other mindset exists in respect of that consequence. It would create serious frictions with basic premises of the contemporary international legal regulation of armed conflict if it were left to the discretion of States whether they desire their party status as a legal consequence of their own or their opponents' acts, as Vattel once suggested.[222] In particular, it would be incompatible with the notion that IHL's applicability (for which identifying party status has significant implications) is generally triggered by objective factual situations.[223] The fundamental rule that armed conflicts exist even if parties do not recognise their existence[224] could easily be defeated if each party were free to deny its own party status.

(2) Subjective dimensions inherent in performing relevant coordinated conduct

Although parties need not intend or accept their party status as a legal consequence of their conduct, subjective elements arguably play a role in establishing that they have performed the relevant conduct in the first place.[225] It is at this level that references to 'belligerent intent' in the context of identifying parties can be situated.[226]

(a) Inherent requirement of subjective dimensions Indeed, the elements set out so far inherently contain a subjective dimension. The requirements of performing activities with a sufficiently direct relationship to harm to the adversary in sufficiently close coordination with one's partners cannot be considered fulfilled where the respective entity is unaware of what it is doing, for example as the result of an error or being misled. Rather than as a separate additional requirement, the

[221] Greenwood (n 52) 49; see already A McNair and A Watts, *The Legal Effects of War* (4th edn, CUP 1966) 8 ('[s]o serious a matter as the existence of a state of war is not lightly to be implied'); see also Akande (n 214) 34.

[222] nn 16–17.

[223] Chapter 3.2.

[224] See Common Article 2, which includes situations where neither of the parties recognises the existence of an international armed conflict, an idea which is also true in non-international armed conflicts (Chapter 3, n 8).

[225] On this distinction, see H Kelsen, *Principles of International Law* (Rinehart & Company 1952) 27.

[226] For such references, see eg Ferraro (n 96) 587 ('When fulfilled, these criteria [of the ICRC's SBA] testify beyond reasonable doubt to the existence of belligerent intent'); see also van Steenberghe and Lesaffre (n 122) 14–15.

subjective dimension can, therefore, be thought of as refining and specifying the 'conduct' and 'coordination' elements.

The idea of inherent subjective dimensions is no uncommon conceptual construct. For example, during the ILC's work on state responsibility, Brownlie noted that 'the elements of knowledge were already built into the conditions of aiding, assisting, directing and controlling' and questioned the need to explicitly require such an additional subjective element.[227] More importantly for present purposes, inherent subjective dimensions also inform concepts in contexts related to the present enquiry.

First, the very notions of 'military operations' and, particularly, 'hostilities' (which, as seen above, constitute the granular components of the conflict relationship between adverse parties) have been understood as being directed against the adversary, performed with an adversarial ('hostile') purpose[228]—which may convey a sense that there is an inherent subjective dimension to them.

Secondly, and relatedly, the notion of international armed conflict contains a subjective dimension that is inherent in the concept of what constitutes resort to armed force between States.[229]

Thirdly, the requirement proposed by the ICRC in the context of civilian DPH that an act must be 'specifically designed to [cause harm directly] in support of a party to an armed conflict and to the detriment of another (belligerent nexus)'[230] could arguably also be understood to contain an inherent subjective dimension. This criterion has informed the ICRC's SBA to identifying parties to pre-existing non-international armed conflicts as well.[231] The ICRC insists that the criterion accounts for the objective design of an act rather than the mindset of the respective individual.[232] However, the ICRC also acknowledges that the requirement would not be fulfilled where the individual was 'totally unaware' of its role,[233] suggesting the existence of an implicit knowledge requirement. More generally, the explanation that the purpose of an act must be deduced from its objective design could also be taken to specify the mode of assessment of an inherent subjective dimension. Indeed, as will be explored below, looking at the objective facts is a common way to establish the existence of a subjective element in practice.

227 2577th Meeting of the ILC (1999) I YILC 67, 70 [27].

228 nn 151–152.

229 Chapter 3.2.b.i.

230 DPH Guidance 58 (emphasis omitted).

231 Ferraro (n 95) 1234; above 2.b.ii.(1).

232 DPH Guidance 59–60; for the debates on subjective elements in the expert process preceding the publication of the Guidance, see ICRC, 'Report on the Third Expert Meeting on the Notion of Direct Participation in Hostilities' (2005) 33–34; for criticism of this 'objective' conception of belligerent nexus, see M John-Hopkins, 'Extrapolation of Criminal Law Modes of Liability to Target Analysis under International Humanitarian Law: Developing the Framework for Understanding Direct Participation in Hostilities and Membership in Organized Armed Groups in Non-International Armed Conflict' (2017) 22 JCSL 275, 287.

233 DPH Guidance 60.

However, to analytically refine the understanding of the elements of co-party identification, it is helpful to acknowledge the existence of subjective dimensions in the first place. How this dimension is to be established in practice to accommodate evidentiary concerns regarding mental requirements can then be addressed separately. It must first be clarified what exactly is to be established through the practical assessment, since this will inform what an adequate practical assessment would look like.

(b) Requisite subjective standard If inherent subjective dimensions are accepted in principle, this raises the question of the requisite subjective standard. Although references to 'belligerent *intent*'[234] might suggest an even higher subjective standard, knowledge is a plausible candidate. Arguably, performing military operations with a sufficiently direct connection to harm to the adversary while coordinating decision-making processes relating to such operations with one's fellow co-parties necessarily implies volitional acts with an awareness of what one is doing. Acts stemming from errors or being misled would not suffice.[235] At the same time, a specific intent to cause a certain result cannot be said to be inherent in the elements of a coordinated contribution.

The ensuing question is what 'knowledge' means for these purposes and, particularly, what degree of specificity of knowledge is required. In the present context, the knowledge requirement can be understood as an awareness of the essential factual patterns constituting the coordinated military operations, that they are directly related to harm to the adversary, and the circumstances enabling involvement in the decision-making processes on these military operations. It is not necessary for the respective entity to be aware of every factual detail of the military operations, the harm they will cause, or the exact way in which the entity influences the decision-making.

(c) Establishment in practice In practice, whether or not a collective entity acts with the requisite knowledge will need to be ascertained from some external manifestation of this mindset. This is, to some extent, common to establishing subjective elements in law generally. It is particularly relevant regarding the 'mindset' of States or other collective entities, which can only be 'deducible from what has been said or done'.[236]

The awareness will thus usually be deduced or inferred objectively from the factual patterns surrounding the conduct,[237] unless it is otherwise externally

[234] Ferraro (n 96) 576; van Steenberghe and Lesaffre (n 122) 14–15; in the context of the concept of international armed conflict, see also ICRC Challenges Report (2015) (n 111) 8; Lubell (n 180) 19–20; Melzer (n 143) 247, 250.

[235] For the parallel idea in the context of the creation of an international armed conflict, see Chapter 3, nn 47–51.

[236] B Cheng, 'Custom: The Future of General State Practice in a Divided World' in RSJ MacDonald and D Johnston (eds), *The Structure and Process of International Law* (Nijhoff 1986) 530.

[237] In favour of deducing 'belligerent intent' from factual circumstances, see also eg ICRC Challenges Report (2015) (n 111) 8; van Steenberghe and Lesaffre (n 122) 14–15.

manifested, for example in statements or documents, such as agreements between the respective entities. To determine how much and what kind of evidence is required, it should be considered that co-parties in practice often need to be identified regarding ongoing military operations, with limited time and evidence available. Presumptions of awareness, rebuttable by contrary factual indications (giving rise to suspicions of errors, for example), could facilitate an objective assessment and further accommodate practical concerns.[238] In sum, the knowledge standard and its objective assessment ensure that the inherent subjective dimensions do not undermine the practical workability of the conceptual elements for identifying co-parties.[239]

To illustrate how the inherent subjective dimensions would play out in practice, consider two different scenarios of intelligence provision. Intelligence can be routinely provided under a standing intelligence cooperation arrangement not related to any specific operations, such as the 'Five-Eyes' partnership between Australia, Canada, New Zealand, the UK, and the US under the framework of the UKUSA Agreement[240] or the 'Counter-Terrorism Group' framework of intelligence cooperation between the security services of EU Member States, the UK, Norway, and Switzerland.[241] Such intelligence provision would not, without more, allow for deducing an awareness that this could form part of coordinated military operations entailing a sufficiently direct connection to harm and involvement in the relevant decision-making processes. By contrast, where intelligence is provided as part of an arrangement for concrete operations, the facts will likely allow deducing the requisite awareness. Consider, for example, the provision of intelligence on potential targets provided by the Dutch intelligence services to the Dutch representative at the headquarters of Operation Inherent Resolve in Iraq and Syria[242] or the

[238] See also Melzer (n 143) 250 (suggesting a presumption of 'belligerent intent' in the context of the creation of international armed conflicts). Care should be taken, however, that such presumptions do not circumvent the requirements for identifying co-parties where evidence of their fulfilment is lacking.

[239] For an argument (in the context of complicity) that a standard of knowledge is more compatible with an objective mode of assessment than intent, see Lanovoy (n 41) 235–236.

[240] For the archival sources on the agreement, see National Archives, 'Newly Released GCHQ Files: UKUSA Agreement' June 2010 <https://discovery.nationalarchives.gov.uk/details/r/C11536914>; for background, see S Kim et al, 'Newly Disclosed Documents on the Five Eyes Alliance and What They Tell Us about Intelligence-Sharing Agreements' 25 April 2018 <https://law.yale.edu/mfia/case-disclosed/newly-disclosed-documents-five-eyes-alliance-and-what-they-tell-us-about-intelligence-sharing>.

[241] C DiMario, 'Counter Terrorist Group (CGT)' <https://pilac.law.harvard.edu/europe-region-efforts//counter-terrorist-group-ctg>; German Federal Office for the Protection of the Constitution, 'Counter Terrorism Group (CTG)' <www.verfassungsschutz.de/DE/verfassungsschutz/auftrag/zusammenarbeit-im-in-und-ausland/counter-terrorism-group-ctg/counter-terrorism-group-ctg_node.html>.

[242] Netherlands Review Committee on the Intelligence and Security Services, 'Review Report: On Contributions of the MIVD to Targeting' 3 August 2016 (CTIVD no 50) <https://english.ctivd.nl/investigations/review-report-50/documents/reports/2017/02/23/index> 29–30 (noting that the Dutch

nominations by the Dutch intelligence services of persons to be included in ISAF's targeting lists.[243] Of course, even if a State nominally provides intelligence under a standing arrangement, the circumstances of the specific case could, nonetheless, reveal that the provider was aware that the recipient used the intelligence as part of specific military operations.

v. Illustrations from State practice

To conclude the analysis of the elements of the general framework for identifying co-parties, it is helpful to consider how they may operate practically. This can be demonstrated with further examples from international practice where co-party identification has been assessed along the lines of the parameters suggested here and examples which can plausibly be explained against the background of the framework developed here.

The different types of military assistance that many States have provided to Ukraine and Russia during Russia's full-scale invasion of Ukraine illustrate the distinctions that the legal framework developed above may enable.[244] It has been noted above that Western States considered that their provision of weapons and military equipment to Ukraine, even tanks and combat aircraft, as well as the combat training of Ukrainian soldiers did not make them co-parties.[245] These repeated statements are consistent with the above framework since this assistance does not meet the criterion of a direct connection to hostilities. Russia's claim that military assistance meant that Western States had become parties to the conflict can thus not be sustained based on weapons deliveries.[246] Only Ukraine's use of the weapons and training directly caused military harm to Russia. The same reasoning would apply regarding reported assistance to Russia, such as Belarus's supply of tanks to Russia[247] or Iran's provision of drones and training on their use.[248]

Most of the intelligence that Western services have provided to Ukraine would have to be assessed in the same way.[249] By contrast, the provision of specific

intelligence and security services 'keep [themselves] appraised of the actions of the military coalition in general and the targeting process at the headquarters of the military coalition in particular').

243 ibid 27–28.

244 Parts of the following paragraphs have previously been published in a similar form (Wentker (n 188) 653–654).

245 n 177.

246 'Russia's Lavrov: Do not Underestimate Threat of Nuclear War' (*Reuters*, 26 April 2022) <www.reuters.com/world/russia-says-western-weapons-ukraine-legitimate-targets-russian-military-2022-04-25/>; J Keaten, 'Russia: US Air Defense Systems Could Be Targets in Ukraine' (*AP News*, 15 December 2022) <https://apnews.com/article/russia-ukraine-politics-donetsk-government-united-states-eed3a0fc72e8197182e78dcc73ade45e>.

247 S Kuznetsov, 'Ukraine Bats Away Lukashenko's Border Threats' *Politico* (12 December 2022) <www.politico.eu/article/ukraine-bats-away-lukashenkos-border-threats/>.

248 J Barnes, 'Iran Sends Drone Trainers to Crimea to Aid Russian Military' *NYT* (18 October 2022) <www.nytimes.com/2022/10/18/us/politics/iran-drones-russia-ukraine.html>.

249 See also OSCE Expert Report 2022 (n 169) 5.

targeting data could conceivably make the State providing it a co-party in certain circumstances.[250] The US and other NATO Member States have reportedly confirmed locations of specific targets in real-time during Ukrainian military operations, including against high-ranking Russian generals and the missile cruiser 'Moskva'.[251] Localising and verifying specific targets forms an essential part of the targeting process and thus of a military operation directly harming the opponent party. Reports also indicate a close connection of Ukraine's decision-making processes to the US intelligence, to the point that Ukraine usually would only strike upon US confirmation of the targeting coordinates and refrain from striking if such confirmation was not given.[252] Overall, the reports also imply that the US had knowledge of the role of its targeting assistance.[253] In sum, if the media reports are accurate, the reported patterns of intelligence cooperation seem capable of meeting the legal criteria for co-party status.[254] In this particular context, Russia's above noted claim that the US directly participated in hostilities and coordinated military operations against Russia reflects the criteria of the legal framework as developed above. The US did not comment on its role in the targeting process in detail but merely pointed out that 'the Ukrainians are responsible for finding targets, prioritizing them and then ultimately deciding which ones to engage. The U.S. does not approve targets, nor are we involved in the selection or engagement of targets'.[255] As noted above, however, the US administration has been said to have concluded that providing specific targeting intelligence could make it a co-party.[256] Similar concerns have reportedly led the German government to refrain from making its own intelligence available to Ukraine in real time.[257]

Turning to non-international armed conflicts, statements by the Danish government concerning its participation in the coalition against ISIL are illustrative. When the Danish government decided to extend this contribution by deploying a

[250] M Schmitt, 'Are We at War?' (*Articles of War*, 9 May 2022) <https://lieber.westpoint.edu/are-we-at-war/>.

[251] J Barnes, H Cooper, and E Schmitt, 'U.S. Intelligence Is Helping Ukraine Kill Russian Generals, Officials Say' *NYT* (4 May 2022) <www.nytimes.com/2022/05/04/us/politics/russia-generals-killed-ukraine.html?smid=tw-nytimes&smtyp=cur>; H Cooper, E Schmitt, and J Barnes, 'U.S. Intelligence Helped Ukraine Strike Russian Flagship, Officials Say' *NYT* (5 May 2022) <www.nytimes.com/2022/05/05/us/politics/moskva-russia-ship-ukraine-us.html?smid=url-copy>.

[252] I Khurshudyan et al, 'Ukraine's Rocket Campaign Reliant on U.S. Precision Targeting, Officials Say' *Washington Post* (9 February 2023) <www.washingtonpost.com/world/2023/02/09/ukraine-himars-rocket-artillery-russia/> (describing the targeting process based on an account of a 'senior Ukrainian official').

[253] M Milanovic, 'The United States and Allies Sharing Intelligence with Ukraine' (*EJIL: Talk!*, 09 May 2022) <www.ejiltalk.org/the-united-states-and-allies-sharing-intelligence-with-ukraine/>.

[254] See similarly R Pedrozo, 'Russia–Ukraine Conflict: The War at Sea' (2022) 100 ILS 1, 56.

[255] Khurshudyan et al (n 252) (quoting a Pentagon spokesperson).

[256] n 168.

[257] H Stark, 'Hilfe, die zum Ziel führt' *Zeit* (28 September 2022) <www.zeit.de/2022/40/ukraine-russland-krieg-bnd-geheimdienstinformationen?utm_referrer=https%3A%2F%2Fwww.google.com%2F>.

ground-based radar with associated personnel—while, at the same time, temporarily withdrawing its combat aircraft contribution—it considered that:

> [t]he radar contribution requested by the coalition will be an integral part of the planning and implementation of the international coalition's operations in Iraq and Syria

before concluding that:

> [t]he nature and extent of Denmark's overall active military participation in the international coalition in support of Iraq means that Denmark, together with the other military-active coalition countries, remains a party to the armed conflict against ISIL.[258]

By Denmark's own account, its activities thus constituted an integral part of coordinated military operations, such that Denmark was involved in the decision-making processes. That this happened with the knowledge of the essential elements of the relevant military operations is objectively evident from the circumstances.

Germany's contribution as part of that same coalition may provide another illustration. Although Germany has not itself carried out airstrikes, it has afforded a wide range of support to military operations in close coordination with the other States forming part of the coalition, such as air-to-air refuelling, intelligence gathering through reconnaissance flights, airspace surveillance, and transport.[259] The German government has not explicitly pronounced itself on its potential status as a co-party to the conflict with ISIL. Yet, the mandate for the deployment of the German armed forces, as prepared by the federal government and approved by parliament, at least hints at the view that Germany may indeed be a co-party. The mandate notes that 'the applicable international humanitarian law' regulates the conduct of the German armed forces.[260]

Finally, the instances of practice on aggregated intensity assessments for co-parties in non-international armed conflicts, discussed in the previous chapter,[261]

[258] Danish Foreign Ministry, 'Proposal for a Parliamentary Resolution on the Deployment of an Additional Danish Military Contribution to Support the Effort against ISIL' (8 October 2015) B8 (2015–16) [IV] (translated with DeepL). Placed under the Coalition's operational control with Denmark retaining full command, the radar contribution would 'help to ... coordinate the overall deployment of Coalition aircraft, to separate Coalition missions from each other and from any civilian air traffic, to direct aircraft to and from tankers and to direct them to areas where they will perform their operational tasks' but, as the government stressed, '[t]he aerial image from the Danish radar [would] not be used to detect and identify targets on the ground' (ibid [III]).

[259] German Federal Government, 'Motion: Continuation of the Deployment of Armed German Forces—Securing Stabilisation, Preventing the Resurgence of IS, Promoting Reconciliation in Iraq and Syria' 9 September 2020 (BT Drs 19/22207) [4]–[5].

[260] ibid [7].

[261] Chapter 3.4.a.ii.

provide further illustrations of patterns where findings of co-party status can be explained through the framework suggested here. Consider, for example, how the ICC in *Bemba* found the Central African Republic to be a co-party along with the MLC. That finding was based on the close connection of the Central African Republic government's military support to the MLC's operations and the co-ordination by the Central African Republic government of military operations of different partners.[262] In *Katanga*, the Court similarly concluded that the APC group was a co-party to the Ngiti militia against the background of logistical support to military operations as well as a role in planning and coordinating concrete attacks.[263] Concerning the situation in Afghanistan, the ICC Prosecutor considered the Haqqani Network as a co-party of the Taliban based on evidence of 'joint planning and execution of military operations, at both the strategic (national) level and at the tactical level for specific attacks'.[264]

To complement the general framework drawn up so far, the next section turns to potential special rules for identifying co-parties in specific situations.

c. Special rules for identifying co-parties?

As explained at the outset, special rules for identifying co-parties in specific situations may develop alongside the general framework. Such rules would take precedence over the general framework for the situations that they would cover. Section i. will first briefly recall the persisting special rule on declarations of war. While no other special rules for identifying co-parties are found to exist, sections ii. and iii. will discuss candidates for such rules for specific types of conflicts, activities, and entities.

i. Declarations of war

It has already been noted that declaring war alongside others still provides a route to co-party status.[265] This possibility is best conceived of as a special rule since identifying States declaring war as co-parties would turn on discerning their declared intent to be at war, rather than on whether they meet the elements of the general framework set out above. The continued existence of this special rule is woven into the structure of contemporary IHL through the wording of Common Article 2, and its persistence remains supported by international practice, as seen above.[266] As a historical relic that States have not been willing to extinguish, it testifies to the development of the regulation of war and armed conflict as an

[262] Chapter 3, nn 153–156.
[263] Chapter 3, nn 144–147.
[264] *Afghanistan Investigation Request* (n 212) [58].
[265] Above b.iii.(1).
[266] Chapter 3.2.a.

incremental process and illustrates that the prospects for this process to produce an entirely coherent regulative framework are limited.

ii. Specific types of conflicts and activities: the example of the provision of territory in inter-State settings

Special rules for identifying co-parties could also develop by type of conflict, that is rules applicable to co-party identification in international or non-international armed conflicts only, or for specific types of activities—or specific types of activities if performed in a specific type of conflict. To illustrate, the provision of territory by State A in support of State B fighting State C is a potential candidate for a specific type of activity that could be covered by a special rule if performed in a specific type of conflict. Here, a special rule could govern the identification of A as a co-party to B in the international armed conflict with C.

This special rule would flow from the idea that, in inter-State conflict, the prohibition of the use of force may serve as a yardstick in identifying co-parties and that, in particular, activities specifically covered by the prohibition of aggression would also make the State a party to an international armed conflict.[267] In cases of aggression by allowing territory placed at the disposal of another State to be used for an act of aggression (Article 3(f) of the 1974 Definition of Aggression), this would mean that the State providing the territory would become a party to an international armed conflict with the victim of the aggression. The derivative character of the rule contained in Article 3(f), which presupposes an act of aggression by the State receiving the assistance,[268] can be taken to suggest that the two States would be co-parties to the same international armed conflict, rather than parties to separate conflicts.

If the connection of party status to the prohibition of aggression by providing territory were to be established, the resulting identification of co-parties in such cases might diverge from the result under the general framework set out above. In particular, the rule reflected in Article 3(f) might not necessarily presuppose a direct connection to military operations or hostilities, close coordination along the lines of the general framework, or the same inherent subjective element. For example, Jackson has suggested that mere acquiescence in the use of one's territory for the perpetration of an act of aggression may suffice.[269] This would, without more, hardly evidence sufficiently close coordination to point to co-party status under the general framework.[270]

[267] Above 2.a.iii.

[268] J Quigley, 'Complicity in International Law: A New Direction in the Law of State Responsibility' (1986) 57 BYIL 77, 86.

[269] M Jackson, *Complicity in International Law* (OUP 2015) 142.

[270] See also Upcher (n 44) 54–57 (distinguishing invitations by a neutral State to enter one's territory, which could make a neutral State a party to an international armed conflict, from mere acquiescence in the use of one's territory which the neutral is powerless to prevent. This leaves open cases of acquiescence where the territorial State was not powerless to prevent the use of its territory or take preventive action).

Interestingly, however, some parallels to the elements of the general framework set out here have also been suggested. For example, Kreß has proposed relying on the ICRC's articulation of the 'directness' of civilian participation in its DPH Guidance to determine whether territory has been used to perpetrate aggression.[271] As regards the subjective dimension, Article 3(f) gives no express indication. Aust thus concludes that no subjective element at all is required.[272] By contrast, Jackson has argued that 'placing' one's territory at the disposal of another State presupposes that the territorial State has knowledge of the aggressor's acts.[273] This proposition aligns with the inherent knowledge element that is required as part of the general framework proposed above.

In any event, international practice has not established an explicit connection between co-party identification and the rule reflected in Article 3(f) of the prohibition of aggression.[274] Furthermore, practice on identifying co-parties in the realm of providing territory does not seem to align with the content of the prohibition of aggression. For example, a hint at the notion that more than acquiescence might be required for co-party status was provided in relation to the 1970 US intervention, in the course of the Vietnam War, against bases on Cambodian soil (allegedly) used by North Vietnamese and Viet Cong forces.[275] The US justified its decision not to coordinate this with Cambodia and, in particular, not to seek explicit Cambodian consent for this intervention with its concern not to make Cambodia 'a co-belligerent along with South Viet-Nam and the United States'.[276]

Some practice in this area may actually align with the general criteria suggested here. In particular, to the extent that instances of placing territory at the disposal of other States distinguish, among other things, according to the closeness of the connection of the provision of territory to military operations, they may be read as being consistent with the elements of the general framework.

To illustrate this point, consider the patterns of provision of territory by various States in the course of the Iraq War beginning in 2003. The US identified a number

[271] C Kreß, 'The State Conduct Element' in C Kreß and S Barriga (eds), *The Crime of Aggression: A Commentary* (CUP 2017) 447.

[272] H Aust, *Complicity and the Law of State Responsibility* (CUP 2011) 381.

[273] Jackson (n 269) 141.

[274] In addition to the practice on the identification of co-parties discussed here, conversely, practice supporting the rule in art 3(f) does not seem to draw a connection to party status to an international armed conflict—see ARSIWA Commentary Article 16 [8]; Aust (n 272) 115–120; Jackson (n 269) 137–139.

[275] 'Letter Dated 5 May 1970 from the Permanent Representative of the United States of America to the United Nations addressed to the President of the Security Council' (S/9781).

[276] 'Military Operations in Cambodia: Statement of the Legal Adviser' (1970) 64 AJIL 933, 935; Address to the Nation on the Situation in Southeast Asia on 30 April 1970, Public Papers of President Nixon (1970) 405, 407 ('[T]he aid we will provide will be limited for the purpose of enabling Cambodia to defend its neutrality and not for the purpose of making it an active belligerent on one side or the other'). Suggesting that the Cambodia Operation had nevertheless compromised this explicit aim of the US, Falk commented that the intervention had 'brought additional governments into positions of active co-belligerency' (R Falk, 'The Cambodia Operation and International Law' (1971) 65 AJIL 1, 24).

of States as its 'co-belligerents', namely the UK, Australia, Spain, Poland, Kuwait, and Qatar, because they had 'sen[t] military forces to participate in Coalition combat operations or allow[ed] their territory to be used as a base for such operations'.[277] While the three European States and Australia participated with their own troops in the conflict, it is not reported that Kuwait and Qatar did so. By implication, the US considered these two States as its co-parties based on their role in the conflict by permitting coalition forces to use their territory as a base for military operations against Iraq. The nature of the connection of the contributions to military operations seems to have played a decisive role in this assessment.[278] Kuwait denied any participation in military operations against Iraq,[279] though, importantly, as Corten has pointed out, this was a denial of the facts, not of the legal consequences potentially attached to its acts.[280]

In addition to Kuwait and Qatar, several European States permitted the US to use their territory for military operations against Iraq, notably by granting overflight rights to military aircraft and allowing refuelling and maintenance stopovers. The potentially less direct connection of this territorial support to military operations may have been why the US did not explicitly count these States among its co-parties. The States themselves also considered that they had remained third parties. Italy and Ireland argued that they had practised 'non-belligerency' and 'qualified neutrality' respectively,[281] and Germany maintained that it 'neither directly nor indirectly participated' in the Iraq War.[282] The Federal Administrative Court expressed 'grave concern' as to the compatibility of Germany's activities with international law, including neutrality law.[283] The Court did not suggest, however, that this had made Germany a party to the conflict with Iraq. In his decision not to open investigations against members of the German government for participation in the preparation of a war of aggression, the Federal Prosecutor General found that Germany's granting of overflight rights and other support to the coalition operations had not made it a party to the conflict with Iraq.[284]

Although the justifications for the rejections of co-party status have mostly remained opaque in these instances, the insufficient quality of the contributions to the US operations seems to have played a role. In the parliamentary debate, the Irish government, for example, pointed to its position taken in the First Gulf War (1990–1991) and noted:

[277] OLC Memo (n 161) 44.

[278] See above the text accompanied by n 162.

[279] UNSC, 4726th Meeting (26 March 2003) UN Doc S/PV.4726 14.

[280] O Corten, 'Quels droits et quels devoirs pour les États tiers? Les effets juridiques d'une assistance à un acte d'agression' in K Bannelier, T Christakis, and O Corten (eds), *L'Intervention en Irak et le droit international* (Pedone 2004) 128.

[281] Chapter 2, nn 67–68.

[282] German Federal Parliament, Stenographic Protocol Plenary Session 15/34 (19 March 2003) 2728 (statement by the Chancellor).

[283] Federal Administrative Court, Judgement of 21 June 2005 (n 60) [4.1.4.1.1]–[4.1.4.1.4].

[284] Federal Prosecutor General, 'Decision of 21 March 2003' (2003) 58 JZ 908, 911.

> that any role adopted or action taken by the Government in relation to a Gulf War [*sic*] would constitute participation in that war is, in the last analysis, a question of substance and degree. The Government then and now maintains that merely to permit the use of a civilian airport in this manner is not of sufficient degree or substance to constitute participating in the war. The provision of facilities does not make Ireland a member of a military coalition nor does anybody regard us as such.[285]

To sum up, while this practice does not allow for inferring specific criteria, the above instances can plausibly be explained based on the general framework developed here. More generally, it seems that this general framework can provide appropriate delimitations in identifying co-parties also regarding the provision of territory in international armed conflicts. This framework also avoids applying different criteria for co-party identification depending on whether territory is provided to an aggressor or, for example, to the victim of an aggression and thus keeps the identification separate from the lawfulness of the respective conduct under the *jus ad bellum*.

iii. Specific types of entities

Special rules could also develop for identifying specific entities as co-parties. Such propositions have been made for non-State armed groups and international organisations. Sections (1) and (2) will discuss these propositions and their rationales and find both of them to be neither established nor necessary.

As a prerequisite to these discussions, it should be clarified that such rules would not contravene the principle of the belligerent equality, which 'underlies the law of armed conflict'[286] and remains firmly rooted in international treaty and customary law,[287] notwithstanding occasional contestation.[288] This principle requires that IHL applies equally to all parties to the conflict, regardless of who acts in accordance with the *jus ad bellum*.[289] Leaving aside the unsettled issue of whether and to what extent the principle also applies to non-international armed conflicts,[290] the

285 Irish House of Representatives, 'Daéil Éireann Debate 20 March 2003' vol 563 no 3 <www.oireachtas.ie/en/debates/debate/dail/2003-03-20/4/>.

286 ICRC, 'International Humanitarian Law and the Challenges of Contemporary Armed Conflicts' (2003) 19.

287 V Koutroulis, 'And Yet It Exists: In Defence of the "Equality of Belligerents" Principle' (2013) 26 LJIL 449.

288 M Mandel, 'Aggressors' Rights: The Doctrine of "Equality between Belligerents" and the Legacy of Nuremberg' (2011) 24 LJIL 627.

289 See generally H Lauterpacht, 'The Limits of the Operation of the Law of War' (1953) 30 BYIL 206; H Meyrowitz, *Le Principe de l'égalité des belligérants devant le droit de la guerre* (Pedone 1970); C Greenwood, 'The Relationship between *Ius ad Bellum* and *Ius in Bello*' (1983) 9 Rev Int Stud 221; A Roberts, 'The Equal Application of the Law of War: A Principle under Pressure' (2009) 90 IRRC 931.

290 See generally J Somer, 'Jungle Justice: Passing Sentence on the Equality of Belligerents in Non-International Armed Conflict' (2007) 89 IRRC 655, 663ff; Roberts (n 289) 933, 961; T Gill, 'Reconciling the Irreconcilable: Some Thoughts on Belligerent Equality in Non-international Armed Conflicts' (2022) 51 NYIL 343; in favour of an equality of belligerents principle in non-international armed

principle does not cover the rules on how an entity becomes a party to an armed conflict.[291] Indeed, variations for different entities regarding who qualifies as a party would not mean treating different *parties* differently.[292] The operation of the principle of equal application of IHL to all 'belligerents' presupposes, by definition, that an entity qualifies as a party in the first place. The principle cannot, therefore, have a bearing on how that status is acquired.

(1) Non-State armed groups

It has been suggested that more restrictive rules should govern when non-State armed groups are identified as co-parties to non-international armed conflicts,[293] as compared to those that apply to other potential parties, namely only where they 'actually participate in hostilities'[294] or where there is 'some armed violence between each armed group and their common opponent'.[295] If framed in these terms, it may already be questioned to what extent such proposals would indeed prove more restrictive than the elements of the general framework suggested here. An actually more restrictive rule would consist, for example, in requiring that the armed group carries out 'attacks' itself (rather than relying on the broader concepts of 'military operations' or 'hostilities', as proposed above) or indeed in requiring that the activities of the armed group separately meet the intensity threshold for the existence of a non-international armed conflict in the relationship with the adverse side.[296]

At present, such a more restrictive rule is not borne out by international practice, as attested by the instances reviewed in Chapter 3. Non-State armed groups have been identified as co-parties whose activities did not separately fulfil the intensity threshold and who did not carry out attacks either.[297]

conflicts, see ICRC, 'Position Paper—ICRC Engagement with Non-State Armed Groups: Why, How, for What Purpose, and Other Salient Issues' (2020) 102 IRRC 1089, 1094.

[291] For suggestions that this principle requires uniformity in the criteria for identifying parties to armed conflict, see eg T Rodenhäuser, *Organizing Rebellion: Non-State Armed Groups under International Humanitarian Law, Human Rights Law, and International Criminal Law* (OUP 2018) 78 fn 108; Verlinden (n 45) 144; with respect to UN peace operations, see Maganza (n 137) 217, 220.

[292] D Akande, 'Classification of Armed Conflicts: Relevant Legal Concepts' in E Wilmshurst (ed), *International Law and the Classification of Conflicts* (OUP 2012) 68 (in the context of UN peacekeeper's involvement in armed conflict).

[293] These discussions and the present section address non-State armed groups as parties to non-international armed conflicts only, rather than the special case of non-State entities qualifying as parties to international armed conflicts under API, art 1(4) (on this, see Chapter 1.2.b.i.).

[294] Lubell (n 180) 26; R Bartels, 'When Do Terrorist Organisations Qualify as "Parties to an Armed Conflict" under International Humanitarian Law?' (2017) 56 MLLWR 451, 473. In the context of the US's associated forces doctrine, Ingber similarly traces an 'active hostilities' test as one approach existing within the US administration (Ingber (n 86) 94–97).

[295] Zwanenburg (n 120) 53.

[296] Presumably, a special rule would still require additional elements, such as coordination and the subjective dimension suggested in the general framework above. In this respect, no suggestions to differentiate between armed groups and other entities seem to have been made.

[297] Chapter 3.4.a.ii.(2).

The development of such a rule is, nonetheless, conceivable. However, it is arguably unnecessary. The rationale for a more restrictive approach is to accommodate normative concerns about the authority of a State party to a non-international armed conflict to target a broader range of individuals if an additional armed group becomes a co-party on the adverse side.[298] This concern has arisen mainly against the background of expansive US targeting practices, based partly on permissive invocations of the alleged party status of opponent groups to armed conflicts with the US.[299]

Crucially, however, the general framework proposed here would arguably provide sufficiently robust requirements that do not allow for arguments taking loose cooperation between armed groups as a starting point for potentially unbounded targeting practices. It should also be kept in mind that the fulfilment of the requirements must be deduced from the factual circumstances. Therefore, invocations of co-party status that are not backed by factual evidence would not be in line with the general framework. The problem with such abusive invocations would be compliance with the general requirements, rather than the standards set by those requirements in the first place.

More generally, focusing purely on the additional permissions following from an armed group's co-party status for the opponent State party does not do justice to the broad range of legal implications connected to party status. It is true that for the armed group itself, the same permissions would not arise, thus creating an imbalance with the State side.[300] However, potential normative benefits in terms of protection and accountability should not be ignored.[301] As discussed above, such benefits may, for example, flow from restrictions imposed on non-State parties to armed conflict and from implications of party status under international criminal law.[302]

(2) International organisations involved in peacekeeping operations

Particular restrictions in the identification of party status have also been proposed for Peacekeeping Operations. In this respect, it has been suggested:

> that a United Nations force and national units operating in association with it … will be regarded as parties to an armed conflict only when they have engaged in hostilities on a scale … considerably higher than that which is used … for other purposes.[303]

[298] On the connections between the regime of targeting individuals and the party status of non-State armed groups, see generally Chapter 1.4.a.i.(2). For a discussion of the normative concerns related to targeting authority, see Chapter 3.4.a.iii.

[299] See generally Ingber (n 86) 98–107.

[300] See Chapter 1.3.b.

[301] Chapter 3.4.a.iii.

[302] Chapter 1.3.a.iii. and Chapter 1.4.b.ii.

[303] C Greenwood, 'International Humanitarian Law and United Nations Military Operations' (1998) 1 YIHL 3, 25.

The underlying traditional vision from the early days of the UN was that:

> the United Nations, acting on behalf of the organized community of nations against an offender, has a superior legal and moral position as compared with the other party to the conflict.[304]

Here, too, a special rule to this effect would be conceivable. However, such proposals do not seem to have sufficiently crystallised in practice to reflect positive international law[305]—identifying parties is subject to the same rules where peace operations are involved.[306] A special rule in this sense would also appear problematic, as relying on the motives or moral causes of the acting entities sits ill with the general scheme of IHL applicability. The scheme is based not on motives or causes for action but, rather, on the factual situation on the ground.[307] Different standards for operations involving international organisations might also provide avenues and incentives for States to organise military operations so as to avoid the implications that would flow from their own party status.

d. Temporal scope of party status

Having developed elements to identify an entity as a (co-)party and having assessed potential special rules for this identification, a final crucial specification pertains to the extension of this status in time. When does it begin and when does it end? Chapters 3 and 4 have so far demonstrated that finding that an armed conflict exists and that specific entities are parties to the conflict are different matters. This is also true for the temporal scope of such findings. In multiparty armed conflicts, the temporal scope of the armed conflict sets the outer limits of the temporal scope of any entity's co-party status. Within these confines, as a rule, party status extends for as long as an entity meets the requirements set out in the previous sections. This section will explain how this basic rule plays out by showing, first, when party status begins, secondly, when it ends, and, thirdly, to what extent legal consequences of party status can extend beyond its termination.[308]

304 Report of the Committee on Study of Legal Problems of the United Nations, 'Should the Laws of War Apply to United Nations Enforcement Action?' (1952) 46 ASIL Proc 216, 217.

305 For reviews of practice on this point, see C Wiesener, 'The Application and Interplay of Humanitarian Law and Human Rights Law in Peace Operations, with a Particular Focus on the Use of Force' (PhD, EUI 2015) 68–77; E Nalin, *L'Applicabilità del diritto internazionale umanitario alle operazioni di 'peace-keeping' delle Nazioni Unite* (Editoriale Scientifica 2018) 102–126.

306 T Gill et al, *Leuven Manual on the International Law Applicable to Peace Operations* (CUP 2017) 93.

307 Chapter 3.2.

308 Parts of this section have been published previously in a condensed form (Wentker (n 188) 652–653).

i. Beginning of party status

Once the criteria for the existence of an international or non-international armed conflict are met overall, the (co-)party status begins as soon as the prospective party has made a sufficiently coordinated contribution with the requisite direct connection to military operations or hostilities, as specified above. This may, but need not, coincide with the beginning of its engagement. Thus, for example, Denmark assessed that its initial military contribution to the fight against ISIL, which consisted in deploying a cargo aircraft, had not yet made it a party to the conflict, but that it had only become a party once it had extended this contribution.[309] For contributions consisting of recurrent acts, some repetition may be helpful evidence to establish that a contribution meets the requirements.[310] Depending on the circumstances, however, the very first acts of a contribution may already suffice to establish that this is the case, such as the first airstrikes by different States joining the US efforts against ISIL in Syria and Iraq discussed in Chapter 3.[311] Similarly, as seen above, the ICC in *Bemba* considered the MLC as a party to a non-international armed conflict alongside the Central African Republic government from the first days of the group's intervention on the Central African Republic's territory.[312]

ii. Termination of party status

Party status necessarily ends with the end of the conflict, which is 'notoriously difficult' to pin down in practice.[313] A commonly adopted requirement for this assessment in international armed conflicts is the 'general close of military operations'.[314] As Pictet noted, 'in most cases the general close of military operations will be the final end of all fighting between *all* those concerned'.[315] For non-international armed conflicts, the ICTY requires a 'peaceful settlement' for the conflict to cease.[316] The ICRC emphasises that this should be understood as a 'factual and lasting pacification', evidenced by the 'cessation of all hostilities between the parties to the conflict and the absence of a real risk of their resumption'.[317]

Conversely, even during the armed conflict, an individual entity's co-party status may, nonetheless, end in two main scenarios. First, party status ends once a party ceases to meet the structural requirements for qualifying as a potential

[309] *Danish Manual* 56.
[310] Ferraro (n 96) 586.
[311] Chapter 3, nn 121–128.
[312] *Bemba* (Confirmation of Charges) (n 210) [249]ff.
[313] N Derejko, 'A Forever War? Rethinking the Temporal Scope of Non-International Armed Conflict' (2021) 26 JCSL 347, 348.
[314] Drawing on the language of GCIV, art 6(2), see notably *Gotovina* (Trial Judgment) IT-06-90-T (15 April 2011) [1694]; *GCI Commentary* [277], [494]; see also M Milanovic, 'The End of Application of International Humanitarian Law' (2014) 96 IRRC 163, 174.
[315] *Pictet Commentary GCIV* 62 (emphasis added).
[316] *Tadić* (Decision on the Defence Motion for Interlocutory Appeal on Jurisdiction) IT-94-1-A (2 October 1995) [70].
[317] ICRC Challenges Report (2015) (n 111) 10–11; see also *GCI Commentary* [491]–[494].

party—particularly if an armed group is no longer sufficiently organised. Secondly, party status ends once a co-party's activities no longer meet the requirements for identifying it as a party in the first place. Conceptually, the analysis is simply a reversal of establishing the beginning of party status.[318] It would thus not be necessary for an entity to fully disengage from the conflict and entirely stop its coordinated contribution.[319] A change in the quality of the contribution (such that it no longer meets the requirements) could already entail that the respective entity is to be considered a third party rather than a party.

Nonetheless, it seems reasonable, in practice, to presume that an entity remains a co-party until that presumption is rebutted by an externally discernible manifestation of a significant change of the contribution or its cessation. A changed pattern over a prolonged period can be helpful evidence in this respect. This would avoid the legal uncertainty that could otherwise result from 'revolving door' situations or simply from the fact that the relevant changes may not be instantly evident to other actors that need to make the assessment in the context of ongoing operations.[320] Brief interruptions of a contribution may thus not suffice. For example, the Netherlands and Belgium established a rotation plan, and each took turns of several months to carry out airstrikes with the coalition against ISIL.[321] The close coordination and mutual support, regardless of whose turn it was to carry out the strikes at a given point in time, would militate against considering the co-party status of one of the two States as terminated with every rotation.[322]

Party status does not end merely because a specific type of activity is temporarily or permanently suspended, so long as the respective co-party's overall contribution still meets the requirements for identifying the entity as a party. For example, Denmark first temporarily and then permanently suspended carrying out airstrikes against ISIL. Nonetheless, the Danish government assessed that the range of activities through which Denmark continued to contribute to the coalition efforts against ISIL entailed that '[t]he nature and extent of Denmark's total active military participation in the international coalition in support of Iraq mean[t] that Denmark remains a party to the armed conflict against ISIL'.[323] Similarly, the fact

[318] Weizmann (n 43) 225, 232; similarly Milanovic (n 314) 170 (regarding the scope of application of IHL).

[319] For a suggestion that a lasting disengagement or a prolonged cessation of the activities is required, see Verlinden (n 15) 157.

[320] *Gotovina* (Trial) (n 314) [1694] (for parallel considerations regarding the termination of an armed conflict).

[321] Global Coalition, 'Belgium: A Committed Member of the Coalition' 26 January 2017 <https://theglobalcoalition.org/en/belgium-a-committed-member-of-the-coalition/>; Belgium, 'Prolongation de la contribution à la coalition internationale contre DAESH en Irak' 10 July 2015 <https://news.belgium.be/fr/prolongation-de-la-contribution-la-coalition-internationale-contre-daesh-en-irak>.

[322] See also R van Steenberghe, 'La légalité de la participation de la Belgique à la lutte armée contre l'Etat islamique en Irak' (2015) 134 Journal des Tribunaux 641, 641.

[323] Danish Foreign Ministry, Proposal B8 (2015–16) [V] (translated with DeepL); for the same assessment concerning the temporary interruption of airstrikes in 2015/16, see ibid [II]–[IV]; *Danish Manual* 56.

that Canada ceased its airstrikes in Iraq and Syria in 2016 arguably did not end its party status, since it continued various other aspects of its contribution, including 'air-to-air refuelling and aerial intelligence, surveillance, and reconnaissance missions in support of coalition air operations' as well as 'efforts to train Iraqi security forces'.[324]

iii. Temporal extension of legal consequences attached to party status

The end of an entity's party status does not necessarily mean that no further legal consequences will flow from this status. The point in time at which an entity must have been a party is to be discerned by carefully interpreting the specific rule that attaches legal consequences to party status.

While obligations relating to the conduct of hostilities will typically not apply to a former party once it ceases to be a party,[325] many obligations regarding protected individuals will extend beyond this point in time. Some obligations that are activated while an entity is a party will still need to be discharged after its party status ends. For example, a former party's obligations to care for a wounded individual do not simply end because it ceases to be a party.[326] Other obligations may even be activated after the cessation of hostilities but still entail consequences for former parties, such as obligations to search for and collect the dead and account for the missing,[327] obligations relating to persons deprived of their liberty,[328] or obligations to take measures regarding explosive remnants of war.[329]

The exact temporal extent of a former party's obligations will need to be established on a case-by-case basis for each specific rule.[330] It seems reasonable that a party's obligations would, at least, extend to those situations where the facts activating the obligation arose while the entity was still a party. A former party

[324] Canada, 'Canadian Armed Forces Cease Airstrike Operations in Iraq and Syria' 17 February 2016 <www.canada.ca/en/department-national-defence/news/2016/02/canadian-armed-forces-cease-airstrike-operations-in-iraq-and-syria.html>; Canada, 'Canada Renews Its Military Contribution to Support Stability in the Middle East' 18 March 2019 <www.canada.ca/en/department-national-defence/news/2019/03/canada-renews-its-military-contribution-to-support-stability-in-the-middle-east.html> (concluding that Canada had remained a party).

[325] By contrast, some such party obligations could theoretically already cover conduct *preceding* the beginning of the entity's (co-)party status, such as precautionary measures relating to the very military operation through which the entity becomes a party. This problem is similar to whether the law of international armed conflict already covers the 'first strike' that gives rise to the international armed conflict (for the debates on this point in the context of the killing of the Iranian General Soleimani in early 2020, see eg UN Special Rapporteur on Extrajudicial, Summary or Arbitrary Executions, 'Report: Use of Armed Drones for Targeted Killings' UN Doc A/HRC/44/38 (15 August 2020) Annex [15]–[39]; O Corten et al, 'L'Exécution de Qassem Soleimani et ses suites: Aspects de jus contra bellum et de jus in bello' (2020) 124 RGDIP 41, 64.

[326] See eg GCI, arts 12, 15; GCII, arts 12, 18; API, art 10; Common Article 3(2); APII, arts 7–8; *CIHL* rr 109–111.

[327] See eg GCI, art 15; GCII, art 18; GCIV, art 16; API, art 33(1); APII, art 8; *CIHL* rr 112–117.

[328] On the temporal scope of such obligations, see eg GCIII, art 5; APII, art 2(2).

[329] Protocol V CCW, arts 3–6.

[330] For the scope of IHL generally, see Derejko (n 313) 11ff (suggesting a 'functional approach' that distinguishes the temporal scope of application of each rule).

would thus, for example, bear obligations to collect those individuals killed while it was a party. To what extent it would still bear such obligations if the killing occurred only after it ceased being a party seems less certain. For some obligations, this may be the case. For example, the obligation to clear remnants of war covers 'all explosive remnants of war in territory under [the party's] control'.[331] This suggests that the obligation extends to remnants of explosives used after the respective entity's party status ended.

Such differentiation is required not only for obligations addressed to parties but also, for example, as regards the legal position of individuals. To the extent that the applicability of a rule depends on the nature of the connection of an individual to a party, the application of the rule can be activated only while the respective entity is a party. Specific protective rules may, nonetheless, provide for continued protection independent of party status. For example, an individual will be a combatant only for such time as the State, of whose armed forces the individual is a member, remains a party. Once fallen into the hands of the enemy, however, the end of the State's party status does not affect the individual's secondary status as prisoner of war 'until their final release and repatriation'.[332]

4. Conclusion

Chapter 4 has developed an account of the legal criteria for establishing co-party status. Within the parameters that Chapter 3 has drawn from the notions of armed conflict, Chapter 4 has discerned concepts for understanding the identification of co-parties as a distinct legal analysis. The account provides a common analytical framework for all constellations of co-party identification. Grounded in the structure of the legal system regulating armed conflict, the framework builds on concepts proposed by approaches to co-party identification in specific settings and is informed by international practice.

The relevance of this account will now be made more tangible in Chapter 5. Chapter 5 completes Part II of the book by drawing out central legal implications, which flow from identifying collective entities as co-parties to multiparty armed conflicts under the legal criteria discerned in Chapters 3 and 4.

331 Protocol V CCW, art 3.
332 GCIII, art 5(1).

5

Operationalising Party Status

Cooperation and the Implications of Identifying Co-parties

1. Introduction

To further demonstrate why and how the framework proposed in Chapters 3 and 4 is practically significant, Chapter 5 delves into the legal implications of identifying collective entities as co-parties to multiparty armed conflicts under this account.[1] In doing so, the chapter draws together the analysis of the two parts of the book. It specifies what follows from the analysis in Part I on the parties' legal position in light of the legal framework for their identification presented in Part II.

As a starting point, co-parties are 'fully fledged belligerent[s]'.[2] Identifying co-parties therefore comes with all the legal implications at various levels that ordinarily flow from the international legal position of parties, as set out in Part I of the book. To illustrate, for Germany, being identified as a co-party to the non-international armed conflict with ISIL[3] would mean bearing central sets of obligations under international humanitarian law (IHL).[4] Conversely, the relation of a co-party with non-party States with respect to the conflict is governed by the rules applicable between parties and third parties.[5] Whether the US support to Kuwait during the Iran–Iraq War violated neutrality law thus turned on whether Kuwait was indeed to be identified as a co-party to Iraq as alleged by Iran.[6] For individuals, their connection to a co-party impacts the nature and scope of their legal protections as well as their rights, obligations, and criminal responsibility.[7] For instance, whether al-Shabaab qualified as a co-party to al-Qaeda in the conflict with the US in Somalia[8] would have played a role in the targetability of its fighters under IHL by the US,[9] but also possibly in establishing their liability for potential

[1] Parts of this chapter have previously been published in a similar form (A Wentker, 'Partnered Operations and the Positive Duties of Co-parties' (2022) 27 JCSL 159).
[2] M Greenspan, *The Modern Law of Land Warfare* (University of California Press 1959) 531.
[3] Chapter 4, text accompanied by nn 259–260.
[4] Chapter 1.3.
[5] Chapter 2.
[6] Chapter 4, nn 55–59.
[7] Chapter 1.4.
[8] Chapter 4, n 91.
[9] See Chapter 1.4.a.i.(2).

Party Status to Armed Conflict in International Law. Alexander Wentker, Oxford University Press. © Alexander Wentker 2024.
DOI: 10.1093/oso/9780198900900.003.0006

war crimes under international criminal law (specifically for those war crimes that require the perpetrator to have a specific connection to a party and, at a general level, as a factor in the nexus assessment).[10] And the impact of al-Shabaab's potential co-party status alongside al-Qaeda against the US on the legality of US strikes against members of that group would also have mattered to whether other States acted lawfully. For example, the finding would indirectly matter to assess whether Germany (as a third State) violated its duty not to aid or assist the parties' IHL violations by allowing the US to operate the strikes from German territory.[11]

To what extent each set of implications of party status is relevant to a particular party in a given case depends on various factors pertaining to the factual circumstances of the case. An important factor for co-parties will be their role within the cooperation scheme with the fellow co-parties. A division of labour between co-parties may entail that, for example, some co-parties do not themselves carry out attacks. Accordingly, certain obligations specifically regulating the conduct of attacks by a party may not be activated for all co-parties, such as the prohibition to carry out indiscriminate attacks.[12] Consider, for example, the role of States like Germany or Italy in the conflict with ISIL or the US in the conflict with the Houthis alongside the Saudi-led coalition—assuming, for the sake of the illustration, that the respective States indeed qualified as co-parties.[13] Although certain implications of party status may only be activated if a co-party carries out specific activities, Chapter 5 illustrates that a range of significant implications will be relevant to all entities identified as co-parties under the framework developed in Chapters 3 and 4.

What is more, Chapter 5 demonstrates that party status has specific implications for the relationship between multiple co-parties—in other words, the chapter spells out the specific practical meaning of *co*-party status. The chapter does so by focusing on one emblematic set of such implications related to a key issue frequently surfacing in cooperative conflict settings, namely to what extent cooperation partners bear obligations under international law regarding the conduct of their partners. Among other similar examples of current or recent conflicts, the US's support of the Saudi-led coalition in Yemen raised questions as to what the US was legally required to undertake regarding the conduct of the coalition.[14] Likewise, following Russia's military intervention alongside Syrian government

[10] See Chapter 1.4.b.ii.(1).

[11] On this duty, see Chapter 2.3.c.; on the factual relevance of Germany's support in this case, see Administrative Court of Cologne, Judgment of 27 April 2016 (4 K 5467/15) [6]–[7], [12] (summarising the submissions of a Somali plaintiff on the involvement of the Ramstein airbase in US strikes in Somalia).

[12] API, art 51(4)–(5); *CIHL* r 11.

[13] Chapter 4, nn 259–260, 197–203.

[14] O Hathaway et al, 'Yemen: Is the U.S. Breaking the Law?' (2019) 10 Harv NSJ 1, 67–71; J Hursh, 'International Humanitarian Law Violations, Legal Responsibility, and US Military Support to the Saudi Coalition in Yemen: A Cautionary Tale' (2020) 7 JUOFIL 122, 147–154.

forces, Russia was publicly criticised for not taking steps to prevent Syria from using prohibited weapons and deliberately targeting civilians.[15] Similar questions also existed for the members of the multinational coalition that took action against ISIL as part of Operation Inherent Resolve.[16]

The central argument of Chapter 5 is that co-parties have duties to take positive steps vis-à-vis the conduct of their fellow co-parties in an armed conflict. The background to this argument is the debate on the extent to which States have a duty to ensure respect for IHL by others under Common Article 1 and customary international law. As shown in Chapter 2, particular controversy revolves around the question as to whether this 'external' element of the obligation to respect and ensure respect also entails a duty to take *positive* steps (in addition to a duty to refrain from aiding, assisting, and encouraging violations of IHL). Chapter 2 suggested that a critical reason for this particular opposition is that imposing such duties on *all* States is perceived to create tensions in the overall structure of how international law allocates obligations in armed conflict between parties and third parties. Such duties would seemingly demand abandoning the posture of abstention that international law generally requires of third States.

Bracketing the question of whether *third parties* have such positive external obligations, Chapter 5 takes the structural tensions underlying the unsettled state of this debate as a point of departure for arguing that *parties* to a conflict do have obligations to take positive measures regarding the conduct of others, namely vis-à-vis their fellow co-parties in the same armed conflict. This crucial nuance is not sufficiently accounted for in the debates, which often do not distinguish between whether the duties would be borne by co-parties or by parties. The chapter shows why our understanding of how IHL allocates obligations in cooperation settings benefits from fully appreciating the duties among co-parties vis-à-vis their fellow co-parties' conduct.

For co-parties, the role (that accompanies their party status) as a central duty bearer under IHL translates into what they must do in relation to conduct by their fellow co-parties. These duties stem from multiple legal bases. On the one hand, there are obligations addressed to parties in the realms of both the conduct of hostilities and the protection of individuals that encompass positive duties regarding fellow co-parties. On the other hand, the general obligation to ensure respect for IHL requires that co-parties take measures to ensure that their fellow co-parties also respect IHL. The chapter explains that the general system of duty bearers under IHL entails that the case for such duties as between co-parties is structurally stronger than it is for third parties. These different sets of duties of co-parties

[15] J Borger, 'Russia May Share Criminal Responsibility for Assad's Use of Barrel Bombs, UK Says' *The Guardian* (30 September 2015) <www.theguardian.com/world/2015/sep/30/russia-syria-barrel-bombing-international-law-uk> (quoting the UK Foreign Secretary as considering Russia to bear an obligation to '[a] least stop [IHL violations] from happening').

[16] See also below 2.a.i.

complement each other to form a robust network of positive duties vis-à-vis fellow co-parties. The network reflects that parties have a central role in ensuring that armed conflicts are carried out in accordance with the protective purposes of IHL. This account is thus built into the very structure of the allocation of obligations under IHL. As will be seen, the account is, therefore, structurally less exposed to the opposition that positive duties to ensure respect otherwise face.

Against this background, Chapter 5 argues that a better understanding of the positive duties among co-parties is crucial for IHL to effectively fulfil its protective purposes in cooperative settings. At a general level, accounting for the duties of co-parties presents a more refined conception of the allocation of obligations under the legal framework that regulates armed conflict. This conception is particularly relevant to cooperative settings as it may help mitigate the risk of diffuse responsibilities in such settings.[17] At the same time, the account traces how party status translates into positive obligations that must be fulfilled by cooperation. In that sense, Chapter 5 suggests a way in which IHL may harness potential protective benefits of cooperation in armed conflicts.[18]

To advance the main claim of the chapter, section 2 argues that different sets of obligations of co-parties contain a positive duty dimension vis-à-vis fellow co-parties. It shows how these duties complement each other. Section 3 demonstrates the implications of the resulting network of duties and their contribution to a more refined understanding of the allocation of duties in armed conflict.

2. Legal bases for different sets of positive duties of co-parties vis-à-vis their partners' conduct

Two sets of obligations provide the legal bases for the duties of co-parties in relation to conduct of their fellow co-parties. First, duties to take positive steps vis-à-vis the conduct of co-parties flow from specific obligations addressed to the parties to the conflict in the realms of the conduct of hostilities and the protection of individuals. Secondly, such duties can be derived from the general obligation to respect and ensure respect for IHL in its specific application to parties vis-à-vis their fellow co-parties. The two sets of duties differ in their scope and content and thus complement each other to form a web of obligations to take positive steps vis-à-vis the conduct of one's partners. This network of obligations defines the relationship between co-parties as structurally apart from that of third parties towards parties.

[17] On this risk, see generally eg ICRC, 'Allies, Partners and Proxies: Managing Support Relationships in Armed Conflict to Reduce the Human Cost of War' (April 2021) 21.

[18] On such benefits, see generally ibid 24–28.

a. Duties with respect to fellow co-parties flowing from specific party obligations

Certain obligations that address parties to armed conflicts can, in their application to co-parties in multiparty conflict settings, be understood to entail positive duties with respect to the conduct of one's fellow co-parties. This is the case as regards both the conduct of hostilities and the protection of individuals in situations of armed conflict.

i. Conduct of hostilities: precautions vis-à-vis fellow co-parties

As regards the conduct of hostilities, the general duty to take precautions may serve as a central illustration of a duty that requires parties to take positive measures vis-à-vis the conduct of their fellow co-parties. The obligation requires that '[i]n the conduct of military operations, constant care shall be taken to spare the civilian population, civilians and civilian objects'.[19]

At the outset, the room for construing the duty to take 'constant care' is provided by the broad scope of the duty. First, as seen in Chapter 4, the notion of 'military operations' covers a considerably wider range of activities as compared to 'attacks'.[20] The obligation would, therefore, also apply to co-parties who do not carry out attacks themselves[21] but who, for example, provide air-to-air refuelling or logistical support (such as transporting troops to front lines) as part of military operations coordinated among multiple partners. Secondly, the scope of the requirement to take 'constant care' is understood to be broad and covers all stages and aspects of a military operation, from its planning to the execution process.[22] The rule has thus been referred to as a 'principle of precaution'[23] that should 'animate all strategic, operational, and tactical decision-making'[24]

[19] API, art 57(1); *CIHL* r 15; on precautions in military operations concerning the environment, see also ibid r 44.

[20] Chapter 4, nn 147–149.

[21] J-F Quéguiner, 'Precautions under the Law Governing the Conduct of Hostilities' (2006) 88 IRRC 793, 797.

[22] *Tallinn Manual 2.0* 477; ILA Study Group, 'The Conduct of Hostilities and International Humanitarian Law: Challenges of 21st Century Warfare' (2017) 93 ILS 322, 381; G Corn, 'War, Law, and the Oft Overlooked Value of Process as a Precautionary Measure' (2015) 42 Pepperdine LR 419, 430–442.

[23] *CIHL* r 15; G Corn, 'The Invaluable Civilian Risk Mitigation Contribution of Recognizing the Value of Precautionary Measures' in R Geiß and H Krieger (eds), *The 'Legal Pluriverse' Surrounding Multinational Military Operations* (OUP 2019) 225; M Sassòli and A Quintin, 'Active and Passive Precautions in Air and Missile Warfare' (2014) 44 Isr YHR 69, 75; A Cohen and Y Shany, 'Beyond the Grave Breaches Regime: The Duty to Investigate Alleged Violations of International Law Governing Armed Conflicts' (2012) 14(2011) YIHL 37, 46.

[24] G Corn, 'Precautions to Minimize Civilian Harm Are a Fundamental Principle of the Law of War' (*Just Security*, 8 July 2015) <www.justsecurity.org/24493/obligation-precautions-fundamental-principle-law-war>.

so as to best serve its purpose and effectively operationalise the protection of civilians.[25]

Against this background, it can be reasonably argued that the requirement to take 'constant care' also applies to the interactions between multiple co-parties in the conduct of military operations. Accordingly, where contributions by multiple co-parties are intertwined in coordinated military operations, the obligation of each party to take all feasible precautions to spare civilians can be understood as encompassing steps to ensure that civilians are spared by the military operations as a whole, including the contributions made by one's fellow co-parties. In that sense, the intertwined nature of coordinated contributions by different cooperation partners—which allows their identification as co-parties under the framework suggested in this book—means that the obligation extends to precautions vis-à-vis one's co-parties' activities. Chapter 4 argued that the degree of coordination required for establishing co-party status can be understood to be such that each co-party is involved in the decision-making process regarding whether and how military operations are conducted.[26] Since the obligation to take constant care covers the entire strategic, operational, and tactical decision-making process, each co-party must use the role it has within that process regarding its co-parties to ensure that civilians are spared.

Just like other precautions, measures vis-à-vis one's co-parties must be taken only when it is feasible for the respective party. The obligation prescribes conduct rather than a result,[27] and it is set out in terms of a due diligence standard.[28] 'Feasible' is generally understood to mean precautions that are 'practicable or practically possible taking into account all circumstances ruling at the time, including humanitarian and military considerations'.[29] The US, however, takes a narrower view and considers that only those practicable precautions would have to be taken that are also 'reasonable'.[30] To establish which steps a co-party can feasibly take

[25] A Haque, *Law and Morality at War* (OUP 2017) 154–155; A Cohen and D Zlotogorski, *Proportionality in International Humanitarian Law: Consequences, Precautions, and Procedures* (OUP 2021) 177–178; Corn (n 22) 424; Corn (n 23) 225.

[26] Chapter 4.3.b.ii.

[27] On the distinction, see generally J Combacau, 'Obligations de résultat et obligations de comportement: Quelques questions et pas de réponse' in D Bardonnet (ed), *Mélanges offerts à Paul Reuter: le droit international, unité et diversité* (Pedone 1981); R Pisillo-Mazzeschi, 'The Due Diligence Rule and the Nature of the International Responsibility of States' (1992) 35 GYIL 9, 30, 46–49.

[28] G Venturini, 'Les Obligations de diligence dans le droit international humanitaire' in S Cassella (ed), *Le standard de due diligence et la responsabilité internationale* (Pedone 2018) 137; M Longobardo, 'Due Diligence in International Humanitarian Law' in H Krieger, A Peters, and L Kreuzer (eds), *Due Diligence in the International Legal Order* (OUP 2020) 188–189.

[29] UK, Statement on Ratification of AP I (28 January 1998) 2020 UNTS 75, 76; Germany, Statement on Ratification of AP I (14 February 1991) 1607 UNTS 526, 529; for similarly worded statements by other States, see *CIHL* vol II 360–361; see also CCW Protocol II, art 3(4); CCW Protocol III, art 1(5); Amended CCW Protocol II, art 3(10); *Galić* (Trial Judgment) IT-98-29-T (5 December 2003) [58] n 105 (with reference to further practice); *HPCR Manual* 26.

[30] US, 'Comments on ICRC Memorandum on the Applicability of International Humanitarian Law in the Gulf Region' (11 January 1991) in S Cummins and D Stewart (eds), *Digest of United States Practice in International Law 1991–1999* (International Law Institute 2005) 2057, 2063; 'Remarks by

vis-à-vis its fellow co-parties, important factors include the degree of coordination and the extent to which the position of the respective co-party permits exercising influence on how its partners carry out their contributions to the military operations.

In practical terms, precautionary measures among co-parties could, for example, consist of assisting partners at the stage of planning or executing military operations by setting up and carrying out appropriate processes for the selection and verification of targets that anticipate sufficient precautions to spare civilians. This could happen through consultation with fellow co-parties on the precautionary measures that they take, in providing expertise and technological means, in sharing intelligence to enable appropriate target selection and verification processes, or in cooperating in gathering such intelligence.

To illustrate, consider the measures taken by the Netherlands in relation to its contribution to the multi-State coalition against ISIL. The Dutch contribution included not only airstrikes but also providing intelligence on potential targets for coalition operations.[31] A report to the House of Representatives by an independent review committee into the contributions of the Dutch intelligence and security services in identifying targets examined the precautionary procedural framework of the intelligence provision. The report found that

> [f]or the purpose of providing these reports, the MIVD [Dutch Intelligence and Security Services] has established and presented a specific procedure to the Dutch Minister of Defence, who has approved it. This procedure provides for additional safeguards, such as a mandatory prior review by the legal department of the MIVD as well as additional reports. In the context of this procedure, the MIVD reviews whether the data to be provided pertains to a legitimate military objective ... as defined in international humanitarian law.[32]

The report also highlighted the relevance to the MIVD of 'considerations concerning potential collateral damage' and noted, more generally, that

> the MIVD keeps itself appraised of the actions of the military coalition in general and the targeting process at the headquarters of the military coalition in

Defense Dept General Counsel Paul C. Ney Jr. on the Law of War' (*Just Security*, 28 May 2019) <www.justsecurity.org/64313/remarks-by-defense-dept-general-counsel-paul-c-ney-jr-on-the-law-of-war/>; *US Manual* 192–195.

[31] Netherlands Review Committee on the Intelligence and Security Services, 'Review Report: On Contributions of the MIVD to Targeting' 3 August 2016 (CTIVD no 50) <https://english.ctivd.nl/investigations/review-report-50/documents/reports/2017/02/23/index> 29.

[32] ibid.

particular. For example, the MIVD asks for feedback from the Dutch representatives at the headquarters on the targeting process of the military coalition.[33]

The measures taken, as regards the Dutch intelligence contribution, effectively operate as precautions to prevent or limit potential harm to civilians from the coordinated military operations of the coalition.

The importance of cooperation in gathering and sharing intelligence among co-parties relevant to precautionary processes has been recently illustrated by a case that also concerns the Dutch contribution to Operation Inherent Resolve. An interrogation of the Dutch Minister of Defence in the House of Representatives in 2020 concerning civilian casualties resulting from Dutch airstrikes in Hawija in 2015 revealed that the Dutch 'Red Card Holder', representing the Netherlands at the joint operations centre, had not been aware of US intelligence that indicated risks of civilian casualties from the airstrikes.[34] In response to this, the Dutch government reportedly instructed its Red Card Holder to proactively request such information from partners.[35]

In the aftermath of a military operation, the cooperated collection of information can also be crucial to conducting investigations into potential harm to civilians.[36] It has been suggested that 'monitoring the effects of military actions through investigation of possible violations arguably constitutes a "feasible precaution" against disproportionate harm'.[37] The duty of a party to take precautions may thus comprise a duty to investigate where feasible.[38] The duty to take precautions regarding the conduct of fellow co-parties would, therefore, also entail a duty to investigate potential IHL violations of other co-parties.[39] Such a duty could be meaningful, particularly if one's co-party is not itself in a position, without support from its co-parties, to investigate all civilian casualties of its military operations, as

33 ibid 30.

34 Netherlands, Parliamentary Debate Nr 71 item 7 (2019–2020) 14 May 2020 <https://zoek.officielebekendmakingen.nl/h-tk-20192020-71-7.html>.

35 L Treffers, 'Dutch Defence Minister Announces Fresh Transparency Moves' (*Airwars*, 7 July 2020) <https://airwars.org/news-and-investigations/minister-announces-fresh-transparency-moves/> (referring to a letter to members of parliament dated 29 June 2020); for a more general discussion of the ensuing legal case and its implications, see S Tosun, 'Victims of Hawija v. The Netherlands: Proportionality and Precaution under Mounting Pressure' (2022) 51 NYIL 409.

36 N Lubell, J Pejic, and C Simmons, *Guidelines on Investigating Violations of International Humanitarian Law: Law, Policy, and Good Practice* (ICRC and Geneva Academy 2019) 15, 20.

37 Cohen and Zlotogorski (n 25) 214.

38 Cohen and Shany (n 23) 46–47; M Lattimer, 'The Duty in International Law to Investigate Civilian Deaths in Armed Conflict' in M Lattimer and P Sands (eds), *The Grey Zone: Civilian Protection between Human Rights and the Laws of War* (Hart 2018) 42.

39 On the related issue of duties to investigate war crimes in military coalition contexts, see J Sexton, 'How Does the Obligation to Investigate Alleged Serious Violations of International Humanitarian Law Apply in ad hoc Military Coalitions?' (2022) 60 MLLWR 188.

the Netherlands made clear regarding its operations as part of Operation Inherent Resolve.[40]

In addition to 'active' precautions, positive steps regarding the conduct of fellow co-parties may also be required as part of the obligation to take 'passive' precautions against the effects of attacks (by the adverse side) on civilians.[41] Accordingly, each co-party would, for example, not only have to remove civilians under its control from the vicinity of military objects[42] and avoid locating military objectives near civilians,[43] but also have to take steps towards its fellow co-parties to ensure that they take those same passive precautions to the extent that such steps are feasible. This could be particularly relevant for co-parties operating extraterritorially, for example, alongside another State fighting armed groups on its territory.

Understanding passive precautions in these terms, when applied to co-parties, is consistent with the reference in Article 58 API to individuals 'under their [ie the parties'] control', which does not preclude each party also bearing duties towards individuals under the control of its co-parties. More generally, this approach is in line with the broad and flexible scope of the obligation to take precautions against the effects of military operations as well as with the purpose of ensuring the effective protection of civilians. The rationale is the same as the one applied to the obligation to take active precautions. If multiple co-parties cooperate to enhance their military capabilities, they must also cooperate in the deployment of their defensive capabilities to fulfil their duties as defending parties. The fact that the respective civilians are under the control of a fellow co-party (rather than one's own control) will determine what measures are feasible. Feasible measures could include assisting the respective co-party with removing civilians from the military objectives, identifying military objectives located near civilians and alerting co-parties, or providing expertise to another co-party on where military objectives may be located.

In summary, the duties of parties to take precautions vis-à-vis the conduct of their fellow co-parties aptly illustrate how obligations addressed to parties to an armed conflict translate into positive external duties for co-parties.

ii. Protection of individuals

Positive duties towards fellow co-parties also flow from obligations addressed to parties in the realm of protecting individuals affected by armed conflict. This is illustrated by the obligations to search for, collect, protect, and care for the wounded, sick, and shipwrecked, search for the dead, and prevent them from

[40] Netherlands, Parliamentary Debate, 14 May 2020 ('The Netherlands on its own does not have sufficient capacity and capabilities to gather intelligence ... to be able to deal with such a conflict ... We can only do these things as part of a coalition' (translated with DeepL); see also Treffers (n 35).

[41] API, art 58; *CIHL* rr 22–24.

[42] API, art 58(a); *CIHL* r 23.

[43] API, art 58(b); *CIHL* r 24.

being despoiled, and search for missing persons.[44] These obligations can be understood as encompassing the duties of a party to take positive steps so that its fellow co-parties (also) search for, collect, care for (etc) the protected individuals in compliance with their own obligations in that respect. The argument for this account proceeds as follows.

At the outset, it is important to note that these obligations are activated irrespective of what specific activities a co-party engages in. Unlike, for example, obligations incumbent on detaining powers (which only apply to a State conducting detention operations),[45] the obligations to search for, collect, and care for wounded, sick, shipwrecked, missing, or dead individuals address all parties to the conflict. There are no textual or contextual indications or reasons stemming from the object and purpose of these obligations[46] that would confine them to those parties that have inflicted the casualties, or more generally, have used means or methods of warfare that have affected the respective individuals in such a way that they now require protection. The treaty provisions only speak of the 'parties'. Since other provisions (such as those addressed to detaining powers) are explicitly limited to parties engaging in certain conduct, a systematic interpretation does not support such limitations to be implicitly assumed. This is also in line with the object and purpose of these provisions. The purpose is to protect individuals because of their present condition,[47] rather than to regulate specific acts by parties that inflict casualties or to attach consequences to such acts. This protective purpose would be undermined if it was necessary, in every instance, to determine who exactly brought about the individual's condition. In practice, that will often not be possible. The ICRC, therefore, rightly notes that these obligations:

> apply equally to the Party to the conflict that inflicted the casualties (*and its allies to the extent that they are also Parties to the conflict*) and to the Party to the conflict to which the casualties belong[48]

and that:

> [i]n situations in which multinational or coalition forces are engaged as Parties to a conflict, it may also mean that a Party that has not participated in a particular

[44] GCI, art 15; GCII, art 18; GCIV, art 16; API, art 33; *CIHL* rr 109, 112–114, 116–117.
[45] Even in multiparty settings, there will—as a matter of international law—always be only one detaining power regarding each detained individual, see *GCIII Commentary* [1519]–[1523].
[46] See VCLT, art 31(1). As noted above, the considerations underlying this interpretation of the relevant treaty law also informs the scope of co-parties' obligations under customary international law, whether by way of interpreting custom or as part of the process of identifying their existence and content. See Chapter 2, nn 43–44.
[47] See eg API, art 9(1) ('intended to ameliorate the condition of the wounded, sick and shipwrecked').
[48] *GCII Commentary* [1632] (emphasis added).

> engagement nevertheless needs to assist in search, collection and evacuation activities if it is present in the area of an engagement.[49]

Accordingly, *all* (co-)parties bear these obligations vis-à-vis *all* protected individuals. This includes situations where several co-parties coordinate their operations, for example by dividing up different tasks or geographical zones in military operations. In such cases, working with one's co-parties can be an essential—and sometimes even necessary—way to protect individuals who are, for example, located in areas where one's co-parties operate. This arguably means that obligations to take 'all possible measures'[50] towards protected individuals entail a duty to take positive steps, if possible, to ensure that fellow co-parties also protect individuals and thus comply with their own protection obligations.

Similar to the obligation to take precautions vis-à-vis the conduct of fellow co-parties, the obligations discussed in this section are obligations of conduct and subject to due diligence standards.[51] Only those steps that are 'possible' in light of the circumstances must be taken.[52] In practical terms, this could mean assisting fellow co-parties with the search, identification, or treatment of individuals, for example by providing the necessary expertise, personnel, facilities, and material resources or by cooperating in the collection and sharing of information that may facilitate the identification of individuals.[53]

To sum up, the notion that it is the primary role of parties to ensure the protection of individuals in armed conflict is specified for the situation of co-parties by the positive external dimension of party obligations to protect individuals who are affected by armed conflicts.

b. General duty to ensure respect for IHL by fellow co-parties

In addition to the duties to take certain positive steps vis-à-vis one's co-parties as part of party obligations in the realms of the conduct of hostilities and the protection of individuals, co-parties also bear a general duty to take positive steps to ensure respect for IHL by their fellow co-parties.

To buttress this proposition, it is helpful to recall the resistance observed in Chapter 2 against positive external duties to ensure compliance under Common Article 1 and customary international law.[54] Section 1 of this chapter has suggested

[49] *GCI Commentary* [1490].
[50] GCI, art 15; GCII, art 18; *CIHL* rr 109–113.
[51] *GCI Commentary* [1485]; *CIHL* 402; Longobardo (n 28) 190.
[52] *GCI Commentary* [1485]. Some relevant provisions even point to specific circumstances that may play a role, for example GCIV, art 16 ('[a]s far as military considerations allow').
[53] See also eg ICRC (n 17) 63, 67, 107–109.
[54] Chapter 2, nn 245–252.

that this resistance can be accounted for by the tensions between such duties and the posture of abstention which is otherwise required of third parties in armed conflicts. The point here is not whether these tensions are insurmountable or whether there are good reasons to simply adjust the posture required of third parties by embracing positive external compliance duties. Instead, the point is that the concern associated with this departure from a detached posture arises only for third parties vis-à-vis the parties, but not for parties vis-à-vis their fellow co-parties. And, indeed, as section 3 will demonstrate, some illustrations from international practice indicate that this account of the general duty to ensure respect as it applies to co-parties faces less opposition than the positive external duties for third parties.

Accordingly, there is a stronger case for arguing that co-parties have a general duty to take positive steps to ensure compliance by their fellow co-parties, regardless of whether those duties are also accepted for third parties. This is because the respective postures of (co-)parties and third parties in armed conflict differ structurally, as noted at the outset of this book. Construing the general duty to ensure respect for IHL as entailing positive duties vis-à-vis fellow co-parties coheres with the overall primary role of parties to ensure that armed conflicts are conducted in accordance with IHL. Such an account of the general duty to ensure respect fits neatly into the framework of duty bearers under IHL, which, as section 2.a of this chapter has demonstrated, already imposes positive duties on parties with respect to both the conduct of hostilities and the protection of individuals, arguably with implications for the duties of co-parties vis-à-vis one another. These systematic considerations inform an interpretation of the terms of Common Article 1 'in their context'[55] as well as an account of the customary law obligation to ensure respect that is consistent with the legal framework regulating armed conflict as a whole.[56]

In practical terms, positive measures to ensure respect for IHL by fellow co-parties under Common Article 1 may range from diplomatic dialogue or protest and legal assistance to 'conditioning joint operations on a coalition partner's compliance with its obligations'.[57] In choosing and implementing these measures, co-parties must exercise due diligence.[58] What and how much action is required will depend on the prevailing circumstances, including the factual capacity to influence one's partners.[59] In general, co-parties may have greater discretion under the broad, general duty to ensure respect than they have under the more specific positive party duties discussed in the previous section. The position of parties within

[55] VCLT, art 31(1).
[56] On the underlying methodological questions in determining the scope of customary rules, see Chapter 2, nn 43–44.
[57] *GCIII Commentary* [214].
[58] R Geiß, 'The Obligation to Respect and to Ensure Respect for the Conventions' in A Clapham, P Gaeta, and M Sassòli (eds), *The 1949 Geneva Conventions: A Commentary* (OUP 2015) 123; Longobardo (n 28) 185–186.
[59] Longobardo (n 28) 186; *GCIII Commentary* [198].

the regulatory scheme of IHL suggests, however, that more can be expected of co-parties than of third parties under Common Article 1.

In conclusion, there are different legal bases for the obligations of co-parties to take positive measures vis-à-vis their fellow co-parties. This raises the question of how these different sets of obligations relate to each other, to which the following section now turns.

c. The complementary relationship between the different sets of duties

The different sets of obligations of co-parties vis-à-vis their fellow co-parties complement each other. Figuratively speaking, the duties that co-parties have in this respect as part of their party obligations may be imagined as 'narrow [in their scope of application], but deep [in their content]', whereas the duty flowing from the general obligation to ensure respect would be 'wide [in its scope of application] but shallow [in its content]'.[60]

For activities where there are no specific duties imposed on parties that can be construed as encompassing duties vis-à-vis one's co-parties, the general duty to ensure respect would be relevant. Thus, to the extent that the positive duties of parties with an external dimension among co-parties remain sectorial rather than comprehensive, they leave gaps for the operation of the general duty to ensure compliance with IHL by one's co-parties.

Conversely, for activities that are regulated by specific positive duties vis-à-vis fellow co-parties, these duties are not made redundant by a general obligation to ensure respect by one's co-parties. This is because these duties have a different content from the general obligation to ensure respect. In addition to being somewhat more specific—with the advantages of greater clarity and legal certainty as to their contours—these obligations may reach wider and ask more from the co-parties bearing them.

For example, when specific positive measures vis-à-vis one's co-party can feasibly be taken to ensure that civilians are spared, the obligation to take *all* feasible precautions would entail that all of these measures must be taken.[61] The same

[60] For the use of this model to contrast competing visions of Common Article 1, see R Geiß, 'Common Article 1 of the Geneva Conventions Scope and Content of the Obligation to "Ensure Respect"—"Narrow but Deep" or "Wide and Shallow"?' in H Krieger (ed), *Inducing Compliance with International Humanitarian Law: Lessons from the African Great Lakes Region* (CUP 2015) 441 (drawing on the Report of the Secretary-General on Implementing the Responsibility to Protect (12 January 2009) UN Doc A/63/677 (10(c))).

[61] W Boothby, *The Law of Targeting* (OUP 2012) 130–131 ('[A]ll practicable measures must be taken ... and ... action which could be taken but is not is as much indicative of a breach of the provision as action that is directly contrary to any of the precautions'); Corn (n 24) ('In fact, Article 57 imposes an obligation to take precautions unless doing so is not feasible ... Article 57 appears to establish a presumption that precautionary measures will be implemented, qualified by a feasibility limitation'); see also Haque (n 25) 155; though note N Neuman, 'A Precautionary Tale: The Theory and Practice

would be true of duties to protect individuals by taking 'all possible measures'.[62] Such party obligations may be more demanding than the general duty to ensure respect, which might leave a co-party with greater discretion as to how it ensures respect.[63] Indeed, although both the activity-specific duties and the general obligation must be fulfilled by exercising due diligence, what is considered sufficiently diligent conduct may vary in meeting different obligations.[64] More generally, understanding obligations that are specifically addressed to parties as wider-reaching than the general duty of all States to ensure respect for IHL is consistent with the overall structure of the legal system of IHL and the central position that parties have—notably as duty bearers—within that regulatory framework.

Moreover, the activity-specific party duties include, but may also go beyond a requirement that co-parties ensure that their fellow co-parties respect their own party obligations under IHL. Since all co-parties are bound by the underlying obligations—for example, to take precautions or to take care of protected individuals—the requirement to take positive steps vis-à-vis one's fellow co-party is directed structurally at inducing or facilitating a behaviour by that co-party to which that co-party itself has a duty. In other words, an element of ensuring respect is inherent to these duties. Yet, unlike the general duty to ensure respect, the duties to take positive steps flowing from party obligations do not end there. They are not confined to positive action that would be required to prevent a co-party from violating its own party obligations, not if further action is 'feasible' or 'possible'.

To illustrate this point, imagine a scenario in which co-party A has relatively more limited technological capabilities at its disposal than co-party B and diligently uses these means in the most feasible way to implement precautionary measures. Nonetheless, if co-party B can feasibly share its enhanced technological capabilities with co-party A such that co-party A can take more effective precautions, for example, by drawing on more reliable intelligence or by using more precise weapons, co-party B would arguably have an obligation to assist co-party A in that respect as part of its obligation to take precautions in military operations.[65]

The broader underlying point is that the positive obligations of co-parties depend on what co-party B itself can do, rather than on what its fellow co-party A can do. And this is also relevant if co-party A fails to diligently use its own, relatively

of Precautions in Attack' (2018) 48 Isr YHR 19, 27 (emphasising the flexible nature of the duty to take precautions).

62 nn 50–52.
63 *GCIII Commentary* [199].
64 Longobardo (n 28) 195.
65 On the relevance of the technological means available to a State for establishing the feasibility of precautions, see Sassòli and Quintin (n 23) 84–85; K Trapp, 'Great Resources Mean Great Responsibility: A Framework of Analysis for Assessing Compliance with API Obligations in the Information Age' in D Saxon (ed), *International Humanitarian Law and the Changing Technology of War* (Brill 2013) 156, 164–165.

limited, capabilities. As a case in point, recall the example of Russia's intervention alongside Syria in the armed conflict with Syrian opposition forces, or the US's support to the Saudi-led coalition in their armed conflict with the Houthis (assuming for the sake of the argument that the US's involvement in the conflict sufficed to render it a party).[66] What precautions Russia and the US would have to take vis-à-vis Syria and the Saudi-led coalition, respectively, would depend on Russia and the US's own technological means (for example, regarding the collection of targeting intelligence), regardless of whether Syria or Saudi Arabia could otherwise be expected to deploy those same means.

In light of the complementary character of the different sets of positive duties of co-parties vis-à-vis their fellow co-parties, the next section considers the rationale underpinning them and the wider implications that flow from them.

3. A network of mutual positive duties vis-à-vis fellow co-parties: rationale and ramifications for allocating obligations in cooperation settings

The different sets of obligations explored in section 2 of this chapter form a robust network of positive obligations among co-parties vis-à-vis each other's conduct. While that network tends to be overlooked, section 2 has shown that it is consistent with the wording of the relevant obligations and built into the very structure of the international legal regulation of armed conflict. This account of the obligations of co-parties reflects the central role of parties to ensure the protection of individuals in armed conflict and specifies the implications of this role for the interaction between multiple parties on the same side of an armed conflict.

In doing so, the account offers a crucial nuance to the debate on positive external duties to ensure respect for IHL by others. Indeed, the different sets of duties among co-parties avoid central concerns that have been associated with positive external duties to the extent that these are only relevant as regards duties imposed on third parties. These duties do not involve a departure from the established postures required of parties and third parties as distinct duty bearers within the overall structure of the allocation of obligations in armed conflicts.

Accordingly, they are also less vulnerable to the normative criticism of overextension levelled against the duty to respect and ensure respect for IHL.[67] Moreover, the advantage of legal certainty gained by emphasising negative duties, which are

[66] For the controversies on this point, see Chapter 4, nn 202–203.

[67] V Robson, 'The Common Approach to Article 1: The Scope of Each State's Obligation to Ensure Respect for the Geneva Conventions' (2020) 25 JCSL 101, 114; M Schmitt and S Watts, 'Common Article 1 and the Duty to "Ensure Respect"' (2020) 96 ILS 674, 706; R Goodman, 'Two U.S. Positions on the Duty to Ensure Respect for the Geneva Conventions' (*Just Security*, 26 September 2016) <www.justsecurity.org/33166/u-s-positions-duty-ensure-respect-geneva-conventions/>.

somewhat more 'clear-cut',[68] is more relevant to conceptualising the legal position of third parties than that of co-parties. Further, the positive duties of co-parties also do not run the risk of providing incentives for increased third-party involvement,[69] which may complicate and in certain circumstances prolong armed conflicts.[70] More generally, the perceived benefits traditionally associated with the posture of abstention required of third parties would not be affected, particularly the function of preventing armed conflicts from expanding and escalating.[71] At the same time, an account of the duties of co-parties, as advanced, here yields normative benefits. It translates the protective purposes underlying the duties addressed to parties to armed conflict to multiparty settings, and spells out the meaning of these duties in such settings.

These considerations suggest that there is considerably less ground for contesting the duties of co-parties vis-à-vis their fellow co-parties. This is also illustrated by instances in recent international practice, which can plausibly be read as indications that the account of the duties of co-parties may indeed face less opposition. For example, the US State Department only objected to the view that Common Article 1 imposed positive duties on the US 'vis-à-vis *not only our partners*, but all States and non-State actors engaged in armed conflict',[72] leaving room for the possibility that such obligations might exist with respect to 'partners'.[73] Although this could theoretically include instances where the US acts in partnership with others while itself remaining a third party to conflicts, the statement was made against the background of the current practice in the US-led campaign against ISIL—a conflict to which the US undoubtedly was a party—and other 'coalitions and partnerships' in 'current U.S. military operations'.[74] Implicitly, a limitation to duties vis-à-vis fellow co-parties may therefore have been the underlying idea.

A statement at the Security Council by the US Mission to the UN in 2019 points in a similar direction. Concerning the Turkish offensive in north-east Syria at the time, the statement noted that:

[68] H Krieger, 'Rights and Obligations of Third Parties in Armed Conflicts' in E Benvenisti and G Nolte (eds), *Community Interests across International Law* (OUP 2018) 456.

[69] ibid 467.

[70] See eg A Aydin and P Regan, 'Networks of Third-Party Interveners and Civil War Duration' (2011) 18 EJIR 574, 586–587; D Cunningham, *Barriers to Peace in Civil War* (CUP 2011) 126–129; D Balch-Lindsay and A Enterline, 'Killing Time: The World Politics of Civil War Duration, 1820–1992' (2000) 44 ISQ 615, 632–633; P Regan, 'Conditions of Successful Third-Party Intervention in Intrastate Conflicts' (1996) 40 JCR 336, 346–347.

[71] C Chinkin, *Third Parties in International Law* (Clarendon Press 1993) 300; M Bothe, 'The Law of Neutrality' in D Fleck (ed), *The Handbook of International Humanitarian Law* (4th edn, OUP 2021) 603.

[72] B Egan, 'Keynote Address' (2016) 110 ASIL Proc 300, 306–307 (emphasis added).

[73] See also O Hathaway and Z Manfredi, 'The State Department Adviser Signals a Middle Road on Common Article 1' (*Just Security*, 12 April 2016) <www.justsecurity.org/30560/state-department-adviser-signals-middle-road-common-article-1/>.

[74] Egan (n 72) 306.

> Turkey must protect civilians in northeast Syria. We also expect Turkey to abide by its commitments to prevent ISIS from regaining a foothold in Syria, and to ensure the secure, humane detention of ISIS fighters. We remain deeply troubled by reports that Turkish Supported Opposition forces deliberately targeted civilians. If verified, these actions may constitute war crimes, and we urge our Turkish partners to immediately investigate these incidents and hold accountable any individuals or entities involved. Turkey is responsible for ensuring its forces and any Turkish-supported entities act in accordance with the law of armed conflict.[75]

The reference that Turkey must ensure that its partners comply with the law of armed conflict concerned a conflict in which it is plausible that Turkey and the non-State armed groups supported by Turkey were co-parties,[76] and it was made in the context of a statement that emphasised aspects of Turkey's obligations as a party, including notably the protection of civilians.

Similarly, other instances of practice seem to suggest that positive external duties may be accepted in instances of co-party status. For example, the then UK Foreign Secretary reportedly considered Russia to be legally required to prevent the Syrian regime from certain violations of IHL following Russia's intervention as a (co-)party to the conflict alongside the regime.[77] At the same time, as a practical matter, recent litigation on arms exports concerning the conflict in Yemen has revealed that the UK government seems to determine its approach and duties regarding IHL violations by others based on whether or not the UK considers itself a party to that conflict. The government stressed that:

> neither the MOD [Ministry of Defence] nor the FCO [Foreign and Commonwealth Office] reaches a conclusion as to whether or not an IHL violation has taken place in relation to each and every incident that comes to its attention. This would simply not be possible in conflicts to which the UK is not a party, as is the case in Yemen.[78]

[75] M Barkin, 'Remarks at a UN Security Council Briefing on the Humanitarian Situation in Syria' 24 October 2019 <https://usun.usmission.gov/remarks-at-a-un-security-council-briefing-on-the-humanitarian-situation-in-syria-21/>.

[76] For some factual background on Turkey's operations, see C Gall and P Kingsley, 'Turkish Forces Escalate Campaign in Syria Against Kurdish-Led Militia' *NYT* (11 October 2019) A11 <www.nytimes.com/2019/10/10/world/middleeast/syria-turkey-offensive.html>. Based on the limited available information, it is, however, also possible that some of the entities supported by Turkey were too closely connected to Turkey to be considered (co-)parties in their own right.

[77] Borger (n 15) ('The airstrikes, said Hammond, changed Russia's legal position as a party to the conflict. "Now the Russians ... have a shared responsibility. They may arguably have a legal exposure to this barrel bombing activity. Barrel bombing ... breaches international humanitarian law ... At least stop that from happening. Use your leverage"').

[78] *The Queen (on the application of Campaign against Arms Trade) and the Secretary of State for International Trade and Amnesty International, Human Rights Watch UK and Oxfam International intervening* [2019] EWCA Civ 1020 [83] (quoting a ministerial statement on this point).

These concerns have been acknowledged by the High Court, which found that:

> there would be inherent difficulties for a non-party to a conflict to reach a reliable view on breaches of International Humanitarian Law by another sovereign state.[79]

As a final illustration, the UN has explicitly embraced its duty to take positive steps to ensure respect by its co-parties in situations where the UN considers itself a party by virtue of the involvement of Peace Operations under UN aegis in the conflict:

> where the non-UN security forces are party to an armed conflict and the UN becomes a party to that conflict, too—something that may occur precisely because the UN is providing support to those forces ... international humanitarian law, as reflected in common article 1 of the Geneva Conventions, requires that the Organization take such action as is within its power to try to make sure that the non-UN security forces conduct their operations in a manner that respects their obligations under international humanitarian law.[80]

It cannot be said that international practice has established an 'agreement'[81] in the sense of a 'common understanding' between the High Contracting Parties[82] to the effect that the relevant IHL treaty obligations encompass positive duties vis-à-vis fellow co-parties.[83] The instances reviewed here also do not in and of themselves reflect a general practice accepted as law such that specific rules of customary international law can be said to have emerged to this effect.[84] Nonetheless, these instances may be taken into account as a supplementary means of interpreting the general duty to ensure respect and the duties addressed to parties in the realms of the conduct of hostilities and the protection of individuals.[85] They may also be considered in establishing the scope of the customary international law obligations in this respect.[86] In particular, statements from States that otherwise object to positive external duties under IHL suggest that the pushback against such duties in

[79] *The Queen (on the application of Campaign against Arms Trade) and The Secretary of State for International Trade and Amnesty Int'l, Human Rights Watch UK and Oxfam Int'l intervening* [2017] EWHC 1726 (QB) [181].

[80] Statement at the ILC by the Under-Secretary-General for Legal Affairs and Legal Counsel (23 May 2013) <http://legal.un.org/ola/media/info_from_lc/ILC%20Legal%20Counsel%20statementrev3may20.pdf> 20.

[81] VCLT, art 31(3)(b).

[82] It should be noted that the US is not a contracting party to API and the UN is not a contracting party to any IHL treaty.

[83] Chapter 3, n 167.

[84] ICJSt, art 38(1)(b).

[85] Chapter 3, n 169.

[86] For the methodological issues in this respect, see n 46.

international practice may actually be confined to duties for third parties.[87] For co-parties, the duties may be, accordingly, more readily accepted in practice.

Crucially, even under an expansive approach to the positive external duties of third parties, which does not share the concerns of sceptics in this respect, the account of the duties of co-parties developed in this chapter would, nonetheless, remain relevant. This is because the network of duties among co-parties, as discerned here, would set co-parties as structurally apart from the potential positive external duties of third parties in several ways.

First, the positive duties of co-parties vis-à-vis their fellow co-parties would be more wide-reaching than the potential positive duties of third parties vis-à-vis parties. As section 2 of this chapter has argued, the duties addressed to the parties regarding the conduct of hostilities and the protection of individuals impose more concrete and stringent requirements than the general duty to ensure respect for third parties. For this reason alone, potential external compliance duties of third parties can never quite reach the duties of co-parties. In addition, it may even be that the general duty to ensure respect by others under Common Article 1 and customary international law would be more demanding in what it requires from co-parties than from third parties.

Secondly, the duties of co-parties would also be borne by parties other than States, namely non-State armed groups and international organisations. If non-State armed groups are co-parties to an armed conflict, they bear party obligations encompassing duties vis-à-vis their fellow co-parties in the realms of the conduct of hostilities and the protection of individuals under Common Article 3, APII (where applicable), and customary international law.[88] As parties to non-international armed conflicts, armed groups could also arguably bear such positive external duties as part of the general obligation to ensure respect for IHL as a matter of customary international law.[89] By contrast—unlike States—non-State armed groups are not addressees of IHL (and are thus not bound by the general duty to ensure respect) when they do not qualify as parties to an armed conflict. For international organisations, in turn, it remains to be settled as to whether they bear a duty to ensure respect for IHL if they, for example, mandate or coordinate a multinational military operation without qualifying as parties to the conflict.[90] Conversely, when they are (co-)parties, there appears to be no reason why they should not bear the obligations of co-parties identified in this chapter as a matter of customary international law with respect to their fellow co-parties.[91]

87 This is also true of positions such as that of the Canadian government, which entirely rejects the applicability to third parties of the general duty to respect and ensure respect for IHL (see Chapter 2, n 251).

88 For example, *CIHL* rr 15, 109, 112–114, 116–117.

89 ibid r 139. See Chapter 2.3.c.i.

90 Chapter 2, n 212.

91 For the UN's view to this effect, see n 80.

For all these reasons, the network of positive duties among co-parties set out in this chapter is significant. If this network of obligations is better understood and implemented, it may prove to be an important step towards ensuring that the protective purposes of IHL are fulfilled effectively, specifically in situations of co-operation between multiple parties. In this respect, it is worth recalling that all co-parties bear these duties, and, therefore, these duties mutually reinforce one another between the cooperating parties. For example, if co-party A can feasibly assist co-party B in taking precautions or caring for protected individuals, co-party A has a positive duty to provide this assistance and co-party B has a corresponding duty to seek such assistance from co-party A as part of their own obligation to take positive steps vis-à-vis their co-parties. In other words, co-parties are under a mutual duty to cooperate in fulfilling their party obligations.

4. Conclusion

From the perspective of protecting human beings affected by an armed conflict, cooperation entails the risk that capabilities to inflict harm are amplified while responsibility is diffused among partners.[92] Conversely, cooperation may enhance capacities to achieve greater standards of protection.[93] Chapter 5 has shown one way in which the international legal regulation of armed conflict accounts for the risks and makes use of the potential benefits of cooperation in terms of protection. In multiparty armed conflicts, co-parties bear complementary sets of mutual duties to take positive steps vis-à-vis each other's conduct in the conflict. The account of the duties of co-parties presented here clarifies the allocation of obligations in cooperative settings. It can thus contribute to mitigating the risks that responsibility is diffused. Engrained into the established structure of the international legal regulation of armed conflict, the network of positive obligations to ensure the protection of individuals in cooperation with fellow co-parties also exploits potential protection benefits of cooperation in armed conflict.

[92] n 17.
[93] n 18.

Conclusion

This book examined why party status to armed conflict matters in international law and how it is established. Based on an analysis of the legal position of parties to an armed conflict within the international legal system, the book has developed an account of the legal framework for identifying parties. The following conclusions can be drawn from this inquiry.

The prism of the multifaceted legal position of parties to armed conflicts helps us grasp the complex structure of the contemporary international legal regulation of armed conflict as well as its development. Party status is central to all levels of the structure of this legal system.

As to what party status means for the respective entity itself, the blurring of the old divide between peace and war as two separate spheres of international law entails that being a party no longer frees a State from all peacetime constraints, as being 'at war' signalled traditionally. Yet, parties remain key addressees of obligations and, in a more nuanced way, permissions under international law in armed conflict.

Moreover, parties are also central regulatory reference points for other addressees of international law in armed conflict. First, the protection, rights, obligations, and responsibility of individuals depend, to varying extents, on their relationship to parties. This shows how the humanisation and individualisation of the regulation of armed conflict have inextricably intertwined the collective and the individual levels of the regulation of armed conflict. In that sense, the findings of the book are in line with Welsh's wider observation on the current state of the individualisation of warfare that 'there remains strong evidence for the continued influence of forms of collective authority, agency and subjectivity both in theory and in practice'.[1]

Secondly, the legal position of collective entities that do not qualify as parties—referred to in this book as third parties—is also regulated through obligations and rights in the relationship with parties. Obligations and rights of parties and third States under neutrality law require and ensure that third States are detached from

[1] J Welsh, 'The Individualisation of War: Defining a Research Programme' (2019) 53 Annals of the Fondazione Luigi Einaudi 9, 18.

Party Status to Armed Conflict in International Law. Alexander Wentker, Oxford University Press. © Alexander Wentker 2024.
DOI: 10.1093/oso/9780198900900.003.0007

the conflict. This position is further refined by obligations prohibiting third parties to contribute to violations of international law by parties, including, particularly, as part of the duty to respect and ensure respect for international humanitarian law (IHL).

The regulation of war as a concern to the international community as a whole has thus established an increasingly nuanced system of different addressees, in which parties continue to hold a central place. Accordingly, conceiving of the regulation of armed conflict as centred around parties does not mean understanding armed conflict in terms of bilateralism. Instead, it allows envisaging how other addressees are integrated into this regulatory architecture. These additional layers in the legal framework of armed conflict complement the primary role of parties to ensure that armed conflicts are conducted in accordance with the protective purposes of IHL.

The findings on the legal position of parties are relevant to identifying who qualifies as a party in two ways. On the one hand, the findings specify which legal implications may flow from identifying parties and in what ways this identification is, therefore, legally significant. On the other hand, the picture that emerges from the analysis of the legal features of party status also subtly informs the vision underlying international law of who is to be identified as a party. Party status has a central position within the regulation of military operations in armed conflict and protection needs connected to those operations. That central position presumes that parties have a key role in deciding and implementing those operations in the first place.

Against this background and in response to the challenges presented by cooperation practices in armed conflict, the book has proposed an account of the legal criteria for identifying parties. A common analytical framework has been developed to identify parties to conflicts with multiple parties on the same side; the book has labelled these parties as 'co-parties'. The elements of this framework can be summarised as follows.

The analysis of multiparty conflicts has revealed that the concepts of international and non-international armed conflict set the outer parameters of the framework, but also that these concepts need to be complemented with concepts capturing the identification of parties as a distinct legal inquiry. Accordingly, under the proposed framework, each party must individually meet those criteria for the existence of an armed conflict which concern the nature and structure of parties, particularly the organisation requirement in non-international armed conflicts. Conversely, the criteria regarding the conflict as a whole may be fulfilled jointly by all potential co-parties. That is, the contributions of all potential co-parties can be aggregated to assess whether there is resort to armed force for an international armed conflict or protracted armed violence for a non-international armed conflict.

Within these parameters, each potential co-party must make a contribution that can be attributed to it and that is directly connected to harm to the adversary. The contribution must be coordinated with fellow co-parties so that each co-party is involved in the decision-making processes on the coordinated military operations. Although no intent to be a party is required, a subjective requirement of knowledge about the facts and circumstances constituting the relevant coordinated contribution is inherent to these elements.

The question of what makes entities co-parties is common to a range of different cooperation scenarios. The single analytical framework proposed in this book can, in principle, be applied to identify co-parties in all of these scenarios, whether the conflict is an international or a non-international armed conflict, whether the co-parties are States, international organisations, or non-State armed groups, whether or not their conduct would independently fulfil the conflict-related requirements for the existence of an armed conflict, and whether their contribution is made before or after these criteria have first been met.

In practical terms, the framework proposed in the book may, therefore, serve as an analytical roadmap in actual conflict settings to establish whether a particular State, international organisation, or non-State armed group is a party to a conflict and what legal consequences flow from that finding. As such, it may also be of use to the potential parties themselves, as well as to third parties, international and domestic courts, and humanitarian organisations. The roadmap would have to be further specified and operationalised by those actors through an application to concrete conflict settings, in dialogue with further scholarship. It is hoped, however, that it can provide a useful starting point for such analyses.

The framework for identifying co-parties also allows for a refined account of the allocation of obligations in armed conflict, which may both contribute to mitigating the risk of a diffusion of responsibility in cooperation settings and harness the potential of cooperation for enhanced protection capacity. Emblematically, this has been shown through the duties—flowing from being identified as a co-party—to take positive steps vis-à-vis the conduct of fellow co-parties in armed conflict. In addition to a general duty to ensure respect for IHL by fellow co-parties, co-parties bear a range of specific duties entailed in obligations that are addressed to parties. In the realm of the conduct of hostilities, these duties include taking feasible precautions so that civilians are spared by the coordinated military operations of all co-parties and thus also by the contributions of one's fellow co-parties. In the realm of the protection of individuals, co-parties' obligation to search for, collect, and care for wounded, sick, shipwrecked, missing, or dead individuals requires taking positive steps so that their fellow co-parties also search for, collect, and care for the protected individuals. These complementary sets of obligations form a robust network of positive duties vis-à-vis fellow co-parties.

More widely, this analysis of party status enhances our understanding of the architecture of the international legal regulation of armed conflict and its ability to respond to the complex realities of contemporary armed conflicts. The account of party status presented in this book reveals often overlooked ways in which the established structures of this body of law enable addressing challenges to the effective protection of individuals that are raised by increasingly widespread and varied patterns of cooperation. Even as the international regulation of individuals and third parties in armed conflict develops further, a clear understanding of the status of parties still has much to offer.

Bibliography

Books

Abi-Saab R, *Droit humanitaire et conflits internes: Origines et évolution de la réglementation international* (Henry Dunant Institute 1986)

Akande D, Rodin D, and Welsh J (eds), *The Individualization of War: Rights, Liability, and Accountability in Contemporary Armed Conflict* (OUP 2023)

Allott P, *The Health of Nations: Society and Law beyond the State* (CUP 2002)

Antonopoulos C, *Non-Participation in Armed Conflict: Continuity and Modern Challenges to the Law of Neutrality* (CUP 2022)

Aquinas T, *On Law, Morality, and Politics* (William Baumgarth and Richard Regan (eds), Hackett 1988)

Aust H, *Complicity and the Law of State Responsibility* (CUP 2011)

Bedjaoui M, *Law and the Algerian Revolution* (International Association of Democratic Lawyers 1961)

Berber F, *Lehrbuch des Völkerrechts*, vol II (2nd edn, CH Beck 1969)

Bluntschli J, *Das moderne Kriegsrecht der civilisirten Staten* (Beck 1866)

Boothby W, *The Law of Targeting* (OUP 2012)

Bos M, *A Methodology of International Law* (Elsevier 1984)

Bothe M, Partsch KJ, and Solf W, *New Rules for Victims of Armed Conflicts—Commentary on the Two 1977 Protocols Additional to the Geneva Conventions of 1949* (reprint edn, Nijhoff 2013)

Bowett D, *United Nations Forces: A Legal Study of United Nations Practice* (Stevens 1964)

Brownlie I, *International Law and the Use of Force by States* (Clarendon Press 1963)

Calvo C, *Le Droit international: Théorique et pratique*, vol IV (5th edn, Rivière 1896)

Cameron L and Chetail V, *Privatizing War: Private Military and Security Companies under Public International Law* (CUP 2013)

Carron D, *L'Acte déclencheur d'un conflit armé international* (Schulthess 2016)

Castrén E, *The Present Law of War and Neutrality* (Suomalainen Tiedeakatemia 1954)

Chinkin C, *Third Parties in International Law* (Clarendon Press 1993)

Cicero MT, *Philippics* (Shackleton Bailey D tr, Harvard UP 2009)

Clapham A, *War* (OUP 2021)

Cohen A and Zlotogorski D, *Proportionality in International Humanitarian Law: Consequences, Precautions, and Procedures* (OUP 2021)

Corten O, *The Law against War: The Prohibition on the Use of Force in Contemporary International Law* (Hart 2012)

Crawford E, *The Treatment of Combatants and Insurgents under the Law of Armed Conflict* (OUP 2010)

Crawford E, *Identifying the Enemy: Civilian Participation in Armed Conflict* (OUP 2015)

Crawford E, *Non-Binding Norms in International Humanitarian Law: Efficacy, Legitimacy, and Legality* (OUP 2021)

Crawford J, *The Creation of States in International Law* (2nd edn, Clarendon Press 2006)

Crawford J, *State Responsibility: The General Part* (CUP 2013)

Cullen A, *The Concept of Non-International Armed Conflict in International Humanitarian Law* (CUP 2010)

Cunningham D, *Barriers to Peace in Civil War* (CUP 2011)

d'Aspremont J and de Hemptinne J, *Droit international humanitaire: Thèmes choisis* (Pedone 2012)

David É, *Principes de droit des conflits armés* (5th edn, Bruylant 2012)

Dawidowicz M, *Third-Party Countermeasures in International Law* (CUP 2017)
de Vattel E, *Le Droit des gens, ou, Principes le la loi naturelle, appliqués à la conduite aux affaires des nations et des souverains*, vol III (Fenwick C tr, Carnegie Institution 1916)
de Visscher C, *Theory and Reality in Public International Law* (Corbett P tr, 3rd edn, Princeton UP 1968)
de Wet E, *Military Assistance on Request and the Use of Force* (OUP 2020)
Delerue F, *Cyber Operations and International Law* (CUP 2020)
Derejko N, *Identifying Non-International Armed Conflict: International Law and Practice* (CUP forthcoming)
Dinstein Y, *War, Aggression and Self-Defence* (6th edn, CUP 2017)
Dinstein Y, *Non-International Armed Conflicts in International Law* (2nd edn, CUP 2021)
Dinstein Y, *The Conduct of Hostilities under the Law of International Armed Conflict* (4th edn, CUP 2022)
Doswald-Beck L (ed), *San Remo Manual on International Law Applicable to Armed Conflicts at Sea* (CUP 1995)
Drew P, *The Law of Maritime Blockade: Past, Present, and Future* (OUP 2017)
Fazal T, *Wars of Law: Unintended Consequences in the Regulation of Armed Conflict* (Cornell UP 2018)
Findlay T, *The Use of Force in UN Peace Operations* (OUP 2002)
Frutig A, *Die Pflicht von Drittstaaten zur Durchsetzung des humanitären Völkerrechts nach Artikel 1 der Genfer Konventionen von 1949: Auf dem schmalen Grat zwischen Recht und Moral* (Helbing Lichtenhahn 2009)
Geiß R, *'Failed States': Die normative Erfassung gescheiterter Staaten* (Duncker & Humblot 2005)
Gentili A, *De jure belli libri tres*, vol II (Rolfe J tr, Clarendon Press 1933)
Gill T et al, *Leuven Manual on the International Law Applicable to Peace Operations* (CUP 2017)
Green J, *Collective Self-Defence in International Law* (CUP 2024)
Greenspan M, *The Modern Law of Land Warfare* (University of California Press1959)
Grotius H, *De jure belli ac pacis libri tres*, vol II (Kelsey F tr, Clarendon Press 1925)
Grotius H, *De jure belli ac pacis libri tres*, vol III (Kelsey F tr, Clarendon Press 1925)
Grzebyk P, *Human and Non-Human Targets in Armed Conflicts* (CUP 2022)
Halleck H, *International Law or, Rules Regulating the Intercourse between States in Peace and War* (Bancroft 1861)
Haque A, *Law and Morality at War* (OUP 2017)
Harvard Program on Humanitarian Policy and Conflict Research, *Manual on International Law Applicable to Air and Missile Warfare* (CUP 2013)
Hathaway O and Shapiro S, *The Internationalists: How a Radical Plan to Outlaw War Remade the World* (Simon & Schuster 2017)
Haug H, *Neutralität und Völkergemeinschaft* (Polygraphischer Verlag 1962)
Heffter A, *Das Europäische Völkerrecht der Gegenwart auf den bisherigen Grundlagen* (8th edn, Geffcken F, HW Müller 1888)
Henckaerts J-M and Doswald-Beck L (eds), *Customary International Humanitarian Law* vol I (CUP 2005)
ICRC (ed), *Commentary on the First Geneva Convention* (CUP 2016)
ICRC (ed), *Commentary on the Second Geneva Convention* (CUP 2017)
ICRC (ed), *Commentary on the Third Geneva Convention* (CUP 2020)
Iñigo Alvarez L, *Towards a Regime of Responsibility of Armed Groups in International Law* (Intersentia 2020)
Iurlaro F, *The Invention of Custom: Natural Law and the Law of Nations, c.1550–1750* (OUP 2021)
Jackson M, *Complicity in International Law* (OUP 2015)
Jenks CW, *The Prospects of International Adjudication* (Stevens 1964)
Jessup P and Deák F, *Neutrality: Its History, Economics and Law—Vol I: The Origins* (Columbia UP 1935)
Jo H, *Compliant Rebels: Rebel Groups and International Law in World Politics* (CUP 2015)
Kalmanovitz P, *The Laws of War in International Thought* (OUP 2020)

Kammerhofer J, *Uncertainty in International Law: A Kelsenian Perspective* (Routledge 2011)
Kelsen H, *Principles of International Law* (Rinehart & Company 1952)
Kelsen H, *Pure Theory of Law* (Knight M tr, 2nd edn, University of California Press 1967)
Kelsen H, *General Theory of Norms* (Hartney M tr, OUP 1991)
Kennedy D, *Of War and Law* (Princeton UP 2006)
Klein N, *Maritime Security and the Law of the Sea* (OUP 2011)
Kolb R, *Droit humanitaire et opérations de paix internationales* (2nd edn, Helbing Lichtenhahn 2006)
Kolb R, *Ius in bello—Le droit international des conflits armés* (2nd edn, Helbing Lichtenhahn 2009)
Kolb R, Porretto G, and Vité S, *L'Application du droit international humanitaire et des droits de l'homme aux organisations internationales: Forces de paix et administrations civiles transitoires* (Bruylant 2005)
Kunz J, *Kriegsrecht und Neutralitätsrecht* (Springer 1935)
Lanovoy V, *Complicity and Its Limits in the Law of International Responsibility* (Hart 2016)
Lauterpacht H, *Recognition in International Law* (CUP 1947)
Lauterpacht H, *Oppenheim's International Law*, vol II (7th edn, Longmans 1952)
Lauterpacht H, *Oppenheim's International Law*, vol I (8th edn, Longmans 1955)
Lawrence T, *The Principles of International Law* (4th edn, Macmillan 1913)
Lubell N, *Extraterritorial Use of Force against Non-State Actors* (OUP 2010)
Mačák K, *Internationalized Armed Conflicts in International Law* (OUP 2018)
McDougal M and Feliciano F, *Law and Minimum World Public Order* (Yale UP 1961)
McDougall C, *The Crime of Aggression under the Rome Statute of the International Criminal Court* (2nd edn, CUP 2021)
Mackenzie-Gray Scott R, *State Responsibility for Non-State Actors: Past, Present and Prospects for the Future* (Hart 2022)
McLaughlin R, *Recognition of Belligerency and the Law of Armed Conflict* (OUP 2020)
McMahan J, *Killing in War* (Clarendon Press 2009)
McNair A and Watts A, *The Legal Effects of War* (4th edn, CUP 1966)
Martens F, *Traité de droit international* (Léo A tr, Maresq 1883)
Martens G, *Précis de droit des gens, fondé sur les traités et l'usage* (Cobbett W tr, Cobbett and Morgan 1802)
Maurice JF, *Hostilities without Declaration of War: An Historical Abstract of the Cases in which Hostilities Have Occurred between Civilized Powers Prior to Declaration or Warning. From 1700 to 1870* (HM Stationery Office 1883)
May L, *War Crimes and Just War* (CUP 2007)
Melzer N, *Targeted Killing in International Law* (OUP 2008)
Meron T, *The Humanization of International Law* (Nijhoff 2006)
Meyrowitz H, *Le Principe de l'égalité des belligérants devant le droit de la guerre* (Pedone 1970)
Moore JB, *A Digest of International Law, Vol VII* (Government Printing Office 1906)
Nalin E, *L'Applicabilità del diritto internazionale umanitario alle operazioni di 'peace-keeping' delle Nazioni Unite* (Editoriale Scientifica 2018)
Neff S, *The Rights and Duties of Neutrals: A General History* (Manchester UP 2000)
Neff S, *War and the Law of Nations: A General History* (CUP 2005)
Nolte G, *Eingreifen auf Einladung* (Springer 1999)
Nowak C, *Das Interventionsverbot im Bürgerkrieg: Darstellung eines Wandels durch die Bürgerkriege in Libyen, Syrien, Irak, Jemen und Ukraine seit 2011* (Peter Lang 2018)
Nußberger B, *Interstate Assistance to the Use of Force* (Nomos 2023)
Oeter S, *Neutralität und Waffenhandel* (Springer 1992)
Oglesby R, *Internal War and the Search for Normative Order* (Nijhoff 1971)
Okimoto K, *The Distinction and Relationship between Jus ad Bellum and Jus in Bello* (Hart 2011)
Oppenheim L, *International Law: A Treatise*, vol II (Longmans 1906)
Orakhelashvili A, *The Interpretation of Acts and Rules in Public International Law* (OUP 2008)
Papastavridis E, *The Interception of Vessels on the High Seas: Contemporary Challenges to the Legal Order of the Oceans* (Hart 2013)

Park I, *The Right to Life in Armed Conflict* (OUP 2018)
Parlett K, *The Individual in the International Legal System: Continuity and Change in International Law* (CUP 2011)
Parry C, *The Sources and Evidences of International Law* (Manchester UP 1965)
Peters A, *Beyond Human Rights: The Legal Status of the Individual in International Law* (CUP 2016)
Pictet J, *Geneva Convention for the Amelioration of the Condition of the Wounded and Sick in Armed Forces in the Field: Commentary* (ICRC 1952)
Pictet J, *Geneva Convention Relative to the Protection of Civilian Persons in Time of War: Commentary* (ICRC 1958)
Pictet J, *Humanitarian Law and the Protection of War Victims* (Sijthoff 1975)
Pieper U, *Neutralität von Staaten* (Peter Lang 1996)
Plato, *The Laws* (Saunders T tr, Penguin 1970)
Plato, *The Republic* (Lee H tr, 2nd edn, Penguin 1987)
Politis N, *Neutrality and Peace* (Macken F tr, Carnegie Endowment for International Peace 1935)
Portmann R, *Legal Personality in International Law* (CUP 2010)
Prieto Rudolphy M, *The Morality of the Laws of War: War, Law, and Murder* (OUP 2023)
Provost R, *International Human Rights and Humanitarian Law* (CUP 2002)
Quintin A, *The Nature of International Humanitarian Law: A Permissive or Restrictive Regime?* (Edward Elgar 2020)
Redaelli C, *Intervention in Civil Wars: Effectiveness, Legitimacy, and Human Rights* (Hart 2020)
Rodenhäuser T, *Organizing Rebellion: Non-State Armed Groups under International Humanitarian Law, Human Rights Law, and International Criminal Law* (OUP 2018)
Rousseau J-J, *The Social Contract* (Cranston M tr, Penguin 1968)
Ruys T, *'Armed Attack' and Article 51 of the UN Charter: Evolutions in Customary Law and Practice* (CUP 2010)
Sandoz Y, Swinarski C, and Zimmermann B (eds), *Commentary on the Additional Protocols of 8 June 1977 to the Geneva Conventions of 12 August 1949* (ICRC 1987)
Sassòli M, *International Humanitarian Law: Rules, Controversies, and Solutions to Problems Arising in Warfare* (Edward Elgar 2019)
Savage C, *Power Wars: The Relentless Rise of Presidential Authority and Secrecy* (Back Bay Books 2017)
Schabas W, *The European Convention on Human Rights: A Commentary* (OUP 2015)
Schmitt M (ed), *Tallinn Manual 2.0 on the International Law Applicable to Cyber Operations* (CUP 2017)
Seyersted F, *United Nations Forces in the Law of Peace and War* (Sijthoff 1966)
Sivakumaran S, *The Law of Non-international Armed Conflict* (OUP 2012)
Sloan J, *The Militarisation of Peacekeeping in the Twenty-First Century* (Hart 2011)
Stone J, *Legal Controls of International Conflict: A Treatise on the Dynamics of Disputes- and War-Law* (2nd edn, Maitland 1959)
Strupp K, *Grundzüge des positiven Völkerrechts* (2nd edn, Röhrscheid 1922)
Tams C, *Enforcing Obligations Erga Omnes in International Law* (CUP 2005)
Tanaka Y, *The International Law of the Sea* (3rd edn, CUP 2019)
Tucker R, *The Law of War and Neutrality at Sea* (Government Printing Office 1957)
Upcher J, *Neutrality in Contemporary International Law* (OUP 2020)
Van Bynkershoek C, *Quaestiones juris publici libri duo*, vol II (Frank T tr, Clarendon Press 1930)
Villiger M, *Customary International Law and Treaties: A Manual on the Theory and Practice of the Interrelation of Sources* (Kluwer 1997)
Wallace S, *The Application of the European Convention on Human Rights to Military Operations* (CUP 2019)
Walzer M, *Just and Unjust Wars: A Moral Argument with Historical Illustrations* (5th edn, Basic Books 2015)
Wampach C, *Armed Reprisals from Medieval Times to 1945* (Nomos 2020)
Wani K, *Neutrality in International Law: From the sixteenth century to 1945* (Routledge 2017)

Wheaton H, *Elements of International Law* (8th edn, reprint Clarendon Press [1866] 1936)
Wilson H, *International Law and the Use of Force by National Liberation Movements* (Clarendon Press 1988)
Wolff C, *Jus gentium methodo scientifica pertractatum*, vol II (Drake J tr, Clarendon Press 1934)
Yip KL, *The Use of Force against Individuals in War under International Law: A Social Ontological Approach* (OUP 2022)
Zamir N, *Classification of Conflicts in International Humanitarian Law: The Legal Impact of Foreign Intervention in Civil Wars* (Edward Elgar 2017)
Zwanenburg M, *Accountability of Peace Support Operations* (Nijhoff 2005)

Chapters in Books

Akande D, 'Classification of Armed Conflicts: Relevant Legal Concepts' in Wilmshurst E (ed), *International Law and the Classification of Conflicts* (OUP 2012)
Akande D, 'Classification of Armed Conflicts' in Saul B and Akande D (eds), *The Oxford Guide to International Humanitarian Law* (OUP 2020)
Asada M, 'The Concept of "Armed Conflict" in International Armed Conflict' in O'Connell M (ed), *What Is War? An Investigation in the Wake of 9/11* (Brill 2012)
Aust H, 'Complicity in Violations of International Humanitarian Law' in Krieger H (ed), *Inducing Compliance with International Humanitarian Law: Lessons from the African Great Lakes Region* (CUP 2015)
Bartolini G, 'The "Civilianisation" of Contemporary Armed Conflicts' in Ruiz-Fabri H, Wolfrum R, and Gogolin J (eds), *Select Proceedings of the European Society of International Law 2008*, vol II (Hart 2010)
Benvenisti E and Nolte G, 'Introduction' in Benvenisti E and Nolte G (eds), *Community Interests across International Law* (OUP 2018)
Bernhardt R, 'Customary International Law' in Bernhardt R (ed), *Encyclopedia of Public International Law*, vol 1 (North-Holland 1992)
Bernhardt R, 'Article 103' in Simma B (ed), *The Charter of the United Nations: A Commentary* (2nd edn, OUP 2002)
Blum G, 'The Individualization of War: From War to Policing in the Regulation of Armed Conflicts' in Sarat A, Douglas L, and Umphrey M (eds), *Law and War* (Stanford UP 2014)
Blum G, 'The Dispensable Lives of Soldiers' in Ohlin J, May L, and Finkelstein C (eds), *Weighing Lives in War* (OUP 2017)
Bohrer Z, 'Divisions over Distinctions in Wartime International Law' in Bohrer Z, Dill J, and Duffy H (eds), *Law Applicable to Armed Conflict* (CUP 2020)
Bothe M, 'Comments' in Post H (ed), *International Economic Law and Armed Conflict* (Nijhoff 1994)
Bothe M, 'The Law of Neutrality' in Fleck D (ed), *Handbook of International Humanitarian Law* (4th edn, OUP 2021)
Brölmann C and Nijmann J, 'Personality' in d'Asprémont J and Singh S (eds), *Concepts for International Law: Contributions to Disciplinary Thought* (Edward Elgar 2019)
Cathcart B, 'Coalition Warfare and the Future of the Law of Armed Conflict' in Waxman M and Oakley T (eds), *The Future Law of Armed Conflict* (OUP 2022)
Cheng B, 'Custom: The Future of General State Practice in a Divided World' in MacDonald RSJ and Johnston D (eds), *The Structure and Process of International Law* (Nijhoff 1986)
Chetail V, 'Vattel and the American Dream: An Inquiry into the Reception of the *Law of Nations* in the United States' in Dupuy P-M and Chetail V (eds), *The Roots of International Law/Les fondements du droit international: Liber amicorum Peter Haggenmacher* (Brill 2014)
Clapham A, 'The Concept of International Armed Conflict' in Clapham A, Gaeta P, and Sassòli M (eds), *The Geneva Conventions: A Commentary* (OUP 2015)
Combacau J, 'Obligations de résultat et obligations de comportement: Quelques questions et pas de réponse' in Bardonnet D (ed), *Mélanges offerts à Paul Reuter: Le droit international, unité et diversité* (Pedone 1981)

Condorelli L and Boisson de Chazournes L, 'Quelques remarques à propos de l'obligation des Etats de "respecter et faire respecter" le droit international humanitaire "en toutes circonstances"' in Swinarski C (ed), *Etudes et essais sur le droit humanitaire et sur les principes de la Croix-Rouge en l'honneur de Jean Pictet* (Nijhoff 1984)

Condorelli L and Kreß C, 'The Rules of Attribution: General Considerations' in Crawford J et al (eds), *The Law of International Responsibility* (OUP 2010)

Corn G, 'The Invaluable Civilian Risk Mitigation Contribution of Recognizing the Value of Precautionary Measures' in Geiß R and Krieger H (eds), *The 'Legal Pluriverse' Surrounding Multinational Military Operations* (OUP 2019)

Correa C, 'Operationalising the Right of Victims of War to Reparation' in Correa C, Furuya S, and Sandoval C (eds), *Reparation for Victims of Armed Conflict* (CUP 2021)

Corten O, 'Quels droits et quels devoirs pour les états tiers? Les effets juridiques d'une assistance à un acte d'agression' in Bannelier K, Christakis T, and Corten O (eds), *L'Intervention en Irak et le droit international* (Pedone 2004)

Crawford E, 'Who Is a Civilian? Membership of Opposition Groups and Direct Participation in Hostilities' in Lattimer M and Sands P (eds), *The Grey Zone: Civilian Protection between Human Rights and the Laws of War* (Hart 2017)

Crawford E, 'The Temporal and Geographic Reach of International Humanitarian Law' in Saul B and Akande D (eds), *Oxford Guide to International Humanitarian Law* (OUP 2020)

Dill J, '"The Rights and Obligations of Parties to International Armed Conflicts" From Bilateralism but Not Toward Community Interest?' in Benvenisti E and Nolte G (eds), *Community Interests across International Law* (OUP 2018)

Dörmann K and Rodenhäuser T, 'Contemporary Challenges for International Humanitarian Law' in Crawford J et al (eds), *The International Legal Order: Current Needs and Possible Responses Essays in Honour of Djamchid Momtaz* (Brill 2017)

Dörr O, 'Article 32' in Dörr O and Schmalenbach K (eds), *Vienna Convention on the Law of Treaties: A Commentary* (2nd edn, Springer 2018)

Engdahl O, 'Multinational Peace Operations Forces Involved in Armed Conflict: Who Are the Parties?' in Mujezinović Larsen K, Guldahl Cooper C, and Nystuen G (eds), *Searching for a 'Principle of Humanity' in International Humanitarian Law* (CUP 2012)

Finkelstein C, 'The Equality of Combatants in Asymmetric War' in Ohlin J, May L, and Finkelstein C (eds), *Weighing Lives in War* (OUP 2017)

Fleck D, 'The Law of Non-International Armed Conflict' in Fleck D (ed), *The Handbook of International Humanitarian Law* (4th edn, OUP 2021)

Fortin K and Kleffner J, 'Responsibility of Organized Armed Groups Controlling Territory: Attributing Conduct to ISIS' in Bartels R et al (eds), *Military Operations and the Notion of Control under International Law* (Springer 2020)

Furuya S, 'The Right to Reparation for Victims of Armed Conflict: The Intertwined Development of Substantive and Procedural Aspects' in Correa C, Furuya S, and Sandoval C (eds), *Reparation for Victims of Armed Conflict* (CUP 2021)

Gaeta P, 'The Interplay Between the Geneva Conventions and International Criminal Law' in Clapham A, Gaeta P, and Sassòli M (eds), *The 1949 Geneva Conventions: A Commentary* (OUP 2015)

Gaeta P and Jain A, 'Individualisation of IHL Rules through Criminalisation for War Crimes: Some (Un)intended Consequences' in Akande D, Rodin D, and Welsh J (eds), *The Individualization of War: Rights, Liability, and Accountability in Contemporary Armed Conflict* (OUP 2023)

Gasser H-P, 'International Humanitarian Law' in Haug H (ed), *Humanity for All: The International Red Cross and Red Crescent Movement* (Henry Dunant Institute 1993)

Geiß R, 'Common Article 1 of the Geneva Conventions Scope and Content of the Obligation to "Ensure Respect"—"Narrow but Deep" or "Wide and Shallow"?' in Krieger H (ed), *Inducing Compliance with International Humanitarian Law: Lessons from the African Great Lakes Region* (CUP 2015)

Geiß R, 'The Obligation to Respect and to Ensure Respect for the Conventions' in Clapham A, Gaeta P, and Sassòli M (eds), *The 1949 Geneva Conventions: A Commentary* (OUP 2015)

Gill T, 'Belligerents' in Djuić D and Pons N (eds), *The Companion to International Humanitarian Law* (Brill 2018)

Gioia A, 'Neutrality and Non-Belligerency' in Post H (ed), *International Economic Law and Armed Conflict* (Nijhoff 1994)

Greenwood C, 'Rights at the Frontier' in Rider B (ed), *Law at the Centre: The Institute of Advanced Legal Studies at Fifty* (Kluwer 1999)

Greenwood C, 'Scope of Application of Humanitarian Law' in Fleck D (ed), *The Handbook of International Humanitarian Law* (2nd edn, OUP 2008)

Hampson F, 'Afghanistan 2001–2010' in Wilmshurst E (ed), *International Law and the Classification of Conflicts* (OUP 2012)

Heffes E, 'Non-State Actors Engaging Non-State Actors: The Experience of Geneva Call in NIACs' in Heffes E, Kotlik M, and Ventura M (eds), *International Humanitarian Law and Non-State Actors: Debates, Law and Practice* (Springer 2020)

Heintschel von Heinegg W, '"Benevolent" Third States in International Armed Conflicts: The Myth of the Irrelevance of the Law of Neutrality' in Schmitt M and Pejic J (eds), *International Law and Armed Conflict: Exploring the Faultlines Essays in Honour of Yoram Dinstein* (Nijhoff 2007)

Heintschel von Heinegg W, 'Blockades and Interdictions' in Weller M (ed), *The Oxford Handbook of the Use of Force in International Law* (OUP 2015)

Heller K, 'The Use and Abuse of Analogy in IHL' in Ohlin J (ed), *Theoretical Boundaries of Armed Conflict and Human Rights* (CUP 2016)

Hernández G, 'The Responsibility of the International Legal Academic: Situating the Grammarian within the "Invisible College"' in d'Aspremont J, Gazzini T, and Nollkaemper A (eds), *International Law as a Profession* (CUP 2017)

Heyns C et al, 'The Right to Life and the International Law Framework Regulating the Use of Armed Drones' in Akande D et al (eds), *Human Rights and 21st Century Challenges* (OUP 2020)

Hill-Cawthorne L, 'Persons Covered by International Humanitarian Law: Main Categories' in Saul B and Akande D (eds), *Oxford Guide to International Humanitarian Law* (OUP 2020)

Ipsen K, 'Combatants and Non-Combatants' in Fleck D (ed), *The Handbook of International Humanitarian Law* (4th edn, OUP 2021)

Kilibarda P and Gaggioli G, 'The Globalisation of Non-International Armed Conflicts' in Lattimer M and Sands P (eds), *The Grey Zone: Civilian Protection Between Human Rights and the Laws of War* (Hart 2018)

Kleffner J, 'Scope of Application of International Humanitarian Law' in Fleck D (ed), *The Handbook of International Humanitarian Law* (4th edn, OUP 2021)

Kolb R, 'Protecting Powers' in Clapham A, Gaeta P, and Sassòli M (eds), *The 1949 Geneva Conventions: A Commentary* (OUP 2015)

Kooijmans P, 'The Security Council and Non-State Entities as Party to a Conflict' in Wellens K (ed), *International Law: Theory and Practice Essays in Honour of Eric Suy* (Nijhoff 1998)

Koutroulis V, 'Jus ad/contra Bellum' in van Steenberghe R (ed), *Droit international humanitaire: Un régime spécial de droit international?* (Bruylant 2013)

Kreß C, 'The State Conduct Element' in Kreß C and Barriga S (eds), *The Crime of Aggression: A Commentary* (CUP 2017)

Krieger H, 'Rights and Obligations of Third Parties in Armed Conflicts' in Benvenisti E and Nolte G (eds), *Community Interests across International Law* (OUP 2018)

Landais C, 'Entre l'application du droit et les hostilités, cadre légal et règles d'engagement' in Marchand C (ed), *The Distinction between International and Non-International Armed Conflicts: Challenges for IHL? 38th Round Table on Current Issues of International Humanitarian Law* (Franco Angeli 2015)

Lattimer M, 'The Duty in International Law to Investigate Civilian Deaths in Armed Conflict' in Lattimer M and Sands P (eds), *The Grey Zone: Civilian Protection between Human Rights and the Laws of War* (Hart 2018)

Longobardo M, 'Due Diligence in International Humanitarian Law' in Krieger H, Peters A, and Kreuzer L (eds), *Due Diligence in the International Legal Order* (OUP 2020)

Luban D, 'Human Rights Thinking and the Laws of War' in Ohlin J (ed), *Theoretical Boundaries of Armed Conflict and Human Rights* (CUP 2016)

Lubell N, 'The War (?) against Al Qaeda' in Wilmshurst E (ed), *International Law and the Classification of Conflicts* (OUP 2012)

Lubell N, 'Fragmented Wars: Multi-Territorial Military Operations against Armed Groups' in Williams W and Ford C (eds), *Complex Battlespaces: The Law of Armed Conflict and the Dynamics of Modern Warfare* (OUP 2019)

Mancini M, 'The Effects of a State of War or Armed Conflict' in Weller M (ed), *The Oxford Handbook on the Use of Force in International Law* (OUP 2015)

Marxsen C, 'Introduction: The Emergence of an Individual Right to Reparation for Victims of Armed Conflict' in Correa C, Furuya S, and Sandoval C (eds), *Reparation for Victims of Armed Conflict* (CUP 2021)

Massingham E and McConnachie A, 'Common Article 1: An Introduction' in Massingham E and McConnachie A (eds), *Ensuring Respect for International Humanitarian Law* (Routledge 2020)

Mégret F, 'From "Savages" to "Unlawful Combatants": A Postcolonial Look at International Humanitarian Law's "Other"' in Orford A (ed), *International Law and Its Others* (CUP 2006)

Merkouris P, 'Interpreting Customary International Law: You'll Never Walk Alone' in Merkouris P, Kammerhofer J, and Arajärvi N (eds), *The Theory and Philosophy of Customary International Law and Its Interpretation* (CUP 2022)

Milanović M, 'Extraterritorial Derogations from Human Rights Treaties in Armed Conflict' in Bhuta N (ed), *The Frontiers of Human Rights* (OUP 2016)

Milanović M and Hadzi-Vidanović V, 'A Taxonomy of Armed Conflict' in White N and Henderson C (eds), *Research Handbook on International Conflict and Security Law* (Edward Elgar 2013)

Moir L, 'The Concept of Non-International Armed Conflict' in Clapham A, Gaeta P, and Sassòli M (eds), *The 1949 Geneva Conventions: A Commentary* (OUP 2015)

Nasu H, 'The Laws of Neutrality in the Interconnected World: Mapping the Future Scenarios' in Waxman M and Oakley T (eds), *The Future Law of Armed Conflict* (OUP 2022)

Nolte G, 'The Different Functions of the Security Council with Respect to Humanitarian Law' in Lowe V et al (eds), *The United Nations Security Council and War: The Evolution of Thought and Practice since 1945* (OUP 2008)

Orakhelashvili A, 'Article 30 1969 Vienna Convention' in Corten O and Klein P (eds), *The Vienna Conventions on the Law of Treaties*, vol I (OUP 2011)

Peters A, 'Article 25' in Simma B et al (eds), *The Charter of the United Nations: A Commentary*, vol I (3rd edn, OUP 2012)

Quintin A and Tougas M-L, 'Generating Respect for the Law by Non-State Armed Groups: The ICRC's Role and Activities' in Heffes E, Kotlik M, and Ventura M (eds), *International Humanitarian Law and Non-State Actors: Debates, Law and Practice* (Springer 2020)

Ronzitti N, 'Italy's Non-Belligerency during the Iraqi War' in Ragazzi M (ed), *International Responsibility Today: Essays in Memory of Oscar Schachter* (Nijhoff 2005)

Sandoz Y, 'Neutral Powers and the Conventions' in Clapham A, Gaeta P, and Sassòli M (eds), *The 1949 Geneva Conventions: A Commentary* (OUP 2015)

Schöberl K, 'The Geographical Scope of Application of the Conventions' in Clapham A, Gaeta P, and Sassòli M (eds), *The 1949 Geneva Conventions: A Commentary* (OUP 2015)

Schöberl K, 'Multinational Military Operations and the Geographical Scope of the Laws of Armed Conflict in Non-International Armed Conflict' in Geiß R and Krieger H (eds), *The 'Legal Pluriverse' Surrounding Multinational Military Operations* (OUP 2020)

Scobbie I, 'Gaza' in Wilmshurst E (ed), *International Law and the Classification of Conflicts* (OUP 2012)
Suttle O, 'Reasons, Institutions, Authorities: Three Models of Exceptions in World Trade Organization Law' in Bartels L and Paddeu F (eds), *Exceptions in International Law* (OUP 2020)
Szesnat F and Bird A, 'Colombia' in Wilmshurst E (ed), *International Law and the Classification of Conflicts* (OUP 2012)
Trapp K, 'Great Resources Mean Great Responsibility: A Framework of Analysis for Assessing Compliance with API Obligations in the Information Age' in Saxon D (ed), *International Humanitarian Law and the Changing Technology of War* (Brill 2013)
Trapp K, 'Exemptions, Qualifications, Derogations, and Excuses in International Human Rights Law' in Bartels L and Paddeu F (eds), *Exceptions in International Law* (OUP 2020)
Treves T, 'Customary International Law' in Peters A (ed), *Max Planck Encyclopedia of Public International Law* (OUP) <https://opil.ouplaw.com/display/10.1093/law:epil/9780199231690/law-9780199231690-e1393?rskey=lpdCqj&result=1&prd=MPIL>
Venturini G, 'Les Obligations de diligence dans le droit international humanitaire' in Cassella S (ed), *Le Standard de due diligence et la responsabilité internationale* (Pedone 2018)
Vierucci L, 'Private Military and Security Companies in Non-international Armed Conflicts: Ius ad Bellum and Ius in Bello Issues' in Francioni F and Ronzitti N (eds), *War by Contract: Human Rights, Humanitarian Law, and Private Contractors* (OUP 2011)
Weizmann N, 'Ensuring Respect for IHL as It Relates to Humanitarian Activities' in Massingham E and McConnachie A (eds), *Ensuring Respect for International Humanitarian Law* (Routledge 2020)
Wright Q, 'The American Civil War' in Falk R (ed), *The International Law of Civil War* (Johns Hopkins Press 1971)

Journal Articles

Abi-Saab G, 'Whither the International Community' (1998) 9 EJIL 248
'Address of Robert H Jackson, Attorney General of the United States, Inter-American Bar Association, Havana, Cuba, March 27, 1941' (1941) 35 AJIL 348
Akande D, 'Clearing the Fog of War? The ICRC's Interpretive Guidance on Direct Participation in Hostilities' (2010) 59 ICLQ 180
Akande D and Gillard E-C, 'Arbitrary withholding of Consent to Humanitarian Relief Operations in Armed Conflict' (2016) 92 ILS 483
Alexander A, 'A Short History of International Humanitarian Law' (2015) 26 EJIL 109
Alland D, 'L'Interprétation du droit international public' (2013) 362 RCADI 51
Anghie A, 'Finding the Peripheries: Sovereignty and Colonialism in Nineteenth-Century International Law' (1999) 40 Harv ILJ 1
Appicciafuoco L et al, 'Diplomatic and Parliamentary Practice' (2003) 13 IYIL 265
Arguillas M, 'The Non-Traditional Moro Elites and the Organization of Islamic Conference' (2001) 22 Phil PSJ 97
Aydin A and Regan P, 'Networks of Third-Party Interveners and Civil War Duration' (2011) 18 EJIR 574
Bailey S, 'Cease-Fires, Truces, and Armistices in the Practice of the UN Security Council' (1977) 71 AJIL 461
Balch-Lindsay D and Enterline A, 'Killing Time: The World Politics of Civil War Duration, 1820–1992' (2000) 44 ISQ 615
Balladore Pallieri G, 'La Notion de guerre et de combattant dans les conflits armés' (1971) 10 MLLWR 313
Bartels R, 'When Do Terrorist Organisations Qualify as "Parties to an Armed Conflict" under International Humanitarian Law?' (2017) 56 MLLWR 451
Bartolini G, 'The Provision of Belligerent Materials in the Russia–Ukraine Conflict: Beyond the Law of Neutrality?' (2023) 99 QIL 3

Baxter R, 'So-Called Unprivileged Belligerency: Spies, Guerrillas, and Saboteurs' (1951) 28 BYIL 323
Bellal A, Giacca G, and Casey-Maslen S, 'International Law and Armed Non-state Actors in Afghanistan' (2011) 93 IRRC 47
Bellal A and Heffes E, 'Yes, I Do: Binding Armed Non-State Actors to IHL and Human Rights Norms through Their Consent' (2018) 12 HRILD 120
Bellinger J and Haynes W, 'A US Government Response to the International Committee of the Red Cross study Customary International Humanitarian Law' (2007) 89 IRRC 443
Bernstorff J, 'The Use of Force in International Law before World War I: On Imperial Ordering and the Ontology of the Nation-State' (2018) 29 EJIL 233
Bleckmann A, 'Zur Feststellung und Auslegung von Völkergewohnheitsrecht' (1977) 37 ZaöRV 504
Blum G, 'The Dispensable Lives of Soldiers' (2010) 2 JLA 117
Boon K, 'The UN Security Council and Non-State Actors' (2019) 113 ASIL Proc 209
Borchard E, '"War" and "Peace"' (1933) 27 AJIL 114
Borlini L, 'The Security Council and Non-State Domestic Actors: Changes in Non-Forcible Measures between International Lawmaking and Peacebuilding' (2021) 61 Va JIL 489
Borlini L and Kolb R, 'Le Conseil de Sécurité des Nations Unies et les entités non-étatiques' (2021) 125 RGDIP 25
Bothe M, 'Customary International Humanitarian Law: Some Reflections on the ICRC Study' (2006) 8(2005) YIHL 143
Bowett D, 'The Impact of Security Council Decisions on Dispute Settlement Procedures' (1994) 5 EJIL 89
Bradley C and Goldsmith J, 'Congressional Authorization and the War on Terrorism' (2005) 118 HLR 2047
Bradley M, 'Additional Protocol II: Elevating the Minimum Threshold of Intensity?' (2020) 102 IRRC 1125
Breslin A, 'A Reflection on the Legal Obligation for Third States to Ensure Respect for IHL' (2017) 22 JCSL 5
Bridgeman T, 'The Law of Neutrality and the Conflict with Al Qaeda' (2010) 85 NYULR 1186
Buchan R, 'Non-forcible Measures and the Law of Self-Defence' (2023) 72 ICLQ 1
Cassese A, 'The Status of Rebels under the 1977 Geneva Protocol on Non-International Armed Conflicts' (1981) 30 ICLQ 416
Charpentier J, 'Pratique française de droit international' (1977) 23 AFDI 1012
Chasapis Tassinis O, 'Customary International Law: Interpretation from Beginning to End' (2020) 31 EJIL 235
Chesney R, 'Who May Be Killed? Anwar al-Awlaki as a Case Study in the International Legal Regulation of Lethal Force' (2011) 13(2010) YIHL 3
Clapham A, 'Extending International Criminal Law beyond the Individual to Corporations and Armed Opposition Groups' (2008) 6 JICJ 899
Clapham A, 'Booty, Bounty, Blockade, and Prize: Time to Reevaluate the Law' (2021) 97 ILS 1200
Clancy P, 'Neutral Arms Transfers and the Russian Invasion of Ukraine' (2023) 72 ICLQ 527
Cohen A and Shany Y, 'Beyond the Grave Breaches Regime: The Duty to Investigate Alleged Violations of International Law Governing Armed Conflicts' (2012) 14(2011) YIHL 37
Colby E, 'How to Fight Savage Tribes' (1927) 21 AJIL 279
Corn G, 'War, Law, and the Oft Overlooked Value of Process as a Precautionary Measure' (2015) 42 Pepperdine LR 419
Corten O et al, 'L'Exécution de Qassem Soleimani et ses suites: Aspects de jus contra bellum et de jus in bello' (2020) 124 RGDIP 41
Crawford J, 'International Law and Foreign Sovereigns: Distinguishing Immune Transactions' (1983) 54 BYIL 75
Cuyckens H and Paulussen C, 'The Prosecution of Foreign Fighters in Western Europe: The Difficult Relationship between Counter-Terrorism and International Humanitarian Law' (2019) 24 JCSL 537

Daugirdas C and Mortenson J, 'United States Strikes Houthi-Controlled Facilities in Yemen, Reaffirms Limited Support for Saudi-Led Coalition Notwithstanding Growing Concerns about Civilian Casualties' (2017) 111 AJIL 523
David E, 'How Does the Involvement of a Multinational Peacekeeping Force Affect the Classification of a Situation' (2013) 95 IRRC 659
DeCock C, 'Legal Implications Surrounding Operation "Inherent Resolve" in Iraq and Syria' (2017) 47 Isr YHR 69
Del Mar K, 'The Requirement of "Belonging" under International Humanitarian Law' (2010) 21 EJIL
Derejko N, 'A Forever War? Rethinking the Temporal Scope of Non-International Armed Conflict' (2021) 26 JCSL 347
Dill J, 'Do Attackers Have a Legal Duty of Care? Limits to the "Individualization of War"' (2019) 11 IT 1
Dörmann K and Serralvo J, 'Common Article 1 to the Geneva Conventions and the Obligation to Prevent International Humanitarian Law Violations' (2014) 96 IRRC 707
Drew P, 'Blockade? A Legal Assessment of the Maritime Interdiction of Yemen's Ports' (2019) 24 JCSL 35
Dzehtsiarou K, 'Georgia v. Russia (II)' (2021) 115 AJIL 288
Eagleton C, 'An Attempt to Define War' (1933) 291 IC 237
'Effects of a Formal Declaration of War: U.S. Defense Department Statement' (1966) 5 ILM 791
Egan B, 'Keynote Address' (2016) 110 ASIL Proc 300
Eichensehr K, 'Biden Administration Launches Reset in Relations with Saudi Arabia, Withdraws Support for Saudi-Led War in Yemen' (2021) 115 AJIL 545
Engdahl O, 'How does the Involvement of a Multinational Peacekeeping Force Affect the Classification of a Situation: A Rebuttal to Eric David' (2013) 95 IRRC 667
Falk R, 'The Cambodia Operation and International Law' (1971) 65 AJIL 1
Farley B, 'Targeting Anwar al-Aulaqi: A Case Study in US Drone Strikes and Targeted Killing' (2011) 2 AUNSLB 57
Farrant J, 'Modern Maritime Neutrality Law' (2014) 90 ILS 198
Fassbender B, 'The United Nations Charter as Constitution of the International Community' (1998) 36 Colum JTL 529
Fazal T, 'Why States No Longer Declare War' (2012) 21 Secur Stud 557
Fazal T, Irajpanah K, and Schultz K, '*Jus in Bello*, *Jus ad Bellum*, and the Decline in Declarations of War: An Exchange' (2021) 30 Secur Stud 893
Fazal T and Konaev M, 'Homelands versus Minelands: Why Do Armed Groups Commit to the Laws of War?' (2019) 4 JoGSS 149
Fenwick C, '"The Old Order Changeth, Yielding Place to New"' (1953) 47 AJIL 84
Ferraro T, 'The Applicability and Application of International Humanitarian Law to Multinational Forces' (2013) 95 IRRC 561
Ferraro T, 'The ICRC's Legal Position on the Notion of Armed Conflict Involving Foreign Intervention and on Determining the IHL Applicable to This Type of Conflict' (2015) 97 IRRC 1227
Ferraro T, 'Military Support to Belligerents: Can the Provider Become a Party to the Armed Conflict?' (2019) 49 Collegium 47
Ferraro T, 'International Humanitarian Law, Principled Humanitarian Action, Counterterrorism and Sanctions: Some Perspectives on Selected Issues' (2021) 103 IRRC 109
Ferro L and Verlinden N, 'Neutrality during Armed Conflicts: A Coherent Approach to Third-State Support for Warring Parties' (2018) 17 CJIL 15
Focarelli C, 'Common Article 1 of the 1949 Geneva Conventions: A Soap Bubble' (2010) 21 EJIL 125
Fox G, Boon K, and Jenkins I, 'The Contributions of United Nations Security Council Resolutions to the Law of Non-International Armed Conflict: New Evidence of Customary International Law' (2018) 67 AULR 649

Franck T and Rodley N, 'Legitimacy and Legal Rights of Revolutionary Movements with Special Reference to the Peoples' Revolutionary Government of South Viet Nam' (1970) 45 NYULR 679

Gaggioli G, 'Targeting Individuals Belonging to Armed Groups' (2018) 51 Van JTL 901

Gaggioli G and Kilibarda P, 'Counterterrorism and the Risk of Over-classification of Situations of Violence' (2021) 103 IRRC 203

Gal T, 'Unexplored Outcomes of *Tadić*: Applicability of the Law of Occupation to War by Proxy' (2014) 12 JICJ 59

Galand A, '*Bemba* and the Individualisation of War: Reconciling Command Responsibility under Article 28 Rome Statute with Individual Criminal Responsibility' (2020) 20 ICLR 669

Galbraith J, 'Congress Signals Concern over U.S. Role in Aiding Saudi Arabia's Activities in Yemen' (2019) 113 AJIL 159

Galvis Martínez M, 'The "Allegiance" Test: Judicial Legislation and Interpretation of GCIV' (2022) 27 JCSL 21

Gardam J, 'Proportionality and Force in International Law' (1993) 87 AJIL 391

Geiß R and Siegrist M, 'Has the Armed Conflict in Afghanistan Affected the Rules on the Conduct of Hostilities?' (2011) 93 IRRC 11

Giladi R, 'Corporate Belligerency and the Delegation Theory from Grotius to Westlake' (2020) 41 Grotiana 349

Gill T, 'Classifying the Conflict in Syria' (2016) 92 ILS 353

Gill T, 'Some Thoughts on the ICRC Support Based Approach' (2019) 59 QIL Zoom-in 45

Gill T, 'Reconciling the Irreconcilable: Some Thoughts on Belligerent Equality in Non-international Armed Conflicts' (2022) 51 NYIL 343

Gillard E-C, 'Business Goes to War: Private Military/Security Companies and International Humanitarian Law' (2006) 88 IRRC 525

Glennon M, 'How International Rules Die' (2005) 93 Geo LJ 939

Green J, 'The Article 51 Reporting Requirement for Self-Defense Actions' (2015) 55 Va JIL 563

Greenwood C, 'The Relationship between *Ius ad Bellum* and *Ius in Bello*' (1983) 9 Rev Int Stud 221

Greenwood C, 'The Concept of War in Modern International Law' (1987) 36 ICLQ 283

Greenwood C, 'International Humanitarian Law and United Nations Military Operations' (1998) 1 YIHL 3

Greenwood C, 'The Applicability of International Humanitarian Law and the Law of Neutrality to the Kosovo Campaign' (2002) 78 ILS 35

Gross A, 'Human Proportions: Are Human Rights the Emperor's New Clothes of the International Law of Occupation?' (2007) 18 EJIL 1

Guilfoyle D, 'The *Mavi Marmara* Incident and Blockade in Armed Conflict' (2011) 81 BYIL 171

Halabi SF, 'Traditions of Belligerent Recognition: The Libyan Intervention in Historical and Theoretical Context' (2012) 27 AULR 321

Haque A, 'Whose Armed Conflict: Which Law of Armed Conflict' (2017) 45 Ga JICL 475

Hathaway O et al, 'Ensuring Responsibility: Common Article 1 and State Responsibility for Non-State Actors' (2017) 95 Tex LR 539

Hathaway O et al, 'Yemen: Is the U.S. Breaking the Law?' (2019) 10 Harv NSJ 1

Heinsch R, 'Conflict Classification in Ukraine: The Return of the "Proxy War"?' (2015) 91 ILS 323

Heintschel von Heinegg W, 'The United Nations Convention on the Law of the Sea and Maritime Security Operations' (2005) 48 GYIL 151

Heintschel von Heinegg W, 'Territorial Sovereignty and Neutrality in Cyberspace' (2013) 89 ILS 123

Heller K, 'In Defense of Pure Sovereignty in Cyberspace' (2021) 97 ILS 1432

Heller K and Trabucco L, 'The Legality of Weapons Transfers to Ukraine under International Law' (2022) 13 JIHLS 251

Helmersen S, 'The Use of Force against Neutral Ships Outside Territorial Waters' (2022) 35 LJIL 315

Henckels C, 'Permission to Act: The Legal Character of General and Security Exceptions in International Trade and Investment Law' (2020) 69 ICLQ 557
Henderson C and Lubell N, 'The Contemporary Legal Nature of UN Security Council Ceasefire Resolutions' (2013) 26 LJIL 369
Heyns C et al, 'The International Law Framework Regulating the Use of Armed Drones' (2016) 65 ICLQ 791
Hill-Cawthorne L, 'Rights under International Humanitarian Law' (2017) 28 EJIL 1187
Hill-Cawthorne L, 'Common Article 1 of the Geneva Conventions and the Method of Treaty Interpretation' (2023) 72 ICLQ 869
Hoffmann T, 'War or Peace? International Legal Issues Concerning the Use of Force in the Russia–Ukraine Conflict' (2022) 63 Hungarian JLS 206
Hohfeld W, 'Some Fundamental Legal Conceptions as Applied in Judicial Reasoning' (1913–14) 23 Yale LJ 16
Højfeldt Jakobsen H, 'Returning Foreign Fighters: The Case of Denmark' (2018) 100 IRRC 315
Howard L and Dayal A, 'The Use of Force in UN Peacekeeping' (2018) 72 IO 71
Hrnjaz M and Simentić Popović J, 'Protracted Armed Violence as a Criterion for the Existence of Non-international Armed Conflict: International Humanitarian Law, International Criminal Law and Beyond' (2020) 25 JCSL 473
Huneeus A, 'International Criminal Law by Other Means: The Quasi-Criminal Jurisdiction of the Human Rights Courts' (2013) 107 AJIL 1
Hursh J, 'International Humanitarian Law Violations, Legal Responsibility, and US Military Support to the Saudi Coalition in Yemen: A Cautionary Tale' (2020) 7 JUOFIL 122
Ingber R, 'Co-belligerency' (2017) 42 YJIL 67
Ingber R, 'Untangling Belligerency from Neutrality in the Conflict with Al-Qaeda' (2011) 47 TexILJ 75
Irajpanah K and Schultz K, 'Off the Menu: Post-1945 Norms and the End of War Declarations' (2021) 30 Secur Stud 605
Jackson M, 'State Instigation in International Law: A General Principle Transposed' (2019) 30 EJIL 391
Jamnejad M and Wood M, 'The Principle of Non-intervention' (2009) 22 LJIL 345
John-Hopkins M, 'Extrapolation of Criminal Law Modes of Liability to Target Analysis under International Humanitarian Law: Developing the Framework for Understanding Direct Participation in Hostilities and Membership in Organized Armed Groups in Non International Armed Conflict' (2017) 22 JCSL 275
Johnson J, 'National Security Law, Lawyers, and Lawyering in the Obama Administration—Dean's Lecture at Yale Law School, February 22, 2012' (2012) 31 Yale L Pol Rev 141
Johnston K, 'Transformations of Conflict Status in Libya' (2012) 17 JCSL 81
Jorritsma R, 'Where General International Law Meets International Humanitarian Law: Attribution of Conduct and the Classification of Armed Conflicts' (2018) 23 JCSL 405
Junod S, 'Additional Protocol II: History and Scope' (1983) 33 AULR 29
Kalshoven F, 'The Undertaking to Respect and Ensure Respect in All Circumstances: From Tiny Seed to Ripening Fruit' (1999) 2 YIHL 3
Kalshoven F, 'The International Humanitarian Fact-Finding Commission: A Sleeping Beauty?' (2002) 15 Hu V-I 213
Karsten N, 'Distinguishing Military and Non-Military Superiors: Reflections on the *Bemba* Case at the ICC' (2009) 7 JICJ 983
Kelsen H, 'Théorie générale du droit international public: Problèmes choisis' (1932) 42 RCADI 121
Kelsen H, 'Théorie du droit international' (1953) 84 RCADI 1
Kennedy D, 'The Stages of Decline in the Public/Private Distinction' (1982) 130 U Penn LR 1349
Kessler B, 'The Duty to "Ensure Respect" under Common Article 1 of the Geneva Conventions: Its Implications on International and Non-International Armed Conflicts' (2001) 44 GYIL 498

Kleffner J, 'The Legal Fog of an Illusion: Three Reflections on "Organization" and "Intensity" as Criteria for the Temporal Scope of the Law of Non-International Armed Conflict' (2019) 95 ILS 161
Koh H, 'Keynote Address: The Obama Administration and International Law' (2010) 104 ASIL Proc 207
Kolb R, 'La Désuétude en droit international public' (2007) 111 RGDIP 577
Kolb R, 'Commentaires iconoclastes sur l'obligation de faire respecter le droit international humanitaire selon l'Article 1 Commun des Conventions de Genève de 1949' (2013) 46 RBDI 513
Koutroulis V, 'IOs Involved in Armed Conflict: The Material and Geographical Scope of Application of IHL' (2012) 42 Collegium 29
Koutroulis V, 'And Yet It Exists: In Defence of the "Equality of Belligerents" Principle' (2013) 26 LJIL 449
Koutroulis V, 'The Fight against the Islamic State and Jus in Bello' (2016) 29 LJIL 827
Koutroulis V, 'A Clarification of the Geographical and Personal Scope of Multinational NIACs?' (2019) 49 Collegium 35
Kraska J et al, 'The Newport Manual on the Law of Naval Warfare' (2023) 101 ILS 1
Krebsbach R, 'Totality of the Circumstances: The DoD Law of War Manual and the Evolving Notion of Direct Participation in Hostilities' (2017) 9 JNSLP 125
Kreß C, 'Towards further Developing the Law of Non-International Armed Conflict: A Proposal for a Jus in Bello Interno and a New Jus Contra Bellum Internum' (2014) 96 IRRC 29
Kritsiotis D, 'The Tremors of *Tadić*' (2010) 43 Isr LR 262
Lachs M, 'Teachings and Teaching of International Law' (1976) 151 RCADI 161
Lauterpacht E, 'The Legal Irrelevance of the "State of War"' (1968) 62 ASIL Proc 58
Lauterpacht H, 'The Pact of Paris and the Budapest Articles of Interpretation' (1934) 20 GST 178
Lauterpacht H, 'The Subjects of the Law of Nations: Part II' (1948) 64 LQR 97
Lauterpacht H, 'The Limits of the Operation of the Law of War' (1953) 30 BYIL 206
Lazar S, 'Just War Theory: Revisionists versus Traditionalists' (2017) 20 Annu Rev Polit Sci 37
Le Floch G, 'La Désuétude en droit international public' (2007) 111 RGDIP 610
Levie H, 'The Status of Belligerent Personnel Splashed and Rescued by a Neutral in the Persian Gulf Area' (1991) 31 Va JIL 611
Levie H, 'The Falklands Crisis and the Laws of War' (1998) 70 ILS 203
Lieblich E, 'The Facilitative Function of *Jus in Bello*' (2019) 30 EJIL 321
Linderfalk U, 'State Responsibility and the Primary–Secondary Rules Terminology—The Role of Language for an Understanding of the International Legal System' (2009) 78 Nordic JIL 53
Longobardo M, '"Super-Robust" Peacekeeping Mandates in Non-International Armed Conflicts under International Law' (2020) 24 SYIL 42
Lootsteen Y, 'The Concept of Belligerency in International Law' (2000) 166 MLR 109
Lowe V, 'The Impact of the Law of the Sea on Naval Warfare' (1987) 14 SJILC 657
Lowe V, 'The Laws of War at Sea and the 1958 and 1982 Conventions' (1988) 12 MP 286
Lowe V, 'Responsibility for the Conduct of Other States' (2002) 101 JILD 1
Lubell N and Derejko N, 'A Global Battlefield? Drones and the Geographical Scope of Armed Conflict' (2013) 11 JICJ 65
Mačák K and Zamir N, 'The Applicability of International Humanitarian Law to the Conflict in Libya' (2012) 14 ICLR 403
McDougall C, 'The Inspector-General of the Australian Defence Force Afghanistan Inquiry Report and the Applicability of Additional Protocol II to Intervening Foreign Forces' (2023) 105 IRRC 992
Mackenzie-Gray Scott R, 'State Responsibility for Complicity in the Internationally Wrongful Acts of Non-State Armed Groups' (2019) 24 JCSL 373
McLaughlin R, 'United Nations Mandated Naval Interdiction Operations in the Territorial Sea?' (2002) 51 ICLQ 249
McNair A, 'The Legal Meaning of War, and the Relation of War to Reprisals' (1925) 11 GST 29

Maganza B, 'Which Role for Hybrid Entities Involved in Multi-Parties NIACs? Applying the ICRC's Support-based Approach to the Armed Conflict in Mali' (2019) 59 QIL Zoom-in 25
Maganza B, 'From Peacekeepers to Parties to the Conflict: An IHL's Appraisal of the Role of UN Peace Operations in NIACs' (2020) 25 JCSL 209
Mandel M, 'Aggressors' Rights: The Doctrine of "Equality between Belligerents" and the Legacy of Nuremberg' (2011) 24 LJIL 627
Mathias S, 'UN Peacekeeping Today: Legal Challenges and Uncertainties' (2017) 18 Melb JIL 138
Mégret F, '"War"? Legal Semantics and the Move to Violence' (2002) 13 EJIL 361
Melzer N, 'Keeping the Balance between Military Necessity and Humanity: A Response to Four Critiques of the ICRC's Interpretive Guidance on the Notion of Direct Participation in Hostilities' (2010) 42 NYUJILP 831
Meron T, 'International Criminalization of Internal Atrocities' (1995) 89 AJIL 554
Meron T, 'Classification of Armed Conflict in the Former Yugoslavia: Nicaragua's Fallout' (1998) 92 AJIL
Meron T, 'The Humanization of Humanitarian Law' (2000) 94 AJIL 239
Meron T, 'International Law in the Age of Human Rights' (2003) 301 RCADI 9
Mignot-Mahdavi R, 'Rethinking Direct Participation in Hostilities and Continuous Combat Function in Light of Targeting Members of Terrorist Non-State Armed Groups' (2023) 105 IRRC 1028
Milanovic M, 'The End of Application of International Humanitarian Law' (2014) 96 IRRC 163
Milanovic M, 'Special Rules of Attribution of Conduct in International Law' (2020) 96 ILS 295
Milanovic M, 'Intelligence Sharing in Multinational Military Operations and Complicity under International Law' (2021) 97 ILS 1269
'Military Operations in Cambodia: Statement of the Legal Adviser' (1970) 64 AJIL 933
Mortlock D, 'Definite Detention: The Scope of the President's Authority to Detain Enemy Combatants' (2010) 4 Harv L Pol Rev 375
Neuman N, 'A Precautionary Tale: The Theory and Practice of Precautions in Attack' (2018) 48 Isr YHR 19
Neuman N, 'Neutrality and Cyberspace: Bridging the Gap between Theory and Reality' (2021) 97 ILS 765
Nieto Navia R, '¿Hay o no hay conflicto armado en Colombia?' (2008) 1 ACDI 139
Norton P, 'Between the Ideology and the Reality: The Shadow of the Law of Neutrality' (1976) 17 HILJ 249
O'Donnell D, 'International Treaties against Terrorism and the Use of Terrorism during Armed Conflict and by Armed Forces' (2006) 88 IRRC 653
Ohlin J, 'The Combatant's Privilege in Asymmetric and Covert Conflicts' (2015) 40 YJIL 337
Okowa P, 'State Responsibility and Individual Responsibility in Internal Conflicts: Contours of an Evolving Relationship' (2009) 20 FYIL 143
Oswald B et al, 'Peace Forces at War: Implications under International Humanitarian Law' (2014) 108 ASIL Proc 149
Parkerson J, 'United States Compliance with Humanitarian Law Respecting Civilians during Operation Just Case' (1991) 133 MLR 31
Parks WH, 'Special Forces' Wear of Non-Standard Uniforms' (2003) 4 Chic JIL 493
Paust J, 'NIAC Nonsense, the Afghan War, and Combatant Immunity' (2016) 44 Ga JICL 555
Pearlstein D, 'Armed Conflict at the Threshold' (2019) 58 Va JIL 369
Pedrozo R, 'Russia–Ukraine Conflict: The War at Sea' (2022) 100 ILS 1
Petrochilos G, 'The Relevance of the Concepts of War and Armed Conflict to the Law of Neutrality' (1998) 31 VanJTL 575
Pisillo-Mazzeschi R, 'The Due Diligence Rule and the Nature of the International Responsibility of States' (1992) 35 GYIL 9
Polackova van der Ploeg K, 'The Functional Threshold: Direct International Legal Regulation of Collective Nonstate Entities and the Law of International Peace and Security' (2020) 53 NYUJILP 71
Politis N, 'Les Représailles entre États membres de la Société des Nations' (1924) 31 RGDIP 5

Preston S, 'Policy Address: "Legal Framework for the U.S. Use of Military Force since 9/11"' (2015) 109 ASIL Proc 331
'Q&A Session' (2019) 49 Collegium 58
Quéguiner J-F, 'Precautions under the Law Governing the Conduct of Hostilities' (2006) 88 IRRC 793
Quigley J, 'Complicity in International Law: A New Direction in the Law of State Responsibility' (1986) 57 BYIL 77
Regan P, 'Conditions of Successful Third-Party Intervention in Intrastate Conflicts' (1996) 40 JCR 336
Roberts A, 'The Equal Application of the Law of War: A Principle under Pressure' (2009) 90 IRRC 931
Roberts AE, 'Traditional and Modern Approaches to Customary International Law: A Reconciliation' (2001) 95 AJIL 757
Robson V, 'The Common Approach to Article 1: The Scope of Each State's Obligation to Ensure Respect for the Geneva Conventions' (2020) 25 JCSL 101
Rodenhäuser T, 'Armed Groups, Rebel Coalitions, and Transnational Groups: The Degree of Organization Required from Non-State Armed Groups to Become Party to a Non-International Armed Conflict' (2018) 19(2016) YIHL 3
Rodenhäuser T, 'The Legal Protection of Persons Living under the Control of Non-State Armed Groups' (2020) 102 IRRC 991
Roithmaier K, 'Holding States Responsible for Violations of International Humanitarian Law in Proxy Warfare: The Concept of State Complicity in Acts of Non-State Armed Groups' (2023) 14 EJLS 140
Rousseau C, 'Chronique des faits internationaux' (1966) 70 RGDIP 178
Rousseau C, 'Nigéria' (1968) 72 RGDIP 228
Russo F, 'Neutrality at Sea in Transition: State Practice in the Gulf War as Emerging International Customary Law' (1988) 19 ODIL 381
Ruys T, 'Of Arms, Funding and "Non-lethal Assistance"—Issues Surrounding Third-State Intervention in the Syrian Civil War' (2014) 13 CJIL 13
Ruys T, 'The Meaning of "Force" and the Boundaries of the Jus ad Bellum: Are "Minimal" Uses of Force Excluded from UN Charter Article 2(4)?' (2014) 108 AJIL 159
Sassòli M, 'State Responsibility for Violations of International Humanitarian Law' (2002) 84 IRRC 401
Sassòli M, 'Taking Armed Groups Seriously: Ways to Improve Their Compliance with International Humanitarian Law' (2010) 1 JIHLS 5
Sassòli M, 'Active and Passive Precautions in Air and Missile Warfare' (2014) 44 IsrYHR 69
Saul B, 'From Conflict to Complementarity: Reconciling international Counterterrorism Law and International Humanitarian Law' (2021) 103 IRRC 157
Scelle G, 'Règles générales du droit de la paix' (1932) 46 RCADI 327
Schachter O, 'Invisible College of International Lawyers' (1977–78) 72 NULR 217
Schaller C, 'Der völkerrechtliche Rahmen für Waffenlieferungen an die Ukraine' (2023) 60 AVR 439
Schindler D, 'Aspects contemporains de la neutralité' (1967) 121 RCADI 221
Schindler D, 'The Different Types of Armed Conflicts According to the Geneva Conventions and Protocols' (1979) 163 RCADI 121
Schmitt M, 'The Interpretive Guidance on the Notion of Direct Participation in Hostilities: A Critical Analysis' (2010) 1 Harv NSJ 5
Schmitt M, 'Charting the Legal Geography of Non-International Armed Conflict' (2014) 90 ILS 1
Schmitt M, 'International Humanitarian Law and the Targeting of Non-State Intelligence Personnel and Objects' (2020) 30 Duke JCIL 309
Schmitt M and Biggerstaff WC, 'Aid and Assistance as a "Use of Force" under the *Jus ad Bellum*' (2023) 100 ILS 186
Schmitt M and Watts S, 'Common Article 1 and the Duty to "Ensure Respect"' (2020) 96 ILS 674

Schöndorf R, 'Israel's Perspective on Key Legal and Practical Issues Concerning the Application of International Law to Cyber Operations' (2021) 97 ILS 395
Schwarzenberger G, 'Jus Pacis Ac Belli? Prolegomena to a Sociology of International Law' (1943) 37 AJIL 460
Sexton J, 'How Does the Obligation to Investigate Alleged Serious Violations of International Humanitarian Law Apply in Ad Hoc Military Coalitions?' (2022) 60 MLLWR 188
Shniderman A, 'Prove It: Judging the Hostile-or-Warlike-Action Exclusion in Cyber-Insurance Policies' (2019) 129 Yale LJF 64
Shraga D, 'The United Nations as an Actor Bound by International Humanitarian Law' (1998) 5 International Peacekeeping 64
Siekmann R, 'Netherlands State Practice for the Parliamentary Year 1986–1987' (1988) 19 NYIL 279
Simma B, 'From Bilateralism to Community Interest in International Law' (1994) 250 RCADI 224
Sivakumaran S, 'Binding Armed Opposition Groups' (2006) 55 ICLQ 369
Sivakumaran S, 'Re-envisaging the International Law of Internal Armed Conflict' (2011) 22 EJIL 264
Sivakumaran S, 'Exclusion Zones in the Law of Armed Conflict at Sea: Evolution in Law and Practice' (2016) 92 ILS 153
Sloane R, 'The Cost of Conflation: Preserving the Dualism of Jus ad Bellum and Jus in Bello in the Contemporary Law of War' (2009) 34 YJIL 47
Somer J, 'Jungle Justice: Passing Sentence on the Equality of Belligerents in Non-International Armed Conflict' (2007) 89 IRRC 655
Starski P, 'Silence within the Process of Normative Change and Evolution of the Prohibition on the Use of Force: Normative Volatility and Legislative Responsibility' (2017) 4 JUOFIL 14
Sur S, 'La Créativité du droit international' (2013) 363 RCADI 13
Talmon S, 'Determining Customary International Law: The ICJ's Methodology between Induction, Deduction and Assertion' (2015) 26 EJIL 417
Tan F and Zwanenburg M, 'One Step Forward, Two Steps Back? *Georgia v Russia (II)*, European Court of Human Rights, Appl No 38263/08' (2021) 22 Melb JIL 136
Tosun S, 'Victims of Hawija v. The Netherlands: Proportionality and Precaution under Mounting Pressure' (2022) 51 NYIL 409
Tsagourias N and Biggio G, 'Cyber Peacekeeping Operations and the Regulation of the Use of Lethal Force' (2022) 99 ILS 37
'The US Plan to Protect Kuwaiti Ships in the Gulf by Putting Them under US Flags' (1987) 26 ILM 1429
van Poecke T, Verbruggen F, and Yperman W, 'Terrorist Offences and International Humanitarian Law: The Armed Conflict Exclusion Clause' (2021) 103 IRRC 295
van Steenberghe R, 'La Légalité de la participation de la Belgique à la lutte armée contre l'Etat islamique en Irak' (2015) 134 Journal des Tribunaux 641
van Steenberghe R, 'Les Interventions militaires étrangères récentes contre le terrorisme international. Seconde partie: Droit applicable (jus in bello)' (2017) 63 AFDI 37
van Steenberghe R, 'Military Assistance to Ukraine: Enquiring the Need for Any Legal Justification under International Law' (2023) 28 JCSL 231
van Steenberghe R and Lesaffre P, 'The ICRC's "Support-Based Approach": A Suitable but Incomplete Theory' (2019) 59 QIL, Zoom-in 5
Villalpando S, 'The Legal Dimension of the International Community: How Community Interests Are Protected in International Law' (2010) 21 EJIL 387
Vité S, 'Typology of Armed Conflicts in International Humanitarian Law: Legal Concepts and Actual Situations' (2009) 91 IRRC 69
Watkin K, 'Opportunity Lost: Organized Armed Groups and the ICRC Direct Participation in Hostilities Interpretive Guidance' (2010) 42 NYUJILP 641
Weizmann N, 'The End of Armed Conflict, the End of Participation in Armed Conflict, and the End of Hostilities: Implications for Detention Operations under the 2001 AUMF' (2016) 47 Colum Hum Rts LR 204

Welsh J, 'The Individualisation of War: Defining a Research Programme' (2019) 53 Annals of the Fondazione Luigi Einaudi 9

Wentker A, 'Kriegspartei? Sicherheitspolitischer Diskurs und Völkerrecht im Ukraine-Krieg' (2022) 75 DÖV 988

Wentker A, 'Partnered Operations and the Positive Duties of Co-Parties' (2022) 27 JCSL 159

Wentker A, 'At War? Party Status and the War in Ukraine' (2023) 36 LJIL 643

Wéry M, 'La Jurisprudence relative à la clause d'exclusion prévue à l'article 141*bis* du Code Pénal: La difficile application du droit international humanitaire par les cours et tribunaux belges' (2018) 57 MLLWR 103

Wiesener C and Kjeldgaard-Pedersen A, 'Ensuring Respect by Partners: Revisiting the Debate on Common Article 1' (2022) 27 JCSL 135

Wilhelm R-J, 'Le Caractère des droits accordés à l'individu dans les Conventions de Genève' (1950) 32 IRRC 561

Wolfrum R, 'Military Activities on the High Seas: What Are the Impacts of the U.N. Convention on the Law of the Sea' (1998) 71 ILS 501

Worster W, 'The Inductive and Deductive Methods in Customary International Law Analysis: Traditional and Modern Approaches' (2014) 45 Geo JIL 445

Wright Q, 'The Future of Neutrality' (1928) 12 IC 353

Wright Q, 'When Does War Exist?' (1932) 26 AJIL

Yip KL, 'Separation between *jus ad bellum* and *jus in bello* as Insulation of Results, Not Scopes, of Application' (2020) 58 MLLWR 31

Zamir N, 'The Armed Conflict(s) against the Islamic State' (2016) 18(2015) YIHL 91

Zimmermann A, 'Humanitarian Assistance and the Security Council' (2017) 50 Isr LR 3

Zrilič J, 'Armed Conflicts and the Law of Treaties: Recent Developments and Reappraisal of the Doctrine in Light of the Wars in Syria and Ukraine' (2023) 65 Japanese YIL 107

Zwanenburg M, 'Double Trouble: The "Cumulative Approach" and the "Support-Based Approach" in the Relationship between Non-State Armed Groups' (2021) 22(2019) YIHL 43

Zwanenburg M, 'The "External Element" of the Obligation to Ensure Respect for the Geneva Conventions: A Matter of Treaty Interpretation' (2021) 97 ILS 621

Blog Posts

Akande D, 'Embedded Troops and the Use of Force in Syria: International and Domestic Law Questions' (*EJIL: Talk!*, 11 September 2015) <www.ejiltalk.org/embedded-troops-and-the-use-of-force-in-syria-international-and-domestic-law-questions/>

Akande D, 'When Does the Use of Force against a Non-State Armed Group Trigger an International Armed Conflict and Why Does this Matter?' (*EJIL: Talk!*, 18 October 2016) <www.ejiltalk.org/when-does-the-use-of-force-against-a-non-state-armed-group-trigger-an-international-armed-conflict-and-why-does-this-matter/>

Akande D et al, 'The Second Oxford Statement on International Law Protections of the Healthcare Sector during COVID-19: Safeguarding Vaccine Research' (*EJIL: Talk!*, 11 August 2020)

Akande D et al, 'Oxford Statement on the International Law Protections against Cyber Operations Targeting the Health Care Sector' (*EJIL: Talk!*, 21 May 2020)

Aly H, 'Negotiations at Red Cross Conference Shrouded in Global Politics' (*New Humanitarian*, 13 December 2019) <www.thenewhumanitarian.org/news/2019/12/13/Red-Cross-IHL-conference-global-politics>

Blank L, 'Symposium: The Interplay between IAC and NIAC—Questions and Consequences' (*OpinioJuris*, 16 January 2019) <http://opiniojuris.org/2019/01/16/symposium-the-interplay-between-iac-and-niac-questions-and-consequences/>

Chesney R, 'Yemen Is a Hot Battlefield' (*lawfare*, 7 March 2012) <www.lawfareblog.com/yemen-hot-battlefield>

Corn G, 'Precautions to Minimize Civilian Harm Are a Fundamental Principle of the Law of War' (*Just Security*, 8 July 2015) <www.justsecurity.org/24493/obligation-precautions-fundamental-principle-law-war>

Droege C and Tuck D, 'Fighting together and International Humanitarian Law: Setting the Legal Framework (1/2)' (*Humanitarian Law and Policy*, 12 October 2017) <https://blogs.icrc.org/law-and-policy/2017/10/12/fighting-together-international-humanitarian-law-setting-legal-framework-1-2/>

Fortin K, 'Symposium: Further Thoughts on an IAC with Three Parties and the Capacity of Armed Groups to Adhere to International Norms' (*OpinioJuris*, 18 January 2019) <http://opiniojuris.org/2019/01/18/symposium-further-thoughts-on-an-iac-with-three-parties-and-the-capacity-of-armed-groups-to-adhere-to-international-norms/>

Goodman R, 'Al-Qaeda, the Law on Associated Forces and "Belonging to" a Party (Did the New UN Drones Reports Get It Right?)' (*Just Security*, 18 October 2013) <www.justsecurity.org/2191/al-qaeda-law-forces-belonging-to-party-drones-reports/>

Goodman R, 'Is the United States Already in an "International Armed Conflict" with Syria?' (*Just Security*, 11 October 2016) <www.justsecurity.org/33477/united-states-international-armed-conflict-syria/>

Goodman R, 'Two U.S. Positions on the Duty to Ensure Respect for the Geneva Conventions' (*Just Security*, 26 September 2016) <www.justsecurity.org/33166/u-s-positions-duty-ensure-respect-geneva-conventions/>

Gurmendi A, 'The Last Recognition of Belligerency (and Some Thoughts on Why You May Not Have Heard of It)' (*OpinioJuris*, 10 December 2019) <http://opiniojuris.org/2019/12/10/the-last-recognition-of-belligerency-and-some-thoughts-on-why-you-may-not-have-heard-of-it/>

Hathaway O and Manfredi Z, 'The State Department Adviser Signals a Middle Road on Common Article 1' (*Just Security*, 12 April 2016) <www.justsecurity.org/30560/state-department-adviser-signals-middle-road-common-article–1/>

Heintschel von Heinegg W, 'Neutrality in the War against Ukraine' (*Articles of War*, 1 March 2022) <https://lieber.westpoint.edu/neutrality-in-the-war-against-ukraine/>

Labuda P, 'The UN Goes to War in the Central African Republic: What Are the Limits of Peacekeeping?' (*Just Security*, 23 March 2017) <www.justsecurity.org/39151/war-central-african-republic-limits-peacekeeping/>

Mačák K, 'Symposium: Internationalized Armed Conflicts—Four Concluding Thoughts' (*OpinioJuris*, 23 January 2019) <http://opiniojuris.org/2019/01/23/symposium-internationalized-armed-conflicts-four-concluding-thoughts/>

Maganza B, 'Escalation of Violence in Bangui: Has MINUSCA Become Party to a Conflict in CAR, and What Would that Mean?' (*OpinioJuris*, 28 April 2018) <http://opiniojuris.org/2018/04/16/escalation-of-violence-in-bangui-has-minusca-become-party-to-a-conflict-in-car-and-what-would-that-mean/>

Milanovic M, 'Georgia v. Russia No. 2: The European Court's Resurrection of Bankovic in the Contexts of Chaos' (*EJIL: Talk!*, 25 January 2021) <www.ejiltalk.org/georgia-v-russia-no-2-the-european-courts-resurrection-of-bankovic-in-the-contexts-of-chaos/>

Milanovic M, 'The United States and Allies Sharing Intelligence with Ukraine' (*EJIL: Talk!*, 9 May 2022) <www.ejiltalk.org/the-united-states-and-allies-sharing-intelligence-with-ukraine/>

Nikolic J, de Saint Maurice T, and Ferraro T, 'Aggregated Intensity: Classifying Coalitions of Non-State Armed Groups' (*Humanitarian Law and Policy*, 7 October 2020) <https://blogs.icrc.org/law-and-policy/2020/10/07/aggregated-intensity-classifying-coalitions-non-state-armed-groups/>

Nohle E, 'Drawing the Line between Armed Groups under IHL' (*Humanitarian Law and Policy*, 22 July 2016) <https://blogs.icrc.org/law-and-policy/2016/07/22/drawing-line-armed-groups/>

Pobjie E, 'Covid-19 as a Threat to International Peace and Security: The Role of the UN Security Council in Addressing the Pandemic' (*EJIL: Talk!*, 27 July 2020) <https://www.ejiltalk.org/covid-19-as-a-threat-to-international-peace-and-security-the-role-of-the-un-security-council-in-addressing-the-pandemic/>

Pothelet E, 'Symposium: Three Questions to the Author' (*OpinioJuris*, 21 January 2019) <http://opiniojuris.org/2019/01/21/symposium-three-questions-to-the-author/>

Redaelli C, 'A Common Enemy: Aggregating Intensity in Non-international Armed Conflicts' (*Humanitarian Law and Policy*, 22 April 2021) <https://blogs.icrc.org/law-and-policy/2021/04/22/common-enemy/>

Reid J, 'Ensuring Respect: The Role of State Practice in Interpreting the Geneva Conventions' (*ILA Reporter*, 2016) <http://ilareporter.org.au/2016/11/ensuring-respect-the-role-of-state-practice-in-interpreting-the-geneva-conventions-john-reid/>

'Remarks by Defense Dept General Counsel Paul C. Ney Jr. on the Law of War' (*Just Security*, 28 May 2019) <www.justsecurity.org/64313/remarks-by-defense-dept-general-counsel-paul-c-ney-jr-on-the-law-of-war/>

Schmitt M, 'Are We at War?' (*Articles of War*, 9 May 2022) <https://lieber.westpoint.edu/are-we-at-war/>

Weizmann N, 'Are the U.S. and U.K. Parties to the Saudi-led Armed Conflict against the Houthis in Yemen?' (*Just Security*, 22 September 2016) <www.justsecurity.org/33095/u-s-u-k-parties-saudi-led-armed-conflict-houthis-yemen/>

Working Papers, Opinion Papers, Reports, and Theses

Bellal A (ed), *The War Report: Armed Conflicts in 2018* (Geneva Academy 2019)

Crawford J, 'Opinion: Third Party Obligations with respect to Israeli Settlements in the Occupied Palestinian Territories' (Report for the Trade Unions Congress 2012) <www.tuc.org.uk/sites/default/files/tucfiles/LegalOpinionIsraeliSettlements.pdf>

El-Zein J, 'Das Ende des Neutralitätsrechts' (PhD Thesis, University of Cologne 2023)

Kreß C, 'The Ukraine War and the Prohibition of the Use of Force in International Law' (TOAEP Occasional Paper Series No. 13 2022)

Lewis L, Modirzadeh N, and Blum G, 'Quantum of Silence: Inaction and Jus ad Bellum' (2019) HLS PILAC <http://nrs.harvard.edu/urn-3:HUL.InstRepos:40931878>

Lubell L, Pejic J, and Simmons C, *Guidelines on Investigating Violations of International Humanitarian Law: Law, Policy, and Good Practice* (ICRC and Geneva Academy 2019)

Pothelet E, 'Searching for the Nexus: A Proposal to Refine the Applicability of IHL' (PhD, Geneva 2021)

Peters A, 'Direct Rights of Individuals in the International Law of Armed Conflict' (2019–23 MPIL Research Paper Series, 20 December 2019) <https://papers.ssrn.com/sol3/papers.cfm?abstract_id=3506742>

Santos S, 'Evolution of the Armed Conflict on the Communist Front' (Background Paper, Human Development Network Foundation 2005) <http://hdn.org.ph/wp-content/uploads/2005_PHDR/2005%20Evolution_Communist_Conflict.pdf>

Schöberl K, 'The Geographical Scope of Application of International Humanitarian Law' (PhD, Université de Genève 2019)

Talmon S, 'The Provision of Arms to the Victim of Armed Aggression: The Case of Ukraine ' (Bonn Research Papers on Public International Law, 6 April 2022) <https://ssrn.com/abstract=4077084>

Verlinden N, '"Are We at War?" State Support to Parties to Armed Conflict: Consequences under *jus in bello*, *jus ad bellum* and Neutrality Law' (PhD, KU Leuven 2019)

Vermeer Z, 'Intervention by Invitation and the Alleged Prohibition of Military Assistance to Governments in Civil Wars' (DPhil, University of Oxford 2018)

Wentker A, 'Mohammed v Ministry of Defence' (2017) ILDC 2803

Wiesener C, 'The Application and Interplay of Humanitarian Law and Human Rights Law in Peace Operations, with a Particular Focus on the Use of Force' (PhD, EUI 2015)

Newspaper Articles, Press Releases, and Other News Items

Ackermann B, 'Is War on ISIS Illegal?' *NYT* (5 May 2016) A25 <www.nytimes.com/2016/05/05/opinion/is-americas-war-on-isis-illegal.html?searchResultPosition=1>

Barkin M, 'Remarks at a UN Security Council Briefing on the Humanitarian Situation in Syria' 24 October 2019 <https://usun.usmission.gov/remarks-at-a-un-security-council-briefing-on-the-humanitarian-situation-in-syria-21/>

Barnes J, Cooper H, and Schmitt E, 'U.S. Intelligence Is Helping Ukraine Kill Russian Generals, Officials Say' *NYT* (4 May 2022) <www.nytimes.com/2022/05/04/us/politics/russia-generals-killed-ukraine.html?smid=tw-nytimes&smtyp=cur>

Barnes J, 'Iran Sends Drone Trainers to Crimea to Aid Russian Military' *NYT* (18 October 2022) <www.nytimes.com/2022/10/18/us/politics/iran-drones-russia-ukraine.html>

Belgium, 'Prolongation de la contribution à la coalition internationale contre DAESH en Irak' 10 July 2015 <https://news.belgium.be/fr/prolongation-de-la-contribution-la-coalition-internationale-contre-daesh-en-irak>

Bertrand N and Lillis K, 'US Officials Say Biden Administration Is Sharing Intelligence with Ukraine at a "Frenetic" Pace after Republicans Criticize Efforts' (*CNN*, 4 March 2022) <https://edition.cnn.com/2022/03/04/politics/us-ukraine-intelligence/index.html>

Borger J, 'The Austrian Position on Arms Embargo in Syria—Official Document' *The Guardian* (15 May 2013) <www.theguardian.com/world/julian-borger-global-security-blog/interactive/2013/may/15/austria-eu-syria-arms-embargo-pdf>

Borger J, 'Russia May Share Criminal Responsibility for Assad's Use of Barrel Bombs, UK Says' *The Guardian* (30 September 2015) <www.theguardian.com/world/2015/sep/30/russia-syria-barrel-bombing-international-law-uk>

'Bundesregierung: Ausbildung von Soldaten kein Kriegseintritt' *SZ* (2 May 2022) <www.sueddeutsche.de/politik/konflikte-bundesregierung-ausbildung-von-soldaten-kein-kriegseintritt-dpa.urn-newsml-dpa-com-20090101-220502-99-126669>

'Burkina Faso, Mali Say Military Intervention in Niger Would Be "Declaration of War"' (France24, 1 August 2023) <www.france24.com/en/africa/20230801-burkina-faso-and-mali-say-intervention-in-niger-would-be-declaration-of-war>

Canada, 'Canada Renews Its Military Contribution to Support Stability in the Middle East' 18 March 2019 <www.canada.ca/en/department-national-defence/news/2019/03/canada-renews-its-military-contribution-to-support-stability-in-the-middle-east.html>

Canada, 'Canadian Armed Forces Cease Airstrike Operations in Iraq and Syria' 17 February 2016 <www.canada.ca/en/department-national-defence/news/2016/02/canadian-armed-forces-cease-airstrike-operations-in-iraq-and-syria.html>

Canadian Department of National Defense, 'Press Release: First Airstrike Conducted in Syria under Operation Impact' 9 April 2015 <https://skiesmag.com/press-releases/firstairstrikeconductedinsyriaunderoperationimpact/>

Cooper H, Schmitt E, and Barnes J, 'U.S. Intelligence Helped Ukraine Strike Russian Flagship, Officials Say' *NYT* (5 May 2022) <www.nytimes.com/2022/05/05/us/politics/moskva-russia-ship-ukraine-us.html?smid=url-copy>

Dilanian K, 'Biden Administration Walks Fine Line on Intelligence-Sharing with Ukraine' (*NBC News*, 4 March 2022) <www.nbcnews.com/news/investigations/biden-administration-walks-fine-line-intelligence-sharing-ukraine-rcna18542>

France, Press Conference of the Ministry of Foreign Affairs (26 January 2023) <https://twitter.com/francediplo/status/1618906329925718016?s=66&t=yQX2QgElwKQBP1VR-SbK7Q>

Friedman T, 'Syria Says Airman Seized in U.S. Raid Will Not Be Freed' *NYT* (6 December 1983) A 1 <www.nytimes.com/1983/12/06/world/syria-says-airman-seized-in-us-raid-will-not-be-freed.html?searchResultPosition=12>

Fuentes C, 'Salvador's Opposition' *NYT* (16 September 1981) A27

Gall C, 'As Libya Faces a Growing Conflict, Turkey Deploys Troops to Back Its Government' *NYT* (6 January 2020) A6 <www.nytimes.com/2020/01/05/world/europe/erdogan-turkish-troops-libya.html?searchResultPosition=1>

Gall C and Kingsley P, 'Turkish Forces Escalate Campaign in Syria against Kurdish-Led Militia' *NYT* (11 October 2019) A11 <www.nytimes.com/2019/10/10/world/middleeast/syria-turkey-offensive.html>

Ghasemilee S, 'Libyan Rebels, NATO in Joint Military Operations against Qaddafi Forces' (*Alarabiya*, 16 November 2011) <https://english.alarabiya.net/articles/2011/04/16/145587>

Keaten J, 'Russia: US Air Defense Systems Could Be Targets in Ukraine' (*AP News*, 15 December 2022) <https://apnews.com/article/russia-ukraine-politics-donetsk-government-united-states-eed3a0fc72e8197182e78dcc73ade45e>

Khurshudyan I et al, 'Ukraine's Rocket Campaign Reliant on U.S. Precision Targeting, Officials Say' *Washington Post* (9 February 2023) <www.washingtonpost.com/world/2023/02/09/ukraine-himars-rocket-artillery-russia/>

Kuznetsov S, 'Ukraine Bats Away Lukashenko's Border Threats' *Politico* (12 October 2022) <www.politico.eu/article/ukraine-bats-away-lukashenkos-border-threats/>

'Libya Conflict: Turkey Sends Troops to Shore Up UN-backed Government' (*BBC*, 6 January 2020) <www.bbc.com/news/world-africa-51003034>

Muñoz C, 'U.S, Russia Suspend Talks on Joint Operations in Syria as Cease-Fire Deal Fails' *Washington Times* (20 September 2016) <www.washingtontimes.com/news/2016/sep/20/us-russia-suspend-talks-joint-operations-syria-cea/>

Oakford S, 'One American's Failed Quest to Protect Civilians in Yemen' *The Atlantic* (17 August 2018) <https://perma.cc/PM9Q-6H3V>

'Poland Ready to Place All Its MIG-29 Jets at the Disposal of U.S.' *Reuters* 8 March 2022 <www.reuters.com/world/europe/poland-ready-place-all-its-mig-29-jets-disposal-us-2022–03–08/>

'Press Briefing by Press Secretary Jen Psaki, March 3rd, 2022' <www.whitehouse.gov/briefing-room/press-briefings/2022/03/03/press-briefing-by-press-secretary-jen-psaki-march-3rd-2022/>

'Press Point with NATO Secretary General Jens Stoltenberg' 30 September 2022 <www.nato.int/cps/en/natohq/opinions_207788.htm>

'Refueling of Jets in India to Stop' *NYT* (20 February 1991) A13 <www.nytimes.com/1991/02/20/world/war-in-the-gulf-refueling-of-jets-in-india-to-stop.html>

Remarks by Acting Department of State Principal Deputy General Counsel William Castle, 'Congressional Authorizations on Use of Force—Speech at the NYC Bar Association' 11 December 2017 <www.scribd.com/document/366923593/Dod-Acting-General-Counsel-William-Castle-NYC-Bar-Remarks-Aumf-Dec-11#download&from_embed>

'Russia's Lavrov: Do Not Underestimate Threat of Nuclear War' (*Reuters*, 26 April 2022) <www.reuters.com/world/russia-says-western-weapons-ukraine-legitimate-targets-russian-military-2022–04–25/>

Sanger D and Schmitt E, 'Biden Signals Break with Trump Foreign Policy in a Wide-Ranging State Dept. Speech' *NYT* (4 February 2021) A1 <www.nytimes.com/2021/02/04/us/politics/biden-foreign-policy.html?action=click&module=Spotlight&pgtype=Homepage>

Saudi Arabia, 'News Release: The Coalition to Restore Legitimacy in Yemen Announces Resuming Humanitarian and Commercial Access to All Ports under the Control of the Legitimate Government of Yemen' 12 November 2017 <www.saudiembassy.net/news/coalition-restore-legitimacy-yemen-announces-resuming-humanitarian-and-commercial-access-all>

Sermo M, 'La Cobelligérance, acte de guerre ou légitime défense collective?' *Le Monde* (26 May 2022) <www.lemonde.fr/idees/article/2022/05/26/la-cobelligerance-acte-de-guerre-ou-legitime-defense-collective_6127767_3232.html>

Strobel W and Landay J, 'Exclusive: As Saudis Bombed Yemen, U.S. Worried about Legal Blowback' (*Reuters*, 10 October 2016) <www.reuters.com/article/us-usa-saudi-yemen-idUSKCN12A0BQ>

'Swiss Troops Get Lost in Liechtenstein' *NYT* (3 March 2007) A3 <www.nytimes.com/2007/03/03/world/europe/03swiss.html>

Treffers L, 'Dutch Defence Minister Announces Fresh Transparency Moves' (*Airwars*, 7 July 2020) <https://airwars.org/news-and-investigations/minister-announces-fresh-transparency-moves/>

United Kingdom Ministry of Defence, 'Defence in the Media: 18 July 2015' <https://modmedia.blog.gov.uk/2015/07/18/defence-in-the-media-18-july-2015/>

United Kingdom Ministry of Defence, 'UK Embedded Forces' (Statement UIN HLWS139) 20 July 2015 <https://questions-statements.parliament.uk/written-statements/detail/2015-07-20/HLWS139>

United Kindom Secretary of State for Foreign and Commonwealth Affairs, 'Saudia Arabia' (Statement UIN HCWS716) 23 May 2018 <https://questions-statements.parliament.uk/written-statements/detail/2018-05-23/HCWS716>

United States Central Command, 'Combined Joint Operations Center–Baghdad Brings Coalition together for Operation Inherent Resolve' (18 January 2017) <www.centcom.mil/MEDIA/NEWS-ARTICLES/News-Article-View/Article/1052365/combined-joint-operations-center-baghdad-brings-coalition-together-for-operatio/>

United States, 'Central Command News Release: CJTF-OIR Completes Civilian Casualty Investigation' 21 May 2015 <www.centcom.mil/MEDIA/PRESS-RELEASES/Press-Release-View/Article/1093845/cjtf-oir-completes-civilian-casualty-investigation/>

United States, 'Remarks by the President at the National Defense University' 23 May 2013 <https://obamawhitehouse.archives.gov/the-press-office/2013/05/23/remarks-president-national-defense-university>

United States, 'Statement by NSC Spokesperson Bernadette Meehan on the Situation in Yemen' 25 March 2015 <https://obamawhitehouse.archives.gov/the-press-office/2015/03/25/statement-nsc-spokesperson-bernadette-meehan-situation-yemen>

Vakil C, 'Russian Official Claims US Participating in Direct Hostilities with His Country' *The Hill* (7 May 2022) <https://thehill.com/policy/defense/3480589-russian-official-claims-us-participating-in-direct-hostilities-with-his-country/>

'West "Working Hard" to Avoid War' (*Sky News*, 28 June 2022) <https://news.sky.com/video/west-working-hard-to-avoid-war-12641856>

Other Online Resources

Airwars, 'Cause for Concern: Civilians Killed in Coalition Strikes' (August 2015) <https://airwars.org/wp-content/uploads/2015/08/airwars-cause-for-concern-civilians-killed-by-coalition.pdf>

'cooperation, n.' (*OED Online*, OUP September 2019) <www.oed.com/view/Entry/41037>

'coordination, n.' (*OED Online*, OUP September 2020) <www.oed.com/view/Entry/41066>

'cooperation' (*CED Online*, CUP) <https://dictionary.cambridge.org/dictionary/english/cooperation>

'coordination' (*CED Online*, CUP) <https://dictionary.cambridge.org/dictionary/english/coordination>

German Federal Office for the Protection of the Constitution, 'Counter Terrorism Group (CTG)' <www.verfassungsschutz.de/DE/verfassungsschutz/auftrag/zusammenarbeit-im-in-und-ausland/counter-terrorism-group-ctg/counter-terrorism-group-ctg_node.html>

Global Coalition, 'Belgium: A Committed Member of the Coalition' 26 January 2017 <https://theglobalcoalition.org/en/belgium-a-committed-member-of-the-coalition/>

Global Coalition, 'Military: Major General Chris Ghika' 12 July 2019 <https://theglobalcoalition.org/en/on-the-line-major-general-chris-ghika/>

Global Coalition, 'Spain's Military Contribution to the Coalition' 12 June 2021 <https://theglobalcoalition.org/en/spains-military-contribution-to-the-coalition/>

Kim et al, 'Newly Disclosed Documents on the Five Eyes Alliance and What They Tell Us about Intelligence-Sharing Agreements' 25 April 2018 <https://law.yale.edu/mfia/case-disclosed/newly-disclosed-documents-five-eyes-alliance-and-what-they-tell-us-about-intelligence-sharing>

National Archives, 'Newly Released GCHQ Files: UKUSA Agreement' June 2010 <https://discovery.nationalarchives.gov.uk/details/r/C11536914>

RULAC, 'International armed conflict in Ukraine' <www.rulac.org/browse/conflicts/international-armed-conflict-in-ukraine#collapse2accord>

RULAC, 'Military Occupation of Moldova by Russia' <www.rulac.org/browse/conflicts/military-occupation-of-moldova-by-russia>

Index

For the benefit of digital users, indexed terms that span two pages (e.g., 52–53) may, on occasion, appear on only one of those pages.

For page references to cases and other primary authorities, please consult the relevant tables at the beginning of the work.

Afghanistan 32, 70–71, 120, 122–23, 133–34, 141–42, 166, 197–98
aggression, prohibition of 31–32, 60–62, 68, 83–84, 106, 158, 160–61, 199–202, *see also* use of force, prohibition of
al-Qaeda 1–2, 27, 110–11, 123–24, 129, 162–64, 210–11
animus belligerendi *see* intent, belligerent intent
Arab-Israeli conflict 63, 97–98
armed attack *see* self-defence in international law
associated forces 1–2, 27, 123, 129, 162–65, 203n.294
attribution of conduct 24, 86, 100, 105n.68, 167, 174–75

belligerency, recognition of 14, 17–18, 38–39n.193, 69–73
belligerent rights 28n.118, 34
  belligerent rights against neutrals (*see* neutrality)
'benevolent neutrality' *see* non-belligerency

Central African Republic 1–2, 18, 120, 122, 124–25, 144, 189, 197–98, 206
civilian 20–21, 37, 42–43, 81–82, 215, 217–18, 226, *see also* direct participation in hostilities; precautions in attack
  'civilianisation of armed conflict' 37–38
civil war 13–14, 17–18, 72–73, 106
'co-belligerency' 110–11, 152–53, 156, 164, 178
collective security 57–62, 83–84, 155–56, 158
community interest 54–55, 57, 79, 82–83
complicity 61–62, 83–84, 86–88
cumulative approach 168–69
cyberspace 64–65, 76, 77–78, 181, 183–84

declaration of war 96–99, 104, 153, 155–56, 171, 190–91
Definition of Aggression (UNGA Resolution 3314) 83–84, 160–61
Democratic Republic of Congo 1–2, 121–22
direct participation in hostilities (DPH) 37, 39–41, 128, 166–68, 180–81, 192
due diligence obligations 215–16, 220, 221–23

ECtHR *see* European Court of Human Rights
ensure respect for IHL, obligation to 84–91, 212–13, 220–29
equality of belligerents 202–3
European Court of Human Rights 27, 32–34

Falklands/Malvinas War 97–98

Gentili, Alberico 153–54
Grotius, Hugo 19, 28, 153–54, 178
Gulf War (1990–1991) 63–64, 201–2

hostilities *see also* direct participation in hostilities
  cessation of hostilities 206, 208
  conduct of hostilities 35, 37–42, 168, 214–18 (*see also* precautions in attacks and military operations)
  notion of hostilities 101, 175–77
Houthi rebels 139, 142, 187–88, 211, *see also* Yemen
humanisation of international law 3, 34–36, 49–50
humanitarian assistance 81–82
humanitarian relief *see* humanitarian assistance

ICC *see* International Criminal Court
ICJ *see* International Court of Justice
ICRC *see* International Committee of the Red Cross
ICTY *see* International Criminal Tribunal for the former Yugoslavia
IDI *see* Institut de Droit International
ILC *see* International Law Commission
India–Pakistan War (1965) 63, 97–98

individual criminal responsibility in international law 46–48
  nexus (war crimes) 47–48
individualisation of war 3, 34–36, 49–50
Institut de Droit International 72–73
intelligence, provision of 1–2, 37–38, 101, 158–59, 175, 179–80, 181, 185, 187–88, 194–96, 216–17
intent 87–88, 96–97
  belligerent intent 102, 167, 190–91, 193
International Committee of the Red Cross 25, 37, 39–40, 88–91, 102, 165–70, 180–81, 192, 219–20
International Court of Justice 23–24, 31–32, 58, 62, 63, 67, 88–89, 104, 105–6
International Criminal Court 18, 51–52, 105–6, 109–10, 120–21, 122–23, 133–34, 136, 189, 197–98, 206
International Criminal Tribunal for the former Yugoslavia 42–43, 47–49, 99, 100, 105–6, 120–21, 134–35, 178, 206
International Law Commission 24, 28, 62, 86–88
international organisations 16–17, 18–19, 85, 175, 204–5, 228, *see also* NATO; UN peace operation
International Tribunal for the Law of the Sea 76
Iran–Iraq War 63, 97–98, 116–17, 158–59, 179, 210–11
Iraq War (2003) 32, 64, 67–68n.93, 115, 116–17, 159–60, 179, 200–1
ISIL, international military operations against 1–2, 25n.90, 51n.274, 111–12, 114–16, 117–19, 128, 174, 183, 187, 194–95, 196–97, 206–8, 210–12, 216–17, 225
ITLOS *see* International Tribunal for the Law of the Sea

jus ad bellum *see* use of force, prohibition of
jus cogens *see* peremptory norms of international law
just war theory 3n.15, 37–38
  revisionism 3n.15, 37–38

Korean War 63

Lauterpacht, Hersch 14, 72, 155–56, 157, 159–60

Mali 1–2
'measures short of war' 96, 97–98, 141
military operations *see* hostilities

national liberation movement 15, 70–71, 132, 144–45
NATO 188–89
neutrality, law of
  abstention from hostilities and assisting belligerents, obligations of 56–57, 67, 74, 157
  belligerent rights against neutrals 63, 67, 77–79
    jus ad bellum, compatibility with the 77–78
  impartiality, principle of 56–57, 72, 115
  inviolability of neutral States' territory 57, 61–62, 67, 75–77
  prevention of use of neutrality territory by belligerents, obligations of 56–57, 59, 74, 86, 91n.255, 157
  'self-help' measures 75–76
non-belligerency 64, 67, 201
non-intervention, principle of 69, 72–73, 76
non-State armed groups *see also* al-Qaeda; ISIL
  requirement of organization 17–19, 108, 122–23, 132–36, 143, 144, 164–65, 168

Operation Inherent Resolve *see* ISIL, international military operations against
Oppenheim, Lassa 13, 155–56, 157
  Oppenheim's International Law 155–56

peremptory norms of international law 83
precautions in attacks and military operations 208n.325, 214–18
prisoners of war 42, 44, 45–46, 49, 101–2, 131

qualified neutrality *see* non-belligerency

Rousseau, Jean-Jacques 12–13, 35
Russia-Ukraine War 1–2, 27–28, 60–61, 64, 111–12, 179–80, 181–82, 195–96

SCSL *see* Special Court for Sierra Leone
Second World War 1–2, 98
self-defence in international law 59–61, 75–76, 78, 102–3, *see also* use of force, prohibition of
Somalia 164–65, 210–11
sovereignty, principle of 13–14, 69–73, 75, 76, 107, 140
Special Court for Sierra Leone 105–6
state of war 20, 28, 34, 53, 54, 56, 66, 77, 96–99, 102, 155, 190–91

support-based approach (SBA) 165–70, 176, 178, 192

Ukraine *see* Russia-Ukraine War
UN peace operations 1–2, 16–17, 18–19, 205, 227
UN Security Council 2, 22–24, 26, 58–62, 63–64, 68, 78, 81–82, 89, 158, 160–61, 225–26
use of force, prohibition of 22, 28–29, 59–62, 68–69, 75–76, 78–79, 83–84, 98, 103–6, 156, 160–61, 199–202

Van Bynkershoek, Cornelius 153n.9
Vattel, Emer de 13–14, 110–11, 153–54, 191
Vietnam War 97–98, 200

war *see also* declaration of war; state of war
  collective character of war 12–14
weapons, supply of 154, 181–82, 195
Wolff, Christian 153–54

Yemen 3–4, 70–71, 119, 139, 142, 187–88, 211–12, 226

The manufacturer's authorised representative in the EU for product safety is Oxford University Press España S.A. of el Parque Empresarial San Fernando de Henares, Avenida de Castilla, 2 – 28830 Madrid (www.oup.es/en or product.safety@oup.com). OUP España S.A. also acts as importer into Spain of products made by the manufacturer.

www.ingramcontent.com/pod-product-compliance
Lightning Source LLC
LaVergne TN
LVHW011820200926
848484LV00005B/1259
* 9 7 8 0 1 9 8 9 0 0 9 0 0 *